D0806190

SEP - - 2013
37653019312282
Main NonFiction: 5th floor
355.00938 MATTHEW
A storm of spears :
understanding the Greek
hoplite at war

A gift has been made by:

Bobby Roberts

In honor of

CALS

A STORM OF SPEARS

A STORM OF SPEARS

Understanding the Greek Hoplite at War

Christopher Anthony Matthew

CASEMATE
Philadelphia

Published in the United States of America in 2012 by
CASEMATE PUBLISHERS
908 Darby Road, Havertown, PA 19083

Copyright 2012 © Christopher Anthony Matthew

ISBN 978-1-61200-119-7

First published in Great Britain in 2012 by Pen & Sword Military,
an imprint of Pen & Sword Books Ltd.

Cataloging-in-publication data is available from the Library of Congress and
the British Library.

All rights reserved. No part of this book may be reproduced or transmitted in any form
or by any means, electronic or mechanical including photocopying, recording or by any
information storage and retrieval system, without permission from the Publisher in writing.

10 9 8 7 6 5 4 3 2 1

Typeset by Concept, Huddersfield, West Yorkshire.

Printed and bound in the United States of America.

For a complete list of Casemate titles please contact:
CASEMATE PUBLISHERS (US)
Telephone (610) 853-9131, Fax (610) 853-9146
E-mail: casemate@casematepublishing.com

Contents

CENTRAL ARKANSAS LIBRARY SYSTEM
LITTLE ROCK PUBLIC LIBRARY
100 ROCK STREET
LITTLE ROCK, ARKANSAS 72201

Acknowledgements

This research upon which this work is based would not have been possible without the assistance of a veritable (and in some cases literal) phalanx of people. I would like to acknowledge the following individuals, for whose contribution I am greatly indebted.

Dr Ian Plant, and Prof. Samuel Lieu of Macquarie University, for their help and feedback during the research process; my wife, Kate Matthew, for her help, support, participation and infinite patience while I undertook this project; the following members of the Sydney Ancients: David Armstrong, Krishna Armstrong, Paul Fisher, Craig Gascoigne, Mark Kelly, Matthew Knight and Robert Wheeler for their help in putting many current theories into practice; the following people for their participation in the testing used in this research: Kenneth Bow, Rosa Bow, Michelle Hopping, Richard Hopping, Raewyn Ingram and Stephen Smith; Anne Nielsen and Douglas Nielsen for their help with parts of the recreated panoply and testing equipment; Alex Schiebner from Talerwin Forge for his help with the re-created hoplite spear and the target plates used in this research; Darryl Crockett from Ancient Replicas for his help with the re-created helmet and cuirass; David Armstrong (again) for his help with the re-created *aspis*; Jo Whalley (Victoria University of Wellington), Dr Patricia Hannah (University of Otago) and Prof. Margaret Miller (Sydney University) for their advice on several aspects of Greek art; Karl van Dyke (Macquarie University), Dr Sonia Puttock (University of Queensland), Penelope Minchin-Garvin (University of Canterbury), Karen Manning (Harvard University), Dr Lucilla Burn (Fitzwilliam Museum, Cambridge) and Simon Eccles (Glasgow Museum) for their help with/photos of/access to items in the collections of the various museums with which they are associated; Prof. Richard Gabriel (Royal Military College of Canada) and Prof. Jeffrey Schnick (St Anslem College) for their help with the findings of the book *From Sumer to Rome*; Dr Stavros Paspalas and Anastasia Aligiannis (Australian Archaeological Institute at Athens) for their assistance in arranging access to items in the collection of the Deutsche Archaeological Institute at Olympia and the National Archaeological Museum in Athens; and all of my other friends, family, and colleagues for the support, comments and patience they have extended to me during the formulation of this work.

CENTRAL ARKANSAS LIBRARY SYSTEM
LITTLE ROCK PUBLIC LIBRARY
100 ROCK STREET
LITTLE ROCK, ARKANSAS 72201

CM 2011

List of Illustrations

List of Tables

List of Plates

Abbreviations

AA	*Archaeologischer Anzeiger*
AHB	*Ancient History Bulletin*
AJA	*American Journal of Archaeology*
AJPA	*American Journal of Physical Anthropology*
Am. J. Phys.	*American Journal of Physics*
CQ	*Classical Quarterly*
FGrHist	F. Jacoby, *Die Fragmente der Griechischen Historiker* (Lieden, Brill, 1952)
GRBS	*Greek, Roman and Byzantine Studies*
JBT	*Journal of Battlefield Technologyv*
JHE	*Journal of Human Evolution*
JHS	*Journal of Hellenic Studies*
JRMES	*Journal of Roman Military Equipment Studies*
LIMC	*Lexicon Iconographicum Mythologiae Classicae*
MMJ	*Metropolitan Museum Journal*
PAE	*Problemes d'Archeologie et d'Ethnographie*
SAJS	*South African Journal of Science*

Foreword

Writing military history is difficult; writing *ancient* military history is very difficult indeed. Becoming a military historian of the ancient world is no easy task. Most graduate programs in the discipline involve completing the requirements for both classics and history degrees. In addition, one must acquire at least a research knowledge of ancient Greek and Latin, a broad exposure to the secondary scholarship in a variety of modern languages, and a working knowledge of numismatics, art iconography, archaeology, and philology. To write ancient military history also requires knowledge of warfare, including tactics, strategy, the operational arts, logistics, and military biography. Little wonder, then, that so few modern historians are willing to attempt writing about ancient military history.

Once adequately prepared to begin, the would-be historian encounters difficulties inherent in the subject itself. The ancient military historian quickly finds himself a prisoner of the ancient texts upon which his study depends. The single biggest obstacle to our understanding of ancient military history is the lack of reliable evidence. The Greeks' invention of history as a search for a rational explanation and understanding of events expressed in written prose or oral recitation created a means by which ancient historians could record events in a manner still comprehensible in the modern age. Three centuries later, the Greeks passed their invention to the Romans. The consequence was an archive of written texts upon which the modern study of Greek and Roman military history is based. Unfortunately, much of the information in the texts is unreliable, biased, incomplete, and even false.

The accounts of many ancient historians have serious limitations. History written by Greek and Romans was often less concerned with a factual accounting of events than with teaching moral lessons or influencing the behaviour of powerful political classes or individuals. This didactic approach to history focused primarily upon the achievements of great men, treating biography as the history of individuals. Ancient historians expected their work to be recited more than read, and due care has to be taken to remember that the historian was also a rhetorician. The concern for rhetoric led to the incorporation in the texts of speeches attributed to famous generals and kings. Almost all of these speeches are fictitious.

Ancient historical accounts are often unreliable because details and factual accuracy were subordinated to the larger purpose of teaching important lessons.

If the bare facts were insufficient for an effective presentation, the facts could be adorned, modified, or variously combined in the interest of a more dramatic presentation. Names, numbers, exact dates, chronologies, and geographical details were frequently inaccurate, invented, or sometimes omitted altogether. It is difficult to think of a Greek or Roman text that does not suffer from one or all of these shortcomings.

Ancient texts were often written long after the events recorded in them, and only a few address events contemporary with their authors. Ancient historians usually did not check the validity of the sources upon whom they relied. This was mostly impossible in any case since few useable archives existed, and would probably have required lengthy and dangerous journeys to get to them. Some ancient historians are simply repeating accounts of earlier sources in a different, more dramatic fashion. Thus, Livy relies primarily on Polybius' account of the Second Punic War for the military narrative, and Dio Cassius, writing a century later, relies upon Livy for the same war. Sources often cannot be evaluated because while they may have been available to the writer, they have since been lost. The accounts of two of Polybius's most valuable sources, Sosylus and Silenus, Greek 'war correspondents' who travelled with Hannibal, are lost to us. Herodotus' sources for the Persian War are little more than a collection of oral tales and monument inscriptions. There are, however, some exceptions. Arrian's *Anabasis*, dealing with the life of Alexander the Great, is the most trustworthy account of Alexander's life precisely because it is based upon earlier eye-witness accounts by Nearchus, Ptolemy, and Aristobulus, all soldiers who participated in Alexander's campaigns.

Military historians are the prisoners of the texts that survived, and many of these texts were corrupted when translated from Greek to Latin or copied by Medieval monks who often lacked knowledge of the military subjects involved. The most common errors involved numbers. The monks often had limited knowledge of ancient numerical systems, and regularly mistranslated or transposed numerical values, sometimes substituting completely new numbers of their own. The tendency of ancient historians to exaggerate the number of enemy combatants and casualties was thus compounded by the monks' errors. Speed, rates of march, distances, weights, numbers of animals, the widths of rivers and streams, terrain heights etc. are most often expressed numerically, with the result that distortion occurs frequently in information most important to the military historian. The emphasis of ancient writers on the past as giving moral lessons for the present meant as well that there was no necessary virtue in having experience of the events one wrote about. Thucydides' invention of contemporary history, the study of events of one's own time, changed this, and the sub-discipline of contemporary history as a form of historical analysis owes much to this great soldier-scholar.

The ancient texts dealing with military history can be divided into three categories: (1) those written years after the events by writers who had no military experience upon which to draw for their understanding of military events; (2) those whose authors had some military experience upon which to base their analysis; (3) and those whose authors had military experience and participated in the events about which they wrote.

Works by Herodotus (480–425 BC), Appian (95–165 AD), Livy (59 BC–17 AD), and Dio Cassius (164–234 AD), all of whom wrote major treatments of military history but had never seen military service, fall into the first category. Works by Polybius (200–118 BC), Tacitus (56–117 AD), and Arrian (87–145 AD) fall into the category of texts by historians who had some military experience and wrote about events that had occurred long before their own times. The last category comprises the texts of soldier-historians who wrote accounts of the battles in which they themselves fought. This group includes the works of Thucydides, Caesar, Xenophon, and Aeneas Tacticus.

Military experience, alas, is no guarantee of historical accuracy, and even experienced soldier-historians cannot always be trusted to forego the usual biases of ancient historians. Sallust, for example, was an experienced soldier who saw combat in the civil war in Illyricum and Campania, and later in North Africa. Yet *The Jurgurthine War*, his account of the Roman war against Jurgurtha the Numidian, is generally untrustworthy as to numbers, dates, distances, size of forces, etc., all the material of most interest to the military historian. Josephus, another combat veteran who commanded troops both for and against Rome, is a good source for the details of Roman equipment, arms, and artillery, but is otherwise untrustworthy. His primary work, *The Jewish War*, may have been commissioned by the Romans!

Although the shortcomings of the ancient texts were well-known, for many years there was little else upon which historians could draw. The study of ancient military history was left largely to classicists that could read the texts in the original Latin and Greek. Few had been trained military historians, however. Classicists saw military history as a minor field, so that accounts of ancient wars and battles were regarded as only one minor part of the larger text, with little attention given to military history per se. A European university education of the nineteenth century consisted largely of a classical education in which the original texts were read. Some of the university graduates of the aristocratic classes became military officers who studied the accounts of ancient warfare for modern lessons. A number of these soldier-historians (Liddell-Hart, J. F. C. Fuller, Hans Delbruck, Georges Veith, and others) wrote revised accounts of ancient battles based upon their own experiences in war.

In the late nineteenth century, historians sought to bring a more empirical eye to the study of the ancient accounts. Two developments made this possible.

First, the nineteenth century was an age of invention and discovery in which the scientific impulse required carefully measured confirmation of all propositions before they could be accepted as fact. New knowledge from psychiatry, medicine, nutrition, human endurance studies, map making, metallurgy, engineering, etc. became available to military historians who could now apply this to the study of ancient warfare. The nineteenth century also saw the emergence of modern war on an unprecedented scale. Large standing and reserve armies required the management of men and materiel in precise detail. This brought into being tables of organization and implementation. Tables were devised to tell one how much food and water each soldier required to remain in fighting condition, how quickly a brigade could march under different conditions, how many mules and wagons were needed to transport men and supplies over a given distance, how long they could be sustained in the field, what kinds of wounds could be expected from different types of attacks, how many of the wounded would die from hostile fire, accidents, and disease etc. What had once been the 'art of war' was replaced by 'military science'. The military historian now had at his disposal new information and methods that could be applied to the analysis of the ancient texts.

The new approach was further encouraged by the military reserve mobilization system used by the European armies of the day. Almost every male adult between the ages of 18 and 45 was assigned to a reserve unit. In the period between the Crimean War and World War I, many reservists went to war or underwent military training where they became acquainted with the new science of war and its attendant tables, schedules, and measurement. Many of these reserve soliders were professors, graduate students, and university students who took these methods with them back to the universities, creating an impetus for more empirical analysis of the text accounts of ancient warfare.

By the beginning of the twentieth century, the new approach was gaining credibility and military historians began securing positions at European universities, only to have the disruption and carnage of the First World War decimate the ranks of the new scholarship. After the war the survivors who still had posts to go to and students to teach tried to reestablish the new discipline, and a number of ground-breaking empirical works like Kromayer and Veith's *The Battle Atlas of Ancient Military History* and Delbruck's *History of the Art of War* (4 vols.) were produced. The political turmoil following the war and the catastrophe of the Second World War that followed, however, completely eclipsed the study of ancient military history in Europe. The subject had never been popular in the United States, and ancient military history remains today a minor disciplinary emphasis largely in the hands of classicists.

Only in the last two decades can one can detect a re-emergence of the empirical approach to ancient military history prompted by the electronic revolution in information transfer that has brought the content of the world's libraries and the works of distant scholars to the historian's desktop computer. This same revolution has increased personal communication among scholars sharing similar interests and research results. The emphasis on empirical research has added to the tools that the ancient historian can apply to the texts. Lazenby and J. K Anderson's work on Greek warfare, Hanson's study of the Battle of Cannae, and Sabin's research on the battles of the Punic War have added to our understanding of the battle mechanics of close combat, the role played by fear and exhaustion, and the role played by 'battle pulses' in combat. Junkelmann's experiments measuring the speed, loads carried, and endurance of marching soldiers have raised new question about these factors in ancient warfare. Karen Metz's and my efforts at 'experimental archaeology' have provided insights into the killing and wounding power of ancient weapons, work that supplements the earlier efforts of Peter Connolly. Engels' excellent study on the logistics of Macedonian armies has been supplemented by Jonathan Roth's analysis of the logistics of Roman armies from 264 BC to AD 235. These new sources ought to result in a strongly revised understanding of what war was like in ancient times.

Among the most recent of these new empirical works is Christopher Matthew's book, *A Storm of Spears: Understanding the Greek Hoplite at War*. Matthew has all the necessary credentials of a good ancient military historian, including the language skills and an impressive command of the ancient texts. Moreover, he possesses a qualification that most modern historians lack: military experience. Matthew has been an infantry soldier in the Australian army. Nothing is more likely to give one an appreciation for warfare in antiquity than to have been an infantryman. A twenty-mile march, half of it at night, across a water obstacle, on half-rations, with the end of the trek under a hot sun will quickly reveal just how egregiously false the claims of some ancient writers are!

My suspicion is that it was Matthew's military experience in the infantry that led him to his subject, the Greek hoplite infantry phalanx. The subject of hoplite warfare has occupied historians for centuries, and their efforts have produced a large and contradictory literature on the subject. This is because until now, historians have been forced to rely upon the usual text accounts, drawing whatever conclusions seemed to them logical. Chris Matthew's major contribution to the discipline has been to do what no one else has done: using reenactors, equipped with meticulously manufactured replicas of the hoplite's battle kit (helmet, body cuirass, greaves, shield, and dory spear), Matthew subjected them to battle drills, manoeuvres, and endurance tests while carefully photographing them with high speed cameras and measuring their every move for empirical analysis. The result is a treasure trove of empirical findings that call into question many of the claims made by modern and ancient historians about the battle performance of the hoplite soldier and his phalanx. Matthew then revisits the text accounts of the phalanx at war using his empirical findings to evaluate their claims. His analysis shows that much of what has been claimed for hoplite battle performance is dead wrong.

A Storm of Spears makes a seminal contribution to the field of ancient military history, perhaps finally settling one of the more nettlesome problems of Greek military history. The book is well organized, richly supported with photographs and charts in support of its author's findings, and written for both layman and expert in fine prose. Chris Matthew deserves high praise for taking on a very difficult topic and doing an excellent job of illuminating it. The book is a fine work of historical scholarship that is likely to become the definitive disposition on Greek hoplite warfare.

Richard A. Gabriel
Distinguished Adjunct Professor
Department of History and War Studies
The Royal Military College of Canada

Preface

It has been stated that, 'we must ask ourselves what the hoplites in the phalanx were faced with, for they are the key to our understanding ancient Greek warfare'.[1] However, for decades the investigation into hoplite warfare has not been conducted in a manner consistent with this directive. The analysis of the behaviour of the individual combatant on the battlefields of ancient Greece in the fifth and fourth centuries BC, the age of the 'Classical hoplite', has only just begun. Works by Hanson and van Wees, for example, have initiated a trend of examining the environment in which the hoplite found himself in battle. The sights, sounds and emotions experienced by the individual have merely commenced our understanding of the manner in which the hoplite operated under ancient combat conditions.

What these, and many other works, have only begun to appreciate is how the individual hoplite performed within the context of a large-scale battle. This, however, is not a negative reflection on the progress of modern scholarship. The ancient sources rarely deal with the finer aspects of ancient combat and merely place vague details of engagements into their broader narratives. Artistic representations of mass combat are rare, and are subjective in their interpretation due to the medium used and the ability or licence of the artist. The archaeological record allows the researcher to gain an understanding of the arms and equipment of the hoplite, yet cannot illustrate how these weapons were employed without careful and critical analysis.

Additionally, modern scholarship into the nature of hoplite warfare has been conducted at a time when war is no longer undertaken by hundreds, let alone thousands, of heavily armoured warriors wielding spears and shields. As such, scholars have had little opportunity to study the dynamics of this style of warfare directly. Modern scholars derive their hypotheses primarily from the literary, artistic, topographic and archaeological evidence; yet commonly reach vastly different conclusions. This uncertainty indicates that the precise nature of hoplite combat has not yet been fully comprehended.[2] The use of purely theoretical reconstruction does not allow for experimentation that is controlled, measurable and repeatable to confirm any hypothesis. The ability to create tactical simulations and re-constructions (whether computer or paper based) provides a somewhat controlled means of replicating ancient warfare, but is limited to the amount of variables placed into the rules under which they operate. It is unlikely that every possible variable can be considered in such an exercise.[3]

In order to gain a more comprehensive understanding of hoplite warfare, the traditional sources of evidence, and the methodologies used to interpret them, cannot be solely relied upon. Consequently, the structure of this book follows a simple premise: the best way to fully understand what the hoplite in the phalanx was faced with and, in turn, to understand hoplite warfare in even its broadest context, is to re-create the hoplite and his environment by combining both the traditional methods of historical enquiry with the relatively recent concepts of physical re-creation, experimental archaeology and ballistics testing.[4] This allows for a holistic view of the role of the individual hoplite in the wars of ancient Greece to be formulated. To aid this process, an entire panoply of hoplite equipment was created by skilled armourers to be worn and tested in a variety of experiments that analyzed different aspects of hoplite warfare. It was only by bearing the hoplite's equipment, experiencing all of the limitations to movement and the senses that this panoply creates, extrapolating data from the imagery and descriptions provided in the ancient sources, and then attempting to physically recreate, via experimentation, the functions of the hoplite as suggested by these sources, that the true nature of hoplite warfare could be understood. This process, in turn, allowed the validity of the ancient source material and previous scholarship to be assessed.

The design of this project follows a series of progressive examinations with each one building on, and expanding upon, the findings of those preceding it. It begins with an analysis of the hoplite's primary weapon, the thrusting spear; its length, the weight of its constituent parts, and the different ways the artistic record suggests it was wielded. This understanding of the spear's configuration allows for the artistic record, which has long been the sole source of evidence for many scholars examining hoplite warfare, to be compared with the physical characteristics of the weapon itself. Not only does this examination confirm the existence within the artistic record of two previously unidentified techniques for wielding the spear, as depicted by the ancient Greeks themselves, but also demonstrates that all previous scholarship on hoplite warfare has been based upon an incorrect interpretation of the artistic record; thus leaving a new model for the mechanics of hoplite warfare and the need for all previous work to be revised.

However, the dismissal of the last 150 years of scholarship into hoplite warfare cannot be based solely on artistic reinterpretation alone. As such, physical re-creation, experimental archaeology and ballistics testing are subsequently used to examine both the previously and recently identified techniques for wielding the hoplite spear in a series of tests to examine such things as how the spear could be repositioned from one posture to the next within the confines of the massed formation of the phalanx, the strength and angle of impact of attacks made using these techniques, how long such an action could be maintained in combat, how well protected a hoplite was in battle and, therefore, what both he and his opponent would have aimed at during the course of an engagement. The results of these tests are then compared with the literary, artistic and archaeological evidence to correlate (if possible) what the test results say with the ancient sources and the modern theories that have been based exclusively upon an interpretation of them. The results of these examinations confirm that hoplite warfare was conducted in a manner vastly different than is described in all previous scholarship.

This understanding of the functionality of the individual warrior of the Classical Age is then used as the basis for a greater understanding of the mechanics of combat within the broader context of hoplite warfare, including the creation and maintenance of formations, strategy and tactics. Many of these facets can only be understood by first developing a robust understanding of the role of the individual via physical recreation, experimental archaeology and ballistics testing. This allows for many of the scholarly debates that have raged over some of these issues to be more thoroughly addressed than was previously possible. The results of this part of the reappraisal show that much of what has hereto been considered to be the nature of hoplite warfare is either incomplete, inconclusive or simply incorrect.

Chapter 1

The Hoplite Spear

Any reappraisal of hoplite combat must begin with an examination of the hoplite himself. An understanding of the individual, how he functioned on the battlefield, how he interacted with those around him and how his actions dictated, and were dictated by, the actions of others, forms the foundation of every subsequent enquiry into the broader aspects of warfare in ancient Greece. Similarly, an examination of the individual must also have a reference point from which all further investigations into the characteristics of the hoplite will stem. This starting point must be an examination of what Euripides refers to as the hoplite's only offensive resource: the spear.[1] Despite how vital an understanding of the spear's configuration is to the comprehension of how hoplite warfare was conducted, very little analysis of the physical properties of the hoplite's primary weapon has been undertaken by previous scholarship. By examining the available evidence, it is possible to determine the weight of the spear's constituent parts, the overall length of the weapon and, importantly for any examination of the mechanics of hoplite warfare, how the characteristics of the individual parts influenced the functionality of the assembled weapon.

Modern scholarship tends to generalize any reference made to the characteristics of the hoplite spear. In terms of the size of the weapon alone, various estimates have been given ranging from 6–10ft (183cm–305cm) in length.[2] While most scholars agree about the presence of the three main constituent parts of the hoplite spear (head, shaft and butt-spike – see following), very little analysis has been done in terms of gauging the average weights of these parts or, more significantly, how the weights of these parts influence the performance of the weapon itself. This may in part be due to the diverse range of somewhat confusing data that is available for such a study.

The ancient texts provide few technical details of hoplite arms and armour. There are no texts that provide elaborate descriptions of hoplite weaponry in the same manner that writers such as Asclepiodotus and Polybius outline for the Hellenistic phalangite and the Roman legionaries of the second century BC.[3] From the Archaic Period poems of Tyrtaeus to the Classical Age narratives of Herodotus, Thucydides and Xenophon, many details of the physical characteristics of the hoplite spear, such as its weight or length, are not specified. Later passages by Diodorus and Nepos concerning reforms made to Greek military equipment in the mid-fourth century BC, only offer that the spear was lengthened (by either 50 per cent or 100 per cent according to Diodorus and by 100 per cent according to Nepos), without outlining what the length of the original spear was or to what length it was increased.[4]

The lack of uniform, or even detailed, information within the available written evidence can be accounted for through an acceptance that the intended audience for many of these written passages were already in possession of an inherent knowledge of the mechanics of hoplite warfare, much of it gained from first-hand experience, which rendered any such information redundant.[5] This is clearly illustrated by the aforementioned work of Polybius, which detailed the characteristics of the Roman military for a predominantly Greek audience; who would have had a solid knowledge of Greek weaponry but potentially not of that of their contemporary Romans.

The archaeological record is also a limited, albeit still valuable, resource for any attempt to reconstruct the characteristics of hoplite weaponry. Wood will not survive in the archaeological record except under certain conditions. As a consequence, while many of the metallic components of the hoplite spear have been found, the shaft has, for the most part, been absent. What is certain from the archaeological evidence is that the hoplite spear was tipped with a leaf-shaped head of iron or bronze and had a spike, variously referred to in the ancient sources as a *sauroter* (σαυρωτήρ), a *styrax* (στύραξ) or an *ouriachos* (οὐρίαχος), also of iron or bronze, mounted on the rear end of the shaft.[6]

While artistic representations of the hoplite can sometimes confirm the presence of the leaf-shaped head and *sauroter* on the weapon carried by the hoplite, the quality of the imagery is dependent upon the artistic style and talent of the artist, the amount of room that the artist had to work within his respective medium and the scale of the image. Factors such as these make it difficult to examine the characteristics of the hoplite spear based solely on the artistic record. This evidence can only be used in conjunction with the archaeological and/or written records. Nevertheless, by examining the individual constituent parts of the spear's construction and how, when assembled, these individual items influence the dynamics of the weapon, the fundamental details of how the spear was designed to be used can be determined.

The head of the hoplite spear

It is no easy task to attempt to distinguish a series of 'average' characteristics for the head that was attached to the hoplite spear due to the number of different styles found within the archaeological record. Snodgrass, in his examination of Greek armour and weapons, classifies spearheads into fourteen different categories based upon their size, shape, the material they are constructed from and their period of use.[7] Among these classifications, Snodgrass refers to the 'J style' spearhead as the 'hoplite spear *par excellence*'.[8] The 'J style' spearhead is typified by its long socket, its long, narrow, blade, and its sloping shoulders. This type of spearhead saw service in warfare from the late geometric period (c.700BC) onwards.[9] While perhaps not the most common form of spearhead (a distinction probably belonging to those of the smaller 'M style', which had a period of use from the early Protogeometric Age (c.1000BC) to the fall of the Roman Republic (c.31BC)), the 'J style' spearhead is, according to Snodgrass, the style that set the standard as the best type to be used by the hoplite.

Finds of iron 'J style' spearheads at Olympia average 279mm in length, 31mm in width, and have an average weight of 153g.[10] Many finds of spearheads at other locations also seem to fall within the parameters set by the 'J style'. Spearheads excavated from Vergina, some of which Connolly dates to the Greek Dark Age (c.1200–800BC), measure 270–350mm.[11] A damaged spearhead excavated from Corinth measures 175mm in length but it is estimated that it would have been approximately 200mm when undamaged.[12] A spearhead excavated from Olynthus measures 147mm in length. However, two-thirds of its socket is missing and the length of the complete artefact is estimated at 250mm.[13] The longest spearhead excavated from Olynthus, which has been dated to the Classical Era, has a length of 290mm; the smallest complete specimen measures 93mm.[14] In his initial reports, Robinson classified these heads as coming from *sarissae* (the long Macedonian pike), however the length of the larger heads makes it more probable that they belong to spears.[15] Unfortunately, many of these artefacts are not categorized under one of Snodgrass' classifications, nor is sufficient detail provided to classify them, and any comparison with the style of spearhead set by Snodgrass can only be based upon relative length.

The head was attached to the shaft through the use of a tubular socket into which one end of the shaft was inserted. Some examples of spearheads contain a single transverse hole in the wall of the socket where a nail or rivet would have been used to secure the head to the shaft. Other examples of spearheads do not possess this hole and must have been secured to the shaft through the use of some form of adhesive. Sekunda suggests the use of pitch.[16]

Anderson simply summarizes the variance in the available evidence by stating that there is no standard size for the head of the hoplite spear, which ranged in length between 20cm and 30cm.[17] Everson states that spearheads in the ninth and eighth centuries BC ranged between 30cm and 50cm in length but that these weapons were almost certainly for throwing.[18] Everson later states that spearheads did not change in size from the sixth to the fifth century BC without actually outlining the size that the sixth century weapons took.[19] Based upon the work of Snodgrass, the average dimensions of the 'hoplite spear *par excellence*' can most easily be based upon the finds from Olympia. From these finds the 'average' characteristics of the iron hoplite spearhead can be set as follows (table 1).

Table 1: The average details of 'J style' spearheads at Olympia.

Average length	Average max. width	Average weight	Average blade length	Average socket length	Average socket (inner diameter)
279mm	31mm	153g	202mm	77mm	18mm

The *sauroter*

Similar problems are encountered when attempting to distinguish an 'average' set of characteristics for the *sauroter* – the large 'spike' on the rear end of the spear. Like the spearhead, many modern works provide only a generalized reference to the shape and/or size of the *sauroter*. Hanson, for example, states that the *sauroter* ranged in size between 5cm and 20cm.[20] Anderson likewise provides a range of up to 40cm in length.[21] Snodgrass states that the size of the *sauroter* was 'no less than 40cm'.[22]

The most common shape of the bronze *sauroter* is a solid pyramidal or conical spike (referred to hereafter as the 'long point'). Other examples possess either a 'short point' or a 'small knob'. The base of the common 'long point' measured between 20mm and 30mm across at its widest point. It was mounted onto the shaft by a tubular socket approximately 19mm in diameter, designed to fit onto the end of the shaft. Like the spearhead, in some cases, a single rivet passed through a transverse hole in the socket in order to secure the spike in place. Other examples of the *sauroter* lack this transverse hole for a rivet and can only have been attached to the end of the shaft through the use of some form of adhesive.

Across the archaeological record examples of spear butts vary in their size, shape and the material they are constructed from. A bronze 'long point' *sauroter* discovered in Athens in 1971 measures 21.6cm.[23] A *sauroter* from Locris measures 40cm.[24] Yet another, from Arcadia, measures 42.3cm.[25] Spear-ends recovered from Olynthus range in length from a fragmentary artefact 5cm long to a complete *sauroter* of 21cm.[26] As with the spearhead, the most detailed records are those for Olympia where the following average sizes for different types of *sauroter* can be found (table 2).

Table 2: Average dimensions for examples of the *sauroter* at Olympia.[28]

Sauroter style	Average length (mm)	Average max. width (mm)	Average weight (g)	Inner socket diameter (mm)
Bronze long point	259	21	329	18
Bronze short point	160	21	237	19
Bronze small knob	221	24	689	25
Iron long point	301	25	545	23
Iron short point	203	23	308	22

At Vergina a small 'butt-spike' measuring 6.3cm was recovered from Tumulus LXVIII Grave E.[27] Many small spear-ends, of a similar length, have also been recovered from Olympia.[29] These examples appear to be more of a 'butt-cap' than a 'butt-spike'. A 'butt-cap' is suggested by the diminutive noun *styrakion* (στυράκιον) used by Thucydides to distinguish it from the more elongated *styrax* (στύραξ).[30] These appear to be the ends of javelins rather than the ends of thrusting spears (see following and figure 1).

Thus any range given by previous scholars for the size of the *sauroter* that includes the length of the *styrakion* must be revised. Based upon the archaeological evidence for Olympia, the common bronze 'long point' *sauroter* averaged 259mm in length, had an average maximum width of 21mm and an average weight of 329g.

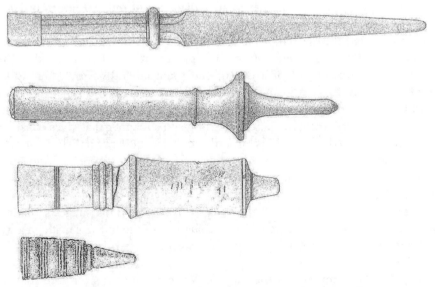

Figure 1: Examples of the different styles of *sauroter* and *styrakion*.[31]

The shaft of the hoplite spear

Both Tyrtaeus and Homer refer to the spears used by the Greeks as being constructed from ash wood (μελίας).[32] Xenophon and dedicatory statements attributed to Nicias and Anyte also confirm the use of Cornelian Cherry (κράνεια) in the construction of spear shafts.[33] The use of pine or olive wood in the spear's construction has also been suggested by some scholars without providing any supporting references.[34] Xenophon states that spoke shaves were carried by an army on the march.[35] This suggests that, no matter which species of wood the shaft was initially manufactured from, replacement shafts could, and would, be fashioned from whatever timber was available to an army in the field.[36]

Regardless of which wood was used in the construction of the hoplite spear, the ancient texts omit details of the diameter of the shaft or how its ends were shaped to accommodate the mounting of both the spearhead and the *sauroter*. In many artistic representations the spear shaft is shown only as a single straight line of uniform thickness. Markle suggests that the average diameter of the shaft was 25mm as this would provide sufficient strength to prevent breakage and to take the force of any thrust made with the weapon.[37] Hanson also offers a diameter of 25mm.[38] Fox, who studied the properties of Cornel wood, concluded that it 'is so tough that it need not be thick when very long'.[39] A shaft with this diameter would necessitate the reshaping of the ends to fit into the socket of the head and *sauroter*; both of which have a smaller average inner diameter.[40]

The size of the socket for both the spearhead and the *sauroter* suggests that the shaft of the weapon may have had a diameter of only 19mm in order to easily fit into these mountings. However, when assembling the re-created spear made for use in this research, it was found that a shaft with a diameter of 19mm does not possess enough inner strength to prevent it from bending and flexing under its own weight and/or the weight of the head and *sauroter*. Due to the point of balance for the weapon (see following), a spear with a 19mm shaft exhibits a considerable 'droop' towards the forward end of the weapon. When moving, the entire weapon bounces and flexes in a manner that gives considerable movement to the head. This 'droop' and flex would have only been negated by a thin shaft made from an extremely hard and rigid wood. However, an army on the march would have had no guarantee of consistently obtaining such timber. Shafts with a diameter of 19mm are also very easy to break (see Chapter 10, The Use of the *Sauroter* as a Weapon). This suggests that the hoplite spear was not constructed using a shaft of 19mm but was made in a way that better self-supported the weight of the weapon, regardless of the density of the wood.

The Achilles Amphora in the Vatican Museum, suggests that the shaft on some spears may have been tapered along its entire length with the rearward end thicker than the front (plate 1.1). Sekunda suggests that this tapering was a by-product of the rounding process used to create the shaft.[41] Matthews suggests that the shaft of the spear may have been as thick as 50mm in diameter at the rear tapering to 30mm at the forward tip.[42] However, not only would a shaft of this configuration make the spear excessively heavy and unwieldy, but the larger diameters of both end of the shaft would require a great deal of reshaping in order to accommodate the 19mm sockets of the spearhead and the *sauroter*. A tapered shaft is also unlikely to have been fashioned by a soldier in the field to the correct shape. If the tapering was too acute, and the front end of the weapon too thin, an amount of bounce and flex would be experienced and the thinner tip of the spear would be susceptible to easy breakage. It would have been difficult to adequately fashion, and balance, a tapered spear shaft without the use of specialized wood-working equipment and expert craftsmen. Xenophon suggests that the shaping of spear shafts was an acquired skill.[43] Xenophon also refers to craftsmen who accompanied a Spartan army when it was in the field.[44] Whether a spear maker (δορυξός) was among these craftsmen is not detailed but is definitely possible.

The presence of spear makers in Aristophanes' *Peace* suggests that the manufacture of spears was at least a specialized industry within the urban environment of the fifth-century city-state, much in the same way that shield manufacture was.[45] Strabo cites the presence of an armoury (ὁπλοθήκη) in Massilia.[46] Dionysius of Syracuse hired numerous professional armourers from across the Greek world to equip his troops for an impending war with Carthage.[47] Similarly, Agesilaus established numerous weapons 'factories' in Ephesus for an impending campaign, with prizes awarded for the most skillfully made and beautifully adorned weapons.[48] This suggests the presence of professional, or at least highly skilled, weapon makers. Whether they arrived with Agesilaus as part of his army or were already present in Ephesus is not stated.[49]

Due to the difficulty in fashioning a tapered shaft, it can be concluded that only experienced spear makers would have created weapons with this kind of shaft; if weapons with tapered shafts were indeed ever made. Xenophon's reference to carried spoke shaves and shaft fashioning by an army in the field is more likely a reference to the manufacture of cruder replacement shafts by the individual hoplite while on campaign.

Therefore, there are two possible methods of construction for the hoplite spear:

1. A shaft fashioned by a professional, or at least highly skilled, craftsman with a gradual taper along its entire length, as suggested by the Achilles Amphora (plate 1.1). The forward end of the shaft would need to have had a diameter of no less than 19mm to comfortably fit into the socket

of the spearhead. The shaft may have then tapered so that it had a diameter of 25mm at the point just before the mounting of the *sauroter*. The rearward end of the shaft would need to have a section reshaped to create a smaller 'tongue' that would insert into the socket of the butt-spike (figure 2).

2. A shaft fashioned by an army on the march, by a less skilled craftsman, or by a craftsman who wanted to produce a weapon with a straight shaft. Such a shaft would have had a uniform thickness along its entire length of approximately 25mm. Those sections that inserted into the head and *sauroter* would have to be reduced and reshaped in order to fit into a socket with a smaller diameter of approximately 19mm (figure 3).

The length of the hoplite spear

To what length were these spear shafts made? Kromayer and Veith, from an analysis of representations of the spear in vase paintings, calculated that the average length of the weapon was approximately one and a half times the height of its bearer.[50] Hanson suggests that the average hoplite was 170cm tall.[51] Angel also provides a figure of 170cm, while Gabriel and Metz base their conclusions on a height of 172cm.[52] The bodies of Spartans discovered in the Kerameikos have been measured and, although the results of the forensic analysis into their stature have not yet been released, their height is said to be the same as that of a modern man; suggesting a height of around 170cm.[53] Two other bodies excavated from the area of the Herian gates north-east of the Kerameikos (now T35 (case 111) and T37 (case 112) in the National Archaeological Museum Athens) dating to the mid-fifth century BC, one of a young adult male and the other of a mature male, were measured at 180cm and 175cm respectively. Unfortunately, comparative data for the supposed burial site of the Theban Sacred Band at Chaeronea is not readily available as the details of this site have only received brief mention in texts and journals, photographs of the finds have never been published and the site has not been re-excavated since the nineteenth century.[54] Vegetius states that, for the Romans, both cavalrymen and front-line legionnaires should be between 172cm and 177cm in height, suggesting that an average height of around 170–172cm for the Greek hoplite is not implausible.[55]

Assuming that a figure of 170cm is correct, Kromayer and Veith's estimations place the length of the hoplite spear at approximately 255cm (8ft 4in), which is located in the centre of the range given by modern scholars. Even assuming a ±10 per cent variable margin of error still gives the length of the spear a range of between 230cm and 280cm, well within the boundaries set by recent scholarship. Subtracting an average length of 27.9cm for the spearhead

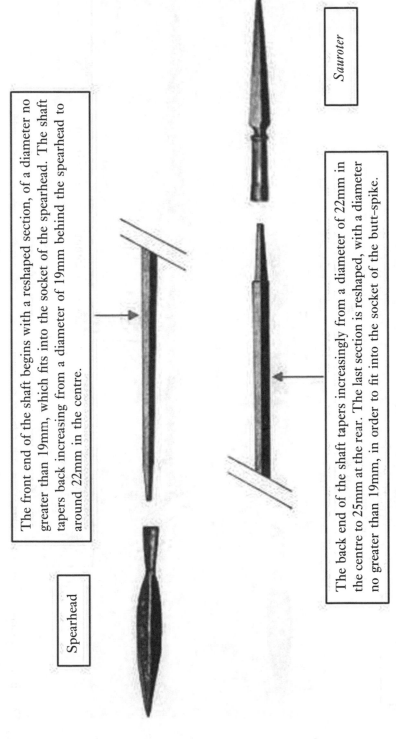

Sauroter

The front end of the shaft begins with a reshaped section, of a diameter no greater than 19mm, which fits into the socket of the spearhead. The shaft tapers back increasing from a diameter of 19mm behind the spearhead to around 22mm in the centre.

Spearhead

The back end of the shaft tapers increasingly from a diameter of 22mm in the centre to 25mm at the rear. The last section is reshaped, with a diameter no greater than 19mm, in order to fit into the socket of the butt-spike.

Figure 2: The construction of a hoplite spear with a tapered shaft.

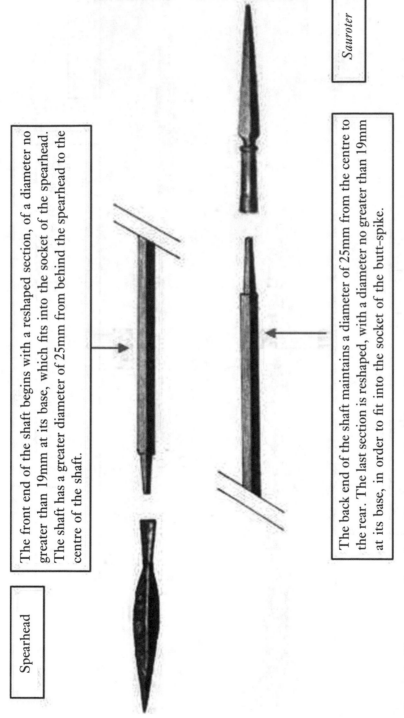

Sauroter

Spearhead

The front end of the shaft begins with a reshaped section, of a diameter no greater than 19mm at its base, which fits into the socket of the spearhead. The shaft has a greater diameter of 25mm from behind the spearhead to the centre of the shaft.

The back end of the shaft maintains a diameter of 25mm from the centre to the rear. The last section is reshaped, with a diameter no greater than 19mm at its base, in order to fit into the socket of the butt-spike.

Figure 3: The construction of a hoplite spear with a 25mm diameter shaft.

and 25.9cm for the *sauroter* from an overall length for the weapon of 255cm, gives a length for the spear shaft itself of around 201cm (not including the tongues that insert into the socket of the head and *sauroter*).

The archaeological record provides only one instance where the length of a shafted weapon can be determined with a high probability for accuracy. The grave excavated at Vergina, which contained the aforementioned *styrakion* (6.3cm), also contained its corresponding head (27.5cm), in situ, with fragments of wood present in the interval between them from a shaft 188.2cm in length; significantly shorter than the estimates made based on the findings of Kromayer and Veith. The overall length of the weapon recovered from Vergina calculates to only 222cm, also far shorter than the predicted length of the spear; with the size of the smaller *styrakion* contributing to this shorter length. If the length of the *styrakion* is replaced with the average length of the *sauroter* (25.9cm) the overall length of the weapon recalculates as 242cm; still shorter than the estimated length for the spear.

The fashioning of replacement shafts by an army in the field suggests that there may not have been an overall standard length for the hoplite spear as replacement shafts would likely have been fashioned from whatever wood was available, and may have been cut to a length only approximating the size of the lost shaft or in replication of weapons belonging to other members of the phalanx. However, the available evidence suggests that the common length for the weapon was somewhere around 250cm with the shaft itself around 200cm in length.

The weight of the hoplite spear

How much did such a lengthy weapon weigh? Markle compared the characteristics of the wood of the *Cornus florida L*, a heavier member of the same family as the Cornelian Cherry, and determined that the density of the wood was approximately the same.[56] During further examinations, Markle determined that oak also possessed similar qualities to that of Cornel wood (although which specific species of oak was not specified).[57] He concluded that the weight of Cornel wood was 13.6g per cubic inch.[58] Basing calculations on a spear shaft approximately 213cm in length, with a uniform diameter of 25mm, and omitting the reshaped tongues for the mounting of the head and *sauroter*, Markle calculated that the weight of the shaft alone would be in the vicinity of 907g.[59] Thus, an average spear shaft 200cm in length, and also with a diameter of 25mm, would weigh 850g. By attaching an average spearhead of 27.9cm in length and 153g in weight, and an average *sauroter* of 25.9cm in length and 329g in weight, the average hoplite spear would have been around 253cm in overall length with a total weight of 1,332g; not far from the estimates based upon the findings of Kromayer and Veith (table 3).

Table 3: The estimated characteristics for various examples of hoplite shafted weapons.

Source	Spearhead dimensions	Butt-spike dimensions	Shaft dimensions	Total length and weight
Kromayer and Veith	27.9cm[##] 153.0g	25.9cm[##] 329.0g	201.2cm[**] 856.8g[#]	255.0cm[*] 1,338.8g
Excavated weapon – Vergina	27.3cm 97.0g	6.3cm 90.0g	188.2cm 801.4g[#]	222.0cm 988.4g
Average Hoplite spear	27.9cm[##] 153.0g	25.9cm[##] 329.0g	200.0cm 850.0g[#]	253.0cm 1,332.0g

[*]   Based on the estimate of length being 1½ times the height of a 170cm tall hoplite
[**] Determined by subtracting the average length of spearheads and butt-spikes from the total length
[#]   Based on the results of calculations conducted by Markle
[##] Average dimensions found in the archaeological record for Olympia

The shorter length and lower weight of the weapon excavated from Vergina, along with the attachment of a *styrakion* to its shaft rather than a *sauroter*, suggests that it is something other than the hoplite spear, most likely a javelin.

The balance of the hoplite spear
The balance of the spear is an important factor in determining how it could be wielded. It has been suggested that the *sauroter* acted as a counterweight to the spearhead.[60] However, even a cursory examination of the unequal average weights of the spear's constituent parts indicates that the spearhead and *sauroter* cannot act as a simple offsetting counterweight to each other. The point of balance for the average hoplite spear (as given in table 3) can be calculated using the following formula (figure 4).

Had the mass of the spearhead and *sauroter* been similar or equal, such as for the weapon excavated from Vergina, the point of balance for the weapon would be situated halfway along its length. It can therefore be concluded that the heavier *sauroter* does not simply offset the weight of the spearhead, as suggested by some scholars, but dramatically shifts the point of balance towards the rear end of the weapon. If the spear possessed a tapered shaft, the point of balance for the spear would move further back towards the rear, depending upon the exact level of tapering along the shaft and the redistribution of weight that this would cause. It is possible that smaller, lighter, butt-spikes were affixed to tapered shafts, and that larger heads were combined with heavier ends so as to keep the location of the point of balance relatively consistent regardless of

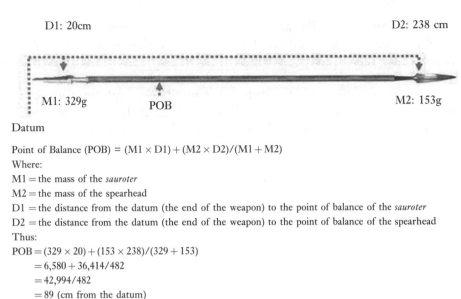

D1: 20cm

D2: 238 cm

M1: 329g   POB

M2: 153g

Datum

Point of Balance (POB) = $(M1 \times D1) + (M2 \times D2)/(M1 + M2)$
Where:
M1 = the mass of the *sauroter*
M2 = the mass of the spearhead
D1 = the distance from the datum (the end of the weapon) to the point of balance of the *sauroter*
D2 = the distance from the datum (the end of the weapon) to the point of balance of the spearhead
Thus:
POB = $(329 \times 20) + (153 \times 238)/(329 + 153)$
    = $6,580 + 36,414/482$
    = $42,994/482$
    = 89 (cm from the datum)

Figure 4: Calculation of the point of balance for the average hoplite spear.

the manner in which the spear was constructed. This would account for the variances in both size and weight for examples of the spearhead and *sauroter* found in the archaeological record. However, if a weapon with a tapered shaft broke while the hoplite was in the field, it is unlikely that he would have been able to fashion a similarly tapered replacement with his spoke shave. The characteristics of the replacement shaft would thus alter the dynamics of the weapon (potentially significantly). This suggests that a shaft with a uniform diameter, for which replacements could more easily be created, was the more common type of shaft used in the manufacture of the hoplite spear.

Additionally, some examples of the *sauroter* (such as #6848 in the National Archaeological Museum, Athens) possess an extra lead weight that has been wrapped around the spike or socket in order to add to the overall mass of the butt-spike. This is a clear indication of a *sauroter* that has been affixed to a spear that has been too light to create the correct point of balance for the weapon. The weight of the *sauroter* has therefore been altered through the addition of a supplementary weight to shift the point of balance of the weapon further to the rear.[61]

The rearward point of balance for the hoplite spear (regardless of the style of shaft) can be seen in the Achilles Amphora. The image on this vase is one of the few pictorial references of a hand-grip, presumably of hide or cloth, wrapped around the shaft of the spear (see plate 1.1).[62] The positioning of this grip clearly complies with the calculated point of balance for the weapon.[63]

A re-examination of the archaeological and artistic evidence, as well as modern estimates and calculations for the characteristics of the hoplite spear, demonstrates that the average hoplite weapon was approximately 2.5m in length, had an iron head weighing around 153g and bronze *sauroter* weighing 329g affixed to either end of a shaft that had either a uniform diameter of 25mm or tapered from 19mm at the front to 25mm at the back. The overall weight of the spear was over 1.3kg and had a point of balance approximately 89cm from the rear end of the weapon.[64]

Chapter 2

Wielding the Hoplite Spear

How then, was this weapon held by the individual hoplite? The identification of how the spear was wielded for battle is paramount for the comprehension of the larger mechanics of hoplite warfare. However, there is only limited evidence that can aid this determination. The archaeological record can only allow for the the balance, weight and size of the weapon to be ascertained. The ancient literary sources are of little use as most accounts do not go to the desired level of detail. The earlier writing of Tyrtaeus, for example, recommends that combatants should 'reach forth and strike the foe' (δηΐων ὀρέγοιτ᾽ ἐγγύθεν ἱστάμενος).[1] This suggests that some form of thrusting motion (i.e. 'reaching') was employed in combat but provides no details of the techniques involved in this action. Much of the literature contemporary with the Classical Period is similarly ambiguous. Xenophon's account of the battle of Coronea tells us that the Spartans engaged the Thebans when they were 'within spear thrust of the enemy' (εἰς δόρυ ἀφικόμενοι ἔτρεψαν τὸ καθ᾽ αὑτούς); again suggesting that some form of thrusting motion was utilized without providing details of the stance that this attack was made from.[2] Euripides' statement that hoplites stood 'side by side and fought spear level with spear' (ᾧ ξύνοπλα δόρατα νέα νεῳ) suggests that hoplites adopted a uniform stance throughout their ranks in combat but provides no details of what the posture actually was.[3] Due to the nature of this evidence, modern research has relied upon an analysis of the only source that provides a clearer picture of hoplite combative postures: the artistic record. However, an examination of scholarship's reliance upon this source demonstrates that previous research into hoplite warfare has been based upon an incomplete, and in many places incorrect, appraisal of the available evidence.

Based upon the selective use of the artistic record as a source of evidence for hoplite combat, current convention holds that there were two different postures that the hoplite could use to wield his spear in battle; the 'low' and 'overhead' positions.[4] Both stances are commonly depicted in vase illustrations and relief carvings (plates 2.1 and 3.1). The 'overhead' is the most commonly depicted of all of the combative postures. Within a test sample of 188 illustrated vases taken from a random selection of the artistic record, incorporating more than

480 individual figures in what could be classed as a combative posture with a shafted weapon, approximately 60 per cent of all of the images show the overhead technique in use.

In the images of the overhead position, the hoplite stands with his left leg forward, the shield is on the left arm and the weapon is held above the head, poised to strike. In the low stance, the placement of the feet is generally the same with the left leg forward, and the shield is still on the left arm, but the spear is held low, between the level of the ribcage and the thigh rather than above the head. As noted, all previous scholarship on hoplite warfare has been based upon a method of fighting utilizing these two techniques for wielding the spear (hereafter referred to as the 'low/overhead two-stance model'). However, this model is incomplete. The artistic record also contains pictorial references of a third combative posture: the 'underarm' technique (plate 4.1). Despite the existence of this stance within the artistic record, the underarm stance has, until now, remained almost completely unexamined by modern historians research-ing ancient warfare.[5]

Upon initial inspection, the 'underarm' stance appears to be merely an elevated version of the low stance with the spear held higher, tucked into the armpit, while the footwork and shield placement remain the same. It is possible that the majority of previous scholars have considered the 'low' and 'underarm' postures to be one and the same and this may account for the lack of analysis of this technique. However, when physically replicating these postures as part of the testing of various aspects of hoplite combat, it was found that there are enough differences between the two, in terms of how the weapon is held, to class them as two separate combative postures (see following). On this basis alone, all previous models of hoplite warfare cannot be considered complete.

One of the major differences between the three postures is the position of the hand and wrist when gripping the shaft of the weapon. When wielding the spear in the 'overhead' position, for example, the forearm is almost vertical, below the weapon, and perpendicular to the axis of the shaft. The wrist is flexed only enough to allow a natural grip on the spear, which is supported in the saddle between thumb and forefinger. The palm of the hand is located on the outer side of the shaft facing towards the hoplite. The fingers curl over the top of the shaft and the weapon is secured by the thumb, which curls beneath it. Regardless of whether the spear is elevated through the extension of the arm, or lowered to the point to where the spear rests on the shoulder, the placement of the hand, wrist and forearm remain unaltered.

The grip of the 'low' stance shares many similarities with that of the 'over-head' posture. The forearm is similarly perpendicular to the shaft, although in this case it is above it rather than below it, and the wrist is also only flexed enough to provide a natural grip on the weapon. The palm remains on the outside of the shaft, but the fingers curl beneath it while the thumb curls over the shaft to secure the grip. Similar to the overhead posture, the placement of the hand, wrist and forearm does not significantly alter as the elevation of the weapon changes and any adjustment to the angle of pitch for both postures is made via the lateral movement and flex of the wrist. However, the major difference between the 'low' and 'overhead' positions is that the positioning of the thumb and forefinger is effectively reversed. In the 'overhead' position the thumb and index finger are situated at the rear of the grip, towards the rear of the weapon, whereas in the 'low' position the thumb and forefinger are towards the front (plate 5.1).

The dynamics of the 'underarm' posture are vastly different to either the 'low' or 'overhead' techniques. The spear is held tucked beneath the armpit with the upper arm placed over the weapon. Unlike any other stance, the forearm is not situated perpendicular to the weapon but can be placed above, beneath or alongside the shaft running roughly parallel to the long axis of the spear. Depending upon the placement of the forearm, the hand can be similarly situated above, beneath or alongside the shaft creating different, and variable, methods of support for the weapon. The spear is further supported by clenching it between the ribcage and the upper arm. These characteristics are what clearly distinguish the 'underarm' posture as a third hoplite combative technique (plate 5.2).

Additionally, unlike the 'low' and 'overhead' postures, any alteration to the pitch of a spear held in the 'underarm' position is made through the vertical movement of the entire forearm, pivoting at the elbow, using the muscles of the upper arm rather than solely relying on the flex of the wrist. The elevation of the spear can be altered slightly through the lowering of the arm at the shoulder joint to a small degree. If the weapon is lowered further, the arm disengages from the shaft as the weapon descends, and the posture moves naturally into a 'low' stance. The spear can also be elevated by rotating the shoulder and raising the entire arm above the head while keeping the grip in position. In doing so the spear moves out from the armpit and is held away from the body in a posture similar to the 'overhead'. Importantly, in adopting such a posture, the position of the hand remains the same with the thumb and forefinger towards the front. This position, which can be considered a fourth combative technique, and is hereafter referred to as the 'reverse' position, is also evidenced in the artistic record (plate 6.1).

The identification of a third and fourth technique employed for the use of shafted weapons by the hoplite, means that much of what is presently under-stood as the nature of warfare in Classical Greece needs to be re-examined. The further reappraisal of the characteristics of the spear and the way it is shown to be wielded in the artistic record indicates that there are two weapons with vastly different configurations being displayed in vase paintings and other artistic sources. This, in turn, demonstrates that previous scholarship's reliance on the low/overhead two-stance model as a means of explaining the mechanics of hoplite warfare has been greatly misplaced.

Chapter 3

Spears, Javelins and the Hoplite in Greek Art

An analysis of the artistic representation of the hoplite in combat, and a comparison of these images with other sources of evidence, demonstrates that there are two differently configured shafted weapons being depicted in the artistic record. The first is the thrusting spear; commonly shown held in either the low or underarm posture. The other is the javelin. Contrary to current scholarly convention it is this weapon, and not the spear of the Classical hoplite, that is regularly depicted being held in the overhead position. Furthermore, there are numerous, previously unidentified, indicators within the evidence to support this conclusion. Consequently, as the overhead posture has been a fundamental element of all previous scholarship on hoplite warfare, any model that has been based upon the use of the overhead posture cannot be considered correct.

The artistic record has always been one of the primary sources for any work on the Greek hoplite. However, the fact that both the underarm and reverse postures have not been previously identified, much less examined for their viability as a method of wielding the spear, indicates that this source has not been appropriately analysed. According to Sparkes, the 'study of vase-painting over the past century has been concentrated on the matter of connoisseurship – that is, the attribution of vases to individual painters on the basis of style.'[1] As such, the interpretation of hoplite combative techniques has been a relatively minor aspect of artistic assessment. The lack of any comparative analysis of the artistic medium against other sources is nowhere more apparent than in the representation of the hoplite spear in vase illustrations. Any attempt to correlate the artistic representations of hoplite weaponry with the characteristics of the spear itself clearly highlights the differences between the two. In many cases the features of the actual spear and its artistic counterpart fail to correspond with one another. This suggests that many of the weapons shown in these images are not the thrusting spear of the hoplite but something else entirely. Within the artistic record there are several indicators that identify this other weapon as the javelin.

The balance of the weapon

One of the primary indicators that there are two differently configured weapons being portrayed in the artistic record is how the balance of the two weapons is represented in the images. Depending upon the stance in which the hoplite is depicted, there is a great disparity between where the weapon is shown to be held and the point of balance for the actual spear. In some instances it is not possible to determine the exact location of the grip on the weapon in the artistic record. The fragmentation of the pottery or masonry, the scale of the image and/or the degradation of any painting have removed this level of detail. Similarly, in scenes containing multiple figures, the features of one figure will often obscure those of another. Within the test sample used for this research, the location of the grip could clearly be determined for 340 individual figures.

Within the artistic record, around 86 per cent of all figures adopting an overhead posture are shown to be gripping their weapons by the centre of the shaft. This is in direct conflict with the physical properties of the spear's point of balance, which suggests that the weapon shown in these images possesses a different configuration to the thrusting spear of the Classical hoplite. Interestingly, 82 per cent of the weapons shown wielded in the underarm position are gripped at the correct point of balance for the spear. Images of weapons held in the low stance are almost evenly split between being held in the centre and rear of the shaft. This difference in the location of the grip poses several possibilities:

1. That the weapons depicted in the overhead position are meant to be wielded in the centre of the shaft but that in a minority of cases the artwork has simply been rendered inaccurately by the illustrator;
2. That the weapons depicted as held in the underarm position are meant to be wielded by the rear of the shaft but that in a minority of these cases the artwork has been rendered inaccurately by the illustrator; and/or
3. Weapons of both configurations could be held in the low position.

A further analysis of the artistic record, and comparison with the properties of the hoplite spear, confirms that there are two different weapons being portrayed: the thrusting spear being wielded in the underarm and low positions and the javelin shown held in the low and overhead positions.

The one thing that would give a shafted weapon a central point of balance would be the absence of a *sauroter*. The majority of weapons shown in the overhead stance within the test sample are devoid of a *sauroter* on the end of the shaft and this accounts for where the weapon is shown to be held in the imagery. While it must be conceded that this omission may be due to the scale of the image, it is curious that the spearhead is able to be depicted in these same images while the *sauroter* is not; even though they share many dimensional characteristics such as their relative length. It may be that the observer is meant to assume that a *sauroter* is present on the end of the weapon. However, the central location of the grip would suggest otherwise.

It is also possible that the omission of the *sauroter* in some cases may be due to artistic licence or error. However, it seems incomprehensible that a feature of the Classical Age spear, which the archaeological record suggests was relatively commonplace, would be omitted from such a vast majority of vase illustrations by artists from different regions and decades. It can only be concluded that the omission of the *sauroter* was a deliberate act on the part of the artist due to the weapon being depicted not actually possessing one. It seems most likely that the end of many of these weapons was, as depicted, unadorned. It is also possible that weapons shown with a central point of balance may have had the smaller *styrakion* attached to it. The size of the *styrakion* would make it impossible to depict in all but the largest-scale artworks and accounts for its lack of depiction in vase paintings. Finds of the *styrakion* at Olympia indicate that the average diameter of the socket for the *styrakion* was 16mm. This is a smaller diameter than that of the socket for both the spearhead and the *sauroter*. This suggests that the *styrakion* was affixed to a weapon with a thinner shaft than that of the spear.

Constructing the javelin with a thinner shaft would make it lighter and easier to throw. The thinner shaft of the javelin, being predominantly a single-use weapon, would also not have to withstand the same stresses undergone by a spear through continuous probing and jabbing in combat; and therefore would not require a thicker shaft. As such, the weapon uncovered at Vergina by Petsas, is most likely a javelin. This provides an actual length for the javelin and a means of calculating its balance. The find at Vergina measured 222cm in overall length (head 27.5cm, shaft 188.2cm, *styrakion* 6.3cm). Calculations show that the Vergina weapon possessed a central point of balance, consistent with the characteristics of the javelin and with the weapons shown held in the overhead stance in the artistic record (figure 5).

This location for the point of balance complies with the optimum point to grip a shafted missile weapon.[2] The removal of the *styrakion* was found to have only a marginal impact on the location of the point of balance; shifting it only 3cm forward of that for a javelin equipped with a *styrakion*. However, the absence of a small 'butt-cap' does not overly affect the flight of the missile. Cotterell and Kamminga have determined that if the point of balance is behind the midpoint of the shaft, the flight of a javelin is almost impossible.[3] The word *styrakion* has been variously translated as 'javelin spike', 'javelin head' and 'spear butt'.[4] However, it seems most likely that the *styrakion* was attached to the rear end of the javelin, with a shaft 16–19mm in diameter, rather than to

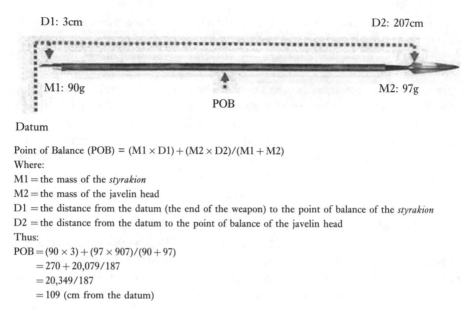

Figure 5: The calculation of the point of balance for the 'Vergina javelin'.

the larger spear. These results demonstrate that the rear end of the shaft of the javelin could have been left bare or adorned with the *styrakion* with only a marginal variance in the balance of the weapon. This suggests that the 'unadorned' shafts of the weapons depicted held in the overhead stance may be an accurate representation of one configuration for the javelin.

Conversely, depictions showing the spear held by the rear third of the shaft commonly have the *sauroter* represented. This is particularly prevalent in depictions of the underarm stance. Regardless of whether the *sauroter* is actually depicted or not, the rearward location of the grip indicates a rearward point of balance for the weapon. Subsequently, a large weight, most likely the *sauroter*, can be assumed to be present on these weapons, which distinguishes them as the thrusting spear of the Classical hoplite rather than the centrally balanced javelin. Additionally, Cotterrell and Kamminga's conclusions further indicate that the rearwardly balanced hoplite spear could not have been used as a missile weapon, and that the javelin must therefore possess a different configuration.

The representations of a centrally balanced weapon held in the overhead posture also raise a question of logic. If these weapons are assumed to be accurate depictions of the thrusting spear of the hoplite, as they are in all previous scholarship, it is odd that a thrusting weapon two and a half metres in length is designed and constructed in a way that requires it to be gripped by the centre of its shaft, negating half of its length. Throughout history, most spears, swords, pikes and other thrusting weapons have been balanced so that the majority of their length is forward of the weapon-bearing hand or hands. When the advances made by Greek city-states in areas such as architecture, geometry, engineering, mathematics and the sciences are considered, it seems absurd to assume that there was something backward about their technology for war. Yet this principle, based upon an interpretation of a centrally held weapon borne over the head, has become one of the fundamental maxims of every previous analysis of ancient Greek warfare. This conclusion seems particularly odd when it is considered that modern scholarship has assumed that the hefty *sauroter* was always affixed to the rear end of the hoplite spear. It seems much more logical to conclude that the weapons shown held centrally are configured differently to the thrusting spear and are, in all likelihood, missile weapons.

It appears that what clearly differentiates the two weapons is the location of their point of balance and how this corresponds with the manner in which they are depicted in art. This is one of the indicators that clearly demonstrates the presence of two different weapons within the artistic record. The first is the thrusting spear, commonly shown held in the underarm and low positions, gripped at its correct point of balance towards the rear of the shaft despite whether a *sauroter* is shown in the image or not. The second is a javelin that would possess a central point of balance regardless of the presence of a *styrakion*. The javelin is commonly wielded using both the overhead and low techniques. Importantly, the central balance of the weapon shown in the overhead posture means that it cannot be the thrusting spear of the hoplite as has been commonly considered by previous scholarship.

The length of the weapon
Another clear indicator that the weapon shown in the overhead stance is something other than the hoplite spear is the length of the weapon being portrayed. Kromayer and Veith have stated that the length of the spear, as depicted in the artistic medium, equates to 1.5 times the height of the bearer.[5] However, this is not an entirely accurate statement. Similar to the location of the grip, the length of the weapon varies depending upon the position in which it is portrayed. The average lengths of weapons relative to bearer height, per combative stance, are shown below (table 4).

As can be seen, the weapon held in the overhead position is generally much shorter than the height of the person wielding it. Using the estimated figure of 170cm for the average stature of a hoplite places the length of this weapon at only 151.5cm. This is far shorter than the estimated length of the spear (255cm) and is even much shorter than the javelin found at Vergina (222cm). The weapons shown wielded in both the low and underarm positions also

Table 4: Weapon length versus bearer height in the artistic test sample.

Stance	Average length of weapon versus bearer height
Overhead	0.891 times bearer height
Low	1.165 times bearer height
Underarm	1.279 times bearer height

measured shorter than Kromayer and Veith's conclusion but, unlike those shown in the overhead position, are still longer than the height of their bearer (calculating to a weapon length of 198.0cm and 217.4cm respectively). Both of these measurements are also outside the estimated lengths provided for the hoplite spear.

It is generally only when the spear is shown in a non-combative context that the weapon's length equates to 1.5 times bearer height. In scenes where the spear is shown to be at rest, such as on the Achilles Amphora (plate 1.1), or when the spear is shown carried sloped over the shoulder by a hoplite on the march, the length of the weapon more commonly conforms to the estimates of Kromayer and Veith. This difference in length is most likely due to the amount of space available to the artist to depict their chosen scene. In images where the spear is depicted vertically, particularly on large vessels like *amphorae*, the weapon can be depicted longer due to the amount of space along the vertical axis of the vessel. On smaller vessels such as *kylikes*, or in large-scale images, superfluous detail, such as the tip or end of the weapon, is often made to project beyond the margins of the illustration, still providing a perception of length. In some cases, parts of the image's decorative border are even erased in order to accommodate the size of weapons and/or figures within the image; again giving an impression of length or size.

With limited space available, there is much less scope for the accurate depiction of length for a weapon held horizontally, as in a combative scene. By their very nature, a combat scene will include at least two figures, and possibly more, all vying for space in the one image. Clearly the limited space would require the artist to compress horizontal dimensioning in order to accommodate the scene. The weapons in these images could not be depicted in their accurate, albeit scaled, dimensions without leaving considerable space between the figures or by having the heads of the weapons project beyond their intended targets; two aspects that may not have been conducive with the artist's stylistic considerations.

The entire scale of the image could have been reduced in size to allow for the accurate depiction of weapons and distancing, but this reduction in scale would also result in a corresponding reduction in the size and detail of the figures involved – the main focus of the illustration itself. The only method for the vase illustrator to depict combat with the protagonists in close proximity to each other, and still be able to place sufficient detail in larger-scale vase imagery, is to reduce the length of any weapon that is depicted horizontally. Unfortunately, the characteristics of the lateral spacing between figures and their weapons appears to be an area of artistic analysis which has yet to be fully examined. Richter's study of foreshortening, linear perspective and distance in Greek art for example, only analyzes how features such as ships, buildings and furniture appear much smaller in scale to their occupants in vase illustrations.[6]

However, the limitation of available space does not account for the shorter depiction of weapons held in the overhead position compared with those in both the low and underarm postures. Weapons shown in the low or underarm positions are reduced in length but are depicted with only a marginal reduction; they are shorter than Kromayer and Veith's estimate of 1.5 times bearer height, but are still longer than the height of the bearer themselves, thus providing a sense of overall length to the weapon. Conversely, weapons shown in the overhead position are generally much shorter than their bearer's height. Interestingly, the depiction of the overhead posture actually provides the artist with more available space and in many cases the weapon could have been depicted to a more accurate length if it was intended to be a representation of the thrusting spear. This is particularly so if the weapon is also meant to be displayed with a central point of balance as both ends of the shaft could be easily placed behind other figures within the image, or projected beyond the margins, without compromising the perception of length. However, this appears not to have occurred and it can only be concluded that the weapons shown in the overhead stance are meant to be depicted as short-shafted weapons. This may be an artistic convention to distinguish the javelin from the longer thrusting spear.

The difference in the length and the thickness of the shaft of the two weapons can be seen clearly in the famous amphora by Exekias depicting Ajax and Achilles playing dice (c. 530BC), now in the Vatican Museum (plate 6.2).

In this image the two different weapons are easily discernable in the hand of Ajax on the right. One weapon is clearly longer than the other. The shorter weapon also has a much smaller head and thinner shaft than its longer counterpart; identifying it as a javelin rather than a spear. Similar features can be seen in the weapons borne by Achilles on the left. Both the difference in length between the spear and the javelin, and the different postures adopted to wield them, can also clearly be seen in a late fourth century (c.330–310BC) amphora in the Los Angeles County Museum of Art (50.8.16). At the top of this image the hoplite on the left engages in combat using a spear held in the underarm position. A basic *sauroter* is represented and the weapon is held by the rear of the shaft; compliant with its point of balance. Two of his adversaries on the right engage using a low posture while another uses an underarm grip. All three weapons are held by the rear of the shaft, distinguishing them as spears with a rearward point of balance. At the bottom of the image other combatants engage with javelins. Their weapons are shorter than the spears depicted at the top of the image, are held in the centre of the shaft and are wielded in an overhead posture. A spent javelin, or perhaps a spare, can be seen embedded in the ground beneath the middle figure (plate 7.1).

A long spear and short javelin has been commonly used to explain the weapons in vase paintings, such as on the Chigi Vase, where two shafted weapons are depicted being held by the one individual (see plate 8.1).[7] However, this conclusion has not been carried on to other areas of artistic analysis or examinations of hoplite warfare. Snodgrass, for example, has commented that 'it is curious that in early art, hoplites are shown thrusting [presumably in the overhead manner] while they are carrying a spare spear in their left hand and that it is a measure of our ignorance that we cannot pronounce the function of the second spear.'[8] This statement appears quite odd when, in an earlier work, Snodgrass states that the long and short–shafted weapons found in early graves are a spear and a javelin respectively.[9] A grave containing two long spears is said to have been an indication of wealth.[10] Everson claims that in this case both weapons were for throwing before closing for melee combat with a sword.[11] Hurwitt oddly claims that the weapon shown held above the head on the Chigi Vase is the spear and the secondary weapon in the left hand is the javelin.[12] Lorimer states that those weapons held at the slope in the image are not borne by the hoplites at all but by unseen servants positioned behind the rank; a hypothesis that has been subsequently dismissed.[13] Lorimer and Mitchell also state that spears were never thrown, even when two were carried; Lorimer oddly states that hunters threw their spare weapons but does not attribute this practice to hoplites.[14]

With the weapons held above the head placed into their correct context as javelins and not thrusting spears as is assumed, Snodgrass' conundrum regarding the second weapon can be definitively addressed. The Chigi Vase, for example, does not display hoplites preparing to engage in the thrusting combat of the Classical Age, but portrays a scene based on an earlier form of warfare, reminiscent of the works of Homer, where a javelin is initially thrown at an opponent before the commencement of thrusting combat with a secondary weapon.[15] It has also been stated that javelins disappear from the artistic record around 640BC.[16] Everson gives a date for its disappearance as 520BC.[17] Van Wees claims that two javelins are still depicted in Athenian art as late as 480BC.[18] However, these positions all require revision. It is not the javelin that disappears from the artistic record, but the bearing of a secondary weapon. The representation of the use of the javelin continues through the depiction of the overhead stance in art and the shorter weapon shown held in this posture. The portrayal of the javelin in art has been dismissed by many as heroic and unrealistic.[19] Again, the dismissal of the javelin as a heroic concept in art is only partially correct. It is true that the javelin is reflective of the heroic style of fighting, but so too is the posture used to wield it. Modern scholarship cannot be entirely to blame for this 'ignorance' as Snodgrass labels it. The lack of any analysis of the underarm stance as a third combative posture left little option but to assume that the overhead stance was a depiction of the thrusting spear in action. Much of what has been determined about hoplite warfare would not hold true if thrusting combat was confined to the only other stance that scholars assumed the hoplite could use: the low stance.

Depictions of the *agkule*

The most conclusive evidence that the short-shafted weapons held in the overhead posture in Greek art are the javelin and not the thrusting spear is the representation of the use of the *agkule* (ἀγκύλη), or throwing loop, in these images. The *agkule* was a thong, presumably of leather or cord, which was attached to the mid-point of the shaft (μεσάηκυλον) of the javelin.[20] The *agkule* was used by inserting the index and/or middle finger into a loop created by the thong in order to gain greater leverage when the weapon was cast.[21] The thong was affixed between the tip and the mid-point of the shaft at the optimum point to generate this leverage.[22] Thus any weapon in the artistic record that displays the use of the *agkule* can be classified as a javelin rather than a spear. On the far left of panel IV of the Chigi Vase, for example, four shafted weapons stand upright and at rest. An *agkule* is clearly visible attached to the shaft of each of these weapons, distinguishing them as javelins rather than thrusting spears (plate 8.1).

An early Corinthian *alabastron* in Berlin also contains two shafted weapons of different lengths in a 'still life' illustration of an early hoplite panoply. The shorter javelin is clearly distinguishable by its attached *agkule*.[23] The javelins on the Chigi Vase are likely to have a *styrakion* mounted on the rear end of the shaft, although this detail is obscured by other features of the image, as this is what would allow them to be thrust upright into the ground as depicted. The Chigi Vase also shows the wielding of *agkule*-equipped javelins by hoplites in the overhead position. While the pigment representing the line of the *agkule* itself has degraded, or was not initially shown, the weapon-bearing hand of the foremost hoplite of the left-hand formation clearly shows the index finger raised for the use of the *agkule* and the javelin (plate 8.2).

It can therefore be concluded that the weapons shown held above the head on the Chigi Vase are javelins and not thrusting spears.[24] The depiction of the throwing hand in this manner can also be seen on the javelin throwers on the LA County amphora (plate 6). This confirms the depiction of javelins rather than spears in the hands of these figures also. The positioning of the fingers to use the *agkulē* is an element of the overhead stance found in many other artistic representations dated well after the Chigi Vase, although it may not be shown on every figure within the same image (see plate 2.1).

On the Toledo *kylix* (cup) (top right on plate 2.1), for example, only one figure clearly shows the fingers raised in the use of the *agkulē* for the throwing of the javelin. However, the other weapons in the image have a similar configuration, particularly their central point of balance, and are also likely to be javelins. This suggests that not all javelins had a throwing loop attached to them and may be another reason, other than scale or degradation, for why not all weapons depicted held in the overhead stance show the presence of an *agkulē* or the raising of the fingers to use it.

Both van Wees and Krentz identify the weapons shown on the Chigi Vase as javelins but fail to connect this conclusion, or the overhead posture, with subsequent depictions involving the same stance or weapons with similar configurations.[25] Similarly, Salmon, Snodgrass and Lorimer identify the throwing loops but do not connect these, or the use of the overhead stance, with the use of the javelin.[26] Boardman identifies the weapons as spears with no reference to the javelin.[27] Similarly, Hanson labels an early black figure depiction of a hoplite in the low stance as demonstrating 'spear thrusting'.[28] This labelling also requires correction as both the *agkulē* and the insertion of the index and middle fingers are clearly visible in this image, marking this weapon as a javelin carried in the low position rather than the thrusting spear. Jarva, who both identifies the throwing loops on the Chigi Vase and interprets the use of the overhead stance in Geometric art as a depiction of casting the javelin, offers no explanation for the retention of this posture in later art when missile warfare had been replaced by the thrusting phalanx.[29] Sekunda calls the image on the Chigi Vase 'Homeric' due to the lack of the *sauroter* and the bearing of two spears but does not connect either of these observations with the use of the overhead stance to wield the javelin.[30] In a confusing set of statements, Everson interprets the figures on a seventh century (c.680BC) Corinthian *aryballos* (narrow-necked flask) wielding weapons in the low position as thrusting with spears and those in the overhead position as throwing javelins.[31] However, in the next paragraph of his work he states that those in the overhead posture on the Chigi Vase (made only thirty years later) are representative of the thrusting phalanx.[32] Not only do these conclusions seemingly conflict, but Everson also labels the weapons held at the slope on the Chigi Vase as for throwing and identifies the throwing loops on the resting javelins to the left of the image as well.[33] Representations such as the Chigi Vase may reflect Homeric 'mass combat', but not the 'massed combat' of the Classical phalanx as Krentz differentiates the two.[34] Salmon also offers that the emerging phalanx warfare of the seventh century BC, which may be depicted in the Chigi Vase, may not necessarily resemble the Classical phalanx of two hundred years later.[35]

The identification of the *agkulē* and the positioning of the hand to use it clearly distinguishes the weapon commonly depicted in the overhead posture as the javelin and not the thrusting spear. Consequently, previous scholarship, including hypotheses that claim that images such as the Chigi Vase are the earliest pictorial references to the thrusting phalanx, or that date the emergence of phalanx warfare based upon these illustrations, is incorrect and needs to be re-evaluated accordingly.[36]

The overhead posture

Another indicator that the overhead posture represents the use of the javelin is that the positioning of the body is more consistent with a throwing, rather than a thrusting, action and has artistic parallels with representations of the use of the javelin by non-hoplites. Scenes involving light troops, cavalry, hunters and athletes regularly depict the use of the javelin in the overhead posture, commonly with the fingers positioned to use the *agkulē*. In many instances the configuration of the weapon and the posture of the bearer correspond with the short weapons and overhead stance used in the portrayal of hoplites wielding the javelin. The overhead posture also finds parallels with the actions of a modern athlete casting the javelin, in which the athlete begins with the centrally balanced javelin in the overhead position, and then draws their arm back to gain leverage for the throw. The extension of the arm behind the caster to gain leverage also finds parallels in artistic representations such as the *Poseidon of Artemision* in the National Museum, Athens (15161) and on the north frieze of the Siphnian Treasury at Delphi, which clearly show the raised fingers used in association with a throwing loop and the wielding of a weapon with a point of balance forward of the centre of the shaft. (see plate 2.1). Thus it is likely that these depictions are also of the casting of either a javelin or some other shafted missile.

Depictions of athletes and cavalry with the javelin in vase illustrations fall into two categories within the artistic record. Some are shown with the javelin angled upwards, throwing in competitions where distance is the primary goal as in the modern athletic event. This is confirmed by the writings of Xenophon who advises javelin-armed cavalry to throw the missile angled upwards to get the best range.[37] Other images show the javelin held level or angled downwards, aimed at specific targets.[38] Most representations of hoplites in the overhead stance fall into this second category. The javelin, angled downwards, is directed at a specific target, generally another figure in the vase painting. Additionally, the downward angle of many of the weapons depicted in the overhead stance may be an accurate representation of what happens to a shafted missile held in this position. The manner in which the hand grasps the shaft in the overhead position results in the grip being much stronger towards the back, due to the placement of the thumb and forefinger, with a weaker, more open, grip towards the front. As such, shafted weapons held in this position tend to naturally 'droop' towards the forward tip unless the arm is drawn back behind the body, which allows the palm to better support the shaft of the missile.

Vegetius states that, for the Romans, standing with the left foot forward is the best posture for throwing the javelin.[39] Markle states that this would have been a natural position for any Greek similarly casting a missile.[40] Images of hoplites in combat are generally shown with the left foot forward, regardless of whether they are armed with the spear or the javelin. Not only is this the best way for wielding the javelin, but this footwork is the only way for a hoplite to position his body in order to effectively use his shield and the rest of his panoply (see Chapter 4, Bearing the Hoplite Panoply). It is only the positioning of the upper body that changes with the weapon. Thus the depiction of an upper body posture more conducive with the casting of a missile is yet another indication that the weapons shown held in the overhead position in Greek art are javelins and not the thrusting spear as has been previously assumed.

The angle of impact

Perhaps the most telling sign that the overhead position was not used to wield the thrusting spear in combat comes from the damage left by weapons on the armour worn by the hoplite. Any thrusting attack delivered with a weapon held in the overhead position will follow a downward-curving trajectory (see Chapter 6, The Reach and Trajectory of Attacks made with the Hoplite Spear). However, there is no evidence of any weapon impacting with a piece of hoplite armour in this manner. A forensic survey of more than 300 helmets, 100 greaves, shields, breastplates, thigh guards and groin protectors (dated from the eighth to the fifth centuries BC) housed in the collection of the Deutsche Archaeological Institute at Olympia in Greece found evidence of weapon impacts on more than 150 pieces of defensive armour. Of these, not one helmet had been struck with a weapon following the downward-curving trajectory of an overhead thrust; all damage had been received from weapons following a shallow upward path (for example, see plate 9.1). This is consistent with strikes delivered with weapons carried in the underarm position (see Chapter 6, The Reach and Trajectory of Attacks made with the Hoplite Spear). The archaeological evidence also demonstrates that wounds received to the lower limbs, as indicated by damage sustained to the greaves and thigh guards, are also the result of blows delivered at a relatively flat downward angle; delivered from either a low or underarm position at a low 'opportune target'. There is little evidence that a sharply decending overhead strike was ever brought to bear against a low target. The nature of this evidence confirms the use of the underarm and low techniques to wield the spear and indicates that the overhead technique was not used by the hoplites of ancient Greece to engage in melee combat. Consequently, the depictions of the use of the overhead stance to wield a shafted weapon therefore must be representations of the use of the javelin.

The themes of the illustrations

The propensity for the depiction of the javelin in art, in an age where missile warfare had been replaced by the thrusting phalanx, can be accounted for by the themes of the combative imagery. Contemporary combat scenes are infrequently depicted in the artistic record. There are far fewer scenes commemorating the Persian Wars, for example, than there are for the labours of Heracles or of the gods.[41] During the Peloponnesian War, the depiction of combat on vases became markedly less popular, possibly due to the undesirability of glorifying war while one was raging against fellow Greeks.[42] The dedication of arms and armour at cult centres like Olympia may have also declined at this time for similar reasons.[43] The most common combative scenes are those that are Homeric, heroic or mythological in theme. The epic cycles appear to have had a strong influence on the themes of vase illustrations as early as the seventh century BC, even though many of the depicted scenes bear no correlation to the extant written epics.[44] Characters such as Achilles and events such as conflicts with Amazons, take pride of place in the catalogue of combat scenes in the artistic record. This may have been due to the influence of oral traditions, folklore and the increased interest by other genres of art, such as drama, sculpture and mural painting in mythological and legendary scenes during the late Archaic Period.[45] It has been suggested that 'vase paintings show mythological scenes with contemporary armour'.[46] This is undoubtedly the case with respect to items such as helmets. Characters such as Achilles or Hektor are unlikely to have worn the later-style Corinthian helmets with which they are so regularly depicted. Lorimer claims that it is a moot point whether the art has a heroic theme or not.[47] However, surely the theme of the illustration would have a major impact on how any combative scene was portrayed. While much of the arms and armour may be contemporary, the style of fighting is commonly reflective of an earlier age; especially the Heroic individual combat of epic poetry.

A minority of vase illustrations show the thrusting spear, long and equipped with a *sauroter*, held in the overhead fashion. This may be a representation of a contemporary weapon placed into an earlier context. In many instances these spears are still shown with the weapon held in the centre of the shaft, contrary to the weapon's point of balance. An even smaller minority of images show the spear held correctly by the rear of the shaft yet still raised above the head. This is also likely to be a depiction of a contemporary spear, held by its correct point of balance, but placed in an anachronistic context; the missile warfare of an earlier age. It has been suggested that many of the poses found in Greek art were copied from one artist to the next, until their popularity and versatility became a standard artistic convention.[48] The occasional depiction of a centrally balanced weapon in the underarm position, and rearwardly balanced spears in the overhead position, suggests that in some instances the artists may have been using models, or at least contemporary weapons as props, when constructing a scene with a Homeric or mythological theme.[49] The use of models is confirmed by Xenophon who refers to a woman who posed for artists.[50] It is possible that models acted out some heroic scenes while bearing contemporary arms and armour in an archaic context. This scene would have then been transferred by the artist into his respective medium. In some cases the characteristics of these contemporary weapons may have been incorrectly incorporated into the scene. Lowenstam suggests that many Archaic illustrations with 'Homeric' themes pre-date the written record of the epics.[51] As such, the scenes could only have been based upon the artist's imaginative interpretation of an oral tradition. If, within these oral traditions, the spear is used as a missile weapon as regularly as it is in the later 'Homeric' versions of the epic, then it is little wonder that the majority of the images show the spear/javelin held in an overhead posture representative of a throwing action.

Thus, the use of the overhead stance satisfies several criteria for the vase illustrator. It places the scene in an antiquated context. Those viewing the piece will recognize the heroic nature of the scene through the regular depiction of the shorter javelin and the overhead posture used to wield it. Other features, such as the depiction of the Dipylon or Boeotian style shield, chariots, or the bearing of a secondary weapon, similarly place the scene into an earlier context.[52] The heroic nature of the overhead stance also adds dramatic effect to the illustration. The characters in the painting take up a larger area of the available space and strike an imposing figure when portrayed in the overhead posture, creating a stronger presence within the illustration. This secures their place as the focus of the image. In many illustrations that show a confrontation between two figures, it is common that the victor is represented adopting the overhead posture while the vanquished is not.[53] This is similar to, and may have been influenced by, the 'smiting poses' often attributed to kings and heroes in earlier Assyrian and Egyptian art, which show a weapon wielded above the head being brought down upon a subjugated victim. Chase claims that the eastern influence on Greek design can be seen as early as Mycenaean and Homeric period shield devices.[54] The Assyrian influence can also be seen in the eighth century (c. 725BC) '*kegel-helm*' found in Argos.[55] Avenues of trade between early Greece and the East allowed for the migration of peoples, the transference of goods and for the transmission of artistic styles.[56] It is therefore possible that aspects of eastern art, including the 'smiting pose', were also transferred to Greek culture.[57] The club, sword or mace often associated with the eastern representations was merely replaced with the contemporary Greek weapon of the time: the javelin or thrown spear. This trend in imagery would have continued until it became a fully ingrained convention among Greek artisans, even into the Classical Age when the javelin was no longer used and the overhead posture rarely adopted on the battlefield. Everson claims that the conventions of late Geometric period art depicting battle scenes, including the depiction of the spear and the javelin, continued into the Hellenistic Era.[58] This being the case, the depiction of the use of the javelin in the overhead posture would have also translated into the art of the Classical Age.

The naked hoplite

Both Bonfante and Lorimer claim that the nudity common to vase illustrations may also place them into a heroic context.[59] While this may be so, what the depiction of the naked hoplite and the overhead posture allowed was for more of the musculature of the human body to be represented. This was an important consideration to sculptors such as Pythagoras, Lysippos, Pheidias and Polyclitus and was often a bone of contention among their critics.[60] It seems likely that vase illustrators would have operated under similar artistic considerations. The importance of the human body in Greek art also draws parallels between the athletic contests of the gymnasium and the martial contests of the battlefield; much in the way that the works of Pindar draw similar parallels between the gymnast and the hoplite.[61] Contests such as the race in armour (ὁπλιτοδρόμος), individual duelling in armour (ὁπλομαχία), the mounting/dismounting of moving chariots (ἀποβάτης) and even such demonstrations as the Pyrrhic Dance (πυρρίχη) or the 'shield' dance (εὐανδρία) are all derived from martial activities.[62] Both athletic and martial contests require a level of manly courage (ἀρετή), involve toils (πόνοι) and dangers (κινδῦνοι), and result in esteem for the victors.[63] Golden claims that heroic excellence in sport is more akin to individual combats than to hoplite warfare.[64] While it is true that these qualities differ somewhat between the athlete and the hoplites who fought in the phalanx, there are more similarities between the athlete and the heroic individual combatant commonly depicted in vase paintings. Prize amphorae awarded to athletic victors commonly show a scene of the event on the vase. Thus it can be concluded that those awarded to winners of the duelling in armour and the chariot mounting also depict scenes from that particular event. Both of these events echo the Homeric style of warfare.[65] It is no coincidence that the prizes given for the *hoplomachia* (duel in armour) show an archaic style of combat: recognizable by the depiction of the overhead stance and use of the javelin.[66]

The desire for the artist to display as much of the human body as possible also explains why hoplites are regularly depicted with either their helmets pushed back off their heads or with the check flaps raised while engaged in combat. Clearly this cannot be based on an actual battlefield precedent. There would be no point in wearing any style of helmet in this manner while fighting as it would negate much of the protection that it was designed to provide. The most likely reason for the portrayal of the helmet in this way was so that the illustrator could display the face of the figure.[67] Whether this was because the illustration depicted an actual person, or merely to display the illustrator's skill as a facial artist (or both), is indeterminable. Everson suggests that this was one reason why Athena was commonly depicted wearing the open-faced Attic-style helmet with the cheek flaps raised.[68]

The naked hoplite also depicts the dual ideals of heroism for the Greek infantryman and the cowardliness of their opponents. In images where the opponent is clearly identifiable, such as a Persian or Amazon, the opponent is regularly depicted fully clothed while the hoplite is commonly naked. This creates two inter-related subconscious connections. Firstly, the opponent is often clad in clothing different to that of the Greeks, representative of their 'foreignness'. In many vase illustrations both the Persians and Amazons are depicted clad in similar garb which, Bonfante suggests, implies that the Persians are being depicted as effeminate.[69] Early proto-Corinthian vase illustrations began a stylistic convention of distinguishing men from women by depicting the men naked and the women clothed. This stylization continued into the Classical Period and may be the basis for Bonfante's hypothesis. However Homer, in some of the earliest literary references to the Amazons, calls them the 'equals of men' (ἀντιάνειραι) and it is therefore unlikely that any comparison of the Persians to the Amazons is meant to portray them as effeminante as Bonfante suggests.[70] The association of the Persians with the Amazons is more likely to be a comparison of the Persian invasions of the early fifth century BC to the very first major invasion of Greece by a hostile force from the east: the Amazon invasion of Attica and the defence of Athens by Theseus.[71] In this legendary war the Amazons, like the later Persians, invaded the precincts of the city of Athens. In both confrontations, the invader was eventually repelled by the steadfast resoluteness of the Athenian hoplite. Thus depictions of the Amazons in Persian garb not only signify that both races come from the 'un-Greek' east, but are simultaneous commemorations of Greek victories over similar invasions as well.

Additionally, the hoplite in these images is shown in his naked glory; trim and muscled from his time in the *gymnasion*. This is a direct comment by the Greeks on Oriental cultural practices.[72] Furthermore, the hoplite is seen as engaging in combat with very little protective armour. The hoplite is placing himself at great risk, in the best tradition of the mythological hero, for the defence of his native land. The cowardly opponent, alternatively, engages with all of his or her available defensive accoutrements. This, again, is a Greek commentary on the heroic nature of the hoplite and, more than anything else, is representative of the 'un-Greek' nature of their adversaries.[73]

It has been suggested that the emergence of the naked hoplite in Greek art is reflective of a correspondingly real reduction in the amount of armour or clothing worn on the battlefield, or worn by the everyday citizen of Ancient Greece.[74] This seems unlikely.[75] Even a cursory examination of grave *stele* and monumental friezes will demonstrate the widespread use of clothing and armour well into the fourth century BC. It must be remembered that vase illustrations are not photographs and are meant to convey an artistic 'message' rather than accurately record an event. Just because nudity is commonly depicted in the artistic record does not necessarily mean that it is an accurate portrayal of real life. Many of the works of da Vinci, Michelangelo and Botticelli, for example, also contain nudes or partial nudes. However, this does not reflect a corresponding lack of clothing in renaissance Italy. While the trend in Greek art moves towards nakedness, there is no other analogous source for a reduction in armament. In some instances, the figure within the image is even portrayed in 'Heroic nudity' while clutching all of the elements of his panoply.

There are also numerous references in the ancient texts to the clothing worn by the hoplite and the everyday citizen of the *polis* (city-state).[76] Xenophon describes hoplites wearing armour in the fourth century BC, while the art contemporary with the time period generally depicts hoplites as naked.[77] If only one source should be believed, the military background of Xenophon would clearly give his narratives precedence over artwork. Other ancient literary sources also contain a vast number of references to hoplites wearing both clothing and armour, similarly while the hoplite was depicted as naked in contemporary artworks. Aeschylus, states that the Greeks at Troy became sick when their clothes became wet (ἔμπεδον σίνος ἐσθημάτων).[78] When the Chians evacuated Leuconia, they were permitted to leave the city with only one tunic and one cloak.[79] The red cloak of the Spartans was worn in battle to instill fear into the enemy and to hide any spilt Spartan blood.[80] Plutarch mentions that even Greek peasantry were clothed and Pausanias describes Arcadian peasants as wearing sheep-skin cloaks.[81] Chares' troops in Thrace are said to have possessed several cloaks to ward off the winter cold.[82] Plutarch also details the uncommon practice of Phocion of travelling unshod (ἀνυπόδητος) and without garments (γυμνὸς ἐβάδιζεν) while on campaign until adverse weather forced him to put his shoes and his cloak back on.[83] The imagery of such an anecdote would only be powerful if was not a common practice to go unadorned and barefoot. Similarly, Iphicrates is said to have worn thin clothing and gone barefoot so that he would undergo the same hardships as some of his men to stop them complaining.[84] This suggests that he had commonly worn better clothing and footwear prior to this incident and that most of his men were clothed; albeit poorly so. There are also numerous references to the production of workable cloth such as coarse and fine flax, hemp, silk and spun wool; all of which could be turned into clothing.[85] If the Greeks were truely naked as some suggest, then it can only be concluded that the majority of this cloth was either used for other purposes or that there was simply a vast amount of unused cloth lying around ancient Greece.

For the use of armour, Solon is described as wearing armour in the sixth century, as is Archidamus in the fifth.[86] Bodies of the enemy slain in battle were commonly stripped of their arms and armour in order to erect battlefield trophies.[87] The plays of Aristophanes describe how armour became tarnished when hung above the fireplace. They describe people donning armour for battle, and even feature a 'cuirass-seller' (θωρακοπώλης) as one of the characters.[88] Even the earlier poems of Alcaeus refer to linen corselets, greaves and tunics.[89] Those involved in the retaking of Thebes in 379/8BC are detailed as wearing armour, as are the Sacred Band at Chaeronea, the Thessalians a Cynocsephylae and both liberators of Syracuse, Dion and Timoleon.[90] Plutarch's account of the second invasion of Sparta by Thebes in 362BC details the exploits of Isidas of Sparta specifically because he went into battle naked and was later fined for being so foolhardy as to go into combat without wearing any armour.[91] Breastplates and cuirasses were also dedicated at cult centres like Olympia but are unlikely to have been made specifically for this purpose.[92]

Footwear is mentioned nineteen times in the works of Homer alone and is just as prevalent in other Greek literary texts.[93] There are also artistic representations and archaeological evidence for footwear going back to at least the fourteenth century BC.[94] Combellack suggests that references by ancient authors to the barefoot training of Spartan youths are to directly contrast against the common practice of wearing footwear in other city-states.[95] All of these passages indicate that during the eighth to fourth centuries BC, tunics, cloaks, armour and footwear were commonly worn, and that the naked hoplite depicted in vase paintings, and of some modern theories, was not the standard of the time despite artistic suggestions to the contrary. Everson states that hoplites in the seventh century BC fought naked and that this translated into an artistic tradition by the fifth century, when the wearing of only tunics into battle was the standard as the practice of wearing of bronze armour had ceased.[96] Clearly this conclusion does not agree with the literary sources or with the finds of armour in the archaeological record.

During the Peloponnesian War it may have been the case that many hoplites were sent into the battle without much of the basic panoply due to the need to place larger armies into the field quickly and for longer periods of time. The armour makers of the city-state may not have been able to keep up with the demand and those without access to cuirasses or helmets that they could borrow would have been deployed with only the basic equipment for battle.[97] The necessitity to place armies into the field quickly may explain why, when the Athenian city-state began to issue arms and armour to its citizens after the battle of Chaeronea in 338BC, only a spear and shield were provided.[98] This may also explain the rise in popularity of simple helmets such as the conical *pilos*. This style of helmet would have been much easier, and more importantly faster, to mass produce than the more elaborate Corinthian version, and the need to outfit large groups of new hoplites rapidly explains the rise in its popularity during the time of the Peloponnesian War and afterwards. As such, at engagements like the battle of Leuctra, there would have been older hoplites wearing the full panoply, poorer hoplites with only certain elements of the panoply, and newer hoplites possibly with only a spear, shield and *pilos* all mixed into the phalanx together due to time, age and level of wealth. However, it is unlikely that any of them fought naked. The only heavy infantry that may have made a conscious decision not to wear heavy armour, despite their means, would have been those who served as marines (ἐπιβάται) in the fleets of the various city-states. This would have provided them with the possibility of swimming to safety should their ship sink in battle. Yet even here the likelihood of a totally naked hoplite is doubtful.[99]

Interestingly, of combatants in vase illustrations, it is only the Greek hoplite that undergoes this artistic metamorphosis towards nudity. In images where Greek deities are engaged in combat they are not generally depicted naked, although they had begun to be depicted so in sculpture by the end of the fifth century.[100] As scenes involving gods are clearly mythological in theme, the trend of depicting them clad in armour and clothing cannot be due to an attempt to place them in an earlier context. Otherwise, they would be depicted naked as are the heroes in illustrations with a Homeric theme. If the depiction of the naked hoplite was a referral to an actual downward trend in the amount of armour worn, it seems odd that images of combative Greek gods would not also be depicted in this way unless due to a sense of reverence and propriety. The Archaic poet-philosopher Xenophanes states: 'mortals seem to have begotten the gods to have their own garments, voice and form'.[101] Again, it seems odd that the gods are clad in the garments of mortals if both hoplites and peasants alike were commonly naked as some suggest.

The identification of the overhead posture common to Greek art as the use of the javelin counters the commonly held scholarly convention of the use of the overhead stance to wield the thrusting spear in combat and leaves a 'new model' of hoplite combative techniques incorporating both the low and under-arm postures. With this conclusion, all previous scholarship on the nature of hoplite warfare is clearly in need of revision. However, as the overhead stance has been a fundamental component of all previous scholarship on the subject, the last 150 years of historical enquiry into ancient Greek warfare cannot simply be dismissed on the basis of artistic re-interpretation alone. This is where the relatively recent practices of physical re-creation and experimental archaeology can act as a tool to test the validity of existing theories and to aid in the formulation of new ones. This process allows for a critical re-examination of the ancient evidence, and a comparison of it to modern theories, to be conducted. The results of this further investigation confirm that the overhead stance was not used by the hoplites of ancient Greece and that the warfare of the time was conducted with the hereto unidentified underarm technique.

Chapter 4

Bearing the Hoplite Panoply

The Argive shield, known in Greek as the *aspis* (ἀσπίς) or the *hoplon* (ὅπλον), is one of the most recognisable features of the hoplite.[1] The construction and encumbrance of this piece of defensive equipment dictates how it could be wielded and, more than any other aspect of the hoplite panoply, how the hoplite must position his body for battle. The positioning of the body would, in turn, influence how effectively the spear could be wielded and thus the effectiveness of any combative posture adopted to employ it. Despite how essential hoplite body posture is to the functionality of the individual on the battlefield, the manner in which the hoplite positioned himself has remained inadequately, and in some cases inaccurately, analyzed by modern historians. Through an examination of what the hoplite needed to achieve through his body posture, how this dictated the positioning of his body, and how this positioning was recorded in the artistic record, the way in which the Classical hoplite bore his panoply can be determined.

Any body posture that an individual can adopt for combat, regardless of the mode of warfare being employed, must comply with certain criteria in order for that posture to be effective. This principle holds true regardless of the historical time-period being analyzed and regardless of the weapon with which the combatant is armed. For the Classical hoplite, armed with a long thrusting spear and the large *aspis*, any adopted combative posture must have:

(a) Allowed the shield to be positioned in such a way so that it could be used defensively;

(b) Allowed the hoplite to move without restriction, particularly in a forward direction;

(c) Provided stable footing to enable the hoplite to remain upright during the rigours of close combat;

(d) Allowed the hoplite to maintain his position within the phalanx and conform to any limitations of space dictated by that formation; and, most importantly;

(e) Allowed the weapon arm to be positioned naturally and provided with a free range of movement so that the hoplite could engage an opponent offensively.

The most fundamental aspects of the positioning of the body in conformance with these criteria are primarily dictated by the characteristics of the hoplite's shield.

The *aspis* was a cumbersome piece of equipment; constructed from a blank of wooden beams glued together and turned on a lathe to create a bowl-shaped wooden core between 80cm and 122cm in diameter and 10cm deep with a 5–7cm offset rim running around its circumference. This core may have had its inner and/or outer surface lined with hide. Archaeological remains show that some shields had their rims faced with a reinforcing layer of bronze. Towards the end of the Classical Period, the outer surface of some shields was entirely faced with a layer of bronze half a millimetre thick.[2] It has been suggested that the reason for the variance in the diameter of the shield was that it was custom made to suit individual bearers.[3] Estimates for the weight of the shield range between 6kg and 8kg.[4]

The shield possessed a central armband called the *porpax* (πόρπαξ), which Euripides suggests was also custom made to suit the forearm of the bearer, and a cord known as the *antilabe* (ἀντιλαβή), which ran around the inner rim of the shield, passing through attachments at evenly distributed points around its circumference, to provide a grip for the left hand.[5] Sekunda claims that all shields were the same size and could have been used by anyone.[6] However, the archaeological and literary evidence clearly do not support this claim.

The natural location for a shield to provide any level of protection to the bearer is across the front of the body (it cannot provide any protection if it is not positioned between the bearer and any attack made against him). However, the ancient sources provide few details as to how the body was positioned to bear a shield with the weight and configuration of the *aspis* for battle. It has been suggested by modern scholars that the left shoulder was placed under the upper rim of the shield in order to take some of its weight.[7] Both the literary evidence and the nature of the shield itself comply with this conclusion. Philostratus, in his work on gymnastics, describes an athlete running with a hoplite shield as having 'well developed shoulders and supple knees in order that the shield may be easily carried and supported by these parts'.[8] This suggests that the weight of the *aspis*, even in athletic contests, was taken on the shoulder. Theocritus states how Heracles was taught to 'keep his shoulder behind his shield and lean towards his man' (ὑπ' ἀσπίδι ὦμον ἔχοντα ἀνδρος), also suggesting that the weight of the shield was taken on the shoulder.[9] Euripides' *Trojan Women* describes how the rim of the shield borne by Hektor was stained by the sweat from his beard.[10] This passage suggests that the upper rim of the *aspis* was situated close to the level of the jaw, further suggesting that the shield was placed on the shoulder.

In fact, it is the concave shape of the *aspis* that allows for this positioning to be possible. When carried, a shield with this configuration can be easily supported by the left shoulder while the forearm is inserted through the *porpax* and the left hand grips the *antilabe*. A shield that does not possess the bowl-like curvature of the *aspis*, or a central armband, cannot be placed upon the shoulder to support its weight. This suggests that these two features of the hoplite shield were conscious considerations in its design.

One aspect vital to the correct portage of the shield, and which indicates that each shield must have been custom made to suit the individual bearer, is that the length of the *antilabe* has to be compatible with the length of the bearer's arm in order to carry the shield correctly. To work effectively, the cord of the *antilabe* must be drawn tight by the left hand. This has two effects. Firstly, pulling on the *antilabe* draws the forearm through the *porpax*, up to the point where the edge of the *porpax* sits in the crook of the elbow, and keeps it in place. By maintaining the tension on the *antilabe*, and the *porpax* in the crook of the arm, the left arm bends slightly, reducing the angle between the forearm and upper arm to less than ninety degrees. This positions the shoulder directly over the *porpax* and under the highest point of the shield's rim; allowing it to be placed comfortably upon the shoulder so that its weight can be supported.

If the cord of the *antilabe* is too long, and therefore hanging too loose, the left arm will not be fully drawn into the *porpax*. As the bearer moves, the shield will slide down the forearm until the *antilabe* becomes taut. This results in the *porpax* sitting on the middle of the forearm instead of in the crook of the elbow; placing considerable stress on the muscles of the upper and lower arm. Also, by having the elbow further back, the high point of the shield's rim is not inline with the shoulder, and so the shoulder cannot be placed under it to support the weight. Having the elbow further back also creates an imbalance in the distribution of the weight of the shield upon the arm itself; there is more of the shield forward of the elbow than there is behind it (figure 6).

This imbalanced distribution of the shield, and improper placement of the shoulder to support it, would also occur if the *porpax* was too small for the bearer to insert his arm all the way up to the crook of the elbow. Similarly, if the opening was too large, the arm/elbow would be situated higher than the centre of the shield, thus limiting how the shoulder could be used to support its weight. This complies with the inference from Euripides that the *porpax* was custom made to suit the bearer.

The effect of gravity on an imbalanced distribution of weight causes the right side of the shield to 'droop' downward as fatigue sets in, pivoting the arm at the elbow, unless substantial counter-force is applied using the muscles of the arm. This greatly tires the arm and has a follow-on effect on how the shield can be carried. As the arm's muscles become more fatigued, the arm naturally

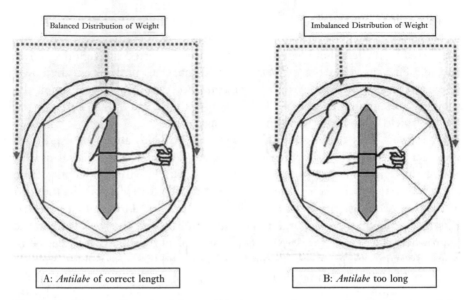

Balanced Distribution of Weight

Imbalanced Distribution of Weight

A: *Antilabe* of correct length

B: *Antilabe* too long

Figure 6: How the length of the *antilabe* is proportionate to the distribution of the shield's weight upon the arm.

tends to straighten under the force of the shield's weight until the arm is almost vertical. At this point the entire weight of the shield is supported only by the grip of the left hand on the cord of the *antilabe*, further adding to the fatigue of the left arm. When the arm is in this vertical position, there is no way that the shoulder can be placed under the rim to support the shield. Everson states that the dual grip configuration of the *aspis* allowed more weight to be born by the left arm itself.[11] However, if the dual grip system is configured correctly, the weight of the shield is taken by the shoulder, not the arm; the arm is merely used to keep the shield in place. Thus the very length of the *antilabe* is one of the features that allows the shield to be carried correctly. This also confirms that the shield must have been custom made to suit the individual.

Additionally, by constructing the shield in such a manner that the cord of the *antilabe* runs around the inner rim, once it is drawn tight, inward pressure is exerted evenly around the entire rim of the shield, concentrating it inwards onto the *porpax* and the elbow in the centre. This creates a very stable and very controllable facing for the shield. It has been suggested that the *antilabe* functioned in a similar manner to the *upozoma* (ὑπόζωμα) – a cable truss used in ship construction to keep ship hulls from bending under pressure.[12] Bradford and Anderson claim that the corded *antilabe* was knotted around the rim in various sections so that if one broke the shield could be spun and a new hand grip used.[13] This assumption cannot be correct. Not only does the rigid mounting of the *porpax* prevent the shield from being used in anything but in its original position or completely upside down, but having the cord knotted to its attachment points prevents it from being pulled taut. If the sections of cord were not of a length that would allow for the application of tension, the shield could not be carried correctly.

Similarly, Matthews suggests that the *antilabe* could be lengthened to create a shoulder strap for the shield.[14] If this practice was ever undertaken by a hoplite on the march, he would have to ensure that the cord was retied correctly (i.e. to the correct length) prior to battle or he would not be able to carry his shield in the proper manner.[15]

Some artistic representations of the shield, such as on the north frieze of the Siphnian treasury at Delphi, suggest that in some cases the *antilabe* may have only been some kind of handle; possibly a single section of cord tied to two attachment points.[16] For this style of grip to work, the handle would need to be situated where the bearer could grasp it, and be long enough that it could be pulled taut so that the shield could be carried correctly. This would be further confirmation for the customizing of the shield to suit each bearer. It is possible that these images only demonstrate the section of the *antilabe* that the hand grasps, with the remainder of the cord omitted, due to scale, the medium used and/or the degradation of any paint. While the use of a simple handle makes the shield less controllable than the corded *antilabe*, the limited number of shield remains in the archaeological record cannot confirm the use of one style of grip over another and it appears that either style may have formed part of a shield's construction.

Further confirmation of the customizing of the shield comes from the nature of the arm itself. The stature of an individual can be estimated from the length of the bones of the arm and, inversely, the length of the arm can be estimated from the overall stature of a person, using the 'regression formulae' of forensic science.[17] The formulae for the calculation of stature for males using the length of the humerus bone and radius bone of the upper and lower left arm are as follows:

Stature $= 3.1906 \times$ humerus length $+ 64.19$cm (standard deviation ±4.03)

Stature $= 4.1780 \times$ radius length $+ 68.13$ cm (standard deviation ±4.21)

By inserting the estimated average stature of the hoplite (170cm) into these formulae, the length of the arm bones can be estimated at an average of: humerus $= 33.16$cm (deviation 29.13–37.19cm), radius $= 24.38$cm (deviation 20.19–28.59cm). An arm of this length is well suited to a shield with an inner diameter of no less than 80cm (figure 7).

A shield of this size neatly sits on the shoulder of an arm of this length. If the overall arm were longer, it could not be positioned where the shoulder was

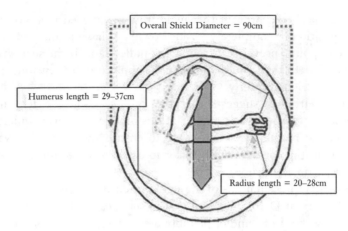

Figure 7: The relationship between the long bones of the arm and the diameter of the shield.

situated under the highest curve of the rim while the forearm was inserted through the *porpax*. This explains why there is no evidence for an *aspis* with a diameter less than 80cm. It can also be concluded that shields with greater diameters were either made for people with longer arms or that they possessed an *antilabe* of a length suitable enough to allow it to be grasped and drawn tight by a bearer. Thus, contrary to Sekunda, an individual could only correctly bear a shield greater than or equal to the diameter to which his arm would fit, with only minor adjustments to the length of the *antilabe* and if his forearm fit through the *porpax*. Indeed, this may have been why a corded *antilabe* was used instead of a rigid handle; cords could be adjusted to suit the individual bearer. A person who tried to use a shield belonging to another (so long as it was of adequate diameter and with an accommodating *porpax*) need only adjust the length of the *antilable* to be able to carry it correctly. Had the grip been a rigid handle, it may have been incorrectly located with no means of alteration. This further supports the conclusion that hoplite shields were custom made to suit each bearer. What has not been appropriately examined by modern scholarship is how a shield with such an individual configuration dictates the body positioning of the hoplite while conforming to each of the necessary criteria for an effective combative posture.

(a) Body posture and the defensive positioning of the shield

Van Wees states that in order to place the shield upon the left shoulder it was necessary for the hoplite to stand in a side-on fashion with 'left shoulder and shield turned towards the enemy, left foot forward, right foot placed well back for balance', comparing hoplite body posture to that of a modern fencer (figure 8).[18]

However, a side-on posture only satisfies some of the criteria necessary for an effective combative stance. Defensively, standing side-on positions the shield to the front, the upper rim is level with the jaw as per the ancient descriptions, and it is correctly supported by the left shoulder. The large diameter and offset rim of the shield provide excellent body coverage for the bearer from jaw–line to knee. The shield can be braced in position by the shoulder, arm and outward pressure exerted with the left leg; further stabilizing its defensive facing. Standing side-on to an opponent also creates the smallest target profile of the upper body, and places many of the vital organs of the body at the furthest distance from any attack. In many artistic representations of the hoplite, the torso is shown 'front-on' to the viewer, particularly in depictions of the low and overhead postures. However, in these same images, the legs are usually shown in profile, which is almost physically impossible to achieve, and it is unclear, from the artistic perspective at least, whether this contortion of the body is meant to represent a side-on posture with the legs portrayed incorrectly, is artistic error or is meant to represent something else entirely. Consequently, the use of a side-on posture cannot be verified based exclusively upon the artistic record.

Using artistic examples van Wees hypothesizes that, when in a side-on position, the left arm was extended so that the lower rim of the shield 'projected a couple of feet in front of its bearer'. He further offers that the projected lower rim could be used in an offensive capacity to strike at an opponent.[19] Luginbill offers a similar offensive possibility.[20] To adopt this position, the elbow of the shield bearing arm has to be raised and the weight of the shield taken off the shoulder to be supported only by the muscles of the upper arm. This counters van Wees' own conclusion, and that of other scholars, that the shield was designed so that its weight could be carried on the shoulder.

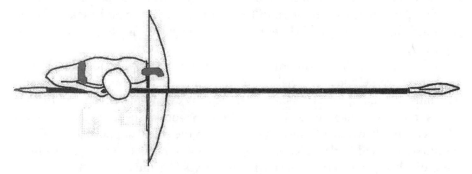

Figure 8: The position of the body and feet of a hoplite in the side-on position.

The weight of an *aspis* held in this position cannot be maintained for a long time and it is unlikely that this was a standard placement for the shield. Additionally, very little energy is created by raising the elbow, nor can the arm be extended forward without the straightening of the arm, suggesting that the lower rim was not used to strike at opponents. It is further unlikely that the shield would be positioned in this way to even parry an attack as the angle of the shield would simply deflect any incoming strike dangerously towards the head. Moreover, any strike that impacted with the shield while it was held in this position would cause it to rotate on the arm back towards the vertical, which would greatly expose the bearer.

Van Wees also uses the same artistic evidence to suggest that the hoplite could run or kneel with the upper body rotated into a side-on posture.[21] However, it is almost impossible to run or squat with the body contorted in this manner; particularly if trying to extend the lower rim of the shield at the same time, and even more so if armour is being worn. Interestingly, both of the images used by van Wees are devoid of any armour on the upper body. Even so, rotating the torso to this extent while running or squatting places considerable stress on the lower back, making it unlikely that a hoplite would turn his upper body completely side-on while performing these actions. The vase paintings used to justify a side-on posture for running and squatting hoplites can be, at best, described as uncertain regarding the extent to which the torso should be considered rotated. Additionally, the statue used by van Wees as an example bears a Boeotian-style shield, which is carried differently to the *aspis*.[22] Consequently, none of the imagery used by van Wees to formulate his hypotheses can be used to confirm how the hoplite bore his panoply or the adoption of a side-on posture by a hoplite in battle.

Nor is it likely that the hoplite simply stood front-on to an opponent. From a defensive perspective, a shield suspended from the shoulder when in this position will remain to the left side of the bearer, with its face perpendicular to any attack from the front, leaving the body exposed to attack. To move the shield to a defensive position in front of the body, it must be taken off the shoulder and held across the front with the weight borne solely by the arm (figure 9).

In doing so, the shield still protects the bearer from jaw-line to knee and just covers the whole body (the right shoulder and arm are somewhat exposed). The only way to improve the body coverage is by extending the left arm further across the body than its natural position. Sekunda suggests that hoplites advanced into battle in a front-on posture with the shield supported on the left shoulder and held to the side, only to reposition the shield across the front of the individual prior to the clash of the phalanxes.[23] Similarly, Matthews states that the shield was only supported by the shoulder when not in combat and

Figure 9: The position of the body and the feet of a hoplite in a front-on position.

that the shield was moved across the front of the body (which must also assume the adoption of a front-on posture by the hoplite) when two opposing sides were 200m apart.[24] The positioning of the shield to the side of the bearer is common within the artistic record and may be the source of this conclusion. However, advancing in this manner would expose the hoplite to enemy missiles, whether the javelins of the Archaic Age or the archers seen at Marathon or those encountered during the march of Xenophon's mercenaries. To provide any level of protection against these missiles the shield must have been positioned across the front of the body.

Furthermore, a shield held across the front of the body is liable to injure its bearer during the rigours of combat if a front-on stance is adopted. Supported solely by the arm, a shield held across the front of the body in this manner has nothing bracing it in place. A strike made against the shield would force the rim into either the bearer's face or thighs, depending upon where the shield was struck, causing potential impact damage as well as angling the shield so that the attack would deflect into the bearer's head or lower limbs. The development of open-faced styles of helmet, the irregular use of the greave and the abandonment of thigh guards all suggest that the shield was not placed in a position where it would cause injuries, either directly or indirectly, to the face or lower limbs. If the shield is held away from the body to potentially alleviate this risk, the arm becomes quickly fatigued. Clearly, this is not a stable defensive position for the shield to be in and cannot be considered conformance to the first necessary criteria for an effective combative posture. Standing front-on also creates the largest target area of the body and places the vital organs of the chest and abdomen in direct line with any spear thrust made by an opponent to the front. As the level of fatigue in the shield-bearing arm increased, more and more of the body would become vulnerable. It can thus be concluded that the shield cannot be effectively used in a defensive manner when the body is positioned front-on. This factor alone makes it seem highly improbable that this was the attitude adopted by a hoplite for combat.

The most likely posture that a hoplite would have adopted for battle is a compromise between a front-on and a side-on position; an oblique posture with the left foot forward, the feet well apart and the right foot back, and with the upper torso rotated to the right by approximately forty-five degrees (figure 10).

The representation of the body in the artistic record is more conducive with this oblique body posture than the completely side-on stance proposed by van Wees. The frontal view of the torso in Archaic Greek art is most likely a representation of this oblique posture with the body viewed frontally due to the ease of depicting it so, and with the legs in profile, until the trend of depicting the body in a three-quarter view, which provides a sense of spatial depth and a more accurate portrayal of an oblique posture, began in later periods.[25] The literary evidence also suggests the adoption of an oblique body posture.

Euripides' *Phoenician Women* describes the 'Thessalian Feint'; an evasive manoeuvre where the combatant is advised to step back with the left foot and strike an opponent as he stumbles forward.[26] This suggests that the hoplite stood with the left foot forward in a manner conducive with the oblique posture. It is unlikely that this passage is a reference to the side-on posture as it is difficult to step back with the left foot from a totally side-on stance without first moving into an oblique position. Similarly, Theocritus' description of Heracles 'leaning' at his opponent with his shoulder behind his shield also suggests the use of an oblique posture.[27] In his work on boar hunting, Xenophon advises those wielding a spear to also stand with the left foot forward and the legs not much further apart than in wrestling.[28] Arrian refers to a Greek practice of wearing only one greave upon the shin of the leg that was extended forward.[29] This also suggests the adoption of an oblique body posture. The practice of wearing one greave may have begun in the Mycenaean period.[30] However, due to the stylization and limited detail of early art there is some

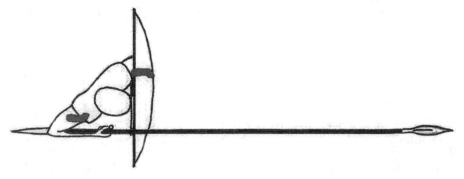

Figure 10: The position of the body and the feet of a hoplite in an oblique position.

debate as to which leg is actually being represented with the greave.[31] Luginbill interprets this practice as the adoption of a side-on posture.[32] However, it seems more likely that this practice, and its artistic representation, should be interpreted as belonging to the left leg of a hoplite in an oblique body posture.

Defensively, positioning the left foot forward in the manner of the oblique posture causes the torso to naturally rotate, or allows it to be easily rotated, so that the chest faces to the front-right. This presents the left shoulder forward enough to allow the shield to be both supported by the shoulder and, importantly, positioned in a defensive manner across the front of the body, while being braced in position with the left leg. Contrary to the side-on posture, standing, walking and running are all physically achievable with little or no discomfort when the torso is rotated in an oblique manner, even when wearing a cuirass. This posture presents the body as a slightly larger target area to any attack coming directly from the front than the side-on posture, but the body is completely covered by the surface of the shield and the organs of the upper body are placed at an angle away from any attack. The left side of the body is, however, still vulnerable to any blow that pierces the shield. Xenophon's account of the death of Leonymus describes how he was killed by an arrow that passed through his shield and impacted with his side.[33] With the adoption of an oblique posture to bear the shield, this description must be of an injury sustained to the left side of the body.

This correlates with the archaeological evidence for the body posture of the hoplite. In the majority of cases, the weapon damage sustained to hoplite helmets and armour is to the front-left side of the head, the outside-front of the left greave, the inside-front of the right greave or the left side of the armour. The location of this damage is consistent with the regular adoption of an oblique body posture, with the left leg forward and the body rotated slightly to the right, to carry the panoply; thus presenting the outside of the left leg, inside of the right leg and left side of the head and body towards the angle of any attack delivered by a facing opponent wielding a weapon in their right hand.[34]

The right side of the body is referred to as 'the unprotected side' by both Thucydides and Xenophon.[35] This has been interpreted by some scholars as the shield not adequately covering the right side of the hoplite.[36] This conclusion can only be based upon the assumption that the hoplite fought in a front-on posture, which seems unlikely. Van Wees, in his interpretation of a side-on posture, explains that while the right side is not directly protected by the shield, and is therefore the 'unprotected side', the body placement in a side-on stance still prevents this side of the body being injured by direct attack.[37] He further states that by standing side-on, hoplites 'found themselves behind the centre of their shields, well covered on both sides'.[38] This conclusion is also true of the oblique posture. A body placed in an oblique fashion is still fully covered by the face of the shield, with the 'unprotected' right side of the body angled away from any frontal attack. This side of the body would only be vulnerable to any flanking attack that came against the right side of the phalanx. Based upon the analysis of how the shield could be borne in each of the three possible combative postures, it is clear that it can only be used defensively in an oblique or side-on position; thus conforming to the first necessary criteria for a combative technique.

(b) Body posture and movement without restriction

The ability to charge and/or advance were vital aspects of the mechanics of hoplite combat. If the two opposing sides were unable to advance upon one another, the battle would simply not take place. However, not all of the possible combative postures allow this to be accomplished without impediment. Standing side-on greatly restricts the movement of the hoplite. To advance while maintaining this posture movement is limited to a shuffling side-step, conforming to van Wees' comparative analogy with the modern fencer. While it is possible that a hoplite could slowly advance into combat with the body in such a manner, it seems improbable that any charge or moderately paced advance, such as those seen at Delium and Coronea, could be made in such a posture. Similarly, it is unlikely that the front-on posture was adopted as forward movement is also restricted. With the shield held across the front of the body in a front-on posture, the legs are not provided with enough room to facilitate running or walking. The shield could be held forward of the body but, as noted, this places considerable muscular stress on the shield-bearing arm. Standing obliquely allows the hoplite to advance by merely stepping or running forward, without altering his body posture or the positioning of his shield.

Certain styles of hoplite helmet additionally restrict the movement of the head when in a side-on posture. The elongated cheek flanges on the Corinthian-style helmet common to the Classical Period, for example, extend below the jaw-line to provide additional protection to the neck and throat. When wearing this style of helmet it is impossible to turn the head fully to the side as the cheek flanges connect with the chest/cuirass and inhibit the full rotation of the head. This means that any hoplite standing side-on would have found it impossible to see his primary opponent directly over his left shoulder. The cheek flanges of the Corinthian helmet similarly connect with the cuirass when standing in an oblique posture. Importantly though, in the oblique position this occurs at the point where the head is facing directly forward due to the angled shape of the lower rim of the cheek flanges (plate 10.1). Had the cheek flanges of the Corinthian helmet been 'squared off' along their lower edge, the ability to turn the head would be similarly inhibited by the helmet. This suggests that the angular cheek flanges of the Corinthian helmet were conscious design considerations to conform with the oblique body posture adopted to bear the hoplite panoply correctly. Forward motion, either at a run or a walk, together with an unimpeded motion of the head, is available only in the oblique posture. Therefore the oblique stance is the only position that allows the shield to be supported by the shoulder in a defensive manner and allows the hoplite to move effectively: conforming to the first two necessary criteria for an effective combative posture.

(c) Body posture and firm footing in combat

The works of Tyrtaeus comment on the necessity for combatants to stand 'firm-set astride the ground' (στηριχθεὶς ἐπὶ γῆς) but provide no details of posture.[39] Vegetius refers to a positioning of the body for the Romans with a preferred foot 'forward in combat' depending upon the weapon used.[40] This indicates that for the Archaic Greeks and the succeeding Romans the placement of the feet was an important aspect of their body positioning for combat. The Classical Greek hoplite is unlikely to have been any different. The ability to transfer the body's centre of gravity and provide stable footing is crucial to maintaining balance on terrain that is soft, uneven or covered with the detritus of battle. Arrian states that infantry 'push with their shoulders and sides' (τοὺς ὤμους καὶ τὰς πλευρὰς αἱ ἐνερείσεις).[41] The noun used (ἐνερείσεις – derived from the verb ἐρείδω) has several definitions, including to push (with), thrust (with), lean in (with) or lay (upon). However, it is clear that, in all of these interpretations, the body is positioned so that one shoulder is further forward than the other. This suggests the adoption of either an oblique or side-on position. An analysis of how the body's centre of gravity, and hence balance, can be altered in the three combative stances demonstrates that the oblique posture is the most efficient footwork for hand-to-hand combat.

Standing side-on allows the hoplite to brace himself to a considerable degree against any impact with his shield. The rearward right leg, with the foot turned outwards, provides solid support for the body to resist any force exerted against the shield or body. The placement of the feet in a side-on posture also provides a good way for the hoplite to exert his own counter-pressure against this force by leaning towards the enemy and pushing using his shoulder and the strength of the right leg. However, a person positioned side-on has little means of altering the body's centre of gravity in every direction. By leaning left or right (i.e. towards or away from the enemy), the hoplite can easily adapt to the changing pressures exerted against his shield. However, a side-on posture provides no means of adaptation to forces exerted from either side, such as jostling from within one's own formation or an attack from the flank, in order to remain upright during the rigours of combat. The placement of the feet in this manner means that the hoplite can be easily knocked sideways (across the face of the phalanx) by the application of pressure from this direction. Consequently, a side-on posture, while providing a solid base for bracing the body against direct impacts from the front, does not provide the most stable footing for the endurance of close combat conditions.

Standing front-on provides the least stable footing of all three postures. A hoplite standing in this position would simply be knocked backwards by the application of force against his shield or body, unless the members of the file behind him were pressed against his back (which in itself assumes the use of the unlikely front-on posture), as no leg is placed to the rear to brace the body in position and to resist any backward momentum. While it is likely that this form of compression did occur in the event of two phalanxes colliding at a run (see Chapter 13, The Hoplite Battle: Contact, *Othismos*, Breakthrough and Rout), it seems unlikely that hoplites could maintain such a close proximity to other members of their own files during any form of advance, and the individual hoplites must have been separated by at least a small margin at the moment of impact. Clearly the front ranks of any such formation would have been very unstable at this moment if they had adopted a front-on posture. A front-on stance also provides no means for the hoplite to apply his own counter-pressure against any force from the front. Counter pressure from a front-on body position can only be applied by leaning towards the enemy, but does not utilize the muscles of the legs unless a forward step is made, or a leg is positioned rearward, to supply leverage to the push. In either case, by doing so the body naturally adopts an oblique posture.

Standing obliquely with the feet shoulder width apart and the left foot forward (or 'firm set astride the ground' as Tyrtaeus describes it or with 'the legs not much further apart than in wrestling' as Xenophon would have it) is the most efficient position for the transference of body weight and the body's centre of gravity. This is particularly so if the legs are slightly bent with the knee joints unlocked as this allows the individual to slightly squat; both lowering and stabilizing their centre of gravity. Bent legs with the knee joints unlocked are another feature common to the artistic record that can be considered an accurate depiction of a particular aspect of hoplite combative postures. With the legs bent and the knees unlocked, the hoplite would be able to lean in to any impact (as per Theocritus' description of Heracles), braced in position by the rearward right leg. The unlocked knees allow the legs to flex or compress and so absorb any pressure, regardless of the direction from which it has come. The stability of this footwork is also increased if the rearward foot is turned slightly outwards. This ability to strengthen the posture is not available to any of the other stances unless significant alterations to the position of the rest of the body are made. In the confines of close combat, an oblique posture, even with the smallest stride distance between the feet, allows the hoplite to use the strength of the rear leg to press forward and maintain his balance at the same time. As such, Arrian's statement that infantry 'push with their shoulders and sides' is most likely a description of combat conducted in an oblique posture. Thus the physical, literary and artistic nature of the footwork involved in hoplite combat also indicates that the oblique body posture was adopted to bear the panoply in battle.

(d) Body posture and conformation to the limitations of the phalanx

The hoplite of the Classical Age did not fight as an individual but as part of the larger phalanx. As such, his body posture was also dictated by the restrictions imposed by the spacing within this formation. Asclepiodotus states that formations could be deployed in one of three orders: a close-order, with interlocked shields, with each man one *pēchus* (πῆχυς), or 45cm, from those around him on all sides (τό πυκνότατον, καθ' ὃ συνησπικὼς ἕκαστος ἀπὸ τῶν ἄλλων πανταχόθεν διέστηκεν πηχυαῖον διάστημα); an intermediate-order (also known as a 'compact formation') with each man separated by 2 *pēcheis*, or 90cm, on all sides (τό τε μέσον, ὃ καὶ πύκνωσιν ἐπονομάζουσιν, ᾧ διεστήκασι πανταχόθεν δύο πήχεις ἀπ' ἀλλήων); and an open-order with each man seperated by 4 *pēcheis*, or 180cm, by width and depth (τό τε ἀραιότατον, καθ' ὃ ἀλλήλων ἀπέχουσι κατά τε μῆκος καὶ βάθος ἕκαστοι πήχεις τέσσαρας).[42] The intermediate-order spacing is also described by Polybius as being used by the Macedonians and the close-order formation is noted by Arrian.[43] These spacings are based on a conversion from an early-Attic *pēchus* equal to 45cm. It is unlikely that Asclepiodotos, Polybius or Arrian based their measurements on the smaller Macedonian *pēchus* of 34cm as this seems to be an incredibly small interval to expect someone to conform to in a close-order formation while wearing armour, bearing a shield and wielding a weapon.[44]

Cawkwell claims that any reference to the Macedonians, which would include the works of Asclepiodotus, Polybius and Arrian, cannot be used in the same context for hoplite armies.[45] Contrary to this, there is evidence to suggest that at least some elements of the Macedonian army were equipped as standard Greek hoplites throughout the course of the campaigns of Alexander the Great and into the time of the Successor kingdoms.[46] Diodorus for example, describes the Macedonian veterans at Hallicarnassus in 334BC as deploying in a formation with 'interlocked shields' (συνασπίσαντες).[47] It is unlikely that troops bearing the smaller (64cm) Macedonian *peltē* would have been able to deploy in a manner where their shields interlocked while the *sarissae* of the first five ranks of their formation projected between the files.[48] These troops must have been carrying shields with a diameter more akin to the Greek *aspis* and using one-handed weapons held above the row of interlocking shields as the left hand would no longer be free to help wield the *sarissa*.[49] Antipater's Macedonian troops are described as armed with spears rather than *sarissae* and may have also been bearing the larger Greek *aspis*.[50] The 'Alexander Sarcophagus' of King Abdalonymus of Sidon (fourth century BC), now in Istanbul Archaeological Museum, clearly shows Macedonian troops bearing the hoplite *aspis* in what may be portrayals of the hypaspists or 'shield bearers'.[51]

The troops in this frieze are also shown using single-handed weapons rather than the *sarissa*. It additionally seems inconceivable that the Macedonian infantry would have used the *sarissa* when storming strongholds such as Tyre (which was taken through a breach in the wall), Gaza (which was stormed with assault ladders) or marching up the steep wooded slope to the Rock of Aornus.[52] They must have used shorter hoplite-style weapons, or at least only swords, under circumstances such as these. The elite Foot Companion regiment, for example, was one of the first into the breach at Tyre.[53] It must be concluded that these 'phalangites' were not equipped with the *sarissa* during this phase of the assault but must have been using smaller weapons of some kind. They may have still been carrying the small Macedonian shield, although, as artworks such as the 'Alexander Sarcophagus' suggest, some units, most likely only the contingents of hypaspists and allied and mercenary hoplites, may have been carrying the larger *aspis*.[54]

It has been suggested that the hypaspist units were equipped with both hoplite and phalangite equipment: the hoplite panoply for sieges and for more mobile actions such as at the Hydaspes River, where they accompanied Alexander's cavalry across the watercourse in order to execute a flanking manoeuvre, and the *sarissa* and *peltē* for more set-piece engagements.[55] However, this seems unlikely as it would create problems with logistics (carrying two sets of arms and armour per man) and deployment (making sure everyone was armed the same for each battle). As such, the hypaspists, in the time of Alexander at least, may have only been equipped with a hoplite panoply. Regardless of whether some or all of the Macedonian army was equipped as hoplites or phalangites, or whether some units were equipped as both, it seems implausible that an army as professional as the Hellenistic Macedonians would train troops in the use of one set of drills for the use of the *sarissa*, and expect troops armed as hoplites to effectively use a different set of drills under similar circumstances. None of the extant military texts relating to the Macedonians suggest the use of a dual system of deployment and armament. It seems more likely that a standard set of formations was used by the Macedonians, based upon those of the earlier hoplite armies, which could be utilized with either panoply with very little variation (see Chapter 12, Phalanxes, Shield Walls and Other Formations). As such, many aspects of the Macedonian footsoldier, such as the formations and intervals outlined by authors such as Asclepiodotus, can also be considered those of the Greek hoplite so long as any variance in the panoplies is considered.

For the Classical hoplite, the minimum spacing between each member of the phalanx is limited by the diameter of the shield. Krentz discounts this conclusion based upon the spacing of Asclepiodotus' intermediate-order (90cm) and the diameter of the Macedonian shield (64cm).[56] However, he fails to consider the use of the *aspis* in the context of the same formations. Thucydides states that hoplites often sought extra protection behind the overlapping sections of the shield belonging to the man to their right.[57] It is clear from this description that there is a large section of shield projecting beyond the bearer to the left, behind which a neighbouring hoplite could take shelter. Thus the interval of the close-order formation that Thucydides describes has to be less than the 90cm diameter of the hoplite shield itself.

The diameter and construction of the *aspis* further dictates that a member of a phalanx in close-order is unable to move any closer to the man to his right than the amount of shield that projects to the left of that man. Thus the minimum frontage per man in a close-order formation is the distance from one man's left elbow to the next man's left elbow, if they wish to maintain the tightest shield wall possible. For hoplites bearing shields 80–100cm in diameter in an oblique posture, this spacing equates to approximately 45cm: the same interval outlined by Asclepiodotus for the close-order formation used by the Macedonians (figure 11).[58]

Asclepiodotus' intermediate-order spacing of 90cm is the same as the average diameter of the *aspis* and can thus be considered an achievable interval between the files of the hoplite phalanx. This formation provides a moderate defensive capability while facilitating movement due to the increased spacing between each man.[59] Similarly, the hoplite panoply easily allows the individual to fit into an open-order formation of 180cm per man. The contemporary texts provide no direct details of the size of the spacing used for the formations of hoplite armies in Classical Greece. However, contrary to the claims of Cawkwell, formations using all three intervals detailed by Asclepiodotus are only achievable by troops equipped as hoplites and there is little reason to discount the attribution of these spacings to the Classical phalanx.[60]

In a close-order formation, a body positioned side-on can fit into a space limited to 45cm in width. However, the limitations of this stance suggest that it was not adopted as it does not satisfy several of the other required criteria for an effective combative posture. Additionally, a hoplite larger than 45cm in width would not be able to conform to the interval. Similarly, an average person standing front-on will occupy a 45cm frontage with just the width of their body. The members of the phalanx would literally be 'shoulder to shoulder' leaving little room for the movement of the weapon arm. Tyrtaeus

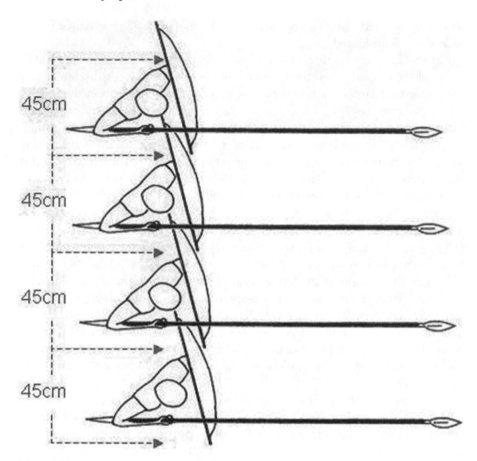

45cm

45cm

45cm

45cm

Figure 11: How hoplites in an oblique body posture conform to Asclepiodotus' close-order interval of 1 cubit (45cm) per man.

describes hoplites as standing 'beside each other' (παρ' ἀλλήλοισι μένοντες) while in formation, a phrase that Edmonds translates as 'shoulder to shoulder', in a passage meant to convey the impression of the hoplites standing side by side.[61] It is only with the adoption of an oblique posture that the phalanx can accommodate members with a shoulder width larger than 45cm. The body easily fits diagonally within the interval, thus providing the weapon arm with sufficient room to move in the gap between the shield and the shoulder rather then being squashed together 'shoulder to shoulder' as Edmonds interprets it (see figure 11). In doing so, none of the other criteria to which the oblique posture complies, are dramatically affected or require alteration. Thus a hoplite of any girth could be accommodated within the uniformly spaced interval of the phalanx only by adopting an oblique body posture. This again suggests that this was the way in which the hoplite stood to bear his panoply correctly for battle.

(e) Body posture and natural movement of the weapon arm

One of the most important aspects of any combative posture is the ability to act offensively. It is in this capacity that van Wees' comparison between the hoplite and the modern fencer fails when compared with what is physically achievable. For the fencer, the weapon arm is held to the front of the body and thus has full range of movement to lunge, thrust and parry. This is not so for the ancient hoplite who, if a side-on stance were assumed, has the weapon arm positioned to the rear of the posture, while the shield is supported by the left shoulder across the front. The positioning of the body in this way greatly restricts the movement of the weapon arm. Any attacking action that is made with either spear or sword must pass across the front of the body and navigate around or over the shield. The construction of the shoulder joint makes this a very awkward and restricted mode of attack. The rigid shoulder and pectoral sections of a cuirass additionally impede the movement of the arm when in this position to the extent that the spear can only be thrust forward a few centimetres (see Chapter 6, The Reach and Trajectory of Attacks made with the Hoplite Spear). Consequently, it can be concluded that a side-on posture would only be beneficial as a defensive mechanism for hoplites experiencing a large amount of pressure (such as a push or strongly delivered attack) from the front. The ability to exert greater counter-pressure, and to brace oneself more solidly, via a side-on posture means that under certain circumstances hoplites may have adopted this posture to resist a superior attack from the front at the expense of their own offensive capabilities.

By standing obliquely, the shoulder is not limited in its range of motion – the position of the body creates a natural gap between the shield and the right shoulder (see figure 11). The ball and socket construction of the shoulder is in no way impeded when the torso is positioned in this oblique angle to the front as thrusts do not have to be made across the body. The angle of the body also alleviates any restriction to the movement of the arm imposed by the armour as experienced in the side-on posture. The gap between shield and shoulder provides the hoplite with a full range of motion for the weapon arm with which to engage effectively.

It is possible to thrust from a front-on stance but this is extremely constricted due to the limited space between the shield, the shoulder and the weapon-bearing hand. Due to these confines, the arm can not sit naturally beside the body but must be folded back with the elbow projecting rearwards (see figure 9). This makes wielding the spear in this manner quite taxing on the muscles of the right arm even before any sort of thrusting action is undertaken in combat. The only way to alleviate this contortion of the weapon arm is to place it in a more natural position. However, in doing this the hand is dangerously situated forward of the protective covering of the shield. Both of these attributes of a front-on posture suggest that it was unlikely to have been used by the hoplite. Thus the ability to employ the weapon arm without restriction is only available when an oblique posture is adopted.

The following table (table 5) summarizes the required criteria that any posture a hoplite could adopt must satisfy in order to be considered viable for combat and how the different postures conform to these requirements.

As can be seen, it is only by positioning the body in an oblique position that a hoplite can satisfy all of these criteria. The ability to use the shield defensively while still supported by the shoulder, the ability to move forward with stable footing, the freedom of movement provided for the weapon arm, and a frontage that conforms to the limitations of a formation deployed in any interval suggest that this was how the hoplite stood to both correctly bare his panoply and engage in combat with the thrusting spear. This stance also complies with

Table 5: A summary of the necessary criteria for an effective hoplite combative posture per stance.

Criteria	Front-on stance	Side-on stance	Oblique stance
Allow the shield to be positioned in such a way so that it could be used defensively	No	Yes	Yes
Allow the hoplite to move without restriction, particularly in a forward direction	No	No	Yes
Provide stable footing to enable the hoplite to remain upright during the rigours of close combat	No	No	Yes
Allow the hoplite to maintain his position within the phalanx and conform to any limitations of space dictated by that formation	No	No	Yes
Allow the weapon arm to be positioned naturally and provided with a free range of movement so that the hoplite could engage an opponent offensively	No	No	Yes

many of the aspects of hoplite body posture depicted in the artistic record and among the scant references to it in the literary evidence. The adoption of an oblique body posture to bear the panoply will further affect how the spear could be wielded, both in terms of the reach and trajectory of any thrust made and how the positioning of the spear could be altered. An analysis of how this body posture affects the use of the spear further indicates that the overhead stance of current convention could not have been used by the hoplite to wield his weapon in battle.

Chapter 5

Repositioning the Spear in 'Hoplite Drill'

It is unlikely that the hoplite engaged in combat using only the one combative technique. Whether through the process of deployment, the natural dynamics of fighting with a thrusting weapon, or through simple fatigue, the hoplite undoubtedly moved through a variety of positions during the course of an engagement. However, no ancient text comprehensively details the movements employed by the individual hoplite to alter the positioning of his spear in preparation for, and to engage in, battle. To rectify this deficit, and in an attempt to better understand the processes of hoplite warfare, modern scholarship has compiled a series of positions and movements that can be considered the basics of 'hoplite drill' with the spear. However, there is a lack of consensus about how some of these positions were achieved. This indicates that the components of 'hoplite drill' are far from fully understood. A comprehensive analysis of the proposed drill movements demonstrates that none of these models can be considered correct; they are all simply unachievable by a hoplite within the formation of the phalanx. Nor do these models comply with what little literary evidence is available. Consequently, the results of this analysis demonstrate that the basics of 'hoplite drill' are something vastly different to the current models.

There is little available evidence to indicate the presence of a set of standardized movements with the spear that the term 'hoplite drill' would suggest. The literary sources do refer to instances, such as the teaching of combative arts under the tutelage of the *hoplomachoi*, where it can be assumed that students were taught a series of spear techniques to be used in battle.[1] What is unfortunately lacking is any reference to what these techniques actually were, how the hoplite was able to change from one to the other, or how standardized these techniques were across all of the city-states of ancient Greece. As a consequence, modern scholarship on the warfare of the hoplite has pieced together a limited corpus of techniques and poses based upon an interpretation of combative and non-combative images within the artistic record. From this source, four standardized positions for the hoplite have been proposed: standing at attention/rest with the *sauroter* planted in the ground and the spear held vertically, with the shield either on the left arm or placed on the ground and leaning against the left leg; marching with the spear angled back over the right shoulder; the low combative posture; and the overhead combative posture.

The failure to include both the underarm and reverse postures within this group of techniques means that all previous models of 'hoplite drill' are, at best, incomplete. Additionally, the presence of these four techniques (not including the underarm and reverse stances) in every model of 'hoplite drill' is as far as modern scholarship goes in agreement with itself. The problem with modern 'hoplite drill' arises from the way the hand grips the weapon in the two combative techniques that are part of the proposed models.

As previously noted, when the spear is held in the low position the thumb and forefinger are towards the front of the weapon. This placement of the hand is also the same when the spear is held in the underarm and reverse positions, when it is held sloped over the shoulder and when standing at attention. However, in the overhead position, the thumb and forefinger are situated to the rear (see pages 16–17). As such, the spear can not be moved from any other posture directly into the overhead position without the spear ending up pointing backwards and the *sauroter* projecting forwards (plate 11.1).

Connolly and Hanson suggest that the hoplite was trained in a few set moves, such as changing from the low to the overhead position, without providing any supporting references or details of how this may have been achieved.[2] Lazenby admits that it is difficult to envisage how the change from one posture to another was accomplished.[3] To circumvent this problem, and the lack of confirmatory ancient evidence, some scholars have proposed three techniques for reversing the grip on the weapon so that it could be moved into the overhead position with the spearhead pointing forwards: hereafter referred to as the 'left hand method', the 'throw and catch method', and the 'stick in ground method'. That three different models exist indicates that no particular option has been universally accepted.

Further to this, each of these models contains the one fundamental underlying flaw. Due to the difficulties in moving directly from the sloped or attention/rest position to the overhead position, it has been suggested that the spear must have been first moved into the low position from whence a change to the overhead position could be made.[4] However the close-order formation, with its row of interlocking shields across the front of the phalanx, is the most commonly described of all hoplite formations (see Chapter 12, Phalanxes, Shield Walls and other Formations). In this style of deployment a low posture could not have been assumed without the shield wall being 'opened' (see page 190–191). However, if all members of the formation conducted this procedure, it would negate the strong level of protection that the shield wall was designed to provide and subsequently weaken the strength of the close-order phalanx.

Additionally, the nearly two metres of weapon that projects forward of the weapon-bearing hand, means that spears held by the rearward ranks that are moved into the low position would project into the interval occupied by at least four men to their front while the phalanx was in close-order, or two men while it was in intermediate order. It seems impossible that a member of anything but the front rank would be able to reposition his spear into the low position without it becoming entangled as there would be no one to his front. Consequently, the three current models for the repositioning of the hoplite spear cannot be accomplished by all members of the most common hoplite deployment. Hanson further suggests that the hoplite phalanxes used the low position for the initial clash of the formations and then moved into the overhead position for the subsequent combat.[5] This conclusion has to assume that only the hoplites of the front rank adopted this position and even then only while in an intermediate or open-order formation. This contravenes the literary descriptions of most hoplite engagements.

It is possible that the move to the low and then to the overhead position was conducted before the phalanx was deployed in close or intermediate order but this seems unlikely. The phalanx would have to have deployed in a very open-order of more than 180cm between each rank to accommodate the length of the weapon, changed the positioning of the spear from sloped over the shoulder to low, then to overhead, and then narrowed the interval between the ranks and files to create a close-order shield wall or intermediate-order deployment. This would result in each hoplite wielding his spear above his head while he waited for the remainder of the phalanx to form up, while he waited to receive an enemy attack or while he advanced to engage. Holding a spear in the overhead position for a prolonged period of time, even without the actions of combat, is extremely taxing on the muscles of the arm. It is unlikely that a hoplite would have had enough strength to actually commit to any fighting once the two lines had met on the field if he had had to hold his spear in this position for any length of time (see Chapter 8, Endurance and Accuracy when Fighting with the Hoplite Spear). Furthermore, hoplites in the rear ranks would have had no need to immediately adopt a combative posture and would have kept their weapons at the slope; either inclined back over their shoulder, or angled forward to help shield the forward ranks from missiles as the later Macedonians did with their *sarissae*.[6] However, once the fighting had commenced, members of the rear ranks would have had no means of moving into a low position and then into the overhead position. Based upon this method of grip alteration, members of the rear ranks of the phalanx would have been unable to engage an opponent should the men before them fall in the fighting.

For the basics of any model of 'hoplite drill' to be considered viable, they must incorporate a method of repositioning the spear that can be done in any formation, under any condition, and without causing undue fatigue to the combatants. This is where the modern processes of re-creation and experimental archaeology come to the fore; they allow for the validity of previous models to be tested in physical reality and for new models of 'hoplite drill' to be formulated if required. The panoply replicated for this study was made specifically with this kind of testing in mind. The results of these tests allow for two inter-related conclusions to be drawn. Firstly, that it is not possible to move the spear from the slope into an offensive overhead position using any of the models forwarded by modern scholarship regardless of the order in which the hoplite may have been deployed. In other words, not one of the proposed models can be considered valid. Secondly, if it is impossible to move the spear into the overhead position, then it follows that the hoplite did not adopt the overhead position to engage in combat with the spear. Subsequently, the current conventions that use the low/overhead two-stance model as a means of explaining the mechanics of hoplite warfare must be corrected.

The problems with the 'left hand method'

One proposed method is that the hoplite used his left hand to achieve a change in his grip on the weapon, which allowed him to subsequently alter his posture. The dual grip system and concave shape of the *aspis* allows for the grip on the *antilabē* by the left hand to be released while the shield remains supported by the shoulder and the forearm inserted through the *porpax*. In the suggested method, the spear is moved from the slope into a low position. It is then raised to a vertical position, close to the left hand, with the tip pointing upwards. The grip on the shield is released, allowing the spear to be transferred to the free left hand. The spear is then re-gripped by the right hand, with the hand reversed, so that the spear can be moved into the overhead position.[7] Markle, in experiments with the cavalry lance, found it almost impossible to alter the posture of the rider without the incorporation of the left hand.[8]

While it may have been possible for the sole mounted participant of Markle's experiments to accomplish a move to the overhead position using this technique, this method possesses several problems in the context of a hoplite within a phalanx. Firstly, this process does not require an initial move to the low position as has been suggested if the spear is held at the slope or at attention/ rest; it can be directly transferred to a vertical position near the left hand – it is only Hanson's suggestion of the hoplite using the low technique for the initial clash that would make the placement of the spear in such a position a requirement of this procedure. Regardless, there are still numerous impediments to the process, which make this technique impossible for a hoplite to achieve. From either a sloped or the unlikely low position, it is easy to move the spear into a vertical position, release the grip on the shield with the left hand, transfer the spear and then re-grip the shaft with the right hand reversed as per the beginning moves of the suggested process (plate 12.1).

However, once this position is reached, it is almost impossible to raise the spear up into the overhead position. If an attempt is made to simply raise and rotate the spear while keeping the shield in its protective position across the front of the body, the shield and left arm inhibit the movement. If the left arm and shield are moved out of the way (by being moved to the left side of the body) to allow free movement of the spear, this also presents several problems. Firstly, it seems unlikely that a move involving the removal of a large piece of defensive equipment would be conducted just prior to, or immediately after, the clash of two opposing phalanxes. This makes this method of re-positioning completely incompatible with Hanson's proposal that the clash was made in the low position before moving into the overhead posture. Additionally, similar to the theory that hoplites advanced into battle with their shield held to their side, it seems highly unlikely that such a move would be undertaken in the presence of enemy archers, slingers or *peltasts* as this would expose the hoplite to volleys of missile fire. Even if the spear is freed from the constraints of the *aspis* and the shield-bearing arm, or even if the spear is somehow moved in front of a shield kept in its protective position, the spear still cannot be raised and rotated into place when the hoplite is wearing a helmet with a crest attached as the spear can become entangled in the crest as the weapon in rotated up into position.

The rider in Markle's experiments was bare-headed and incurred no such impediment. However, even when wearing an un-crested helmet, or no helmet at all, if the shield is moved and the spear freed, the repositioning of the weapon becomes even more problematic within the context of the phalanx. When the spear is held by its correct point of balance and is rotated into position, the tip inscribes a large sweeping arc; extending almost two metres to the right of the hoplite as it is moved into the overhead position (plate 12.1). In even the most open-order formation described in the ancient texts of 180cm per man, this procedure endangers every member of the phalanx around each individual as the weapon is swung into place. This was another problem not encountered in Markle's experimentations with a solitary rider. It is inconceivable that a formation of hundreds, if not thousands, of men could accomplish this manoeuvre without injuring some of their own comrades or simply getting their spears entangled with those around them at the very least. Clearly, such a move could not have been performed if the hoplite was in close proximity to other members of his own phalanx, regardless of order, or in close proximity to an enemy formation. Any assumption that this manoeuvre could have been accomplished in the confusion once the two opposing phalanxes had clashed is completely untenable. In the face of physical reality, this model must be discounted.

The problems with the 'throw and catch method'
Lazenby and Anderson propose that a change in posture could be made only from the low position. They suggest that a spear held horizontally (i.e. in the low position) could have the grip upon it altered, and moved into the overhead position, by raising it above shoulder height, 'tossing the spear upwards a few inches and then catching it again with the grip reversed' (plate 13.1).[9]

The fact that this method requires the adoption of the low position, and the inability for that to be done by anyone other than members of the front rank of an open or intermediate order formation that is not in contact with the enemy, indicates that this method is not a viable means of repositioning the hoplite spear within the context of the most common hoplite deployments.

Anderson suggests that this technique could be accomplished 'easily with little practice' but he cannot have taken the restrictions of the phalanx, or the presence of an opponent to the front, into account.[10] When this process was put into practice it was found that, while it was possible for an isolated individual to alter the position of the spear using this method, it was difficult to accomplish this manoeuvre competently, or with a 100 per cent rate of success, even after 'a little practice'. The Sydney Ancients, a group of re-enactors who specialize in ancient combative techniques who were used in many of the tests involved in this study, previously based all of their drill movements upon modern texts and their own interpretation of the ancient artistic and literary sources. As such, their 'hoplite drill' was based upon the low/overhead 'two-stance model' of current convention and the 'throw and catch' method of repositioning the spear. However some members, even after years of practice and participation, still had trouble using this method and occasionally dropped their weapon during the procedure. The Sydney Ancients also only conducted this manoeuvre when arranged in a single rank, to avoid potential injuries to anyone to the front or rear, and only while there was an intermediate interval between each member of the rank. Nor was this process attempted at a run or rapid advance but only when stationary or walking slowly.[11]

The main problem with this process is that the grip on the weapon has to be fully released, however momentarily. Due to the location of the point of balance for the weapon, the notion that a hoplite deployed anywhere other than in the front rank of a phalanx would be able to toss a spear that projected almost two metres forward of his own body 'up a few inches' without it becoming entangled with those ahead of him is simply unrealistic; unless it is assumed that each rank of the phalanx was separated by at least a full spear length and every man conducted this move in unison. Even the open-order interval described by Asclepiodotus (180cm per man) does not provide sufficient room for this manoeuvre to be performed safely. Such a move in the confines of the phalanx would place many at risk of accidental injury. If this process was attempted just prior to the clash with an opponent, many of the spears of the front rank could have simply been deflected away from their bearer, either by entanglement or due to parrying by the opponent, as the grip on the weapon was released. Nor is it likely that a hoplite in the front rank would be able to undertake this procedure after committing to a first attack from the low position as per Hanson's suggestion of when this alteration of combative postures was made.

There is also the risk that the spear would not be caught at its correct point of balance, or not caught at all, which would make it difficult to fight if this occurred just prior to, or immediately after, a clash with an opposing formation. If only a small percentage of weapons became entangled, dropped or deflected, both the cohesion and the effectiveness of the entire phalanx would be compromised. Like the 'left hand method', it seems highly unlikely that a large formation of hoplites would use this procedure for altering the grip on their weapons and their combative posture, and this proposed method can likewise be considered unviable.

The problems with the 'stick in ground method'

The *sauroter* is utilized in the third proposed technique for altering the grip. In this method, the spear is moved to a vertical position and the *sauroter* is then thrust into the ground, which allows the hoplite to release his grip on the weapon. It is then suggested that the hoplite would be able to re-grip the spear with the right hand reversed, extract the spear from the ground and then raise it into the overhead position.[12] Of all the proposed methods for the alteration of grip and posture, this is the most problematic. The attempt to physically replicate this proposed method clearly demonstrates that the physical aspects of this technique had not been fully considered when it was formulated.

Similar to the 'left hand method', there is no requirement to move the spear into a low position before raising it vertically when using this technique (except within the context of Hanson's suggestion of when this procedure was undertaken). However, there are problems with this model that clearly demonstrate that it too could not have been performed by hoplites deployed in any form of order. Firstly, as the point of balance for the spear is located in the rear third of the shaft, enough of the spear must be allowed to slip through the hand as it is raised vertically so that the *sauroter* will reach the ground as the weapon is driven downwards (plate 15.1).

The natural location for the spear to be thrust into the ground is to the front-right of the hoplite (forward of the level of the shield). This in itself suggests that this procedure could not have been undertaken in the common close-order deployment of 45cm per man. However, once in place, it requires an even more unrealistic level of flexibility and space for a member of a phalanx to extract the weapon and move it into the overhead position. If the spear is simply re-gripped with the hand reversed, extracted and rotated into position, the same problems with entanglement with the crest of the helmet, and of endangering those on either side, are encountered as with the 'left hand method'; making this process impossible within the confines of the phalanx (see plate 12).

Additionally, after allowing some of the spear to slip through the hand so that the *sauroter* can be thrust into the ground, it is impossible to re-grip the weapon at its correct point of balance. This makes moving the spear into an overhead position difficult as the weight of the weapon behind the hand forces the tip to point skyward unless considerable muscular pressure is exerted through the hand to counter the force of gravity. Furthermore, the necessity to thrust the end of the spear into the ground as part of this process means that this manoeuvre can only be done while stationary and could not have been conducted while advancing upon an enemy position; and no member of a formation would be able to alter his posture at his own timing without disrupting the cohesion of the phalanx. If the entire phalanx halted so that the action could be performed in unison, this would present a large, momentarily stationary, target for volleys of missile fire or a counter-charge by the opposing side. It is also highly unlikely that this method could have been undertaken just after two phalanxes had met as per Hanson's suggestion of an initial clash in the low position followed by a move into the overhead.

Other means of completing this manoeuvre are just as problematic and just as unlikely. One possible way of carrying out this technique is for the hoplite to step forward, past his upright spear, and then twist his body so that he can reach behind himself and grasp the spear with the hand reversed, extract the spear and then raise it over his shoulder and into position (plate 15). The only other way to move the spear into position is for the hoplite to similarly step forward of the upright spear and then lean backwards, like some kind of ancient limbo dancer, in order to grab the weapon with the hand reversed, extract the spear and then straighten the body as it is moved into position (plate 16).

Not only do each of these options require substantial room for the weapon to be extracted and moved into position (anyone in the rearward ranks would actually step into the space occupied by the upright spear belonging to the man ahead of him), and still fail to re-grip the weapon at its correct point of balance, but the awkward contortion of the body required to accomplish these techniques make them almost impossible to achieve without overbalancing; particularly in rigid armour and/or when wearing a top-heavy crested helmet. The way the spear comes up and over the right shoulder after it has been extracted in both methods would additionally endanger those in front of any hoplite, whom he would be likely to stab in the back, while the rising *sauroter* would risk injury to those behind the hoplite whom he could not see.

This method also cannot be reversed. If the hoplite somehow managed to get the spear into the overhead position, there is no way to thrust the end of the spear back into the ground should he wish to alter the posture back into the low position. Finally, similar to the 'throw and catch method', the grip on the weapon must be fully released. If it does not stick into the ground adequately, or is knocked by another member of the phalanx as the manoeuvre is performed, the weapon may fall over and would be almost impossible to pick back up again within the confines of the phalanx. It must also be considered, if thrusting the *sauroter* into the ground was the standard method of altering the grip on the weapon, what the hoplite would have done if he was unable to thrust his spear into the ground, such as if the terrain was rocky, a paved courtyard or road, or was strewn with the detritus of conflict. It seems unlikely that the ship-borne hoplites fighting at the battle of Salamis in 480BC thrust their weapons into the deck of a trireme whenever they wished to change posture. Many examples of the *sauroter* also do not possess an elongated spike (see page 5). Weapons with rounded points or small knobs would not be able to be thrust into the ground at all. This in itself suggests that this method for changing the position of the spear was not practised. Any method of grip alteration must be possible on any sort of terrain. From this, and the procedural problems associated with it, it can be concluded that the 'stick in ground method' was not a process employed for altering the grip on the hoplite spear, nor could the *sauroter* have been specifically designed to facilitate any such procedure.

Moving into the underarm position

The only way that a physically achievable series of 'hoplite drill' movements can be formulated, which allows for the hoplite to alter the positioning of his weapon regardless of the interval of the phalanx, the nature of the terrain and/or the speed of any advance, is to replace the low/overhead two-stance model of current convention with the 'new model' incorporating the low and underarm positions. From a marching stance with the spear inclined over the shoulder, the weapon can be easily lowered directly into the underarm position without requiring any elaborate method of altering the grip on the shaft. This allows for the underarm posture to be immediately adopted in a close-order formation as no initial move to the low position is necessary, nor does the weapon move below the level of the interlocking shield wall. As such, the smaller interval of the close-order formation and its protective shield wall are not compromised (plate 17).

The fact that the move to the underarm posture requires no initial move to the low position would allow hoplites in the rear rank of a phalanx to keep their weapons at the slope, angled either backwards or forwards, until a move to a more combative stance was required. Movements from the low position to the underarm are also easily accomplished, by simply raising the spear into the armpit should the hoplite wish to alter his combative posture, to strike at a higher target, or if the formation he was in was closing the intervals of its files from intermediate to close-order (plate 18).

Both of these processes can also be completed in the opposite direction (i.e. from underarm to low or from underarm to sloped), making this drill, unlike any of the proposed methods incorporating the overhead position, dual-directional and very adaptive to the changing circumstances of a hoplite engagement. None of these manoeuvres require more room than that in which the hoplite would have been deployed, nor do they require universal timing within the phalanx unless more than one rank was repositioning their spears at the same time. Nor do such moves endanger or entangle with those around the hoplite as there is no rotation of the spear required to achieve them. Most importantly, the hold on the weapon is at no stage released during the transition. This move can also be conducted when either stationary or on the move, on any terrain, and does not require the involvement of the left hand, or removal of the shield from its defensive position to effect the change.

Interestingly, this series of low/underarm 'hoplite drill' movements is consistent with the few literary descriptions of hoplites altering the positioning of their weapons. Xenophon states that during a demonstration for the queen of Cilicia, Greek mercenary hoplites marched forward and 'when the trumpet sounded, they advanced arms and charged' (καὶ ἐπεί ἐσάλπιγξε, προβαλόμενοι τὰ ὅπλα ἐπῇσαν).[13] During a later engagement, the Greeks were ordered to 'keep their spears on the right shoulder until a signal was given by a trumpet; then, lowering them for the attack, to follow on slowly' (παρήγγελτο δὲ τὰ μὲν δόρατα ἐπὶ τὸν δεξιὸν ὦμον ἔχειν ἕως σημαίνοι τῇ σάλπιγγιν ἔπειτα δὲ εἰς προσβολὴν καθέντας ἕπεσθαι βάδην).[14] Iphicrates is similarly said to have issued orders to 'lower spears' (χλῖναι τὸ δόρυ).[15] Heracles is also said to have learned to fight with the spear couched (δούρατι δὲ προβολαίῳ).[16] The terms used in these passages, meaning to couch, level, lower or present, indicate a move to either the low or underarm position. Had the move been into the overhead position of current convention a word for 'raise' or something similar would most likely have been used; much in the way that Homer and Tyrtaeus describe the missile weapons of the Archaic Age as being 'held aloft' (ανασχόμενος).[17] Lorimer connects a variant of this word with the description of men preparing to throw, but fails to correlate this action with the adoption of the overhead stance.[18] Modern scholarship's failure to associate these ancient references to hoplite drill with the adoption of the underarm stance can only be the result of the omission of the underarm technique from any previous study of hoplite warfare, and the association of the techniques described in the ancient texts with a move to the low position (which cannot have been made under all combat conditions experienced by the hoplite).

It is highly improbable that 'hoplite drill' would incorporate methods that limited how the individual combatant could wield his weapon, how he could alter the position of the weapon, and limit the speed of an advancing phalanx. It is also unlikely that any such method would be dependent upon the type of terrain upon which the hoplite fought or the style of *sauroter* that was affixed to the end of the shaft. Yet this is what current convention would have us accept if the proposed methods of repositioning the spear are followed. However, physical re-creation demonstrates that none of the methods proposed for the alteration of the grip from the attention/slope/low positions to the overhead posture are achievable by a hoplite in the massed formation of the phalanx. This clearly demonstrates that the overhead position of current convention could not have been adopted by the hoplite to wield his weapon in combat. Furthermore, suggestions that the hoplite advanced into battle using the low stance, and then changed into the overhead position for the thrusting combat following the clash of the lines, can in no way be considered correct. The results of the analysis of how the hoplite would have been able to alter his combative posture within the confines of the phalanx, regardless of the mode of deployment, motion or terrain, indicates that the manner in which the hoplite wielded his weapon to engage an opponent was with the 'new model' of the low and underarm techniques.

Chapter 6

The Reach and Trajectory of Attacks made with the Hoplite Spear

As with any hand-held weapon, the reach and trajectory of an attack made with the hoplite spear will influence how efficient that strike will be in a combat situation. The examination of these two factors in relation to the performance of a hoplite wielding his spear in battle indicates that the underarm position is the most effective means for an individual to employ this piece of weaponry. Concurrently, this analysis further demonstrates the unlikelihood of the overhead stance being used by a hoplite to wield a thrusting spear in battle.

Missile weapons, whether they are bows, slings, javelins or rifles, have what are known as both an *effective range* and a *combat range* (also referred to as a *battle range*). The *effective range* is the maximum distance that a projectile (e.g. a bullet, arrow or sling stone) will travel when fired, released or cast. The *combat range* is a measure of the maximum distance at which this weapon can be efficiently used to inflict casualties among enemy combatants. For example, a modern combat rifle may be able to fire a bullet over a kilometre (its *effective range*). However, due to factors that affect the aim, such as line of sight, the diminishing size of targets as distance increases, trajectory etc., the same rifle may only actually be effectual against targets up to a distance of several hundred metres (its *combat range*).

Thrusting weapons have similar characteristics. For the spear of the hoplite, its *effective range* can be considered to be the maximum distance that the spear tip can be projected forward when the weapon-bearing arm is at its full extension. The *combat range* of the spear is therefore how far the spear can be projected forward, connect with a target, and still have enough force and extension of the arm remaining to enable the spear to be driven into that target. Other forms of hand-to-hand combat work on the same principles. In martial arts the *combat range* of a punch, for example, equates to approximately 75 per cent of the full extension of the arm.[1] This is because, as the arm moves towards its full extension, it begins to slow; resulting in a reduction of the impact velocity that can be brought to bear against a target.[2] Additionally, if a punch or kick is delivered at the point where the limb is fully extended, no residual extension remains for the strike to 'penetrate' the target. This is why practitioners of many open-hand combat arts are taught not to punch or kick *at* a target, but rather *through* a target at an imaginary point beyond the area they wish to strike. This ensures that the target is struck prior to the limb reaching its full extension and allows for the punch or kick to be delivered, and followed through, with the maximum amount of force. This is one of the factors that allows martial artists to punch through such things as wooden boards, roof tiles or bricks. As thrusting weapons, such as spears, swords or daggers, act as an extension of the bearer's arm, the optimum *combat range* for these weapons is also when the arm is at 75 per cent of its full extension; with the 'reach' increased by the distance that the tip of the weapon extends beyond the hand wielding it (figure 12).

While it is still possible for soft targets such as flesh, and even the harder surfaces of shields and armour, to be penetrated up to the limits of *effective range* (thus making both *effective* and *combat range* almost one and the same), or for targets to be penetrated at distances closer than when the arm is at 75 per cent of its full extension, the 75 per cent distance provides for the most efficient delivery of force and is therefore the *optimum combat range* for the weapon. The limits of *effective range* will generally remain unaltered; the arm cannot be projected beyond 100 per cent of its full extension, thus allowing for no bio-mechanical means for the *effective range* of the weapon to be increased. The spear could be held further to the rear to increase the 'reach' of the weapon itself, however, this requires that the weapon be held behind its point of balance, making it awkward to wield, and is unlikely to have been a common

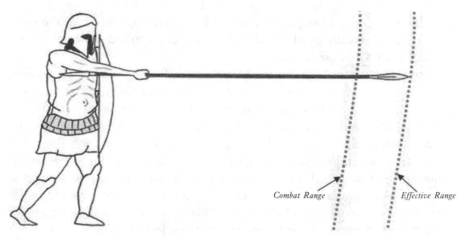

Combat Range   Effective Range

Figure 12: The *effective range* and *combat range* of a hoplite armed with a thrusting spear.

practice. Regardless, the *effective range* will still be at the full extension of the arm and the *combat range* will still remain at 75 per cent of the extension of the arm.

Like many aspects of hoplite warfare, the ancient literary sources provide little help in determining the *effective* or *combat ranges* that the hoplite had with his weapons. As with descriptions of posture, this would have been considered superfluous detail for many readers contemporaneous with the time period and would not have been included by ancient writers in their texts. Passages suggesting that hoplites should 'reach forth and strike the foe', or engage when they are 'within spear thrust of the enemy', indicate the use of some kind of thrusting action but provide no specific reference to the distance at which this attack was made.[3]

Similarly, modern scholarship has not yet attempted to understand the fundamental properties of how the hoplite weapon performed. This lack of analysis may be due to the absence of any suggestive, or confirmatory, detail within the available sources. It also demonstrates another area of modern scholarship where the processes of physical re-creation and experimental archaeology can fill in a gap within the current knowledge base through the testing of the reach of replicated weapons. The lack of any previous examination of this aspect of hoplite warfare may also be due to modern theories being based on a model encompassing only the low and overhead postures. As it was assumed that the hoplite only fought in these two positions, and the low stance could not be used under certain conditions (such as in a close-order formation), deductive reasoning concluded that the hoplite fought by holding the spear above his head when in this deployment. As such, any examination of, indeed even the consideration of, the factors influencing the range of the weapon becomes fundamentally redundant. However, with the identification of the underarm stance as a third combative technique, and the use of the overhead posture to cast the javelin, the physical examination of the *effective* and *combat ranges* of attacks made with the hoplite spear from all possible combative positions becomes paramount to any reappraisal of the mechanics of hoplite warfare.

In order to analyze the *effective range* of thrusts made with the hoplite spear, examinations were conducted using re-enactors from the Sydney Ancients and interested volunteers. The training in hoplite drill undertaken by the members of the Sydney Ancients effectively simulates hoplites with at least some experience in handling their weapons. Conversely, the interested volunteers effectively simulate raw recruits or conscripts with no prior experience of hoplite warfare. Thus the performance of two different levels of hoplite could be co-analyzed. Importantly, the number and variety of shields, cuirasses and helmets owned by the Sydney Ancients also allowed for the volunteers to be equipped with a panoply that fitted them correctly, particularly the shield, so as to remove any interference that ill-fitting equipment may have had on the test results. It also allowed for the influence of different styles of armour on the thrusting action to be observed and recorded. The same spear was used by all participants so that the balance of the weapon was standardized across all of the tests.

Tests examining *effective range* were conducted for the four combative postures found in the artistic record: the overhead; the low; the underarm; and the reverse. The tests were further segregated by an allowable level of body movement simulating two different orders of deployment. In one set of tests the participants were allowed to move their shield during the action of the strike if they wished, simulating the freedom of movement experienced in an open or intermediate-order deployment. In the other set of tests, the participants were required to keep the shield in its protective position across the front of the body, simulating a hoplite in a close-order phalanx with his *aspis* 'locked' into a shield wall. This resulted in a total of eight different variations of thrust and order being examined per participant.

The experiments were conducted in a facility fitted out with testing and recording equipment large enough to accommodate the actions that the participants were to undertake. The room was equipped with a 3 metre long horizontal scale along one wall at a height of 1.2 metres from the floor. The scale was calibrated into alternating black and white sections 200mm in length to allow the differentiations to be easily determined by photography. These sections were further calibrated by centimetres to allow accurate distance measurements to be made by data collectors. A moveable vertical scale, 2 metres in height and with the same calibrations, was used to measure the range and elevation of each thrust. A line was marked on the floor in line with the beginning of the horizontal scale (hereafter referred to as the *zero line*) to indicate where the participants were to stand for each test.

Each participant was tested in turn by having them stand on the *zero line* in a 'ready' position for a particular thrust. The vertical scale was then moved into place until it touched the tip of the spear. The height of the spear tip was read off the vertical scale and recorded on a data sheet. The horizontal distance that the spear projected forward was measured and recorded as the point where the vertical scale intersected the horizontal scale on the wall back to the *zero line* (plate 19).

The movable scale was then withdrawn and the participant performed the actions involved for the required thrust and permissible body movement. This thrust was not done at speed, as would have been the case under real combat conditions, but slowly to ensure safety and to allow measurements to be taken. When the thrust reached the limit of arm extension, the participant held this position while the elevation of the spear tip and the *effective range* of the thrust were measured and recorded, and the actions of the thrust were photographed using still cameras. Any comment that the participant made in relation to how the techniques felt as a combative movement was also recorded. This process was repeated for each type of thrust and permitted level of body movement. The height of each participant, and the length of their right arm, was also recorded so that it could be determined what role stature had in the reach of each type of thrust, and so the *effective range* could be quantified as a percentage of body height.

It must be observed that there are several aspects of the tests different from combat conditions. The terrain upon which they were conducted was the flat surface of the testing room floor and not the open plains of Greece; there was no shoving or jostling against the participant; nor moving targets; nor a need for self defence as would have been necessary in a real battle. All of these factors would undoubtedly influence the *effective range* of a spear thrust. Similarly, the movement of the participant between one test and the next meant that each thrust was not made from the exact same position as its predecessor. Using the *zero line* as a guide, the impact of this last factor was minimized in terms of its influence on the results. In relation to the lack of combat conditions within the test, in the confusion and variability of a real engagement, the exact distance of *effective range* is unlikely to have been paramount to a combatant who would have been more concerned with striking his target than seeing how far forward he could project his spear. These examinations were designed only to provide a basic understanding of the *effective range* of the primary hoplite weapon.

Additionally, as the low position cannot be adopted in a close-order formation while the shield is 'locked' into the shield wall, during the testing process, the participants were allowed to thrust around their shield from the low position so long as the *aspis* was kept in place. If the shield was allowed to be moved, as per an 'opening' of the shield wall, the thrusting action would be the same as for a simulated intermediate order formation. The data for the low stance in close-order is therefore given here only for comparative purposes.

The data collected demonstrates that a hoplite wielding the spear in the underarm position would have held a considerable advantage over those wielding the spear in either the low or overhead positions, even before any strike was made. When standing in the 'ready' position, a spear held in the underarm posture naturally projects further forward of the bearer than in any other combative stance (table 6).

Those wielding the spear in the underarm position begin any thrusting action with their spears projecting further forward than those held in other stances. This equates to an efficient usage of almost an extra 9 per cent of the weapon's overall length. This is due to the positioning of the weapon bearing hand, which is further forward in the underarm 'ready' posture (just behind

Table 6: The projected distance of the spear tip in the 'ready' position per stance, order and participant.

Order	Stance	Projected distance of spear tip in the 'ready' position per participant (centimetres)									
Participant		A	B	C	D	E	F	G	H	I	Avg
Close-order	Overhead	140	145	139	105	100	116	150	135	112	**127**
	Low	130	163	161	111	135	146	159	134	141	**142**
	Underarm	129	166	155	148	155	148	154	151	148	**150**
	Reverse	128	144	147	100	100	140	135	128	135	**129**
Open-order	Overhead	135	135	136	100	116	120	150	108	102	**134**
	Low	135	151	152	137	150	154	161	146	132	**146**
	Underarm	136	160	160	155	158	155	168	146	143	**153**
	Reverse	130	146	136	100	95	124	156	133	137	**129**

the shield and the *zero line*) than in any other. Consequently, the spear itself projects further forward. In comparison, when holding the weapon in the overhead or reverse stance, the hand is beside the head; further back from the shield/*zero line* by approximately 20cm. The minor variances in start position, between the simulated open and close-orders, are clear reflections of how the positioning of the body in relation to the *zero line* altered through the process of the testing. The advantage that the underarm stance possesses in the 'ready' position was also seen in the measurements of the spear at the full extension of its *effective range* (table 7).

Table 7: The projected distance of the spear tip at the *effective range* of the thrust per stance, order and participant.

Order	Stance	Projected distance of spear tip at full arm extension (*effective range*) per participant (centimetres)									
Participant		A	B	C	D	E	F	G	H	I	Avg
Close-order	Overhead	191	178	180	195	220	205	182	181	177	**190**
	Low	195	192	187	190	220	216	222	184	195	**200**
	Underarm	205	212	205	238	230	199	209	240	205	**216**
	Reverse	200	195	185	227	210	153	207	214	212	**200**
Open-order	Overhead	220	215	195	222	222	198	193	196	220	**209**
	Low	240	227	215	251	233	240	230	239	235	**234**
	Underarm	244	231	237	247	238	223	221	242	246	**237**
	Reverse	236	210	202	225	215	179	212	229	240	**216**

As was expected, the permitted movement of the body in the simulated intermediate-order allowed the spear to be thrust further forward than comparative thrusts made under restrictive close-order conditions. In a loose order, underarm and low thrusts are able to be projected almost to the full length of the weapon. This is possible as the rear end of the spear can be advanced almost to where the right hand was situated in the 'ready' position if the body is rotated to the left to follow the action of the strike. Thus the low and underarm techniques are the most efficient use of the length of the weapon itself. The ability for the low and underarm thrusts to be projected further than any other combative technique is attributable to two factors: the natural motion of the arm and the lack of impediment by the panoply.

A thrusting action made from either the low or underarm position follows a natural movement of the arm as the spear is thrust forward to the full extension of the limb. In the underarm action, this is achieved by simply advancing the weapon-bearing hand forward from its starting position. In doing so, the arm is simply straightened; there is no unnatural contortion of any of the joints experienced with the motion. Consequently, there is very little strain on the arm itself in performing this action. With the adoption of an oblique body posture to carry the panoply, the spear naturally sits beside the upper-right rim of the shield. When the strike is made, the spear passes over this same area and the motion is in no way inhibited by the presence of the shield. Thus the underarm thrust can be performed in both a close- and open-order formation without necessitating the removal of the shield from its protective position across the front of the body; giving the hoplite a strong offensive and defensive posture at the same time.

Attacks made from the low position likewise follow a natural movement of the limb as long as the shield is moved aside to prevent contact with the arm as it moves through the motion. As previously noted, this means that the low position could not have been adopted in a close-order while the shield wall is maintained and would have been more commonly used in intermediate-order formations or when pursuing a routed enemy arcoss the battlefield. When committed in a more open-order, without the inhibition of the *aspis*, the weapon-bearing arm is simply swung forward in order to execute the strike. The construction of the wrist allows it to flex as the weapon arm extends forward, which allows the spear to be kept level as it is directed towards the target. This results in a method of delivery that places almost no stress on the muscles and joints of the arm. The finishing position of a low thrust is almost at the same point as that of an underarm thrust due to the arm finishing fully extended and roughly parallel to the ground in both techniques. The main difference is that the low attack is a swinging motion whereas the underarm is a direct forward extension of the limb. In the open-order tests, the *effective ranges* of both the low and underarm thrusts were almost identical.

It was found that the range of the spear thrusts made from both the low and underarm positions were not dramatically affected whether the participant was wearing a metal cuirass, a composite *linothorax* or had no armour on at all due to the natural motions of the arm and oblique body posture adopted to bear the panoply. The different types of helmet worn by the participants during the testing, and the use or lack of greaves, also had little impact on the results. The consensus among the test participants was that these two actions felt the most natural means of attack. This conforms with the conclusion that the 'new model' of hoplite fighting, incorporating the low and underarm techniques, was how the hoplite fought in battle.

Conversely, the overhead position was generally considered to feel awkward as a means of delivering a thrusting action. During the motion of an over-head thrust, the arm cannot follow a natural course of extension and keep the spear level at the same time. The arm can only be presented so far before the wrist locks in position and can be flexed no further. If the arm is extended beyond this point, the construction of the joints result in the spear travelling downwards rather than directly ahead with an unnatural contortion of the limb (see following). This results in a great amount of stress placed upon the arm, particularly the wrist. In a close-order formation the location of the shield rim also inhibits the motion of the arm. If the spear is held close to the body, the right forearm connects with the shield momentarily after commencing the thrust; the arm can only be advanced about 20cm before further motion is prevented by contact with the shield. During the tests, some participants overcame this obstacle by extending the arm to the right and thrusting around the shield itself. This accounts for the vast differences between the start and finish position for these thrusts across the participants (compare tables 6 and 7). While this gave the participants extra reach with the weapon, it also accentuated the stress and contortion experienced by the arm and would not be a viable means of delivery within the confines of a fully deployed phalanx. Even when in an open-order, the ability to move the shield aside did not compensate for the inability to fully extend the arm. This limitation in the extension of the arm was a contributing factor in the thrusts made from the overhead position having the shortest *effective range* in both of the simulated orders. Both the *effective range* and *combat range* of an overhead thrust would be even further reduced if the weapon was held in the centre of the shaft, as per current convention, as this reduces the amount of weapon projecting forward of the bearer.

The rigid shoulder and pectoral sections of metallic body armour were also found to inhibit the forward movement of the arm when the weapon was held in the overhead position. These restrictions were absent in thrusts made from both the low and underarm positions and were another contributing factor to the reduced *effective range* of an overhead thrust. Based upon the analysis of reach, it seems unlikely that the overhead position of current convention could have been adopted to wield a thrusting weapon effectively.

Similarly, all participants stated that thrusts made from the reverse posture felt uncomfortable. However, unlike the overhead thrust, the arm does not encounter any unnatural contortion or locking of the wrist when a thrust is made from the reverse position. As the thumb and forefinger are at the front of the grip, the wrist is able to flex through the motion of the strike, which allows the spear to be kept relatively level. In many respects, a reverse thrust is merely an elevated version of a low or underarm attack. Like the underarm thrust, the reverse action is in no way inhibited by the presence of the shield and so could be delivered in a formation of any order. The one difference is that, due to raising the limb above shoulder height, the arm tends to move downwards as it extends. This downward direction of the spear is accentuated if the wrist is not sufficiently flexed to keep it level and the body rotated into the action. This resulted in a large disparity within the collected data for the ranges of this style of attack (compare tables 6 and 7). Based upon this analysis it seems that a reverse thrust would have only been delivered by a hoplite who, moving from a low or underarm posture, wished to deliver a strong, downward strike over his shield (or his opponent's shield) at an opportune target but would not have been the common method for employing the spear in battle.

Across all of the simulations, the stature of the participant was seen to have had only a slight impact on the *effective range* of the weapon. Thrusts made by shorter participants projected a lesser distance than those of participants of greater height due to the varying lengths of the arm. This created, for example, a range of between 247cm and 221cm for the *effective range* of underarm thrusts made in the open-order. However, when the *effective range* was calculated as a percentage of body height, it was found that all results were only marginally different. This demonstrates that all of the techniques, and the results of the tests examining them, were not dependent upon the stature of the hoplite executing them but upon other bio-mechanical factors to determine their effectiveness.

A further indication of the unsuitability of the overhead posture to wield a thrusting weapon can be seen in the results of the analysis into the trajectory of the four combative techniques. For the purpose of this examination, the trajectory of a spear thrust was defined as any change in the elevation along the path that the spear tip travelled during the action of the thrust. The trajectory for each thrust and order demonstrates that attacks made from the overhead and reverse positions possess the greatest variance in the elevation of their path (table 8).

Table 8: Variations in the elevation of the spear from start to finish per thrust, order and participant.

Order	Stance	Variation between the start and finish height of each thrust per participant (centimetres)									
Participant		A	B	C	D	E	F	G	H	I	Avg
Close-order	Overhead	−5	−1	−15	−5	−18	2	0	−7	6	−5
	Low	4	1	−3	9	17	12	10	−7	11	+6
	Underarm	−9	1	−9	2	0	−3	−5	0	−2	−3
	Reverse	−35	−26	−32	3	−20	−4	−5	5	−13	−14
Open-order	Overhead	−20	−29	−52	−23	−23	0	0	−7	3	−17
	Low	−4	14	0	30	17	19	8	11	20	+13
	Underarm	−2	2	−8	1	−5	3	−3	−4	−8	−3
	Reverse	−47	−20	−13	−9	−22	−5	−2	−5	−20	−16

The downward movement of the arm during the delivery of an overhead strike means that the tip of the spear will descend until the wrist locks, the arm reaches its full extension or it is prevented from extending any further by the restrictions of the panoply. If the shield is moved aside, the spear can continue along its downward path until it impacts with the target or the ground, or until the arm reaches a point where to continue no longer feels 'natural'.

The more distance there is between a hoplite and his target, the more accentuated this downward motion becomes. Thus it is difficult to align the spear with targets beyond the distance that the tip projects forward when in the 'ready' position. Targets at the limit of the *effective range* for the weapon would be very difficult, if not impossible, to hit. Thus both the reach and trajectory of an overhead strike make this method of delivering a thrusting attack extremely ineffective and unlikely to have been used by the hoplite. Thrusts made from a reverse position, where the wrist was not flexed to keep the weapon level, were found to incur similar limitations (plate 16.2).

Thrusts made from a low position in open-order actually increase in height. This is due to the action of the strike inscribing an upward arc. As the hand and the spear travel along this arc, with the wrist flexing to keep the spear level, the elevation of the weapon increases until the motion finishes at the point where the arm is extended laterally and the thrust is completed (plate 17).

Attacks made from the underarm position were found to have the flattest trajectory of any thrust in any order. Following the natural movement of the arm, underarm thrusts encounter few limitations to their movement and project directly ahead. At the full extension of the arm the line between the shoulder and the wrist is generally at a slight downward angle and this accounts for the small variation in the trajectory of the thrust. However, if desired, this can be overcome by a marginal flexing of the wrist. The available body rotation of the open-order resulted in no change to the average variance of the thrust, even though the body could be leaned forward with the action. This would have made the underarm thrust very adaptable to the changing environment of a hoplite engagement while both stable and uniform throughout.

Additionally, the natural movement of the arm in both the low and under-arm strike makes it easy to withdraw any weapon back to its 'ready' position once the attack has been made in preparation for the delivery of another attack. This is accomplished by simply pulling the arm back into position; an action which also follows a natural movement of the arm. Overhead and reverse stikes, on the other hand, are somewhat more difficult to return due to the awkward flexing of the wrist, the weakness of the grip on the weapon, the downward angle of the weapon itself and the path that a withdrawn weapon must follow in order to return to its 'ready' position. The ease or difficulty of withdrawing comitted spears from these positions would have been paramount if the weapon itself became lodged in the shield, armour or body of an opponent. The flat trajectory of the underarm thrust, with is strong grip and use of the muscles of the upper arm, would make the extraction process easy. The awkward and curved trajectory of the overhead and reverse thrusts would have made the extraction of weapons in this position almost impossible. The ability to execute an attack using the underarm technique in any order of deployment, and the ability to easily return the weapon to its 'ready' position, make this the most likely way in which a hoplite wielded his spear in battle.

Another factor that should be considered in relation to the effectiveness of the four combative postures is the strength and stability of the grip on the weapon. It would be a natural reaction for an opponent under attack to attempt to parry the incoming weapon. Thus the strength and stability of the grip is what will determine how, and if, an attacking hoplite could continue with his offensive actions after the first thrust had been deflected. In general, an incoming attack would most likely be parried with the shield. Thus the spear would almost always be deflected to the right of the attacker (as the defender swings his shield to his left to defelect the blow) and never across his body. A spear held in a position that is only supported by the hand and the wrist (i.e. the low, overhead and reverse positions) can be easily deflected with little application of force, either when in the 'ready' position or when extended into the attack, due to the relative weakness of the grip and flexibility of the wrist. Furthermore, due to the rearward position of the spear's point of balance, the amount of weapon that projects forward of the wielder acts as a lever; compounding the ease with which the weapon can be deflected. The inability for both the overhead and reverse thrusts to be projected further than the starting position for the hand mean that the *sauroter* often ends up beside the head at the completion of the strike (see plates 16.1 and 16.2). Should a weapon in this position be parried to the attacker's right, the *sauroter* would be swung dangerously into the head. An attack from either of these postures could also be deflected upwards as it was thrust forward, potentially allowing an opponent to get inside the projected reach of the weapon. It seems unlikely that such methods of attack would be employed if they placed the attacker in as much risk, if not greater risk, than his intended target.

By comparison the underarm thrust is much more secure when in the 'ready' position. Being supported by the hand, wrist and forearm, spears wielded in this manner are more difficult to deflect from the 'ready' position. By additionally having the weapon locked between the upper arm and the body, the posture is relatively elastic. Spears that are deflected tend to naturally 'spring back' into their 'ready' position. The way that the *sauroter* is located beneath the arm when the underarm stance is in the 'ready' position means that the rear of any deflected weapon poses no threat to either the bearer or the rear ranks. Once committed to the attack, the underarm thrust is almost as easy to parry as any other. However, in deflecting an underarm thrust, the entire arm is also deflected because of the nature of the grip on the shaft. Thus the weapon can be brought back into position much more easily by using the muscles of the arm rather than solely relying on counter-torque being applied by the wrist as happens with the low, overhead and reverse thrusts. Underarm thrusts which are deflected when the arm is at its full extension pose little threat to either the bearer or the rearward ranks. As the rear end of the spear is located in line with, or beyond, the rim of the shield as the strike is executed; if the spear is deflected, the *sauroter* merely points towards, or connects with, the bearer's shield, posing no threat to him or those around him.

Van Wees states that the ability to parry requires a certain amount of elbow room.[4] However, the shield can be used to defect attacks even when deployed in a confined close-order formation (see page 191). Snodgrass states that one of the benefits of the *porpax* was that it allowed the shield to be efficiently used to deflect blows.[5] All thrusts are able to be deflected to a certain extent. Some are more easily recoverable than others, and some pose more of a danger to the bearer and his own formation than others. This ability to move the shield to deflect an attack potentially exposes the right side of the body, albeit momentarily. However, it is quite difficult for an attacker to exploit this momentary exposure of his target. It is almost impossible to strike the right side of a facing opponent with a weapon that is wielded in the opposing right hand, particularly when the target's body is angled away from the attack by adopting an oblique body posture. The defender's shield has to be moved a considerable distance to the left to expose enough of the chest, groin or thighs so that they can be easily struck.

Based upon the examination of the reach, trajectory and stability of the four combative postures, coupled with other factors such as the ability to alter the positioning of the weapon, it can be concluded that the manner in which the hoplite employed his spear to engage in combat within the confines of the phalanx was by using a combination of the low and underarm techniques depending upon the interval in which the formation had been deployed. This runs contrary to every previous theory on the dynamics of hoplite warfare and indicates the need for them to be replaced with the new 'low/underarm model' of hoplite combat.

The value of the data gained from this examination is that it allows for a better interpretation of many ancient passages relating to hoplite warfare. Both Aelian and Arrian, for example, state that the spears of the second rank could reach the enemy.[6] Hanson and Matthews suggest that the spears belonging to the third rank could also reach the enemy.[7] Warry suggests that the spears of the first four ranks projected beyond the front of the formation.[8] Blyth suggests that most spears of an eight-deep phalanx could reach the enemy.[9] The understanding of how the spear travels on its path through the action of a strike, and the distance that it can be projected, allows for the validity of these statements to be tested.

For a weapon held by the third rank to reach an enemy as per Hanson's suggestion, the spear has to be able to be thrust forward a distance incorporating the space that the men of the first two ranks occupy and the distance between the front of the phalanx and the opponent. If the enemy was pressed up against the front of the phalanx, this would equate to a distance of 90cm (assuming a close-order deployment of 45cm per man). As such, a spear presented in the 'ready' position of any posture would be able to reach an opponent abutted against the front of the shield wall from the third rank. Only with the adoption of an underarm posture would a member of the fourth rank be able to reach the same target in a close-order formation as per Warry's suggestion. Thus Warry's conclusion seems odd as the underarm technique plays no part in his analysis of hoplite warfare. As the ability to reach an opponent is not attributed to the third or fourth ranks by either Arrian or Aelian, it must be concluded that the enemies they are describing are not pressed against the front of the shield wall, but are being engaged 'at spear length' as per some of the ancient descriptions of hoplite combat.[10]

If the term 'at spear length' equates to the amount of weapon that projects forward of the phalanx, either when in the ready position or when thrust forward, then it is only weapons able to reach this distance from the second rank that can comply with the passages of Arrian and Aelian. Due to the downward trajectory of the strike, an overhead thrust would be unable to reach this distance from the second rank due to the presence of the man in front who would inhibit the action. A reverse thrust may have been able to reach a target at this distance, but its varied trajectory and level of contortion to the arm make its common usage by hoplites in the second rank unlikely. The low posture can only be adopted in a close-order formation when the *aspis* is removed from the shield wall and it is again unlikely that an attack could be delivered from the second rank using this technique due to the presence of the man in front. The only method that would allow for the second rank to engage an opponent 'at spear length' from the front of the phalanx is the flat trajectory of the underarm posture.

When deployed in a close-order formation, the use of the underarm stance positions the spear of each man in a natural 'cradle' created by the intersecting rims of two adjacent shields. This allows for the spear to be held in the 'ready' position for a protracted length of time while reducing the muscular stress incurred by the weapon-bearing arm. This level of support for the weapon is a characteristic of the underarm stance which does not occur with any other posture (plate 18.1).[11]

The adoption of an oblique body posture with the use of the underarm stance also allows members of the second rank of a close-order phalanx to position their spears slightly above those held by the front rank by standing more erect than the members of the front rank, who are in a slight squatting posture (see page 90), and/or marginally elevating the right arm. As such, the spears of the second rank also pass through the lowest point of the inter-locked shield wall created by the members of the front rank but can still be supported by the rims of the second rank shields (which create their own interlocked shield wall). This allows them to present their weapons in a way that provides them with a full range of movement for the weapon arm, and which allows them to engage an opponent 'at spear length' from the formation without endangering the man in the front rank or compromising the ability of that man to effectively engage with his own weapon (plate 18.1).

Homer describes just such a formation in his portrayal of the Greeks awaiting a Trojan attack while standing in an order so close that their shields overlapped, their helmet crests touched and with their spears deployed 'overlaying and underlying each other' (φπάξαντες δόρυ δουρί σάκος σάκεϊ προθελύμνῳ: ἀσπὶς ἄρ' ἀσπίδ' ἔπειδε κόρυς κόρυν ἀνέρα δ' ἀνήρ: ψαῦον δ' ἱππόκομοι κόρυθες λαμπροῖσι φάλοισι νευόντων, ὡς πυκνοὶ ἐφέστασαν ἀλλήλοισιν: ἔγχεα δ' ἐπτύσσοντο θρασειάων ἀπὸ χειρῶν σειόμεν').[12] Murray, in a footnote to his translation, says that the exact interpretation of the word πτύσσοντο, meaning 'doubled up', used by Homer to describe the formation is obscure. Hammond, in his translation, interprets the Homeric formation as presenting a 'serried line of spears'.[13] However, while it is commonly believed that the works of Homer pre-date the Classical phalanx, it is clear that the Homeric warriors are deployed in some kind of defensive formation. The parallels between Homer's description and the characteristics of a close-order phalanx, with the spears of the first two ranks extended forward in the underarm position, are possibly too close to simply dismiss as 'obscure'.

For the members of the second rank to be able to reach an opponent, that opponent cannot have been engaged at the full *effective range* of the weapon borne by the front rank; the arm and weapon of the second rank can simply not be extended far enough to cover both the full reach of the front rank plus the interval separating the two men in the phalanx, even in close-order. For members of an intermediate-order formation, there is no thrust capable of providing enough reach to cover the 90cm interval allotted to the first rank and the distance between the phalanx and the target. Even the longer *effective ranges* of the low and underarm strikes made in a loose order (88cm and 84cm respectively) would not be able to reach an opponent at this distance (figure 13).

The enemy can only have been engaged at the distance that the spear projects forward of the front rank when it is held in the ready position (around 150cm). In this way the reach of an attack made by the second rank (216cm) will cover both the distance between the target and the front of the formation (150cm) and the 45cm space between the first two ranks. Thus members of the

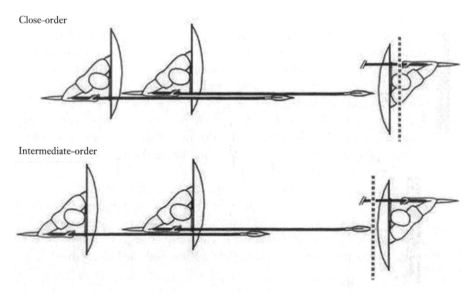

Close-order

Intermediate-order

Figure 13: The *effective range* for the second rank (dotted line) when using the under-arm posture per order of the phalanx.

second rank would have been able to thrust their spears into an opponent's shield, armour or flesh by nearly 20cm. Additionally, an enemy would be engaged by both ranks of a hoplite phalanx at a distance where the front rank had not yet thrusted their weapon forward and had the entire reach of the weapon with which to penetrate the target. Should an attack by the second rank of a hoplite phalanx slay the opponent in the front rank of an enemy formation, the members of the front rank of the phalanx (who had not yet committed to any attack) could easily reach the second rank of the enemy even before they advanced to take the place of their fallen comrades. If the attack of the second rank of hoplites did not slay the enemy, that opponent would be held in place by the spears belonging to both ranks of the phalanx. However, the uncommitted spears belonging to the first rank could easily be driven forward into the opponent while he was kept at bay by the spears of the second rank. Thus hoplite warfare is something of a 'dance in unison' between the members of the first and second ranks of the phalanx with each potentially engaging a different rank of the opposing formation.

Thus it can be concluded that:

1. Both Arrian and Aelian must be describing the offensive capabilities of a close-order hoplite formation using the underarm technique to wield the spear. Due to the reduced reach and impediments caused by the man in the front rank, no attack made with any other technique, including the overhead posture of current convention, is capable of reaching an opponent.
2. Arrian cannot be referring to a formation of Macedonian phalangites as the tips of five weapons project beyond the front of a formation of these troops. This is another indication that much of what has been written by the later military writers can be applied to the hoplite armies of the Classical Period.
3. The opponents that are being engaged in these passages must be separated from the phalanx by the distance that the spear projects forward of the front rank when held in the ready position (a 'spear length' of approximately 150cm).
4. The close-order formation, even though the *effective range* of its members is less than those of the intermediate-order formation, is able to engage with the spears of the first two ranks while the more open and more mobile intermediate formation can only engage with the spears belonging to those in the first rank if its intervals are maintained.

Both Anderson and Cawkwell argue, based on the low/overhead two stance model, that close-order formations could not have been used by hoplites. They attempt to justify this conclusion by stating that the close-order phalanx is too confined for the efficient use of the spear.[14] Gabriel and Metz also claim that it would be hard to use weapons in the press of battle.[15] However, this is clearly not the case for hoplites wielding the spear by the rear of the shaft, in the underarm position and adopting an oblique body posture. Similarly, Hanson states that the *sauroter* was dangerous to those in the rearward ranks, citing a passage in the works of Plutarch (*Pyrrhus* 33).[16] Connolly also states that the *sauroter* could inflict accidental injuries.[17] However, Plutarch's passage refers to the dangers of battle once control of the formation is lost, and the wounding of comrades with both sword and spear in the confusion; he does not specifically mention wounds inflicted accidentally with the *sauroter*. The way that the *sauroter* is positioned when adopting an underarm posture means that members of the rear rank are protected from accidental injury by their own shield positioned across their front (see plate 18). In fact, the 45cm interval of the close-order formation dictates that each rank of the phalanx will create its own interlocked shield wall, which provides protection from any attack (either intentional or accidental) coming from the front. Hanson's conclusion can only be regarded as conjecture based upon a method of fighting incorporating the low/overhead two-stance model and the omission of the underarm posture as a combative technique.

Posture, reach and hoplite combat

An appreciation of the fundamentals of combat with the hoplite spear can be applied to many of the great confrontations of Greek antiquity to gain a more comprehensive understanding of how the engagement played out. This is no more evident than in the reconstruction of engagements where hoplites fought against an opponent who did not fight in a similar fashion; such as at the defence of Thermopylae in 480BC.

Despite claims that no fresh approach seems possible in an analysis of a battle such as Thermopylae, the findings of these tests allow many of the characteristics of this hoplite engagement to be further examined.[18] Herodotus, for example, states that the large casualties suffered by the Persians at Thermopylae were in part due to their shorter weapons.[19] Similarly, the Greek victory at Plataea in 479BC is credited to the superior armaments of the hoplites.[20] Xenophon also describes the later Persians as possessing short spears.[21] What effect did the difference in spear length actually make, and what can this tell us about the course of these engagements?

At Thermopylae, it seems unlikely that the Persians would have been able to maintain any sort of order or formation for their attacks. Herodotus describes the pass as only fifty feet wide. The area beyond the pass, where the Persians encamped and deployed, was much wider.[22] Pritchett can find no reason to question Herodotus' topographical descriptions.[23] Polyaenus states that the

Persian losses were in part due to the terrain on which the engagement was fought.[24] Had the Persians adopted and maintained an intermediate-order formation, the width of the pass would have provided them with a frontage of only seventeen men. Diodorus describes the Greeks as being deployed in a close-order formation to defend the pass.[25] This would create a frontage of around thirty-five men in the available space. Regardless of what formation the Persians initially adopted, or the speed of their assault, the funnelling nature of the terrain would have compressed and slowed their formation as it advanced further into the pass so that it would have been a slow, lumbering mass when it met with the Greek line. Diodorus suggests this was the case by stating that both sides were densely packed (συστάσεως πεπυκνωμένης).[26] It is at this point, where man and metal collided, that the configuration of the Greek weapons gave the outnumbered hoplites an immense tactical advantage.

With the adoption of a close-order formation, there would have been around seventy spears projecting forward of the Greek shield wall; all of which would have been able to engage the front of the Persian line. However, the configuration of the Persian spear meant that the Persians would not have been able to retaliate in kind. Connolly estimates the length of the Persian spear as 2m and Matthews gives a length of 1.8–2.0m, while other scholars simply echo the details provided by Herodotus and Xenophon, referring to them as 'short'.[27] In Persian artistic representations, the length of the Persian spear is portrayed at a height not much taller than the bearer. If the length of the weapon shown in Persian art is set at 200cm as per Connolly, the height of its bearer calculates to around 165cm; close to the figure provided by Hanson for the stature of the Greek hoplite and within the realms of possibility for the height of the average Persian. This suggests that a length of 1.8–2.0m is a reasonable estimate for the length of the Persian spear.

These same images also show that Persian spears were equipped with small, round, counterweights on the rear of their shafts rather than the elongated *sauroter* of the hoplite weapon. An example of just such a spear-butt, now in the Fitzwilliam Museum at Cambridge (ANE.72.1913), is only 63mm long, has a socket 18.9mm in diameter and, importantly, is hollow – which gives it a weight of only 75.75g. Not only does the size of the socket suggest that this was attached to a shaft more akin to a javelin than to a spear, but the lightness of the Persian spear-butt would give the weapon a point of balance slightly forward of centre – much in the same way as the *styrakion* did for the Greek javelin – which also indicates the configuration of a thrown weapon.[28] Many of the Persian contingents are described by Herodotus as being armed with javelins and it may be the case that the shorter Persian spears (called a *paltron*) were designed to be both a missile and a thrusting weapon.[29] Xenophon describes just such a spear, capable of being both a javelin and a lance, used by improvised

Persian cavalry made up of mounted infantrymen.[30] Similarly, Aeschylus describes the Greek weapon as a 'close quarters spear', suggesting a contrast with the Persian weapon, which may have been used at a greater range in a missile capacity.[31] The royal bodyguard of Datames are also described as being armed with missile weapons.[32]

With a capacity to be both a missile and thrusting weapon, the somewhat centrally balanced Persian javelin/spear would have been wielded in the overhead position. Persian cylinder seals depict the weapon being used from such a position for both throwing and stabbing. Herodotus also states that the Persians marched with the tips of their spears pointing down.[33] This practice can be seen in the iconography of Persian coinage dated from the fifth to the fourth centuries BC. It can also be seen in a fragment of wall relief from the North Palace at Nineveh (c.600BC).

Marching with the tip pointing downwards confirms the use of the overhead position to wield the weapon. Unlike the concepts of modern 'hoplite drill', in which it is impossible to move from a position with the spear angled over the shoulder and pointing upwards into an overhead posture, by marching with the tip pointing downwards, the javelin can simply be elevated into an overhead position without requiring any alteration to the grip. From here it is a simple matter to cast or thrust it at a target. Additionally, the weapons shown on the Nineveh relief have throwing loops attached to their shafts; distinguishing them as missile weapons that must have been thrown from the overhead position.

Wielding this centrally balanced weapon in the overhead position, and maintaining some semblance of an oblique body posture as their formation at Thermopylae became compressed, would mean that around 80cm of weapon would have projected forward of each man in the Persian front rank. By using an overhead posture in such confined quarters, it is unlikely that the members of the second and subsequent ranks would have been able to use their weapons except as missiles. However, Diodorus states that all of the attacks delivered during the opening of the battle were made 'in close combat' (τῶν πληγῶν ἐκ χειρὸς γινομένων) rather than with missiles. Employing their spears as stabbing weapons, the Persians in the front rank would have had a reach of no more than 63cm due to the restrictions of the formation and the downward trajectory of the overhead strike. This reach may have been reduced further still by any restriction imposed by the Persian panoply in such confines. If the Persian formation was compressed by the terrain to the point where they crowded each other and/or their shields overlapped, their reach may have been as little as 20cm. Thus the Persians in the front rank would have had an *effective range* of no more than 140cm with their weapons. In comparison, the Greek hoplites of the front rank, using a rearwardly balanced weapon that was longer than the Persian spear, and wielding that spear in the underarm position while adopting an oblique body posture in close-order, would have had an *effective range* of around 220cm; almost a metre's advantage over their opponent. If the Persians somehow managed to move their weapons into either a low or underarm position, the central point of balance of the Persian spear would have provided them with a total *effective range* of no more than 170cm; still not enough to even reach the front of the Greek shield wall. Had the Persians been able to grasp their spear near the rear of the shaft (contrary to the weapon's point of balance) they would have still have been outclassed by the greater reach of the lengthier hoplite spear and could have only engaged the front of the Greek shield wall at the very limits of their *effective range*. Furthermore, all seventy spears of the first two Greek ranks would have been capable of engaging the Persian front line, and the Greek front rank would have also been capable of reaching the second rank of the Persian mass, while not a single Persian would have been able to reach the phalanx with their shorter weapons regardless of the technique they used (figure 14).

Two out of the first three Persian contingents to engage at Thermopylae are described as being armed with short spears while the third bore axes.[34] None of these would have been able to reach, let alone penetrate, the shield wall or the armour worn by the hoplites; nor inflict significant casualties among the Greeks.[35] Diodorus confirms this by stating that the Greeks were afforded much better protection by their larger shields and that this was also a contributing factor to the high number of Persian casualties and the low number of Greek ones.[36] The Greek position only became desperate once their spears began to break on day three of the fighting.[37] This attests to the fact that it was the Greek weapons that gave them a decisive advantage and allowed them to hold off the numerically superior Persians for the first two days of the defence.

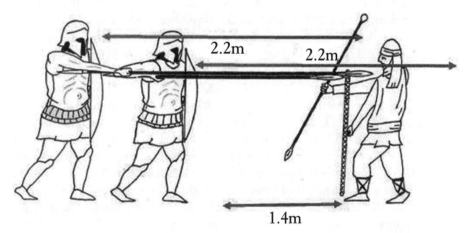

Figure 14: The *effective range* of the Greeks and Persians at Thermopylae.

It was only on the third day that the Persians finally learned the error of their tactics and finished off the Greek position using missiles to overcome the strong defensive and offensive capabilities of the hoplites from a distance.[38] Thus the effectiveness of the hoplite weapon can be seen in the ability of the front rank to hold the Persian line at bay with the length of their spears while they were additionally engaged by the members of the second rank of the phalanx. When an opportune target presented itself during the fighting, the front rank of the Greek phalanx would have had more than enough reach to drive the spear tip into the target.

Had the Greeks employed the overhead posture of current convention, their *effective range* with the weapon would only have been 190cm. While this is still more than the reach of the Persians, the advantage is small (only 50cm), and does not seem to be as noteworthy as Herodotus would imply.[39] This suggests that the Greeks fought in a manner that gave them an even greater advantage and the ancient writers, like Arrian and Aelian, must be describing the benefits of using the underarm technique in a close-order formation. It also seems improbable that either side would engage with a spear at under two metre's distance from their opponent. Herodotus details the equipping of many Persian contingents with weapons much better suited to this sort of close-in fighting such as clubs, maces, axes, daggers and swords.[40] Similarly, the Spartans would have also been better off using their swords at this distance which, Herodotus tells us, they did not resort to until the later stages of the battle when many of their spears had been broken.[41] It seems clear that much of the fighting during the first days of the engagement was conducted with both formations separated by about a Greek spear length, where the Greeks enjoyed a distinct advantage in terms of reach over their opponents. However, it was not only the length of the weapons but the manner in which they were balanced and wielded, combined with the close-order deployment of the phalanx, which gave the Greeks a decisive advantage over their Persian opponents and warranted the reference to this advantage by Herodotus. This would also account for the disproportionate number of casualties among the Persians to those of the Greeks, despite any embellishments that may have been placed upon the figures by pro-Greek historians.[42]

An interesting balance of the offensive and defensive capabilities of the hoplite can be seen in engagements where hoplites fought against other hoplites, but both sides were deployed in different orders, such as when the loose-order Argive formation charged the densely packed Spartan shield wall at Mantinea in 418BC.[43] If both sides were carrying their weapons in the underarm position at the moment the two lines met, the intermediate-order Argive formation would have had greater mobility (hence its charge as described by Thucydides) and a greater reach with their weapons, but would have possessed a reduced defensive capability due to the lack of an interlocking shield wall and could have only engaged with members of its front rank. This would have been counter-balanced by the slow-moving Spartan shield wall; presenting a strong defensive frontage at the expense of a reduction in mobility and the *effective range* of their spear thrusts, but with the ability to engage with the first two ranks of their formation. Thus the overall capabilities of both sides effectively negate each other. This balance of characteristics may account for why casualty figures in hoplite versus hoplite engagements were relatively low until one side broke and fled (see Chapter 13, The Hoplite Battle: Contact, *Othismos*, Breakthrough and Rout).[44]

Through the use of physical re-creation, experimental archaeology and practical testing it can be concluded that the hoplite must have engaged in combat using a combination of the low and underarm techniques to wield the spear. The underarm posture provides the best reach and effective use of the weapon while allowing the shield to be retained in its defensive place in front of the body, regardless of the order of deployment. In a close-order formation, the use of the underarm technique also allows for the first two ranks to engage in accord with ancient descriptions of hoplite combat. Xenophon's account of fighting 'at spear length' appears to be a description of the best environment for an effective combative posture to play a major role and the use of the underarm stance within this context may have been a deciding factor in the outcomes of some of the most notable battles of antiquity. The low stance, while providing a similar *effective range*, requires the removal of the shield from its protective position and can only have been used in instances when its protection was not of paramount concern; such as when pursuing a routed enemy from the field. The test results further confirm the unlikelihood of the overhead stance of current convention being a correct model of the mechanics of hoplite warfare; nor is it likely that the weapon was held in the centre of the shaft as per some currently accepted models. Another indicator that this conclusion is correct is the analysis of how, through the use of a weapon with this reach and trajectory, a hoplite could engage with an opponent once the fighting had commenced.

Chapter 7

The 'Kill Shot' of Hoplite Combat

How did a hoplite employ a spear held in either the low or underarm position during the actual fighting of a hoplite engagement? What target areas, or 'kill shots', did the hoplite aim at on his opponent? Modern theories on the nature of hoplite warfare contain several possible areas that a hoplite could target during combat, with one body area common to most models: the throat. However, like many of the previous investigations into hoplite warfare, the concept of a throat 'kill shot' appears to be misplaced. The available evidence indicates that the most commonly sustained injuries in hoplite warfare were to the region of the chest; with wounds to the upper head, arms and legs making up a much smaller percentage.

There is little or no consensus among modern researchers as to the location of a primary 'kill shot' in hoplite combat, or if one actually existed at all. In fact, one model suggests that there was a variety of areas targeted by the hoplite in battle rather than one over-riding area against which a weapon would be directed. Thus modern scholarship is split into two camps: those who favour a single, primary, 'kill shot' and those that do not. Some scholars state that the primary target of the hoplite in combat was the throat of their opponent.[1] Both Snodgrass and Lorimer state that early vase paintings depict the spear levelled at the region of the throat.[2] This particular characteristic of portrayals of the overhead stance (in most cases) runs through the entire artistic record; from the Archaic Period to the Hellenistic (for example, see plate 8.2).

Hanson, Everson, Gabriel and Metz place the neck and throat in a list of possible target areas, which includes the face, shoulders, groin and thighs depending upon which technique (either low or overhead) was being used.[3] Sekunda simply states that experienced hoplites would aim their blows at targets above or below the shield of their opponent without detailing what these targets were or how these strikes may have been accomplished.[4] The lack of any agreement between the various models forwarded by modern scholarship indicates that this is yet another area of hoplite warfare that is not fully comprehended. Before any attempt to determine what areas on an opponent were targeted by a hoplite in battle, and the location of a primary 'kill shot' (if there was any) can be made, two relevant and important questions must first be addressed:

1. How much of the hoplite was protected, or at least covered, by his panoply?
2. How much of an opponent could a hoplite actually see, and therefore target, when wearing his helmet?

The protection provided by the panoply

The ancient sources provide no direct information as to how much of the body was protected by the armour of the time. An examination of this aspect of hoplite combat can only be conducted using observations and calculations drawn from physical re-creation. A man 168cm tall and weighing 75kg presents a target area of approximately 7,232 square centimetres (cm) when not wearing any armour (plate 19.1).

Opinions as to how much of the head was protected by the Greek helmet vary amongst scholars. Bradford states that the head, cheeks and collar bone were protected by the Corinthian-style helmet.[5] Snodgrass claims that the throat was a vital area of the body protected only by the lengthened cheek flanges of the Corinthian helmet.[6] Anderson states that it protected the back, sides and crown of the head.[7] Lendon calls the Corinthian helmet 'all encompassing' and simply states that it gave good protection.[8] Similarly, Everson states that the Corinthian helmet gave almost complete protection to the head.[9] Everson also claims that the cheek flanges on the open-faced Illyrian helmet protected the throat.[10] However, as this helmet is of an open-faced style, any protection given was to the sides of the neck and not to the throat. Van Wees states that the shape of the cuirass left the throat exposed, which suggests an assumption that the helmet provided little or no protection to this part of the body either.[11] A Corinthinan helmet, regardless of the length of the cheek pieces, reduces the exposed areas of the head, throat and neck to the $181cm^2$ of the openings in the helmet. This represents a reduction in the vulnerable surface area of the head by 75 per cent. The elongated cheek flanges of the helmet alone more than adequately cover the throat and neck from the front. The bronze 'muscled' cuirass, which covers the body from collar bone to waist, further reduces the exposed surface area of the chest and torso to the $420cm^2$ region around the lower abdomen and groin. This area would have been protected to some extent by the addition of a set of leather or linen *pteruges* to the panoply; suspended from the lower rim of the cuirass. When greaves, which Alcaeus states provided protection against missiles, were worn to cover the shins, the vulnerable areas of the legs were lessened to $1,083cm^2$ of the exposed thighs and top of the feet.[12] Thus a hoplite wearing the basic panoply still had approximately $2,787cm^2$

(39 per cent) of their surface area exposed on their arms, legs, groin and face (plate 20.1).

A hoplite engaging in combat while bearing an Argive shield with a diameter of 90cm (itself having a surface area of $6,362\text{cm}^2$ – almost enough to cover the entire body) in an oblique body posture, with the shield supported on the left shoulder, and wielding a spear in the underarm position, greatly reduces the amount of exposed flesh further still. Borne in this manner, the shield completely covers the left arm, the left thigh and the groin (removing 551cm^2, 492cm^2 and 420cm^2 from the amount of unprotected area respectively). The offset rim of the shield extends upwards, further covering the neck and lower face, and protects an area of 78cm^2 left exposed by the openings in the Corinthian helmet. This leaves a total area of 103cm^2 around the eyes and between the nasal and cheek guards exposed above the rim of the shield.

The adoption of an oblique body posture also places the right leg behind the shield and positions it well back from any strike that would impact with the shield, effectively removing a further 340cm^2 from any calculation of exposed area. If a 'shield apron' of hide or cloth was also suspended from the lower rim of the *aspis*, additional protection would be given to the lower legs and feet. 'Shield aprons' appear in some vase illustrations dating from around 475BC. Everson suggests that they may have been used as additional protection against archery fire during the Persian Wars.[13] Lorimer states that it is hard to conceive of a shield that provides protection from shoulder to ankle as is described by Tyrtaeus.[14] However, an *aspis* equipped with a 'shield apron' would give just such cover.[15]

The use of the underarm or low stance to wield the spear additionally places the majority of the right arm in a protected position behind the shield and beside the body, leaving only the forward-facing surface of the right hand exposed: reducing the surface profile of the arm by approximately 509cm^2. Thus a hoplite wearing a full panoply, with the shield supported on the left shoulder and wielding a spear in the underarm position, has only the 103cm^2 of the face, 42cm^2 of the right hand, approximately 50cm^2 around the left knee and 200cm^2 of the top of the left foot exposed.[16] This equates to a total exposed area of only 395cm^2, or 5.5 per cent of the entire body.

The adoption of an overhead posture to wield the spear would leave the underside of the arm exposed. This dangerous aspect of posture is mentioned by Vegetius in relation to the benefits of the Roman legionaire thrusting with his *gladius* rather than slashing with it.[17] While the exposure of the arm in the overhead position does not in itself discount the use of this stance in hoplite combat, such a large area of exposed flesh would make a likely target on a hoplite otherwise covered in armour. A serious wound received to this region would render a hoplite incapable of further offensive action. However, there are no references, either visual or literal, to an injury sustained to the right arm to be found in the available evidence. This is another indication that the overhead stance is unlikely to have been adopted by the hoplite to engage in battle.

Diodorus states that the larger shields borne by the Greeks meant that the Persians who engaged them at Thermopylae found it almost impossible to injure them when they were deployed in a close-order defensive formation.[18] Similarly, Gabriel and Metz, in an examination of the vulnerability of ancient warriors to missile fire, concluded that 'with the shield in place the probability of hitting an exposed area is reduced to almost zero'.[19] Clearly the hoplite was very well protected, if not covered at least, by the elements of his panoply.[20] What is important to note, particularly for the examination of the viability of a throat 'kill shot', is that the throat is doubly protected; first by the elongated cheek flanges of the common Corinthian helmet and secondly by the upwardly extending rim of the shield. Any claim that the head and/or neck of a hoplite were not well protected cannot be accurate unless a more open-faced style of helmet is considered and the protection provided by the shield is removed from the calculation. Within the collection of helmets housed at Olympia in Greece, there is not a single instance of weapon damage below the level of the cheek (for example see plate 9). This is a clear indication of how well the lower parts of the head and neck were protected behind the rim of the shield and that the throat was not a regularly targeted area of the body in hoplite combat.

The available vision of the hoplite in combat

How much of an opponent could a hoplite actually see when bearing his panoply in this manner? Everson merely states that wearing a Corinthian-style helmet would make seeing difficult, while wearing lighter [open-faced?] helmets would have provided better battlefield awareness.[21] Some scholars simply state that the Corinthian helmet would have seriously restricted the hoplite's vision.[22] Again, further investigation into this aspect of hoplite warfare can only be undertaken through physical reconstruction and testing, and then analysing the observations within the context of what information the ancient sources can provide.

The ancient texts contain few references to any impediments to the vision of the hoplite. Thucydides states that '[those who fight in daylight] cannot see everything and, in fact, no one knows much more than what is going on around himself'.[23] Mitchell expands upon this stating that 'the wearer could see nothing except what was directly in front of him'.[24] To examine what these passages may be referring to, and to examine the range of vision provided by the Corinthian-style helmet, a simple test was conducted. A test participant faced a horizontal scale attached to a testing facility wall while extending a spear forward from the underarm position. This placed the participant at a 'spear length' of just over two metres from the wall. The gaze of the test participant was directed beyond the tip of the spear; to where an opponent would be located during an engagement. While the participant maintained this line of sight, markers were moved in from both the left and right until they could be seen at the margins of the participant's range of vision, as provided by the Corinthian helmet, without the participant averting their eyes from the point directly ahead. The angle from the markers to the centre of the face was then measured and combined to give the overall range of vision (plate 22.1).

It was found that with the adoption of an oblique body posture the head naturally rotates slightly to the right so that the axis of the head (and the head's line of sight) is naturally directed towards the tip of the spear. This is an aspect of the underarm technique not found in any other combative posture. The results of this test also showed that, even with the enclosed protection of the Corinthian-style helmet, a hoplite would still possess a lateral range of vision of approximately ninety degrees (forty-five degrees to either side of the axis of the head).

With the shield supported on the left shoulder, the rim, which covers the lower jaw, in no way impedes this range of vision or the ability to look down-wards. Nor does the nasal guard impede any vision due to its close proximity to the face. The upper edge of the eye sockets of the helmet only marginally impede the vertical range of vision and allow objects to be seen up to a height of two-and-a-half metres at the same distance without moving the head (although, as an offset to this minor impediment, the position of the upper rim, and the distance it sits away from the face, does provide a level of shading for the eyes when facing into the sun and affords a certain level of protection against rain). This means that a hoplite wearing a Corinthian-style helmet would have been able to see every part of an opponent, from the top of the crest to the feet, without moving his head or redirecting his gaze when the two were standing a spear length apart. Interestingly, a subsequent examination demonstrated that this is almost the exact same range of vision (apart from the restriction created by the upper edge of the aperture in the helmet) for a head totally bereft of any helmet whatsoever. Blyth determined that the eye holes in the Corinthian helmets of Olympia are almost the same size as the orbital sockets of the skull that house the eyes; although the helmets possess elongated corners.[25] Some helmets display alterations made after initial construction to enlarge the eye holes.[26] It is the size of these eye holes that would have provided a hoplite wearing a Corinthian helmet with an almost natural range of vision.

Wearing another Corinthian-style helmet, based upon a fourth century example, in yet another test, it was found that the range of vision was the same as for its fifth century counterpart. As it is the most enclosed of the common Greek helmets, the Corinthian-style can be considered a 'worst-case scenario' in terms of possible impediments to vision. The test was also conducted while wearing reconstructed versions of open-faced *pilos*, Boeotian and Chalcidian helmets. It was found that the range of vision available when wearing these helmets was the same as being bare-headed or when wearing either of the Corinthian-style helmets.

It must be considered that different helmets have eyeholes spaced at different intervals, even within the same style of helmet, as they were all manufactured by hand, and are therefore all separate pieces of craftsmanship.[27] Similarly, the eyes of each person are spaced differently from one to the next due to the individual features of the skull. As such, the results of these tests would also vary from one person to the next regardless of whether the same helmet was used for each test or whether different helmets were used with different individuals. This explains why some of the helmets identified by Blyth at Olympia demonstrate alterations made after initial construction; the openings for the eyes were enlarged to provide the individual wearing it with an adequate range of vision.

The range of vision of a hoplite wearing a Corinthian helmet also demonstrates that the side-on stance proposed by van Wees could not have been adopted by the hoplite for combat. As the cheek flanges of this style of helmet prevent the head from being fully rotated to the left (see Chapter 4, Bearing the Hoplite Panoply) it is physically impossible for the hoplite to look over his shoulder at the tip of his spear or his target. In contrast, the adoption of the oblique body posture allows the hoplite's line of sight to look directly at where his weapon is aimed (figure 15).

This range of vision allows a hoplite assuming an oblique body posture to see, at a distance of two metres, approximately four metres across the front rank of an opposing formation. This equates to the ability for the hoplite to see up to seven men across the front of a close-order enemy phalanx and up to five men across the front of an intermediate-order enemy formation without adjusting his line of sight (figure 16).

The hoplite would have been able to register movement just beyond the margins of this range, but would have been unable to recognize distinct features without turning his head or averting his gaze. Due to the slight rotation of the head to the right caused by the adoption of the oblique body posture, the hoplite would have seen slightly more to his right than to his left. This in no way endangered the hoplite while in formation as his left was covered, both physically and visually, by the man beside him unless he was at the very

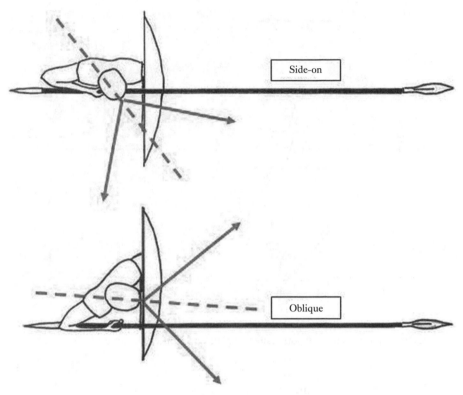

Figure 15: The range of vision (solid arrows) and axis of the head (dotted line) of the side-on and oblique body postures.

extreme left of the formation. Even here, peripheral vision to the left would have only been required to recognize flanking manoeuvres by enemy troops and would not have been vital to the engagement of an immediate opponent to the front.

Additionally, examinations conducted with modern combat veterans and police officers have determined that those undergoing the traumas of combative conditions experience a sense of perceptive narrowing ('tunnel vision') and a heightened sense of awareness to immediate dangers, often to the exclusion of many of the details of the 'bigger picture'.[28] Keegan states that 'battle, for the ordinary soldier, is a very small scale situation'.[29] This would be more so for the Classical hoplite, engaged in close hand-to-hand fighting, than for many a modern soldier. Passages in the ancient texts also seem to refer to this phenomenon being experienced by the hoplite. Euripides declares that 'when you are watching your enemy's spear, you do not know who is brave and who is a coward'.[30] This agrees with modern accounts where combatants or victims of

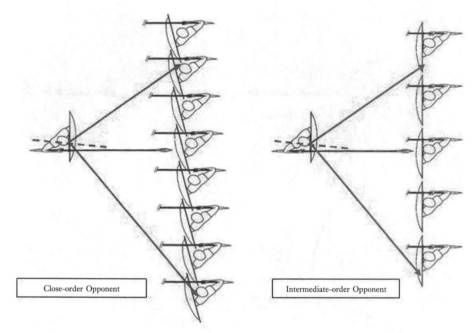

Close-order Opponent

Intermediate-order Opponent

Figure 16: How much of an opposing phalanx a hoplite was able to see.

violent events have concentrated upon a threatening weapon to the exclusion of other visual input. Similarly, Theseus' decision not to ask 'who fought whom' because 'when a man stands face to face with an enemy, he is barely able to see what he needs to' may also be a reference to perceptual narrowing.[31] Thucydides' reference to hoplites only knowing what is going on around themselves may also be a description of the narrowing of focus on the field of battle. Herodotus describes how Epizelus became suddenly blinded at the battle of Marathon after seeing a large, well-armed opponent.[32] It has been suggested that this may be the first recorded case of 'shell shock', but is more likely to be a reference to the acute narrowing of the vision known as 'hysterical blindness'; where a person experiences such an extreme state of fear that the brain actually severs their visual input.[33] What is clear from the test results is that any form of visual narrowing described in the ancient sources cannot be the result of the style of helmet a hoplite chose to wear; it can only be the result of another influencing factor.

This conclusion does not take into account atmospheric impediments to sight such as smoke, fog, dust, sun–glare, precipitation or, as found during one hot summer testing session, insects that get into the helmet. It is also a matter of personal interpretation as to what constitutes 'around oneself' as Thucydides would have it. However, it can be concluded that, contrary to comments made by many recent scholars, all styles of helmet available during the Classical era provided a sufficient range of vision for a hoplite to adequately gauge the happenings in their immediate vicinity. More importantly, these same helmets allowed the hoplite to observe all potential target areas on their opponent at a distance of two metres.

The concept of the throat kill shot

How then do the physical characteristics of the vision, protection, reach and trajectory available to a hoplite committing an attack in combat correlate with the current concept of a throat 'kill shot'? What is immediately observable is that, behind its double layers of protection, a hoplite would not have even been able to see the throat on an opposing hoplite. Additionally, modern models are based only on the one stance: the overhead technique. Those models that include the throat in a list of possible target areas may include the low stance in the hoplite's repertoire (particularly those that list the groin and thighs among other possible target areas), although this is not specified. However, those models that propose a primary 'kill shot' located in the throat cannot have considered that any spear held in the low position (which constitutes one half of the low/overhead two stance model of current convention) is unlikely to point at the throat. While a lack of analysis of both the underarm and reverse techniques can be accounted for, those models that base any analysis of the hoplite 'kill shot' solely upon depictions of the overhead stance can only be considered to be using the available evidence on a selective basis, even from the perspective of current convention.

Furthermore, regardless of the posture used, the double protection given to the throat makes it almost impossible to actually hit that area of an opponent. When in the 'ready' position, weapons held in the underarm posture point directly at the sternum of an opponent. The slight decrease in height along the underarm strike's relatively flat trajectory makes any attack continue to be directed towards the shield or chest without impediment. The pitch of the weapon can be angled upwards towards the head or throat but it is unlikely that even a strong thrust would penetrate both the curved and thicker surface towards the outer rim of the shield and the cheek flanges of the helmet and then continue to impact with the throat.

Strikes made from the low posture follow their upward curving trajectory to connect with an opponent's shield or chest unless the wrist is flexed to direct the strike at a lower or higher target. Even with the wrist flexed, a low thrust will still rise to impact with the shield of an opponent unless the target is abutted up against the weapon when it is in its 'ready' position.

Even the overhead stance of current convention will strike the shield or chest. While angled so as to point at the throat when in the 'ready' position as shown in many vase illustrations, the sharply downward-curving trajectory of an overhead thrust will cause the spear tip to immediately drop below the level of the throat as soon as any attacking action is begun, unless the target is similarly abutted up against the tip of the weapon before the attack is made (see Chapter 8, Endurance and Accuracy when Fighting with the Hoplite Spear). Additionally, to connect with the throat, an overhead thrust would have to follow the unlikely trajectory of passing over the rim of the shield and then somehow turn ninety degrees upwards, before it impacted with the sternum, in order to get under the flanges of the helmet and so impact with the throat if it was not possible to penetrate the shield and helmet with the strike (figure 17).

The throat could also not be attacked with a sword: the hoplite's secondary weapon. Any thrusting action made with a sword would encounter the same limitations as a spear thrust. A hacking weapon such as a *falcata* could in no way be brought to bear against so well a protected area of the body using a downward, slashing, mode of attack.

Based upon the level of protection given to the throat, and the mechanics of how it could be attacked, it appears that the concept of regularly inflicted injuries to the region of the throat cannot be considered valid. This agrees with other sources of available evidence; artistic representations, literary passages and archaeological remains all demonstrate that the chest was more commonly targeted in hoplite battle than any other part of the body.

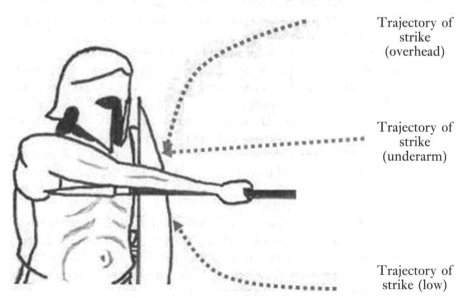

Trajectory of
strike
(overhead)

Trajectory of
strike
(underarm)

Trajectory of
strike (low)

Figure 17: The trajectories of different thrusts and how they naturally impact with the shield.

Artistic evidence of hoplite battle wounds

The artistic record is the very foundation of the concept of the throat 'kill shot' in hoplite combat. Yet the artistic medium itself cannot confirm the existence of wounds commonly received to the region of the neck. As noted, the concept of the throat 'kill shot' is based upon how weapons depicted in the overhead stance generally appear to aim at the throat of an opponent. However, the reliance upon this singular style of depiction as a form of confirmatory evidence contains three inherent problems. Firstly, as the overhead stance is a depiction of the use of the javelin and not the thrusting spear, the use of these illustrations to form the basis of any examination of hoplite combative injuries cannot be considered valid. Secondly, this model assumes that all, or at least the majority, of depictions of the overhead stance show the weapon levelled at the throat. However, this is not always the case. In many artistic examples a weapon held in the overhead stance is levelled at a different area of an opponent's body; anywhere from the head to the feet. Thirdly, there is the location of wounds in the artistic imagery. Regardless of whether the scene is heroic, Homeric, mythological or contemporary in theme, and regardless of which combative posture is depicted, the majority of images in the artistic record show wounds to areas of the body other than the throat. The famous illustration of Achilles attending to the wounded Patroklos (Berlin F2278), for example, clearly shows a wound sustained to the outer side of Patroklos' left arm; an injury that can only have been received from a blow that passed through his shield. Similarly, a *krater* (mixing bowl) ascribed to the Euphronious Painter depicting the death of Sarpedon (NY 1972.11.10) shows bleeding wounds sustained to the chest, abdomen and upper thigh. Other images show strikes made by Greeks passing through the upper cranium of the helmet or penetrating into the chest or legs of their opponents.

The lack of impacting throat wounds cannot be explained by mere artistic convention. In all of the above examples the spear could have easily been drawn so as to impact with the throat if it was the common nature of hoplite combat. That fact that it was not suggests in itself that the throat was not a regularly targeted area. The depiction of other sorts of wounds in vase illustrations clearly demonstrates that the dramatic turmoil of combat was an important aspect of the work of some illustrators. However, this does not explain the lack of images depicting what many modern models suggest was the primary target of the hoplite in combat. One vase illustration that may display this dramatic type of injury, despite Cartledge's claim that no such image exists, is the famous vase by Exekias in the British Museum (1836.2–24.127 (vase B210)) showing the death of Penthesilea at the hands of Achilles.

However, even this vase illustration cannot confirm the throat as the primary 'kill shot' of hoplite combat. Another vase in the British Museum (B209), also attributed to Exekias by Loeschcke but unsigned by the artist, shows a similar scene.[34] However, in this second image Penthesilea is in a different posture and more separated from Achilles, whose weapon is directed against her shield rather than her throat. If these are both the works of Exekias, it is curious that the location of the spear thrust would not be the same if it was based upon some account that suggested that the throat was the main target of hoplite combat; or at least of how Penthesilea was killed. Quintus of Smyrna's literary account of the death of Penthesilea has her riding into battle on horseback where she is initially wounded above the right breast by a javelin. She is finally killed by a spear thrust that passes through the horse and into her lower body.[35] Clearly this cannot be a reference to an injury sustained to the throat while she is on foot as per the Exekias illustration and the alignment of Achilles' spear with what appears to be Penthesilea's throat in the signed Exekias' painting may simply be coincidence due to the placement of the two figures.[36] If the weapon is meant to be interpreted as impacting with Penthesilea's right shoulder rather than her throat, this would at least partially conform with one literary tradition of her death.

Wounds to the head that are inflicted by either thrown or thrusted spears are a minor, but still somewhat common, feature of the *Iliad* (see table 9). Yet it is curious that few vase illustrations with Homeric themes display this kind of injury. Based upon the available artistic evidence, the concept of a throat 'kill shot' as the primary combat strategy cannot be considered valid. The imagery suggests that, instead of the throat, the torso and extremities received wounds more regularly in hoplite combat.

Literary evidence of hoplite battle wounds

This conclusion is also borne out in the literary evidence. By far the most elaborate descriptions of combat come from the Archaic Period though the works of Homer and Tyrtaeus. It is clear that much of the audience of both Homer and Tyrtaeus would have known warfare from first-hand experience and would have therefore expected a certain level of realism within the works. As such many of the wounds described in these texts are most likely based upon injuries that could actually be inflicted.[37] In the *Iliad*, the most descriptive source of Greek warfare for any period, the neck is one of the least targeted of any body area for lethal wounds within the text (table 9).

In the Archaic poems of Tyrtaeus references to injuries sustained to the groin, the chest and the midriff, the most commonly targeted areas in the *Iliad*, can also be found.[38] Of the wounds to the neck in the *Iliad*, there are few passages that refer to a strike specifically aimed at this area of the opponent's body. Achilles, for example, slays Hektor with a strike consciously aimed at the

Table 9: Lethal wounds in the *Iliad* sorted by body area.[39]

Body area where injury is sustained	Number of instances in the *Iliad*	Percentage of total
Chest	67	50.8%
Head	31	23.5%
Neck	13	9.8%
Arms	10	8.3%
Other	6	7.6%
TOTAL	127	100%

region of the neck.[40] Diomedes also aims a strike at the neck of Ajax during the *hoplomachia* at the funeral games of Patroklos.[41]

However, in the narratives and plays of the Classical Period (or those recounting Classical Period events) there is no mention of attacks specifically aimed at the throat or of the receipt of wounds to this area of the body. Hippocrates, who states that the budding surgeon can only gain experience in treating certain types of wounds through military service, includes no description of throat wounds in the entire Hippocratic corpus.[42] If, as modern scholarship suggests, this region of the body was the primary target in hoplite combat, then it seems peculiar that a reference to this type of wound is omitted from such a comprehensive work.[43]

As in Homer, the chest appears to have been the most commonly targeted area in the phalanx warfare of the Classical Age. Euripides' *Phoenician Women* describes weapon strikes aimed at the face and chest while his *Heraclea* details strikes aimed at the shield.[44] Epaminondas received a wound to the chest through the breastplate at Mantinea that was not fatal and is even described as not being incapacitating.[45] Chares was able to display his battle scars and his shield, which had been pierced by a spear, in a boastful gesture to the Athenians; suggesting wounds to the chest and arms.[46] The numerous injuries Agesilaus sustained at Coronea in 394BC are said to have pierced his armour and he was in great pain as a result of them.[47] Brasidas was wounded by a spear that pierced his shield but the wound was so minor that he simply pulled the spear out and kept fighting.[48] There are many other references to chest or abdominal wounds, or attacks directed against the chest or shield, including those on Dion and Timoleon.[49] Plutarch relates that Epaminondas was killed at Mantinea while he was turned about encouraging his troops, the blow most likely delivered to the back.[50] Similarly, Plutarch relates the account of a fallen man who, about to be stabbed in the back, pleads to be stabbed in the chest to avoid the shame.[51] This suggests that the chest, and not the throat, was the regular injury sustained in hoplite combat.

There are also many nondescript references to battle wounds in the sources that do not detail the area of the body that has received the injury. The Spartan king Agesilaus, for example, was wounded fighting against the Thebans in 378BC and yet survived this and many other wounds.[52] Similarly, Alcibiades was wounded at Potidaea, Sphodrias was knocked down three times at Leuctra but got up and continued to fight each time, and Pelopidas received seven wounds at Mantinea before finally collapsing.[53] During the second major battle of the First Messenian War (eighth century BC) many hoplites on both sides attempted to strip the dead only to find that the 'dead' were actually still alive and capable of fighting back.[54] A Spartan mother experienced joy upon receiving news that her son had died bravely in battle from 'many wounds' (τῶν τραυμάτων πολλῶν), none of which could have been immediately fatal.[55] Pytheas, a ship–board hoplite from Aegina, received multiple wounds fighting the Persians when his trireme was boarded. The Persians, out of respect for his bravery, attended his many wounds and later had him exhibit them to their comrades.[56]

The narrative histories also provide details of masses of surviving 'walking wounded' after hoplite engagements.[57] Incapacitated soldiers were abandoned to their fate by the Athenians retreating from Syracuse in 413BC.[58] Some of the Syracusean soldiers were unable to pursue the retreating Athenians as they, too, were incapacitated by injuries.[59] When the Athenians withdrew from Miletos in 411BC the wounded were ordered to be placed aboard ships.[60] At Chalcedon in 409BC, many of the Lacedaemonians and Chalcedonians were disabled by wounds.[61] Aristomenes the Messenian was captured after sustaining many severe, yet non-fatal, injuries.[62] Xenophon's mercenaries also experienced difficulties, both tactically and logistically, due to the number of wounded amongst them.[63] It seems unlikely that any of these reported injuries were to the region of the throat as per the current convention of the 'kill shot'. This is evidenced by the very nature of a wound to this area of the body.

The region of the neck and throat contains many vital areas and features such as the jugular vein, the carotid artery, the thyroid cartilage and the jugular arch, as well as many other nerves and ancillary blood vessels. Injuries to any of these areas are incapacitating if not immediately fatal. For example, the severing of either the jugular vein or the carotid artery will result in a loss of consciousness after approximately five seconds. The victim of such an injury will be beyond medical help after about ten seconds, resulting in death shortly thereafter. The crushing of the thyroid cartilage, through even a reasonably light blow with the hand, will cause the windpipe to swell, causing a suffocating death in a matter of moments. A stronger blow delivered with a spear or sword that pierces the trachea, through either the jugular arch or the thyroid cartilage, spills blood into the windpipe which, due to a reflex action, makes breathing impossible. The victim will choke on their own blood, also in a matter of moments. These were aspects of human physiology well known to the ancient Greeks as is indicated by the account of the death of Hektor in the *Iliad* where the neck is described as the area 'where a wound is most quickly fatal' (ἵνα τε φυχῆς ὤκιστος).[64] Homer specifically mentions that Hektor's trachea is missed by Achilles' spear, which allows him to ask that his body be returned to his father.[65] This further indicates the Greek's knowledge of the vitality of this area to the various functions of the body. Due to the number of vital vessels within the human neck, this ability to continue to speak from a spear wound, which is described as passing through the entire area, must be literary embellishment. Xenophon also comments on the vitality of this area and its need for protection among mounted troops.[66]

The average width of the head of the hoplite spear (31mm) means that any strike that impacted with the neck from the front would have a high probability of impacting with at least one vital area, resulting in the rapid death of the victim. Thus the many references to 'survivable' wounds, and the relatively low casualty figures among the winning side of a hoplite engagement, must be references to injuries and fatalities both aimed at, and received to, areas of the body other than the throat. The mention of survivable head wounds in the Hippocratic corpus must be references to injuries sustained to other parts of the cranium.[67] The commonality of wounds either aimed at the chest or shield, and the occurrences of 'walking wounded' all suggest that the current concept of the throat 'kill shot' has been misplaced.

Like the artistic record, there are also literary passages that refer to wounds to the extremities. Archidamus, for example, was hit in the thigh at Cromnus in 365BC.[68] Plutarch relates several instances of hoplites receiving wounds to the legs and feet. In one case the wounds are so numerous, or so severe in nature, that the recipient is forced to crawl.[69] Lamachus, in Aristophanes' *Acharnians*, describes the piercing wound he has received to the ankle as coming from a 'hostile spear'.[70] The Corinthian Dion was also wounded in the hand by a spear thrust during the siege of Syracuse in 357BC.[71] It is unlikely that many of these wounds were the result of attacks specifically directed against them: it would be extremely difficult to target and hit an opponent's hand during the rigours of combat, for example. As such, many of them are most likely the result of strikes made against another target that the attack has missed only to carry on and impact with another area of the combatant's body. Based upon the literary evidence, this commonly targeted area was the chest and not the throat.

Physical evidence of hoplite battle wounds

The archaeological record is limited in its scope, and therefore in its value, to an investigation of hoplite combative injuries. Flesh will not survive in the archaeological record except under rare conditions. Consequently, the remains of wounds to the soft tissue on victims cannot be easily identified. However, spear wounds are likely to impact with the bones of the body and may allow identification of deeper injuries.[72] Unfortunately, in the majority of the available excavation reports for hoplite war graves, forensic analysis of the remains has not been a focus of the excavators.[73] One of the few clearly identifiable battle casualties in the archaeological record comes in the form of a skeleton belonging to one of the Spartan war-dead excavated from the Kerameikos in Athens who still had a spearhead lodged in his ribs.[74] This was clearly the result of a wound to the chest that was too deep to allow for the extraction of the spearhead before interment. However, this single clear example of a chest wound cannot confirm the regularity of such injuries nor counter the concept of the throat 'kill shot' on its own. It can only be taken in context with the other available evidence.

The archaeological record also provides other clues to the nature of war wounds. Blyth identifies forty-six pieces of armour possibly damaged in battle in the collection of Olympia; mainly helmets and greaves with one groin protector (*mitra*) and one thigh guard.[75] If all of the damage to this armour is the result of impacts sustained in battle, the damage itself is unlikely to be the result of spear thrusts aimed at the throat but to the upper head (in the case of damage to a helmet) or to the legs (in the case of damage to a greave). The thigh and groin wounds may be the result of specifically aimed attacks or of missed attacks aimed at other targets that have impacted with these areas.

The developmental stages of these, and other, pieces of armour used by the hoplite also conflict with the current convention of a throat 'kill shot'. Armour will directly reflect the style of fighting it was designed to protect against. Gabriel and Metz state that in the ancient world the development of better weapons was a direct response to the development of better armour and increased defensive capabilities.[76] For example, they claim that one of the stimuli behind the development of iron-tipped spears was the advances in body armour to resist earlier forms of the weapon.[77] Despite the apparent 'chicken and egg' scenario associated with this conclusion (what actually came first, better weapons or better armour?) it is clear that Greek armour should evolve in response to the style of fighting. However, this does not appear to be the case if the modern principles of the throat 'kill shot' and the use of the overhead stance are followed.

Some scholars have stated that the Corinthian-style helmet fell into disuse towards the end of the sixth century BC and that by the fifth century BC the conical *pilos* helmet was widely in use.[78] This conclusion begs an obvious question: if the throat was the main target of the hoplite, why develop and adopt a style of helmet that afforded no protection to the face or throat and then abandon the use of the Corinthian-style helmet? Other styles of open-faced helmet, such as the Attic or the Chalcidian, also left the face and throat exposed yet these were also developed and adopted during the later Classical Period. Clearly this seems to be an illogical evolutionary path for helmet design to take if the throat was the primary 'kill shot'. Corinthian helmets in the collection of Olympia generally have nasal guards which are thicker than the rest of the helmet.[79] This would suggest that it was designed to protect against blows that would be commonly directed at the face.[80]

The design of the semi-enclosed Thracian/Phrygian-style helmet (c.480BC onwards) appears to be at odds with this trend in helmet development. Everson merely attributes its use to a demonstration of wealth.[81] However, it is depicted in use by the common soldiery on representations such as the Alexander Sarcophagus and this conclusion is unlikely to be correct. As open-faced helmets provide no advantage in terms of the range of vision over the Corinthian helmet (and the Thracian/Phrygian as well), the development of open-faced helmets must be the result of other factors.

There are two characteristics that all open-faced helmets have in common. Firstly, they are all lighter than the Corinthian. The absence of facial and throat protection no doubt requires less metal for the production of open-faced helmets, resulting in their reduced weights. Secondly, open-faced helmets all provide better ventilation for the wearer. In enclosed helmets, such as the Corinthian, an inner felt *pilos* cap was one of the few means of dissipating excess heat.[82] The increased ventilation provided by open-faced helmets was offset by the reduction in the level of protection provided to the head and throat. If the throat was a frequently targeted area, it seems strange that its protection was not retained.

The development of some open-faced helmets is also unlikely to have merely been the result of a desire to create a more easily constructed helmet. The later Attic and Thracian/Phrygian styles, with their moveable cheek guards, involve three separately manufactured components and hinges, and were much more complicated in design than their Corinthian predecessors. Conversely, the simple *pilos* and Boeotian-style helmets were, like the Corinthian, beaten into shape from a single sheet of metal. Their lack of facial protection and basic shape would have required less workmanship to manufacture due to the absence of eye holes and nasal guards. Their simple method of construction may be more representative of the military requirements of the Peloponnesian War period when there was a greater need to quickly arm and equip large numbers of hoplites and place them in the field. Interestingly, some examples of the *pilos* helmet possess cheek and neck guards; suggesting that these examples were made at a time when the rapid equipping of troops may not have been a priority.

Another development concerns the abandonment of the use of arm guards by hoplite infantry in the Classical Era. Evidence indicates that arm guards were used in the Archaic Period but were no longer used by the Classical Period.[83] This disuse can be accounted for when the changes in fighting style of the Greek hoplite are viewed in context with this development. Sekunda suggests that the abandonment of the arm guard was due to the increase in the Persian use of archers as the hoplite would need to be lighter to charge effectively against these missile troops while minimizing the time exposed to their volleys.[84] This explanation seems too simplistic and unlikely. An increase in the use of archers would seemingly necessitate an increase in required protection (for example the adoption of the 'shield apron'), not a reduction. Furthermore, even with the abandonment of the arm guard, the hoplite was still almost fully covered from head to foot with enough armour to protect him against missiles anyway.[85]

The abandonment of the arm guard can be explained by another evolutionary step in the processes of hoplite combat. With the missile-based warfare of the Archaic Period, arm guards, for the weapon-bearing arm at least, would have been almost mandatory. The use of the overhead posture to wield the javelin would have necessitated protection for the exposed arm as it was held aloft. With the advancement of the thrusting phalanx and the disuse of the javelin, arm protection would have been no longer required. This would have been due to the adoption of the underarm stance to wield the thrusting spear, which left very little of the weapon arm vulnerable to injury when it was tucked beside the body and, for the most part, behind the shield. Had the overhead posture been retained for fighting with the spear, protection for the arm would have most likely been also retained. Xenophon states that cavalry in his day still wore arm guards. This was because the cavalry were commonly armed with javelins and thus would have had their right arms exposed.[86] This lends further support to the conclusion that depictions of the overhead stance are representative of the missile warfare of an earlier age rather than that of the thrusting phalanx.

Why aim at the chest?

So why would the area of the chest have been commonly targeted if it was so well protected by the shield and body armour? The answer to this question can be found in a number of factors which, in combination, make the chest area the most likely target against which a spear thrust could be directed. Firstly, it is simply the biggest target area on an opposing hoplite that can be both seen and attacked. By probing and jabbing at an opponent's shield during combat, exploitable 'opportune shots' may have presented themselves as the opponent moved his shield to deflect blows, became fatigued, made errors or merely had his shield broken during the rigours of the contest. This would then leave the torso, the next biggest targetable area on the opponent, exposed. Vegetius states that a wound inflicted by the Roman *gladius* only two inches deep was generally fatal.[87] A wound of this depth, inflicted with the hoplite spear, would have been incapacitating if not similarly fatal. As such, hoplites could ill afford to go into battle without adequate protection for the vital organs and this explains the dual layering of shield and armour to cover the torso.[88] The fact that the throat was also doubly protected by both the cheek flanges of the Corinthian-style helmet and the offset rim of the shield, which are likely to have been conscious considerations in their design, further indicates that the vitality of this area was also recognized by the Greeks. However, this in no manner confirms that the throat was the primary 'kill shot' when engaged in combat.

By concentrating attacks against the most central area of the opponent's body, the hoplite's range of vision would have allowed him to see all of his opponent either directly or in the periphery. This would allow him to observe changes in body posture and movement, keep an eye on his opponent's weapon so as to avoid or deflect attacks, align his own attacks and to exploit opportune targets when they presented themselves. Vegetius states that one of the advantages of a stabbing/thrusting action is that it 'wounds the enemy before he sees it'.[89] Only by keeping an opponent's weapon within his range of vision would a hoplite have had any chance of deflecting or avoiding such an attack.

Lastly, by aiming at the chest, members of the rearward ranks are not endangered by the *sauroter* of the men in the rank before them. If members of both the front and second ranks of a close-order formation focus their attacks at the point directly ahead of where their weapons are pointing when held in the 'ready' position, the *sauroter* is not moved into a position where it could potentially injure the man behind. While it is possible for men in the front ranks to direct attacks at low targets on an opponent, such as the shins or feet, by using the reverse technique to thrust downwards over the top of the shield, this would endanger the man behind with the elevated *sauroter*. Additionally, raising the arm to strike downwards over the shield would push the spear belonging to the man in the second rank upwards so that it could not be brought to bear against a target. An attack at such low targets as the legs could only have been made by momentarily 'opening' the shield wall to attack or when fighting in a more open style of formation where there was little chance of endangering or entangling the members of the second rank.

At Plataea the Spartans aimed their attacks at the chests and faces of the Persians.[90] The small amount of elevation required to aim an underarm attack at an opponent's face lowers the *sauroter*, which does not endanger the rearward man who is protected by his shield from accidental injury. Additionally, the chest of an opponent could easily be targeted by a hoplite in the front rank of the phalanx while the opponent's face was targeted by the man in the second rank. Many helmets in the collection of Olympia contain blade perforations or scarring only on the left side (for example see plate 9).[91] This is clearly the result of a blow delivered by a facing opponent wielding a weapon in their right hand against a head that has been partially rotated, due to the adoption of an oblique body posture, so that its left side has been presented towards the angle of attack. It seems unlikely that a member of the second rank could aim at anything but the upper chest or head of an opponent due to the reach that the members of the second rank had and the obstructions caused by the presence of the members of the front rank, which would prevent them from attacking a lower target. Thus the very configuration of the phalanx dictates that the most commonly targeted areas in a hoplite engagement were those directly ahead of the weapon: the shield, the chest (when exposed) and the parts of the head which were above the rim of the *aspis*.

Are we to believe that all of the evidence for wounds to the shield, torso, head, arms and legs, coming from a variety of sources, is merely the result of poor aim on the part of the attacker; and that the thousands of remaining battlefield casualties, which are only vaguely referred to in mass quantities and tabulated casualty statistics in the ancient texts, are the result of 'kill shots' aimed exclusively at the throat? This seems highly improbable. Yet, this is what we must concede if we are to accept modern scholarship's proposal that the region of the neck was the primary target for the hoplite in battle. Sophocles refers to hoplite combat as 'a storm of spears' (δορός ... ἐν χειμῶνι).[92] It is impossible to conceive that an environment that would warrant such a description would yield so few instances of wounds to the throat if this was the primary 'kill shot' of the hoplite. The lack of any reference to this kind of injury, and the physical mechanics of the phalanx in action, suggests that, in a comparison to the *Iliad* (suggesting the relative realism of its descriptiveness) wounds sustained to the arms, legs and particularly the throat, were not as common in the confrontations of the Classical Age as injuries sustained to the area of the true hoplite 'kill shots': the chest and upper head.

Chapter 8

Endurance and Accuracy when Fighting with the Hoplite Spear

Even though the area of the chest and shield of an opponent was large, and would have been somewhat easy for a hoplite to hit in combat with his spear, if a smaller 'opportune target' presented itself during the course of a battle, could a hoplite have easily hit it, or would it have merely been a matter of luck? Was hoplite warfare merely a frenzied series of ill-aimed and random attacks, or was it more technical and based upon the skill of the combatants? Most importantly, for how long could a hoplite have maintained the physical exertions of combat? The examination of these inter-related facets of hoplite warfare demonstrates that even the most inexperienced hoplite would have possessed enough skill with a spear to hit a small 'opportune target'. However, those who were skilled in the arts of war would have been able to maintain their attacks for a longer period, and with a more consistent level of skill and accuracy, which would have given them a decisive advantage on the battlefield.

Hand-to-hand combat can be broken down into two separate yet inter-dependent criteria. First is the ability to direct strikes at a desired target with a reasonable level of accuracy; for any combative technique to be effective, you have to be able to hit what you are aiming at. Second is the ability to fight in a manner that does not make the body fatigue rapidly so that the processes of attacking and defending can be maintained for as long as possible. Once fatigue sets in, the ability to use any weapon effectively is greatly reduced. The combination of endurance and proficiency is what will determine the effectiveness of an action that is literally a matter of life and death on the battlefield. Unfortunately, the ancient sources are relatively silent on both of these subjects.

No ancient text contains a specific reference to the accuracy of the actions of combat with the hoplite spear. Similarly, the artistic and archaeological records can make no comment on the accuracy of the thrusts to which the images and artefacts relate. As such, modern scholarship has made no attempt to analyze the base level of accuracy for fighting with the hoplite's primary weapon; this aspect is not even vaguely commented on in most modern works on hoplite warfare apart from those theories that suggest the location of specifically targeted areas on the body and the inherent assumption about the accuracy of spear combat that these claims imply.

Similarly, the ancient sources are of little value in determining the levels of stamina and endurance of the individual hoplite in combat. Homer, for example, merely states the obvious when he surmises that a man is unable to fight beyond the limits of his strength.[1] No ancient source directly states, or even hints at, how long the individual hoplite could engage in combat before tiring. What the ancient passages do contain are ambiguous references to the duration of many hoplite engagements. Many ancient sources contain accounts of battles that are described as lasting 'a long time' (ἐπί πολὺν δὲ χρόνον), or a variation of this term, such as Marathon, Thermopylae, the Piraeus and Syracuse.[2] Luginbill states that the evidence for long-duration battles is sketchy and that the term 'for a long time' is a literary construct used by the ancient authors to contrast against relatively quick battles such as Mantinea. Luginbill concludes that all hoplite engagements were relatively short.[3] Munro states that the time may have been measured in minutes yet still be regarded as 'long' under the circumstances.[4] Certainly, the 'Tearless Battle' of 368BC was over almost before it had begun, and therefore must have been of a particularly short duration, but this seems to have been a rare event.[5] In direct contrast are accounts of battles such as that at Himera (480BC), which is said to have lasted from dawn until evening (ἐξ ἠοῦς μέχρι δείης ὀψίης), the second day of the defence of Thermopylae (480BC), which saw the Spartans fighting for the whole day (ἐνημερεύοντες δὲ τοῖς κινδύνοις) and the fighting on Sphacteria (425BC), which also lasted for most of a day (τῆς ἡμέρας τὸ πλεῖστον).[6]

Other engagements, despite their accounts containing no reference to the duration of the conflict, by the very nature of their events, must have taken considerable time to play out. At Coronea for example, both sides deployed and then advanced; both sides then charged and engaged in fighting with the Spartans eventually breaking through on one wing while the opposing Thebans broke through on the other. Both the Thebans and the Spartans then reformed, wheeled about and charged each other; resulting in another bout of heavy fighting before the battle reached its ultimate conclusion.[7] Even if theories suggesting that the actual fighting only lasted several minutes are correct, the time required to perform all of the other accounted manoeuvres would clearly place such a battle among those which lasted 'a long time'.

This highlights one important feature of most forms of combat in general: it is not just the fighting that saps a combatant's reserves of energy, but all of the events leading up to the clash of arms, and the environment of the area upon which the battle is fought, as well. The form in which such a drain on energy could manifest itself is both varied and cumulative in its nature.

The majority of hoplite engagements occurred during the summer period when the land holders who constituted the bulk of the militia hoplite forces were not required to attend to their lands.[8] At Plataea the Greek army deployed on the field for ten days, receiving only limited supplies of rations and water, before the fighting commenced.[9] Fatigue due to hunger, thirst and heat would have undoubtedly affected some of the hoplites. During their retreat from Syracuse in 413BC, the Athenians were additionally burdened by the portage of their own equipment and the stress of incessant attacks from the pursuing Syracusans.[10] Fatigue, injuries, hunger and thirst contributed to such a break-down in morale that the desperate Athenians broke ranks to both cross and drink from the Assinarus River while the Syracusans and their Peloponnesian allies pressed the attack. Thucydides relates how the maddened Athenians trampled each other underfoot in their frenzied attempts to reach the river and how many continued to drink from it even after the water had been stained red with the blood of their fallen comrades.[11] Under such conditions, had the Athenians even been able to deploy in a proper battle line to face the enemy, it is unlikely that many of the hoplites would have had the stamina for a pro-longed engagement. Under similar, if somewhat less dramatic, circumstances, Xenophon's mercenaries marched all the way from Babylon to the Black Sea, through plains and heat, snow and mountainous terrain. Many of the hoplites in the contingent must have been fatigued at the outset of one or more of the engagements they fought. Prolonged exposure to such environmental factors as heat, cold, rain or wind, decrease a combatant's energy reserves and endurance, and consequently affect his level of performance.[12]

A hoplite, or more importantly a hoplite commander, could not guarantee how long a battle he was about to fight would last. Nor could he guarantee the conditions under which the battle would be fought. As such, the hoplite style of fighting had to have been able to endure an engagement of an uncertain, and possibly lengthy, time frame and under all possible conditions. The only way to achieve this would be to use a combative technique that did not quickly fatigue the combatant.

Unlike accuracy, some modern texts on hoplite warfare contain at least a summary statement on the effects of fatigue and the endurance of the hoplite. Many of these passages are merely a conclusion that a hoplite could only fight for a particular length of time before the effects of fatigue set in. However, even amongst these theories there is a vast disparity. Matthews, for example, states that hoplite battles may have lasted for one or two hours.[13] Everson claims that the hoplite could fight for an hour before the effects of fatigue fully set in.[14] Gabriel and Metz, citing Ferrill, state that the hoplite could fight for thirty minutes before becoming exhausted.[15] Hanson, observing students duelling in wood and metal replica panoplies weighing 31kg in 32°C heat, also claims that the hoplite would be exhausted after thirty minutes.[16] Van Wees and Goldsworthy state that fatigue would overcome the hoplite after only a few minutes.[17] Fraser also claims that the hoplite would be exhausted within only five minutes of engaging in combat; a conclusion based upon an extrapolation of how long various sportsmen and animals perform before they are rested.[18]

Fraser's comparison of hoplites to athletes is not entirely without merit for a study of hoplite combat. Pindar draws similar parallels between the toils and courage of the gymnast and those of the hoplite.[19] However, Pindar makes no reference to either stamina or effectiveness. One useful analogy between sport and combat is that, in both activities, as a person becomes fatigued their body movements slow down. As the body tires, breathing becomes shallower and more rapid, oxygen deprivation starves the muscles causing a build up of lactic acid, which in turn slows down the bio-mechanical processes. Consequently, any action involving the further use of these muscles will become weaker and less effective; as will general motor-functions, cognitive ability and levels of accuracy.[20] A lack of sleep, extended periods of physically taxing labour (such as marching) and minimal periods of rest all have similar effects on performance.[21] As such a hoplite who, for whatever reason, was fatigued would not have been able to direct his attacks as accurately as a less fatigued hoplite, may not have had the strength to penetrate the target even if he hit, and may not have even been able to recognize an 'opportune target' when it presented itself. In another correlation between sport and combat, the negative effects of fatigue can be countered to a limited extent through the process of training.

Training, whether it be in a sport or a martial skill, develops ability, confidence, strength and stamina. It is not surprising that many of these characteristics are among those listed by Xenophon for what makes an army impressive.[22] Iphicrates is said to have uttered that 'the untrained lack endurance' (οἱ ἀγύμναστοι οὐ καρτεροῦσιν).[23] For the ancient Greeks, cultural pursuits such as regular training in the *palaestra* or *gymnasion* would have developed physical strength. Practices such as the *hoplomachia* or the *Pyrrhic dance* would have built up aerobic fitness and a limited skill set.[24] The benefit of these limited skills in battle is the very basis for Plato's reported dispute between Nicias and Laches.[25]

Despite this debate, there is little doubt that in hoplite warfare both skill and stamina would have played important roles. But which, if any, was the more important? On this point the opinions of the ancient writers are somewhat diverse. Socrates is said to have stated that the best dancers were likewise the best in war.[26] The Spartans are said to have assigned the greatest merit to endurance.[27] One of the faults of Iphicrates is said to have been that he lacked stamina.[28] Conversely, Epaminondas is said to have expended his greatest efforts on the use of arms; although he did train in both running and wrestling

to a lesser extent.[29] He is also said to have advised that for Thebes to become
the dominant city in all of Greece its citizens must spend time in the military
encampment (i.e. in training with weapons) rather than in the *gymnasion*.[30]
Plato suggests that women should also be trained, either to use the bow like an
Amazon or to bear a shield and spear like Athena, and take their place in the
phalanx to help defend the city-state in times of emergency.[31] This suggests an
emphasis on training in weapon handling skills rather than on physical fitness.
When Messenia was invaded by the Spartans in the eighth century BC, it
was advised that 'anyone ignorant in the art of war was to learn it, and anyone
who knew it was to train in its techniques more vigorously'. After four years of
training, the Messenians finally felt themselves ready to engage the Spartans.[32]
Aristotle states that mercenaries are the best for both attack and defence due
to their expertise with their weapons, with the effect that, when engaging non-
professionals, they are like fully armed troops facing unarmed opponents; a
clear suggestion that Aristotle believed that technical skill was important in
war.[33] Solon is said to have remarked that boxers, short-distance runners and
all other athletes contributed nothing worth mentioning to the safety of the
city-state.[34] This suggests that those who could contribute to the state's defence
were only those skilled in the techniques of combat. Vegetius, in a series of
general comments that hold true as much for the Greeks as they do for the
Romans, states that skill and training produce courage, and that those who fight
with courage and skill are more apt to victory, while an untrained horde that
lacks courage will either be slaughtered or turn in flight; although he does
encourage legionnaires be kept in peak physical condition as well.[35]

   Like Vegetius' advice, it is a combination of both skill and stamina that
would create the most effective warrior. The possession of technical skill is of
limited value without the strength to back it up.[36] Similarly, strength alone can
generally not defeat an opponent who possesses better skill with a weapon.[37]
This is what, as Aristotle points out, separated the two different classes of
soldier found in ancient Greece: the 'professional' and the 'non-professional'
hoplite.

   There is a vast disparity between those who could be classed as 'professional
hoplites' and those who could not. The Spartan hoplite and members of the
Theban Sacred Band could both be considered 'professional' due to their
extensive training.[38] A contingent of one thousand select Argives were also
given extensive military training at state expense, and these troops could
also be considered 'professional' hoplites.[39] However, up to the middle of the
Peloponnesian War, which saw an increase in the use of mercenaries and
protracted campaigning seasons, the majority of hoplites were not professionals;
they held civilian occupations and performed their military duty only when the
need arose.[40] Ducrey argues that Athenian training in the use of formations was

kept only at a rudimentary level as it was seen as an infringement upon the personal freedom of the Athenian citizen. He suggests that they preferred to rely upon the individual courage of their men rather than on blind discipline and that they only resorted to reinstituting the old custom of the *Ephebia* (national service for youths) in 335BC following the defeat of the Greek states by Philip II at Chaeronea in 338BC.[41] Agesilaus is reported to have ordered all of the men among contingents of Spartan and allied hoplites who had 'civilian' vocations to stand up so that he could point out to other commanders that while they had brought farmers and craftsmen to war, Sparta had brought soldiers.[42]

In terms of levels of physical fitness, there would not have been much of a difference between the 'professional' hoplite and the 'non-professional'. As hoplite warfare was reasonably static in nature once two opposing sides had joined, bodily strength and fitness were necessary, but were somewhat secondary to technical skill; there was an initial advance or charge at the outset of the engagement and possibly a secondary charge during the course of the fighting as was seen at Coronea, but for the most part, once the two sides had engaged, there was not a lot of individual movement required by each hoplite other than to perform his offensive and defensive actions (which still require a high level of stamina to be maintained). Whereas many of the farmers, craftsmen and tradesmen who made up the bulk of the citizen militia hoplite forces of the Classical Age would have possessed a certain level of muscular strength and aerobic fitness due to the manual nature of their livelihoods and/ or time spent in the *gymnasion*, the professional hoplite would have developed a similar level of fitness via the activities of his training. The only benefit gained by the professional would have been that his muscles had been conditioned for the rigours of combat, whereas the citizen-soldier would have been used to using his muscles in a different capacity. This agrees with those ancient comments that suggest that strength is secondary to skill in hoplite combat.

Another benefit of regular training and battlefield experience is the conditioning of the mind for the turmoils of war. As an individual becomes more accustomed to a dangerous environment, the level to which their body physically reacts (i.e the release of adrenaline and other hormones, fear, impaired cognitive abilities and motor skills etc.) diminishes.[43] If a person is accustomed to a particular environment, and therefore does not perceive that environment to be threatening or out of the ordinary, they are unlikely to experience the negative physiological effects of fear as someone who feels threatened.[44] Aristotle states: 'The sanguine are confident in the face of danger because they have previously won many victories over many foes'.[45] This sentiment was later echoed by Seneca who states: 'constant exposure to dangers breeds contempt for them'.[46] As such, an experienced and/or 'professional' hoplite would have been able to withstand the physical and psychological pressures of combat more readily. Groups who demonstrate cohesiveness are rarely the same as those who panic.[47] Nepos states that once battle was joined the result of the issue came down to luck and spirit as much as it did fighting skill.[48] These factors partially explain why the morale of Spartan formations rarely failed whereas those of many other city-states did, and why the front ranks of the Spartan phalanx were made up of experienced veterans and officers. The Spartans, having been trained for war from an early age, would have had an almost 'desensitized' attitude to combat. Fear in battle, or even at the sight or approach of an enemy, is a manifestly natural reaction.[49] However, the conditioning and training of the professional Spartan hoplite would have allowed them to function beyond the debilitating effects of fear and so perform more effectively on the battlefield than many 'less professional' hoplites.[50]

Yet what difference would being a professional have made in terms of how well the individual could have wielded the spear? Xenophon states that all men understand war by their very nature and that how to use a weapon can often be determined by simply holding it.[51] Many young Greeks would similarly have been able to guess how to hold a hoplite spear and shield from the balance of the weapon and the dual grip system of the *aspis*. Parents and elders could also have provided limited training through demonstration, instruction and the recounting of personal experiences. Even if events such as the *hoplitodromos* (a foot race run in armour) and the *Pyrrhic dance* did not require the shield and spear to be positioned as they would be for actual combat, they would still need to be held correctly. For the Spartans, their early introduction to the arts of war as part of the *agoge* (the Spartan education system for boys) would have taught the Spartan youths how to correctly hold their weapons. As such, it can be assumed that even the most inexperienced hoplite would have had a general knowledge of how to at least hold his weaponry.

However, many of these same young men (except for the Spartans) would not fully comprehend the dynamics of the panoply's usage in the context of the phalanx until they had received a 'baptism at spear point' on the field of battle itself. Even the *ephebes* of fourth century Athens, which the lexicographer Photius describes as 'young men, new to the skill of battle' (παῖς νέος ἐν αὐτῇ τῇ ἀκμῇ), would have only received limited military training and most of their experience would have been gained 'in the field'.[52] Conversely, young Spartans were initiated to many of the other hardships of war, including cold, hunger, thirst and the endurance of pain as part of their education.[53]

Testing accuracy and endurance

How much difference would this disparity in training have made in the ability of hoplites from different city-states to effectively hit an opportune target in battle and to endure the physical stresses of combat? Due to the lack of direct information in the available evidence regarding the accuracy and endurance of hoplite fighting, a series of re-creative tests were conducted to examine these aspects of ancient Greek warfare. A group of volunteer 'non-professional hoplites' was selected from amongst the members of the Sydney Ancients and other interested individuals. All of the re-enactors possessed full hoplite panoplies and spare equipment was lent to other participants so that every individual bore at least a basic panoply of tunic, shield, helmet and spear. The three main combative stances (low, overhead and underarm) were examined as part of the testing process and the participants were divided into three groups so that each could begin the tests by performing one of the techniques without the influence of any prior level of fatigue.

Each participant stood before a target dummy of hay bales 180cm in height with a life-size silhouette of a human figure attached to it (representing a member of an opposing phalanx). A 10×10cm area representing the throat 'kill shot' of modern theory was outlined on the target and this was the area that the participants were asked to direct their attacks against. This ensured that all of the participants were aiming at the same area of the target so that the accuracy of their attacks could be standardized across the collected data sample. It also allowed for the ease (or difficulty) of hitting the target that forms the basis of many modern models of hoplite warfare to be observed (see Chapter 7, The 'Kill Shot' of Hoplite Combat).

Each target was labelled with a letter designating the participant (for anonymity) and the style of thrust they were performing. Each participant approached their target to a distance they perceived adequate for the delivery of their respective attack and executed five consecutive strikes (hereafter referred to as the 'primary strikes') at the throat 'kill shot' from their assigned posture and at their own pace. All strikes were made from a stationary position. A certain level of shield and body movement was also permitted across all techniques so that the low strike could be more easily performed. Once the five 'primary strikes' had been performed, each participant moved away and engaged in a period of 'simulated combat'. In this action, akin to shadow boxing, each participant engaged against either a static target (e.g. pole or fence-post), or against an imaginary opponent, from their respective posture for a test period of up to fifteen minutes or until they could no longer continue due to fatigue.

When the time had elapsed, or they had 'fought' for as long as they felt they could, the length of time that the participant had lasted in this phase was recorded (rounded up or down to the nearest minute). They then returned to the target and made another five consecutive thrusts (hereafter referred to as the 'secondary strikes'). Each participant was then questioned about their experience and any comments they gave were also recorded on the target. This test allowed several aspects of combat with the hoplite spear to be observed: the accuracy of the primary strikes of the three combative techniques; how fatigue of the weapon-bearing arm influenced the accuracy of the secondary strikes in comparison; and the length of time that the three combative postures could be maintained. This test also allowed for any observations made by the participants on the particular techniques to be recorded. After a period of rest to limit any compromise to subsequent tests, willing participants then went through a second testing session (some even for a third session) using a different technique to gain a broader sample of data. The distance of the primary and secondary strikes from the target area were measured and the location of each impact recorded on separate data sheets for later analysis.

It must be noted that there are aspects of this testing that do not accurately re-create the environment of a hoplite battle. The tests were conducted on a sunny Australian winter's day of 22°C, not during a day that more closely resembled the common Greek summer campaigning season (temperatures would have been in the 30s). Winter was chosen as a testing period to avoid the potential risk of heatstroke in inexperienced test subjects wearing metal armour and it must be assumed that fatigue brought on by summer heat would have reduced the endurance levels of at least some of the participants.

As all the participants were 'non-professional' hoplites, the performance of the test subjects is unlikely to be on a par with that of a 'professional hoplite' of the Classical Age. However, the intermediate skill level of the re-enactors, gained through semi-regular training with the panoply, may more closely reflect the level of skill inherent among the non-professional 'citizen militia' of many Greek city-states, particularly Athenians who had completed their *ephebic* training, and the results can be considered as accurate a reflection of the ability of these hoplites as is practically reproducible in the modern world.

The 'simulated combat' used in the tests would also not accurately reflect battlefield conditions from several perspectives. It is unlikely that the hoplite would have been continuously thrusting during an engagement, but would be using his spear to probe his opponent's defences until a killing blow could be delivered. However, the fatigue experienced by the test subjects brought on by this continuous action would have been partially offset by the corresponding lack of other forms of fatigue, such as would be created by the need for parrying and defending oneself from attacks, and the psychological tensions caused by fear and adrenal stress and their physical side-effects, such as loss of motor skills, auditory exclusion, perceptual narrowing (tunnel vision) and lack of self awareness – all of which are taxing on the body's reserves of energy.[54]

Aristophanes refers to battle as the 'emptier of bowels'.[55] This description is likely a reference to the common battlefield condition where the sympathetic nervous system takes over the body's functions and reserves of energy during a 'fight or flight' situation such as combat, usually to the exclusion of control over the body's digestive and recuperative processes.[56] This physiological condition resulted in over half of Allied combat troops in the Second World War either urinating and/or defecating themselves during battle.[57] Clearly, Aristophanes' description is a reference to similarly extreme states of fear experienced by some hoplites under battle conditions.[58] It is no surprise then that temples to both Fear and Death were established in militaristic Sparta.[59]

A level of tension similar to an ancient hoplite battle, incorporating all of its physiological side-effects, would be impossible to replicate in a test environment without compromising the safety of the participants. As Idzikowski and Baddeley point out, it is almost impossible to gauge the effects of fear in a controlled, yet ethical, test environment as there are simply too many variables involved.[60] The lack of a 'fight or flight' environment resulted in many participants halting their period of 'simulated combat' after only a short period of time at the first onset of fatigue, rather than persevering as would have been required in a life or death situation.[61] The tests were also devoid of impediments such as dust, noise and the detritus of battle underfoot.

Even the target used in the testing itself was not compliant with the physical characteristics of a hoplite engagement. The silhouette on the target was depicted in a front-on position rather than drawn in the oblique posture adopted by the hoplite. Nor was any area on the target silhouette protected by, or even represented as being protected by, armour or a shield. Due to its double protection behind the cheek flanges of the Corinthian-style helmet and/or the offset rim of the *aspis*, the throat on an opposing hoplite would not have been visible during a hoplite engagement. These environmental, conditional and psychological aspects of the hoplite battlefield would all impact on the hoplite's levels of energy and, either directly or indirectly, influence the accuracy of his strike placements and his endurance for battle. As such, it must be conceded that the results of this test cannot be regarded as a truthful reflection of hoplite accuracy and endurance under combat conditions, but are an approximation based upon a standardized set of experiments conducted in an environment with modern best-practice safety parameters for the test subjects. Nevertheless, the results of these tests allow for the baseline accuracy of each style of attack, and the effects of fatigue on the participants performing them, to be analyzed.

The results – endurance
The results of these tests show that attacks made from the low posture were the least taxing on the muscles of the arm. Some participants found it easy to last the fifteen-minute period of 'simulated combat' and commented that they could have easily continued, or were immediately ready to go onto a further session of testing using another posture without rest. This was due to the action of the low thrust merely involving the swinging of the arm forward to the impact

PLATE 1

Plate 1.1   The Achilles Amphora. Attic red-figure amphora by the Achilles Painter (c.450BC) – Musei Vaticani (#16571). (© *Musei Vaticani Archivio Fotografico #XXVII.5.21/1*)

PLATE 2

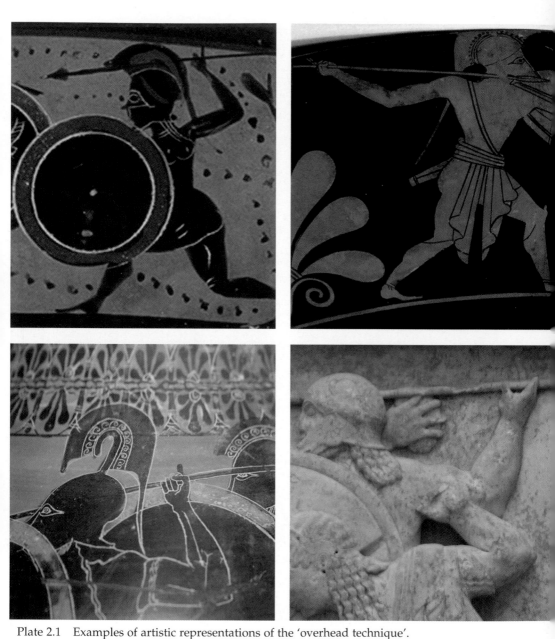

Plate 2.1   Examples of artistic representations of the 'overhead technique'.

Top Left: Band Cup (detail) Group of Villa Giulia 3559 (c.540BC) – John Hugh Sutton Memorial Bequest: The University of Melbourne Art Collection – Classics Collection (1930.0002).

Top Right: Attic red-figure Kylix (detail) by the Euergides Painter (c.520–510BC) – Toledo Museum of Art (1961.25). (© *Toni Marie Gonzales*)

Bottom Left: Attic black-figure Type B amphora (detail) by the Antimenes Painter (c.525–500BC) – The University of Sydney – Nicholson Museum (NM77.1).

Bottom Right: North frieze of Siphnian Treasury, Delphi (detail) c.525BC. (*Author's photograph*)

PLATE 3

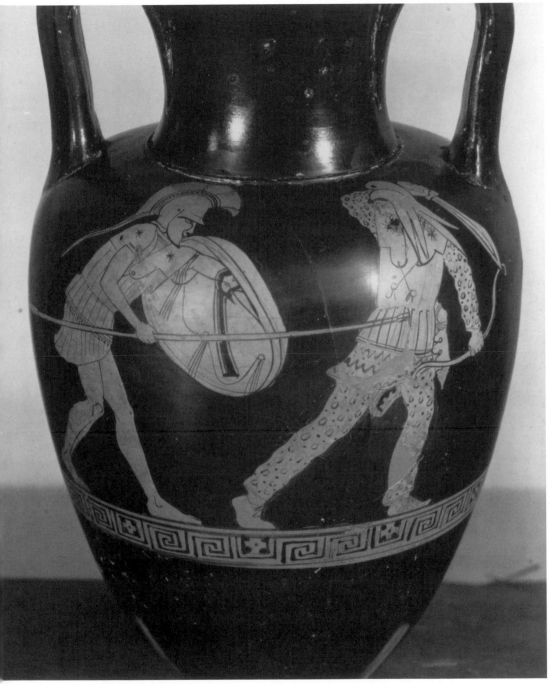

Plate 3.1   Artistic representation of the 'low technique'. Attic red-figure 'Nolan Neck' Amphora (c.480–470BC) – The Rogers Fund, 1906, The Metropolitan Museum of Art, New York (06.1021.117).

(© *The Metropolitan Museum of Art / Art Resource, NY*)

PLATE 4

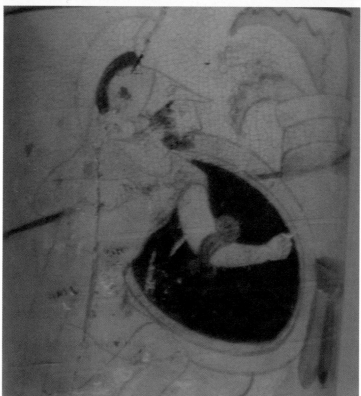

Plate 4.1   Artistic representations of the 'underarm technique'.

Top: Lucanian red-figure Nestoris (detail) attributed to the Choephoroi Painter (c.340–320BC) –
Harvard Art Museum, Arthur M. Sackler Museum, bequest of David M. Robinson (1960.367).
(*Photograph by Junius Beebe © President and Fellows of Harvard College*)

Bottom: White-ground Lekythos (detail) in the manner of the Woman Painter (c.435–420BC) –
National Archaeological Museum, Athens (14517). (*Author's photograph*)

PLATE 5

Plate 5.1   Hand position when using the 'overhead' (*left*) and 'low' (*right*) techniques. (*Author's photographs*)

Plate 5.2   The different possible positions of the hand and arm when using the 'underarm' grip. (*Author's photographs*)

1. with the hand/forearm on top of the shaft.

2. with the hand/forearm alongside the shaft.

3. with the hand/forearm beneath the shaft.

PLATE 6

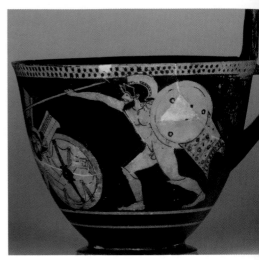

Plate 6.1   Artistic representations of the 'reverse technique'.

Left: Attic volute-krater (detail) by the Woolly Satyrs Painter (c.450BC) – The Rogers Fund, 1907 – The Metropolitan Museum of Art, New York (07.286.84). (*Image ©The Metropolitan Museum of Art / Art Resource, NY*)

Right: Attic cup (c.fifth century BC) – Antikensammlung, Staatliche Museen zu Berlin – Preussischer Kulturbesitz (F2321). (*Photograph by Johannes Laurentius*)

Plate 6.2   Achilles (left) and Ajax playing dice. Attic black-figure amphora by Exekias (c.540–530BC) – Musei Vaticani (#16757). (© *Musei Vaticani Archivio Fotografico #XXXIV.24.86/3*)

PLATE 7

Spears held in the
underarm position

Spears held in the
low position

Javelins held in the
overhead position

Spent javelin?

Plate 7.1   A vase illustration showing the use of the low and underarm postures to wield the spear and the overhead position to cast the javelin. Campanian neck-amphora with heroic battle scene (detail) attributed to the Ixion Painter (c.330–310BC) – William Randolph Hearst Collection, Los Angeles County Museum of Art (50.8.16). (© *2009 Museum Associates/LACMA/Art resource NY*)

PLATE 8

Plate 8.1   Details from the Chigi Olpe (Chigi Vase) (c.640BC) – Museo di Villa Giulia, Rome (#22679).
Top: Javelins with the *agkulē* on the Chigi Vase. (© *Museo di Villa Giulia*)
Bottom: Finger placement for the use of the *agkulē* on the Chigi Vase. (© *Museo di Villa Giulia*)

PLATE 9

Plate 9.1   A spear damaged helmet from Olympia. Corinthian helmet B5213 from Olympia
(c.500BC), one of over 400 pieces of hoplite defensive armour in the collection of the Deutsche
Archaeological Institute at Olympia, Greece, which were examined in November 2008. The wearer
of this helmet has suffered a very heavy blow from a spear high on the left cheek. A couple of
aspects of the perforation in the metal demonstrate the angle and direction that the inflicting
weapon followed. The way in which the lower lip of the perforation is folded inwards, under the
upper lip, shows that the spear which caused this opening struck the helmet at a shallow upward
angle of impact of less than 15 degrees from the horizontal. This angle is more consistent with a
blow delivered from an under arm position which, due to the natural movement of the arm, follows
a fairly flat trajectory. Tearing at the outer edge of the perforation additionally shows that the spear
impacted from the wearer's front left, tearing the metal as it penetrated into the helmet. This is
consistent with a hoplite adopting an oblique body posture, with the feet apart and the left leg
forward, which naturally rotates the head and upper body slightly to the right, thereby presenting
the left side of the head to any attack delivered with a weapon held in the right hand of an
opponent standing directly opposite. The width of this opening suggests that the spear-head may
have penetrated to a depth of up to 15cm; enough to instantly kill the wearer. Importantly, tests
have shown that the overhead strike of current convention is incapable of delivering enough energy
to cause this kind of damage to the curved plate bronze of this helmet; such energy can only be
generated with strikes delivered from the underarm or low positions. For other examples of
damaged helmets and armour at Olympia (without any forensic examination of the damage) see:
P.C. Bol, *Argivische Schilde* (Berlin, Walter de Gruyter, 1989), pp. 3, 14, 115 (catalogue number A244),
pl. 2; E. Kunze, *Bericht über die Ausgrabungen in Olympia V* (Berlin, Walter de Gruyter, 1956), p. 73,
pl. 39; E. Kunze, *Bericht über die Ausgrabungen in Olympia VII* (Berlin, Walter de Gruyter, 1961),
pp. 78, 80, 84, pl.22, 34.1–2, 35.1–2; E. Kunze, *Bericht über die Ausgrabungen in Olympia VIII* (Berlin,
Walter de Gruyter, 1967), pp. 79–80, 124, 126, 138, pl. 30–32, 35, 43.1–2, 59, 63, 72; E. Kunze, *Bericht
über die Ausgrabungen in Olympia IX* (Berlin, Walter de Gruyter, 1994), pp. 61, 71, 89–90, 93, pl. 17,
26.1, 30.1, 31.1–4; E. Kunze, *Beinschienen* (Berlin, Walter de Gruyter, 1991), pp. 54, 86, 89, 91, 93–94,
96, 102–103, 118, pl. 9.4, 12.1, 12.2, 15.3, 18.2, 19.3, 25, 36.2, 50.4; A. Mallwitz, *Bericht über die
Ausgrabungen in Olympia XI* (Berlin, Walter de Gruyter, 1999), p. 18–19.
(© *The Deutsche Archaeological Institute, Athens. Photograph by E.M. Czako*)

PLATE 10

Side-on posture: cannot rotate the head to look to the front.

Oblique posture: can rotate the head and look to the front.

Plate 10.1   How body posture dictates the axis of the head when wearing a Corinthian helmet. (*Author's photographs*)

1. Marching with the spear sloped over the shoulder ...

2. ... then raising the spear without altering the grip ...

3. ... results in an overhead posture with the spear pointing backwards.

Plate 10.2   The problem with moving the spear from sloped over the shoulder directly to the overhead position. (*Author's photographs*)

PLATE 11

1. Begin in, or move to, a low position.

2. Raise the spear vertically.

. Release the grip on the shield and transfer the spear to the left hand.

4. Reverse the grip of the right hand.

Plate 11.1   The beginning moves of the 'Left Hand method' of altering the grip on the weapon. (*Author's photographs*)

PLATE 12

| 1. Move the spear free of the shield. | 2. Rotate the spear above the head … | 3. … and into the overhead position. |

Plate 12.1   The problematic completion of the 'Left Hand method'. (*Author's photographs*)

| 1. Start in, or move to, a low position. | 2. Throw the spear above the shoulder and release the grip. | 3. Catch the spear with the grip reversed. |

Plate 12.2   The 'Throw and Catch method' of altering the grip on the weapon. (*Author's photographs*)

PLATE 13

| 1. Start in, or move to, a low position. | 2. Raise the spear vertically. | 3. Thrust the sauroter into the ground. |

Plate 13.1   The beginning moves of the 'Stick in Ground method' of altering the grip on the weapon. (*Author's photographs*)

| 1. Step forward, reach behind and grasp the spear with the hand reversed. | 2. Extract the weapon from the ground. | 3. Raise the spear into the overhead position. |

Plate 13.2   The problematic 'reach behind' completion of the 'Stick in Ground method'. (*Author's photographs*)

PLATE 14

1. Step forward, lean backwards and grasp the spear with the hand reversed.

2. Extract the weapon from the ground.

3. Raise the spear into the overhead position.

Plate 14.1   The problematic 'lean backwards' completion of the 'Stick in Ground method'. (*Author's photographs*)

1. Marching with spear sloped over the shoulder.

2. Moving the spear ...

3. ... into the underarm position.

Plate 14.2   Moving a spear sloped over the shoulder into the underarm position. (*Author's photographs*)

PLATE 15

1. The low position. | 2. Raising the spear … | 3. … into the underarm position.

Plate 15.1 Changing from the low position to the underarm position. (*Author's photographs*)

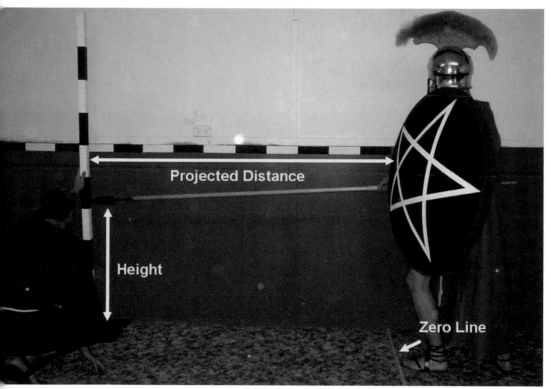

Plate 15.2 Data being recorded for a test participant adopting the low 'ready' position. (*Author's photograph*)

PLATE 16

1. 'Ready' position

2. At full extension.

Plate 16.1   The recording of the *effective range* and trajectory of an overhead thrust.
(*Author's photographs*)

1. 'Ready' position.

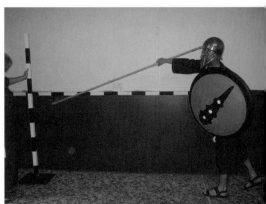

2. At full extension.

Plate 16.2   The recording of the *effective range* and trajectory of a reverse thrust. (*Author's photographs*)

PLATE 17

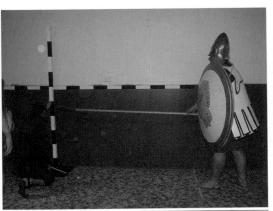

1. 'Ready' position

2. At full extension.

Plate 17.1   The recording of the *effective range* and trajectory of a low thrust. (*Author's photographs*)

1. 'Ready' position.

2. At full extension.

Plate 17.2   The recording of the *effective range* and trajectory of an underarm thrust.
(*Author's photographs*)

PLATE 18

Plate 18.1: A modern reconstruction of a close-order shield wall with the spears held in the underarm position resting in the 'cradles' created by the overlapping shields. (*Author's photograph*)

Plate 18.2   A modern reconstruction of a 2-rank close-order shield wall adopting the underarm 'ready' posture. (*Author's photograph*)

PLATE 19

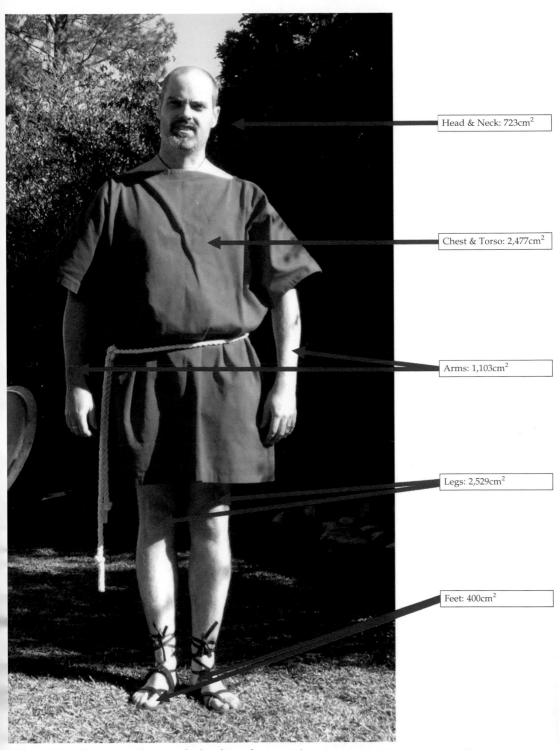

Head & Neck: 723cm^2

Chest & Torso: 2,477cm^2

Arms: 1,103cm^2

Legs: 2,529cm^2

Feet: 400cm^2

Plate 19.1   The exposed areas of a hoplite when wearing no armour. (*Author's photograph*)

PLATE 20

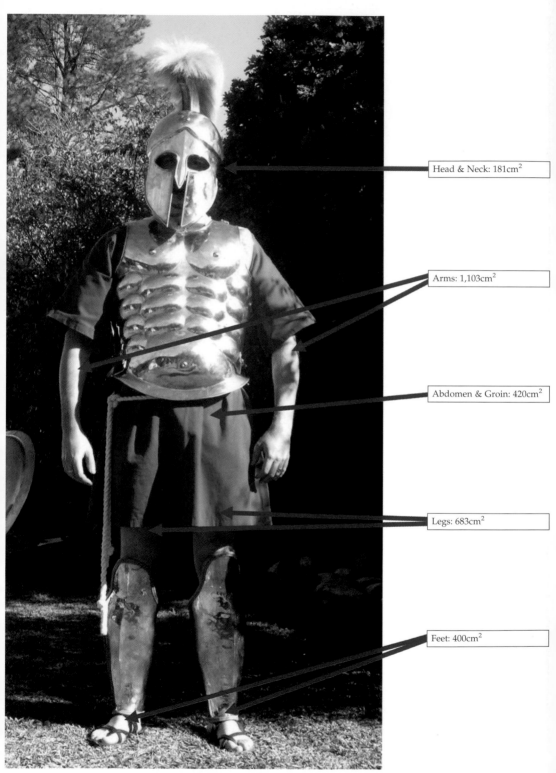

Head & Neck: 181cm^2

Arms: 1,103cm^2

Abdomen & Groin: 420cm^2

Legs: 683cm^2

Feet: 400cm^2

Plate 20.1   The exposed areas of a hoplite wearing a basic panoply. (*Author's photograph*)

PLATE 21

Head: 103cm^2

Right hand: 42cm^2

Left leg: 50cm^2

Left foot: 200cm^2

Plate 21.1　The exposed areas of a hoplite in an oblique posture and wielding the spear in the underarm position. (*Author's photograph*)

PLATE 22

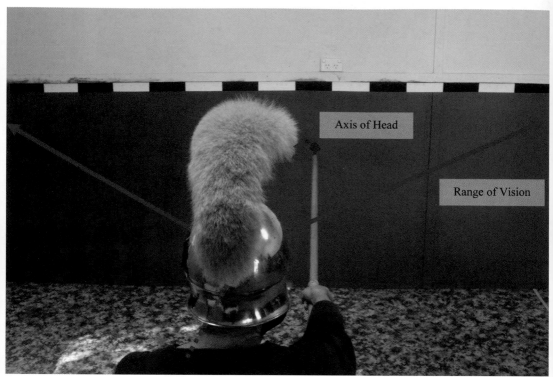

Plate 22.1   The range of vision (solid arrows) and axis of the head (dotted line) when wearing a Corinthian helmet. (*Author's photograph*)

1. The 'ready' position: hand beneath the spear.

2. Committing the attack: hand beside the spear.

3. At full extension: hand on top of the spear.

Plate 22.2   How the wrist can be 'rolled' during the action of an underarm spear thrust to alleviate muscular stress. (*Author's photographs*)

PLATE 23

Plate 23.1   Detail of the plaited hair on a bronze statuette of a Spartan hoplite. Bronze statue of a draped warrior (c.510–500BC) – gift of J. Pierpont Morgan, Wadsworth Atheneum Museum of Art, Hartford USA (1917.815). (© *Wadsworth Atheneum Museum of Art / Art resource NY*)

Plate 23.2   The penetration of 12cm of ballistics gelatine with a *sauroter*. (*Author's photographs*)

PLATE 24

Plate 24.1   Archaic Cypriot statue of Geryon showing how Sekunda believes a shield wall was formed. Cypriot limestone statue of Geryon (early fifth century BC) – The Cesnola Collection, The Metropolitan Museum of Art, New York (74.51.2586). (© *The Metropolitan Museum of Art / Art Resource NY*)

point and back again. There is very little usage of the muscles of the arm as all of the power of the strike comes from the rotation of the shoulder. As such the muscles of the arm do not easily tire. Due to the ease of this action several participants stopped due to what one subject referred to as 'the boredom factor'; there was simply no effort involved or threat to be considered, and this is reflected in many of the recorded durations of around ten minutes. Obviously, in a real combat situation 'the boredom factor' would not have been a consideration! Some participants observed that their hand had begun to ache at the ten-minute mark due to gripping the shaft tightly, but the pain was not sufficient enough to necessitate stopping the action or releasing the grip on the weapon itself. In most cases, the shaft does not have to be gripped as hard as possible, but only with enough force to keep the weapon stable and to prevent it from being knocked out of the hand. Blyth observed that the amount of kinetic energy transferred from the arm to an impacting weapon in the course of a strike was not dependent upon how strongly the weapon was held.[62] When the participants returned to the targets for their 'secondary strikes' it was observed that there was generally no reduction in the speed or power of the thrusts.

Some participants also found that it was also possible to last for fifteen minutes when wielding the spear in the underarm posture even without the 'cradle' of an interlocking shield wall to help support the weapon. Thrusts made from this position were found to be more fatiguing than those of the low stance, due to using more muscles of the arm, but it was commented that the period of 'simulated combat' could have been continued for longer. Most participants began the 'simulated combat' with the spear held between the armpit and the level of the ribcage in the proper underarm position. However, it was observed that as fatigue began to set in, some participants naturally moved into a position more akin to the low stance. This would have been one of the benefits of using these two interchangeable postures on the battlefield should the deployment of the phalanx allow it. In a close-order formation the presence of the shield wall would prevent the easy application of this alteration in technique. However, the support for the weapon provided by the 'cradle' of interlocking shields would also reduce the level of fatigue placed on the arm.

Another factor that reduced the level of fatigue experienced when performing an underarm strike was the ability to 'roll the wrist'. Underarm strikes can be performed by beginning with the hand beneath the spear with the shaft cradled in the palm. As the strike is made the arm and hand can be rotated anti-clockwise as the arm extends so that the strike finishes with the hand on top of the spear with the palm facing down (plate 22.2).

However, the rolling of the wrist is not necessary for the complete execution of the strike. Thrusts could be made with the right hand positioned under the spear shaft through the entire action of the strike. Once fatigue began to set in the grip could be altered so that the hand was on top of the shaft by simply rolling the wrist without affecting the reach, trajectory or power of the thrust. This worked the muscle groups of the arm in a slightly different manner and alleviated the earlier fatigue. The hand could also be moved to a third position on the right side of the shaft to again work the muscles of the arm differently and further reduce muscular stress without compromising the characteristics of the attack. By alternating the manner in which the shaft was gripped, available only to the underarm stance, a fifteen-minute period was endured with very little discomfort by some participants. Like strikes made from the low position, it was observed that the 'secondary strikes' of the underarm posture generally did not demonstrate any reduction in speed or power.

In contrast to this were thrusts made from the overhead position. The act of holding a spear weighing more than 1.3kg above the head and continuously thrusting with it was found to be the most fatiguing of the three tested postures. Indeed, the act of merely holding the weapon aloft, without any thrusting motion, could only be endured for a few minutes before the first signs of muscular fatigue began to manifest themselves. The longest period of 'simulated combat' endured was four minutes, with an average duration of only two minutes. Participants testing this posture reported muscle spasms and shaking of the arm after only a few minutes of thrusting. Unlike the inter-changeable nature of the low/underarm combination, the requirement to alter the grip on the weapon to move from the overhead posture to any other, and the inability to actually do so while bearing the hoplite panoply in the confines of a phalanx (see Chapter 5, Repositioning the Spear in 'Hoplite Drill'), meant that there was no way to alleviate the tension placed on the arm in this posture while continuing with some form of effective offensive action. As fatigue set in, the actions of the thrust slowed and the power behind the thrusts significantly decreased. The strength of the grip on the weapon itself also diminished significantly. One participant observed that after only a few minutes the only thing that was allowing him to keep a hold of the weapon was the leather grip wrapped around the shaft as there was little strength left in his arm or hand.

The awkward and unnatural flexing of the wrist, if combined with the constant jarring of impacts against shields and armour, would have un-doubtedly injured the wrist after only several minutes of actual combat, which would have removed the hoplite's ability to act offensively. The fatigue from the overhead strike also lasted for a considerable period of time once the session of 'simulated combat' had ceased. One subject still experienced muscle spasms after a fifteen-minute period of rest and this caused him to endure only two minutes of thrusting from the otherwise easy low position during a second session of testing.

It was generally observed that, by rocking back and forth with the action of any of the combative techniques, a natural rhythm was created that allowed for some participants to work through minor levels of fatigue. This rocking is not possible in the front-on stance forwarded in some models of hoplite warfare (see Chapter 4, Bearing the Hoplite Panoply). It was also observed that when several participants 'fought' side by side the natural sense of competition resulted in longer durations. A sense of competition would have similarly existed within a hoplite phalanx as is attested to by the awarding of a prize (ἀριστεῖον) to the man judged to be the best and bravest.[63] The 'best men' could also be selected for service in special units such as the *hippeis* (ἱππεῖς); the select men who made up the Spartan royal bodyguard.[64] Xenophon describes *gymnasia* and riding grounds full of men training to be the best in order to earn rewards from their commander.[65] This seems to confirm that it is a combination of both skill and stamina that creates the most effective warriors. Competition could have also simply been based on not wanting to appear a coward, and the simple desire to survive would have also been a strong motivator to persevere through minor levels of fatigue and discomfort.[66]

Modern people are generally unaccustomed to the harsher, more physical, lifestyle of the ancient world, and the levels of fitness and stamina in the test subjects is unlikely to be similar to that of an ancient hoplite (although, physiologically speaking, the human body has changed very little in the last three millennia). As such, the test results cannot be regarded as an accurate reflection of the endurance levels of combatants in the fifth and fourth centuries BC. However, on a comparative basis, the results show that a hoplite would likely to have been able to sustain both the low and/or underarm postures for up to (and possibly exceeding) five times longer than the overhead technique. Even if the length of time that the overhead action could be endured by the test participants is tripled to account for a higher level of stamina in the ancient hoplite, this still equates to an ability to fight in this manner for only between six to twelve minutes. This is far shorter than what most accounts of ancient battles suggest the duration of an engagement was. It can only be concluded that hoplite engagements were fought using a combination of the low and underarm techniques, which would allow for longer periods of fighting.

The results – accuracy

As was expected, the primary strikes proved to be more accurate than the secondary strikes for all three of the tested techniques (table 10).

The results demonstrate that underarm primary strikes were the most accurate, followed by the overhead and finally the low. This can be attributed to several factors. Spears in both the underarm and overhead postures point towards the general region of the throat 'kill shot' highlighted on the targets

Table 10: The proximity of primary and secondary strikes to the target area.

PRIMARY STRIKES

Distance from target	Low thrust	Overhead thrust	Underarm thrust
Within target	55%	74%	83%
1–3cm outside target	30%	23%	10%
4–6cm outside target	8%	3%	7%
7–9cm outside target	5%		
10+ cm outside target	2%		

SECONDARY STRIKES

Distance from target	Low thrust	Overhead thrust	Underarm thrust
Within target	45%	51%	63%
1–3cm outside target	24%	23%	17%
4–6cm outside target	15%	14%	10%
7–9cm outside target		3%	10%
10+ cm outside target	15%	2%	

when in their 'ready' positions. This made it easier for them to strike their targets than thrusts made with the upwardly curving low strike. Participants also commented that it was difficult to estimate the distance that they needed to stand from the target in order for the upward–curving trajectory of the low thrust to hit the area of the throat. This suggests that the low thrust was more commonly directed against larger, and generally lower, targets such as the legs or torso of an opponent, and the legs or back of a fleeing enemy.[67] The ease with which a person can run while adopting the low position suggests that these latter targets were particularly suited to this posture. Similarly, for the overhead strike to be effective, the participant had to stand close enough to the target to counter the downward curving trajectory of the thrust, whereas the strong supportive grip of the underarm stance, its flat trajectory and the axis of the head, which visually aligns the spear to its target, allowed for attacks made from this posture to be delivered with a greater level of accuracy from a greater distance.

All postures demonstrated a reduced level of accuracy in their secondary strikes due to the fatigue of the participants. The low stance experienced the smallest drop in strikes within the target zone of only 10 per cent. However, due to its inherently lower level of accuracy to begin with, this meant that less than half (45 per cent) of the secondary strikes actually hit the target. The overhead posture experienced an approximate 20 per cent reduction in accuracy, but this meant that only just more than half (51 per cent) of the overhead secondary strikes found their target. Even with the short duration of the periods of 'simulated combat' in the overhead position, no participant lasted to the point where they could no longer hold their arm above their head. As such, by standing close enough to the target, the trajectory of the strike caused the weapon to simply fall onto the 'kill shot'. Despite this, some strikes delivered from the low and overhead positions still missed the target by more than 10cm, with some missing the silhouette and one low thrust missing the target altogether.

Underarm secondary strikes also experienced a 20 per cent decrease in accuracy. However, this reduction meant that these thrusts still hit the target in 65 per cent of attacks and after a substantially longer period of endurance than in the overhead posture. The reduction in accuracy can be partially attributed to the participants moving into the low position as they became fatigued and incurring difficulties in alignment and distancing. However, those participants who kept their weapon couched in the armpit and well supported by the forearm demonstrated no reduction in accuracy and in some cases 100 per cent of both primary and secondary strikes fell within the target area. The 'cradle' of the interlocking close-order shield wall would also help guide any thrust onto a target and would no doubt contribute to a higher overall accuracy for the strike.

From the results of the tests several conclusions can be drawn:

1. That while reasonably accurate when the target is close enough to counter the downward trajectory of the thrust, the overhead posture is simply too taxing on the body's reserves of energy to allow the hoplite to fight for more than a few minutes. This does not correlate with the available evidence for the duration of many hoplite encounters. Due to the inability to change posture from the low position or from sloped over the shoulder to the overhead, if a hoplite was to use the overhead position to wield his spear he would need to have adopted it before the phalanx began to advance or charge. As a result, his arm would have been experiencing symptoms of muscular fatigue, and consequently his ability to fight would have been greatly reduced, even before the two opposing sides actually met on the battlefield. It can only be concluded that the overhead posture was not used to wield the thrusting spear in combat. Due to the restrictions imposed by the close-order shield wall, the underarm technique is the most likely mode of delivery for an attack made with the hoplite spear.

2. Both the underarm and low modes of attack could have been maintained by the members of the first two ranks of a phalanx for a period of time of more than fifteen minutes. The additional men in the file would have been able to move forward to replace the fallen or fatigued, allowing for a hoplite engagement to be played out 'for a long time' as some of the ancient accounts suggest. Consequently, those theories that suggest that *all* hoplite battles were relatively short affairs can be dismissed. Those models that propose a limit of endurance of between thirty and sixty minutes appear more viable depending upon the circumstances of the individual engagement.

3. Even an inexperienced hoplite would have had enough skill to be able to hit a small 'opportune target' on an opponent during one of these battles, at a range of two metres, with the underarm thrust in the majority of his attacks; at least until a high level of fatigue had set in. By using any of the other combative techniques, a hoplite's ability to hit a small target would have been limited to the opening minutes of the fighting.

4. Despite this ability/inability to hit a small 'opportune target', it is interesting to note that the majority of strikes that failed to hit the target area, from all three combative postures, still fell into an area smaller in size than the chest or shield of an opponent. This suggests that the chest and shield could have been easily hit during any stage of a battle. This further supports the conclusion that an opponent's shield and chest were the commonly targeted areas of hoplite combat.

5. It is unlikely that hoplite combat was a series of randomly directed attacks but was something more skilful; a form of fighting in which the combatants jabbed and probed at each other's defences until an exploitable target area presented itself.

So where would the experience of a 'professional' hoplite have provided an advantage if even an inexperienced combatant was able to hit a small 'opportune target'? Proficiency with the spear would still have played an important role in deciding a hoplite encounter. Based on the test results, an inexperienced hoplite could have only expected to hit a target with between 83 and 63 per cent of his underarm strikes; a figure that would correspondingly decrease as the engagement progressed for longer. An experienced hoplite, regularly trained to fight, such as a Spartan or a member of the Sacred Band, would undoubtedly possess a higher level of accuracy and, although that level of accuracy would similarly diminish through the course of the battle, its level would always be higher than that of the inexperienced combatant and may have also decreased at a slower rate due to the professional being conditioned for war. Professional hoplites would also have been better skilled in manouevres, defensive techniques and the maintenance of formations. All of these aspects would only further enhance the ability of the hoplite to endure the trials of hand-to-hand combat.[68] The advantage that regular training provided to a hoplite on the battlefield partially explains the longevity of Spartan military dominance and the reasoning behind the formation of 'professional' units by other city-states.

Chapter 9

The Penetration Power of the Hoplite Spear

Herodotus refers to Greek hoplites as 'men of bronze' in a reference to the armour that they wore.[1] However, this armour did not provide total protection against the weapons of the day. The available evidence demonstrates that the shield, the helmet and the cuirass could all be pierced by the hoplite spear. Yet scholarly debate continues over the ease with which a hoplite could penetrate his opponent's armour with his weapons. The examination into the penetrative abilities of the hoplite's primary weapon demonstrates that there are only two methods of fighting that will allow the spear to pierce the bronze plate armour of the hoplite and, in so doing, account for the details of wounds, fatalities and damage found in the source material. These two methods are the low and the previously unexamined underarm techniques.

Evidence pertaining to the penetrative ability of the hoplite spear is both numerous and varied across the available sources. The literary record contains no passage that specifically addresses how easy or difficult it was for a hoplite to pierce the armour worn by an opponent; with the one possible exception being the account of the death of Masistius at the battle of Plataea (see Chapter 10, The Use of the *Sauroter* as a Weapon). What the literary record does contain are numerous accounts of injuries and fatalities inflicted by weapon impacts that penetrate either the shield or the armour. Accounts such as that of Epaminondas receiving wounds through the breastplate at Mantinea, or the numerous injuries that Agesilaus received through his armour at Coronea, suggest that the hoplite spear was capable of penetrating the cuirass. Similarly, the accounts of both Brasidas and Chares suggest that the shield could be penetrated; although in Brasidas' case the penetration was not deep.[2] If it is assumed that the armour worn by the hoplite could not be penetrated, the casualties suffered on both sides of a hoplite engagement can only be the result of wounds received to the 5.5 per cent of the body not covered by elements of the panoply (much of which are areas where wounds would not be fatal). This seems unlikely and similarly suggests that the armour could be pierced.

The artistic record also contains representations of the hoplite spear penetrating both the helmet and the breastplate worn by an opponent (although depictions of the moment of impact in combat scenes are somewhat rare), as well as the representation of wounds sustained to the chest; sometimes with the cuirass still in place and sometimes without. The archaeological record additionally contains evidence that indicates that hoplite armour could be penetrated by the spear. Blyth identified twenty pieces of armour (predominantly helmets) in the collection of Olympia that display battle-related perforations, and a further 150 pieces that display dents and scarring caused by weapon impacts.[3] A more recent survey of armour at Olympia examined twenty-nine examples of weapon impacts that had cleanly perforated the bronze plate, and fifty-six examples of impacts that had resulted in denting and/or scarring (see plate 9). This evidence suggests that, in some instances at least, the bronze armour worn by the hoplite could be penetrated by the weapons of the day. It seems quite reasonable to conclude that the armour worn by the hoplite must have been able to provide at least some form of protection or it would have been made thicker (there is no point wearing armour if it is not going to protect you). Similarly, in a somewhat bizarre balance between defence and offence, this very same armour had to have been able to be penetrated by the spear or something else would have become the hoplite's primary weapon.

Despite this seemingly conclusive evidence for the ability of the spear to pierce hoplite armour, there is some disagreement amongst scholars as to how easily this could be accomplished. Van Wees states that it was quite plausible for the weapons of the hoplite period to penetrate armour.[4] Similarly, Snodgrass claims that the damaged armour at Olympia is proof that it could be easily penetrated.[5] However, Snodgrass fails to appreciate that there are substantially more pieces of armour at Olympia with only dents or scarring than there are with clean penetrations, and there are many other examples of dedicated armour that show no signs of extensive combative damage whatsoever. Counter to these claims, Hanson states that hoplite armour could withstand most impacts, which may have only dented it, unless the strike was delivered at the run to gain extra momentum behind it.[6] Everson states that the curved surface of the muscled cuirass would have been a good defence against glancing blows, but a 'well aimed direct thrust' would have punched through the bronze plate and may only have been stopped by any padding or lining underneath.[7] Despite this lack of consensus among scholars, very little empirical analysis has been undertaken to validate any of these theories.

Blyth, in his examination of the effectiveness of hoplite armour against archery fire, extrapolated from data relating to the velocities that modern athletes can throw various pieces of sporting equipment and adjusted the figures to reflect a thrusting action. He determined that a thrust with a hand-held spear moving at 29.5 feet per second (ft/sec) or 9.0 metres per second (m/sec) could be delivered with an energy of 22.1 foot pounds (fpds) or 30.0 joules (j); half as much energy as that delivered by a missile with a similar weight. Blyth concedes that, due to his estimations, the margin of error for his calculations may be as high as 50 per cent; which would give an upper limit of the energy of a spear thrust of around 33.2fpds (45.0j).[8] He concludes by stating that only blows with an energy in excess of 22.1fpds (30.0j) would be capable of piercing hoplite armour.[9] This suggests that the damaged armour he identified at Olympia may have been the result of 'freak' attacks delivered with a higher than average level of energy or that his own estimations for the energy delivered with a spear thrust may be too low.

In another examination, Gabriel and Metz conducted numerous tests on the effectiveness of various pieces of ancient weaponry, including the spear, using functional replicas. Their data was gathered by filming a man 6ft (183cm) tall and weighing 180lb (82kg), which they concede is taller and heavier than the average ancient warrior, using high-speed strobe photography of ten, thirty and sixty frames per second, while using each of the weapons in front of a graduated scale.[10] Measurements were taken of thrusts made with a spear weighing 1.5lb (680g) from both the low and overhead positions (called the 'underhand' and 'overhand' positions respectively in the text) as well as for the weapon being thrown like a javelin.[11] Measuring the distance that a select point on the weapon travelled between each frame of the strobe photography allowed for the velocity of the action to be determined in feet per second.[12] A velocity of 55.0ft/sec (16.8m/sec) is given for the overhand action and a velocity of 24ft/sec (7.3m/sec) is given for the underhand thrust.[13]

However, the figure given for the velocity of the overhand action (55.0ft/sec or 16.8m/sec) seems exceedingly fast for a method of attack involving a hand-held weapon that is thrust rather than swung. The recorded velocity for a thrusting attack made with a Roman *gladius* is given as only 28.0ft/sec (8.5m/sec), which is not overly different from the velocity given for a low spear thrust of 24ft/sec (7.3m/sec) or the velocity of the spear thrust used by Blyth of 29.5ft/sec (9.0m/sec).[14] The similarity of these figures is no doubt due to both thrusting actions following a similar, and natural, movement of the arm. It seems unlikely that an overhead spear thrust, which follows a somewhat more unnatural movement of the arm and wrist, could be delivered more than twice as fast. This suggests that the figure given by Gabriel and Metz for the 'overhand' technique is for a thrown weapon rather than for a thrust.[15]

The energy delivered by each action (measured in foot pounds) was calculated by inserting the mass of the weapon and the recorded velocity of each action into the following formula used by the US Army Ballistics Laboratory:[16]

$$\text{Energy (fpds)} = \frac{(\text{weight of the weapon}) \times (\text{velocity})^2}{64\,(\text{value of the gravitational constant})}$$

resulting in the following calculated amounts of energy being delivered through the impacting point of the spear:

Overhead (thrown):

$$\frac{1.5\,(\text{weight}) \times 55\,(\text{velocity})^2}{64\,(\text{gravitational constant})} = \textbf{70.8fpds (95.0j) of energy}$$

Low (thrust):

$$\frac{1.5\,(\text{weight}) \times 24\,(\text{velocity})^2}{64\,(\text{gravitational constant})} = \textbf{13.5fpds (18.0j) of energy}$$

The 'killing power' of each action was calculated by examining the area of a wound the weapon would produce upon impact by measuring the circumference of the opening it would create and the size of its impact edge; in this case the tip of the spearhead (table 11).[17]

Table 11: The findings of Gabriel and Metz on the velocity, energy and impact area of a spear.[18]

Action type	Weight (pounds)	Velocity (feet/second)	Impact area	Wound area (circumference)	Impact energy (foot pounds)
Overhead (thrown)	1.5lb (680g)	55.0ft/sec (16.8m/s)	1/32″ (0.7mm)	3.6″ (91.4mm)	70.8 fpds (95.0 joules)
Low (thrust)	1.5lb (680g)	24.0ft/sec (7.3m/s)	1/32″ (0.7mm)	3.6″ (91.4mm)	13.5 fpds (18.0 joules)

The amount of energy required to penetrate bronze armour was tested using 2.0mm thick brass target plates as the amount of energy required to penetrate both brass and bronze is almost identical.[19] Baseline tests using a bow and arrow (the easiest weapon to produce a standardized series of velocities over multiple impacts) concluded that an arrow needed to hit the target with approximately 75.7fpds (103.0j) of energy to penetrate the armour to what was considered a 'killing depth' – the two-inch deep fatal wound described by Vegetius in relation to the Roman *gladius*.[20] The results of this baseline test were then extrapolated to determine the impact energy required for other weapons to pierce the same 2mm thick plate to the 'killing depth'. This was calculated as a function of the weapon's impact area and the size of the opening it created.[21]

From these experiments and calculations, Gabriel and Metz determined that it requires 137.0fpds (186.0j) of energy for a spear to penetrate a 2mm thick bronze plate to a depth that would result in death or serious injury.[22] In comparison, they state that it requires only 2.0fpds (3.0j) of energy to penetrate flesh and 68.0fpds (92.0j) to fracture any bone in the human body apart from the skull, which requires an impact with an energy of 90.0fpds (122.0j) to fracture. A blow to the head with an energy level of between 56.0 and 79.0fpds (76.0–107.0j) would cause unconsciousness.[23]

Based upon these results, Gabriel and Metz conclude that no weapon in the ancient world could be delivered against an opponent with enough energy to penetrate 2.0mm bronze plate armour except for a narrow-headed axe.[24] They state that two opposing hoplites would have found it difficult to deliver a fatal blow with a spear because the energy delivered with their spear thrusts would have been too low to penetrate the armour that they wore.[25] Strangely, Gabriel and Metz later state that 77 per cent of the wounds detailed by Homer are fatal.[26] As the majority of wounds and fatalities detailed in the *Iliad* are to the area of the chest and head (see Chapter 7, The 'Kill Shot' of Hoplite Combat), this statement seems to contradict their own findings. Gabriel and Metz's conclusion also fails to correlate with the other available sources of evidence, all of which suggest that hoplite armour could be pierced. The tabulated results of Gabriel and Metz's tests were later quoted by Hanson, and may be the source of his conclusion that hoplite armour could not be penetrated by the weapons of the time.[27] However, there are many factors that need to be considered in order to make any calculation of the penetrative abilities of the spear accurately reflect the environment of the hoplite battlefield. The refinement of the data gathered by Gabriel and Metz with the combination of these factors demonstrates that the armour worn by the hoplite could be pierced by the spear.

The width of the hoplite spearhead

The width of the common 'J style' hoplite spearhead averages 1.5in (3.8cm) at a point two inches back from the tip due to the angle of its tapering and the minimal amount of ribbing present. This means that a spear equipped with this style of head would create an opening with a circumference approximately 3in (7.6cm) in size when it penetrated a target to the 'killing depth' of two inches. Hoplite spears equipped with any of the smaller, yet still common, types of spearhead (such as the 'E', 'F', 'M' and 'R' styles) would create an even smaller opening when penetrating to the same depth. Thus the figure for the 'wound opening' used by Gabriel and Metz to calculate the required energy to penetrate a 2.0mm thick target plate (3.6in), while no doubt correct for the spear used in their tests, must be adjusted to reflect the narrower head of the hoplite weapon. Recalculating the energy required based upon an average opening of only 3in for the hoplite spear shows that a reduced amount of only 113.0fpds (153.0j) of energy is needed to penetrate a 2.0mm thick target plate to the 'killing depth'.

The thickness of hoplite armour

Additionally, the majority of hoplite armour in the Classical Age was not 2.0mm thick like the plates used in Gabriel and Metz's experiments and calculations. The thickness of both the helmet and the cuirass averages only 1.0mm.[28] The thickness of the armour will influence the ease with which it can be penetrated by a weapon. Put simply: the thicker the armour, the more energy is required for a weapon to penetrate it. The thickness of the armour can be incorporated into the calculation of the energy required to pierce it by the inclusion of an 'energy multiplier' into the equation. Williams, in his analysis of the effectiveness of medieval armour, details a scale of 'energy multipliers' that can be used to reflect the ease (or difficulty) with which armour of different thickness can be pierced (table 12).

Table 12: The 'energy multiplier' required to calculate the penetration of armour of varying thickness.[29]

Thickness of Armour	1.0mm	1.5mm	2.0mm	2.5mm	3.0mm	3.5mm
Energy Multiplier	1.0×	1.9×	2.9×	4.1×	5.5×	7.0×

Based upon Williams' scale it requires almost three times more energy to penetrate a target with a thickness of 2.0mm than it does to penetrate a target with a thickness of 1.0mm to the same depth. Thus the figure of 113.0fpds (153.0j), calculated as the amount of energy required for the hoplite spear to penetrate 2.0mm thick plate, can be reconfigured to only 39.0fpds (52.9j) of energy required to pierce a plate of the same thickness as the armour worn by the Classical hoplite.[30]

The angle of impact and the curvature of the armour

Further still, both the angle at which a spear impacts with a target, and the curvature of the surface of the target itself, will also affect the ease with which it can be penetrated. The arrow impacts conducted by Gabriel and Metz to determine the resistance of bronze plate struck a flat, 2.0mm thick, target inclined at an approximate angle of forty-five degrees. This was done to simulate the downward trajectories of most swung weapons, such as swords or axes; although, as Gabriel concedes, a thrusting weapon such as a spear would impact at a flatter angle.[31] However, the majority of surfaces on hoplite armour are not flat like the targets used by Gabriel and Metz in their testing. The helmet, regardless of style, possesses many rounded surfaces, as does the 'muscled' cuirass with its representative musculature, and both the bell cuirass and composite corslet with their curved 'barrel-shaped' torsos. Williams states that, due to the curvature of the medieval plate cuirass, even a flat thrust connecting with its curved surface will hit at an adjusted angle equivalent to 0–45° from the perpendicular depending upon where on its surface it is struck.[32]

The curves of hoplite armour would have similarly reduced the probability of any thrust impacting perpendicular with its surface and may have caused weaker strikes to simply glance off; as is suggested by Everson.[33] It is only the flatter back panels of the cuirass, which have little or no representative musculature depending upon the style, which would be more prone to weapons hitting at an angle close to the perpendicular. This may account for the number of examples of armour at Olympia that are dented or scarred rather than penetrated. This may have also been one of the reasons for the stylized musculature on the 'muscled' cuirass; the varied contours of its surface would have made it almost impossible for an attack to strike it at the most energy-efficient angle.

Similar to the principles relating to the thickness of the armour, the greater the angle of impact, the greater the amount of energy is required for a weapon to penetrate. In his work, Williams also provides a scale of 'energy multipliers' that can be incorporated into any calculation to reflect the angle (either actual or equivalent) of impact (table 13).

Thus a weapon striking a target at an angle of 45° requires 40 per cent more energy to penetrate to a certain depth than is required to achieve the same result with a weapon impacting the same target at a perpendicular angle. With the incorporation of both 'energy multipliers' for thickness and angle of impact, the readjusted figure of 113.0fpds (153.0j) of required energy for the hoplite spear to penetrate a 2.0mm thick target plate inclined at a forty-five degree angle can be recalculated (again) and tabulated as follows to account for both the thickness of the target and the angle at which the spear strikes it (table 14).

The weight of the hoplite spear

One aspect that is vital in making any calculation of the penetrative abilities of hoplite weaponry is the inclusion of the correct weight of the hoplite spear itself. The stated weight of the weapon used by Gabriel and Metz is 1.5lb

Table 13: The 'energy multiplier' required to calculate the penetration of armour at varying angles.[34]

Angle of impact away from the perpendicular	0°	20°	30°	40°	45°	50°	60°
Energy multiplier	1.0×	1.1×	1.2×	1.3×	1.4×	1.6×	2.0×

Table 14: The energy required to penetrate armour of different thicknesses at different angles.

Angle of impact away from the perpendicular	0°	20°	30°	40°	45°	50°	60°
Thickness of armour	Energy required for penetration – fpds (*joules*)						
1.0mm	28 (*38*)	31 (*41*)	33 (*45*)	36 (*49*)	39 (*53*)	45 (*60*)	56 (*76*)
1.5mm	53 (*72*)	58 (*79*)	63 (*86*)	69 (*93*)	74 (*100*)	85 (*115*)	106 (*143*)
2.0mm	81 (*110*)	89 (*120*)	97 (*131*)	105 (*142*)	113 (*153*)	129 (*175*)	162 (*219*)
2.5mm	114 (*155*)	125 (*170*)	137 (*186*)	148 (*201*)	160 (*217*)	183 (*248*)	228 (*310*)
3.0mm	153 (*208*)	168 (*228*)	184 (*249*)	199 (*270*)	215 (*291*)	245 (*333*)	306 (*415*)
3.5mm	195 (*265*)	214 (*290*)	234 (*317*)	253 (*344*)	273 (*370*)	312 (*423*)	390 (*529*)

(680g) and the weight of the weapon used by Blyth is 1.8lb (800g). Both of these are far too light to accurately replicate the dynamics of a hoplite spear with an average weight of around 3.1lb (1,400g). Gabriel confirms that the spear used in their experiments was devoid of a *sauroter* as most spears in the ancient world, other than those used by the Greeks, possessed no such large weight on the rear end of the shaft.[35] However, the difference in mass between the average hoplite weapon and those used by both Blyth and Gabriel and Metz greatly alters the amount of energy that can be brought to bear against a target. Simply inserting a corrected mass of 3.1lb into the formulae used by Gabriel and Metz (while retaining their figures for velocity) gives the following increased amounts of impact energy:

Overhead (thrown):

$$\frac{3.1\,(\text{weight}) \times 55\,(\text{velocity})^2}{64\,(\text{gravitational constant})} = \textbf{146fpds (198j) of energy}$$

Low (thrust):

$$\frac{3.1\,(\text{weight}) \times 24\,(\text{velocity})^2}{64\,(\text{gravitational constant})} = \textbf{28fpds (38j) of energy}$$

Based upon this, even attacks delivered with the slower velocity of the low thrust recorded by Gabriel and Metz would penetrate 1.0mm thick hoplite armour to a 'killing depth' of two inches so long as its impact connected with the target at an angle close to the perpendicular. Attacks made at the velocity given by Blyth (29.5ft/sec) would be delivered with an energy of 42.2fpds (57.2j), which would penetrate at angles of up to 45°. The results of these recalculations clearly demonstrate that a weapon with a greater mass delivers greater energy and would thus have a higher probability of penetrating a target. As such, it is possible to add another function of the *sauroter* to those already listed by previous scholars: to add to the overall mass of the weapon so as to allow for the easier penetration of an opponent's armour.[36]

The encumbrance of the panoply

However, what effect would a heavier weapon have on the velocity at which it could be delivered? Additionally, how would the armour worn by the hoplite impede these actions and limit or slow the attack? It is unlikely that the extrapolations of athletic data made by Blyth included any consideration of the encumbrance of the hoplite panoply. Gabriel confirms that the test subject used in their experiments was not encumbered by any form of armour, and was therefore not impeded by any of the limitations that this equipment would impose. This was based upon the assumption that Greek armour, other than the early bell cuirass, would not be overly restrictive.[37] However, the results of tests made into the reach and trajectory of different hoplite combative techniques demonstrate that the rigid shoulder sections of the cuirass greatly impede the movement of the weapon–bearing arm in both the overhead and reverse positions. Additionally, the large diameter of the *aspis* would obstruct the full movement of the arm in many postures if it was kept in a defensive position across the body (see Chapter 6, The Reach and Trajectory of Attacks made with the Hoplite Spear).

To determine the effect that the mass of the hoplite spear and restrictions of the panoply have on the velocity of a spear thrust, and to obtain comparative data for all four hoplite combative techniques, a test participant 5ft 5in (168cm) tall and weighing 165lb (75kg) was filmed at a rate of ten frames per second performing attacking actions before a graduated scale while wearing a reconstructed hoplite panoply. Five spear thrusts were delivered from each of the low, underarm, overhead and reverse positions and with a minimal level of shield and body movement. The footage of each thrust was then broken down, and its time index analysed using computer software, so that the velocity of each thrust to its *combat range* (the most effective point of impact for penetration) could be calculated. The average velocity of each series of spear thrusts was then determined (table 15).

The velocities recorded for the low and underarm thrust are similar (although slightly lower) to those given by both Blyth and Gabriel and Metz; possibly due to the extra weight of the weapon involved and the encumbrance of the panoply. Importantly, the velocity recorded for the overhead thrust is vastly lower than the 55.0ft/sec (16.8m/sec) given by Gabriel and Metz. This supports the conclusion that the figure provided in their text is for a thrown,

Table 15: The recorded velocities of spear thrusts made by an encumbered hoplite.

Thrust type	Measured velocity
Low thrust	26.0ft/sec (8.1m/sec)
Underarm thrust	26.6ft/sec (8.3m/sec)
Overhead thrust	21.3ft/sec (6.5m/sec)
Reverse thrust	21.2ft/sec (6.5m/sec)

rather than a thrust, weapon. As was expected, the unnatural movement of the arm as it extends, the limited reach of the weapon and/or the restrictive nature of the shoulder sections of the cuirass all contributed to slower velocities being recorded for the reverse and overhead postures than were measured for the low and underarm techniques. From these recorded velocities, the following amounts of deliverable energy can be calculated (table 16):

Based upon these calculations, an attack made with a spear held in the low position will penetrate 1.0mm thick hoplite plate armour to a 'killing depth' of two inches at angles of impact (whether actual or equivalent) of up to 30°. This agrees with the adjusted findings based upon the velocities recorded by Blyth, and Gabriel and Metz. Due to the ability to keep a spear thrust using the low technique level through the flexing of the wrist, all low strikes can be delivered against a flat surface with an impacting angle less than 30° (although greater angles are possible when the wrist is not flexed). Thus what will prevent a low thrust from piercing an opponent's armour is the curvature of that armour itself, which may increase the effective angle of impact.

Attacks made with the underarm technique will pierce the same armour at angles of up to nearly 40°. Due to the flat trajectory of the underarm technique, most strikes will impact at an angle less than 10° and, again, it is only the curvature of the target that may inhibit penetration. Conversely, the downward-curving trajectory and slower velocity of an overhead thrust would be incapable of penetrating hoplite armour regardless of the angle of impact, as would an attack made using the reverse technique. Consequently, overhead attacks cannot account for the details of wounds and fatalities found in the ancient texts,

Table 16: The energy of spear thrusts made by an encumbered hoplite.

Low	3.1 (weight) × 26.0 (velocity)^2 ÷ 64 (gravitational constant) = **32.7fpds (44.3j) of energy**
Underarm	3.1 (weight) × 26.6 (velocity)^2 ÷ 64 (gravitational constant) = **34.3fpds (46.5j) of energy**
Overhead	3.1 (weight) × 21.3 (velocity)^2 ÷ 64 (gravitational constant) = **22.0fpds (29.8j) of energy**
Reverse	3.1 (weight) × 21.3 (velocity)^2 ÷ 64 (gravitational constant) = **22.0fpds (29.8j) of energy**

nor account for the damage to the armour found at Olympia.[38] This further indicates that the posture that forms the very basis of all previous scholarship into hoplite warfare cannot have been used by the hoplite to wield his weapon in combat.

There are several other factors that will affect the ease or difficulty experienced by a hoplite when attempting to penetrate the armour worn by his opponent. However, many of these factors are difficult to quantify.

Hardness, brittleness and imperfections in the armour

The processes involved in the manufacture of ancient armour can result in varying levels of hardness and/or brittleness in the metal, which can make a cuirass or helmet either harder or easier to penetrate. The process of annealing, the heating and cooling of the metal (either naturally or by quenching depending upon whether it is a ferrous metal like iron or a non-ferrous metal like bronze) relieves stresses in the metal and makes it softer to work with.[39] However, the temperature to which the metal is heated will affect its subsequent hardness. For example, a metal 'partially annealed' to 600°C will be 32 per cent harder than the same metal annealed to a temperature of 800°C.[40] Archaic Era Greek helmets were annealed at around 800°C, which resulted in a bronze with a hardness of 95–100 Brinell (B).[41]

Metal can also be 'cold worked'. As the name suggests, 'cold working' is the shaping of the metal while it is cold. In the case of bronze, it would need to be regularly re-softened by annealing. However, if this is done too often, the structure of the metal can separate, resulting in it becoming brittle and cracking.[42] Many later Corinthian helmets show signs of being 'cold worked'. Due to the partial annealing involved in cold working the bronze, the later helmets have an increased hardness of 160B. This harder metal allowed for helmets and armour to be made thinner (reducing its weight and making the hoplite more mobile) and yet provide a similar, if not better, level of protection than earlier, thicker and heavier elements of the panoply.[43]

The presence of impurities such as carbon or slag in the metal as a result of the smelting, annealing and/or working processes will also influence the hardness and/or brittleness of the metal and may result in weak points in plate armour. The fewer impurities present in the metal, the better the armour will be. For example, the presence of even 1–2 per cent slag in steel armour can reduce its toughness by as much as 25 per cent.[44] Variances in the levels of the components that make up an alloy such as bronze will similarly affect its hardness. The higher the copper content of the bronze, the softer it will be. Most hoplite armour is made of a bronze with a tin content of 7.1–11.8 per cent (average 9.5 per cent); with little change in chemical composition across the Archaic and Classical periods.[45] The addition of other elements into the alloy will also affect the resultant metal. For example, the addition of only 1 per cent phosphorus into the mix (an element common is some modern forms of bronze) can significantly alter the resulting alloy.

As with thickness and angle of impact, the ease or difficulty of penetration will vary with the hardness and brittleness of the armour being struck. However, due to the varied nature of how differences in the hardness of the armour could occur, this cannot be adequately simulated with the simple inclusion of a 'force multiplier' into any calculation. As such, the possibility of a hoplite wearing an inferior set of armour, or of a spear striking a weak point in an otherwise strong set of armour, must remain a possibility but cannot be taken into account empirically.

Padding, linings and clothing

Armour and helmets also do not sit snugly against the body or the head. Due to the nature of the armour and the variances in body shape from individual to individual, there are many places where the surface of the armour sits away from the flesh. Most early Corinthian-style helmets sit away from the surface of the head by about 1cm due to their curvature.[46] Much of this space would have been filled with padding such as the felt *pilos* cap, which was commonly worn under the helmet to help make it sit securely on the head and to help dissipate heat. The presence of linings within the helmet would also aid these processes as would a large mass of hair. It is hardly surprising that the militaristic Spartans placed an emphasis on possessing a full head of long locks or that their hair was regularly dressed prior to battle.[47] A sixth century bronze figurine of a Spartan (possibly an officer) clearly shows his hair plaited into long braids which hang down below the bottom of the helmet. A statuette of a Lakonian warrior from Dodona exhibits a similar hair style. A thick 'padding' of these braids would have acted in a similar capacity to the felt *pilos* (plate 23.1).

By the fourth century BC, the later styles of Corinthian helmets may have sat away from the surface of the head by as much as 2cm due to the repoussé ridging used to reinforce the brow, with possibly 1cm of padding between the sides of the helmet and the head.[48] All of these forms of padding and lining would require a spear thrust to penetrate further, requiring more energy, in order to open the breech in the plate wider so as to allow the tip of the spear to reach a depth that would cause any form of injury. Depending upon the material the lining/inner cap was made from (felt or leather etc.), as well as the presence of hair and how tightly it was plaited, extra padding beneath the helmet would cause greater friction on the surface of the spearhead as it passed through, thus slowing the rate of penetration; again requiring more energy behind the thrust for it to reach an injury causing depth. As well as dissipating heat, the linings of the helmet would also help absorb and dissipate the energy of an impact to the head which may have otherwise resulted in unconsciousness.[49] As a consequence, a spear thrust that impacted with only enough energy to just overcome the plate of the helmet may not have possessed enough residual energy to carry on through the linings, padding and spaces underneath to injure the wearer.

Similarly, the muscled cuirass, and both the 'bell' and composite corslet, do not sit flush against the surface of the body. In many places there are gaps of up to 1cm or more between the body and the inner surface of the armour, depending upon its fit and how tightly it is done up. Linings may have been attached to the undersides of the breastplate to provide a more comfortable (and more secure) fit, padding may have been worn on the shoulders to cushion the weight of the armour and prevent chaffing, and tunics would have been worn beneath them as well. All of these additional layers would have helped prevent a weaker blow from carrying through to injure the body. Thus the claims made by Everson that a 'well aimed direct thrust' may have punched through the bronze plate only to be stopped by any padding or lining underneath is fundamentally correct, even though it is unlikely that this conclusion was based upon the characteristics of the underarm technique.[50]

The effect of momentum

Hanson suggests that the ability of the hoplite spear to penetrate armour was only possible with the addition of the momentum of the advancing phalanx.[51] As Blyth points out:

> ... it may seem that the most effective method of using a hand weapon would be one in which an effective link between the hand and the weapon is maintained during the blow so that some or all of the potential energy of the body is added to the weapon.[52]

However, the transference of the body's potential energy to the impact of the weapon occurs only when the link between the body and the weapon is sufficiently rigid, well supported and, most importantly, maintained.[53] This level of support only occurs in the underarm 'ready' position due to the way the spear is gripped, supported by the forearm and locked in place between the arm and the body. Once the weapon is thrust forward of this position into the attack, the strong link between the weapon and the body is broken. Similarly, the weaker grips of the low, overhead and underarm techniques possess no linkage between the body and the weapon at any point during the process of a strike. Tests conducted by Blyth demonstrate that, regardless of how tight the weapon is held at the moment of impact, little of the kinetic energy of the arm or hand is transferred to the blow if the link between weapon and body is not strong.[54]

Maintaining a strong link between the body and the weapon greatly enhances a weapon's impact energy through the addition of body mass and any momentum into the action. For example, a 154lb (70kg) hoplite charging at 16ft/sec (5m/sec) with the spear held in the well-supported underarm 'ready position' delivers approximately 647fpds (875j) of energy through the tip of the weapon upon impact with a target, so long as the spear is retained in its couched position and not thrust forward into the attack.[55] Once the spear is thrust forward, the strong link between the body and the spear is broken and no transference of potential energy can take place due to the weakened grip and the flexibility of the arm's construction. If the ability of the target to resist penetration is greater than the force applied to it via the point of the weapon, the body and the weapon will move independently.[56] In other words, if a hoplite charging against an opposing phalanx thrusts his weapon forward just prior to the moment of impact, and the thrust did not have enough energy behind it to penetrate the shield or the armour of that opponent, the weapon would simply be forced backwards, potentially out of the hoplite's hand, as the momentum of the charge and thrust continued to drive their body forward.

This partially explains why the members of the front rank of a close-order phalanx would have kept their spears couched (see Chapter 6, The Reach and Trajectory of Attacks made with the Hoplite Spear). Not only did this decrease the distance between the two sides, which allowed the second rank of the close-order formation to engage, but by keeping their weapons in place at the moment two phalanxes met, they presented a well-supported line of spears. Attacking forces who charged against this formation in a more open-order may have simply impaled themselves on the weapons of their enemies due to the impetus of their own attack. Thus Hanson's statement that the armour of the hoplite could be penetrated only with the added energy of the charge is wrong on several points. Firstly, the armour worn by the hoplite could be pierced with a spear thrust delivered by a stationary hoplite. Secondly, the augmentation of momentum to the penetrative power of the spear only occurs with the use of the underarm 'ready' position and not in any of the combative actions of the hoplite; particularly the low/overhead two stance model upon which all of his theories are based.

The effect of fatigue

Fatigue will also reduce the levels at which a blow would be effective against armour. It is most likely that the first deliberate attack made in a combat situation (i.e. not a jab or a probe or a defensive measure, but a fully committed thrust with the intent of penetrating the armour and killing the opponent) will be the strongest. Subsequent thrusts, carried out in battle, will be weaker and slower due to the muscular fatigue of the arm.

Even if the overhead or reverse thrusts were capable of being delivered with enough energy to penetrate an opponent's armour with the first attack, the taxing nature of either technique would make any strike made after the first minute of combat practically useless (see Chapter 8, Endurance and Accuracy when Fighting with the Hoplite Spear). However, a hoplite could not guarantee that his first attack would not be parried or evaded in some other way. As such, hoplite warfare must have involved a method of fighting that allowed the combatants to be effective for a considerably longer period of time; enough time to engage an opponent, probe his defences, defend himself if need be and then, if the opportunity arose, deliver a killing blow against the chest or head with sufficient energy behind it to penetrate the armour and padding deep enough to either kill or incapacitate the enemy. The only combative techniques that allow for this to occur are the low and underarm attacks.

Attacks made using the underarm technique can accommodate up to an 18 per cent reduction in energy (due to fatigue for example) and yet still remain effective against 1mm thick armour if struck perpendicular to the surface. This, combined with the ability to rest the spear in the 'cradle' created by the interlocking shields of the shield wall and fight, even in an intermediate-order formation, for periods of fifteen minutes or more, would have allowed the hoplite to function on the battlefield for a considerably longer period of time than if he had been using the overhead or reverse techniques. Similarly, low strikes can undergo a 14 per cent reduction in energy and still remain effective against targets struck perpendicular. The natural movement of the arm during a low strike, and the minimal levels of fatigue this causes, would have allowed a hoplite to fight almost indefinitely using this method if he had sufficient room to adopt the position.

Where the low thrust would have been the most efficient recourse for the use of the spear would have been during the pursuit of a routed enemy. The low posture is the easiest to run with and a pursuing army may not have necessarily maintained its formation, which would allow the low posture to be adopted. As the back of the cuirass is generally flatter than its front, low spear thrusts would have a higher likelihood of impacting with the back of the cuirass at a perpendicular angle. Even with its lower levels of impact energy, the low thrust would be able to easily pierce the back of a fleeing enemy. The low levels of fatigue brought on by the use of the low technique means that a pursuing hoplite would be able to chase down enemies at will so long as he could continue to run in pursuit.

This accounts for the large differences between the number of casualties sustained by a victorious hoplite army and those sustained by the vanquished. While both sides faced each other on the battlefield, many attacks would have been parried, taken on the shield, or deflected by the curvature of the cuirass or helmet. The number of scarred or dented pieces of armour at Olympia compared with the number with clean perforations attests to the regularity of spear thrusts being turned by the armour. Other impacts would have been delivered at an efficient angle but with insufficient energy behind them; resulting in only shallow penetrations, some of which may have failed to penetrate any padding beneath the armour, with little or no resultant injury. It is these sorts of superficial wounds that would have been sustained by Epaminondas at Mantinea and Agesilaus at Coronea. Some attacks would have been delivered at both an efficient angle and with enough energy and would have slain or incapacitated an opponent. As the battle wore on, both sides would have suffered casualties from these types of attacks. However, in relation to the total numbers involved in the battle on both sides, their numbers would have been small. Thus prior to the moment when one side began to rout, both phalanxes would have suffered approximately 5 per cent casualties. However, once one side broke and fled they left the most vulnerable part of their torso, their backs, exposed to the attacks of the pursuing enemy; resulting in a further 10 per cent casualties or more.[57]

As such, it can be concluded that the curvature of the 1.0mm thick plate cuirass (or its thicker composite equivalent) provided the hoplite with a good deal of protection on the battlefield while he continued to face his enemy. The thickness of the corslet was a compromise between having heavier armour, which would have given better protection at the expense of mobility, and thinner armour that provided enough mobility to allow the hoplite to fight while at the same time providing good protection, when combined with the shield, except against attacks that were delivered with enough force and at the most energy-efficient angle.

It is only the use of the low and underarm techniques by the hoplite in battle that could overcome these defences and so correlate with all of the existing evidence for the nature of hoplite warfare. Not only are the low and underarm thrusts the only ones capable of being delivered with enough energy to penetrate the armour worn by the hoplite, accounting for the wounds and fatalities detailed in the available sources, but they are the only ones that allowed the hoplite to fight for an extended period of time. More than anything else, the inability of a thrust delivered from the overhead position (and similarly the reverse position) to account for the details of wounds and fatalities found in the ancient sources indicates that this method cannot have been used by the hoplite in combat. As such, any model of hoplite warfare based upon the use of this stance cannot be correct.

Chapter 10

The Use of the *Sauroter* as a Weapon

The *sauroter* on the rear end of the hoplite's spear performed a variety of functions: it set the balance of the weapon and added weight to its overall mass, it protected the end of the shaft from the elements and it allowed the weapon to be thrust upright into the ground when not in use. Previous scholarship has also offered several possible offensive uses of the *sauroter* as well. However, these models are based upon scant, often circumstantial, evidence and little analysis of whether the conclusions made conform to even the models of hoplite warfare forwarded by the same scholar. The characteristics and conditions under which it is suggested that the *sauroter* was used offensively, indicate that its employment in this manner is unlikely to have been a common battlefield practice of the Classical hoplite.

The use of the *sauroter* as an ancillary weapon

Some scholars have suggested that the *sauroter* was used as a secondary weapon if the spear borne by the hoplite broke during the course of a battle.[1] Everson claims that this was a feature of earlier, Mycenaean era, warfare, although the basis for this conclusion is not provided.[2] Hanson claims that 'the butt-spike allowed the hoplite a few more thrusts until he was finally forced to go to his secondary, and much less adequate, short sword'.[3] Mitchell states that the *sauroter* was used as a secondary weapon even when two spears were carried, neither of which he claims were thrown.[4] However, it seems unclear why the spike on the end of one spear would be used in combat if a second, intact, spear was still being carried. Sekunda, one of the few detractors of these models, states that there is little evidence for the use of the *sauroter* as a secondary weapon.[5]

There is, in fact, no evidence at all to support the use of the *sauroter* as an ancillary weapon. Diodorus states that once the hoplite had broken his spear, he continued to fight using his sword, not the *sauroter* attached to the remaining section of the shaft.[6] Herodotus states that the Spartans on the third day of the battle of Thermopylae resorted to using their teeth and hands only when both their spears and swords had been broken in the fighting.[7] The Spartans must have drawn their swords as secondary weapons when their spears had become unserviceable and the broken shaft and *sauroter* were most likely discarded on the field as there is no reference to the use of the *sauroter* as a weapon. Xenophon's account of the aftermath of Coronea also details the use of the sword as a secondary weapon as some are still held in the hands of the dead.[8] Broken spears are merely listed amongst the carnage, not cited as weapons. Some theories that offer literary references as support to their conclusions for the use of the *sauroter* as a secondary weapon, cite either a passage of Xenophon (*Hellenica* 6.2.19) and/or a passage of Polybius (6.25.9) as proof of the use of the *sauroter* in this manner. However, neither passage outlines the use of the *sauroter* in a secondary offensive capacity by a hoplite in combat.

Xenophon details the use of the *sauroter* by a hoplite commander to administer an admonishing blow to an insubordinate officer.[9] Striking with the *sauroter* is likely to be the result of an intention to punish the offending individual with a blow from the heavy end of the weapon rather than actually injuring him with a blow using the spearhead. Polybius states that the problem with the Roman cavalry lance is that it does not possess a spike on the end of the shaft and that, if the head breaks, the weapon becomes useless.[10] Hanson interprets this passage as referring to all Roman spears in general; not just the lance of the cavalry. From this he extrapolates that the Roman infantry spear was not as good as that of the Greek hoplite due to its lack of a *sauroter*. He concludes that because the rear end of the Roman infantry spear could not have been used as a secondary weapon, it must have therefore been possible to do so with the *sauroter* of the Greek spear.[11]

Interestingly, the lances carried by Macedonian cavalry were also equipped with a butt-spike.[12] However, when the lances carried by Alexander's cavalry broke at the Granicus, the shattered weapons were abandoned in favour of swords or replacement lances; the butt-spike appears to not have been used as an alternative weapon.[13] Diodorus states that when Alexander broke the tip off his lance he continued to thrust at the unprotected face of his enemy with the jagged end of the shaft.[14] This suggests that even if the *sauroter* was considered as a possible secondary weapon, Alexander had neither the time nor room to re-orientate his shattered lance in the press of battle to bring the butt-spike to bear. Furthermore, Xenophon details the use of the rear end of the spear during mock cavalry battles instead of the spearhead.[15] This suggests that the butt-spike on the end of a cavalry lance could not inflict serious injury, even when used from the back of a moving horse. None of these passages can confirm the common use of the *sauroter* as an offensive weapon even by Greek or Macedonian cavalry.[16] Clearly, none of these accounts can be considered a reference for use of the *sauroter* as a secondary combative weapon by a hoplite, or even extrapolated to assume that it was a standard battlefield practice.

Nor are there any representations of a hoplite engaging an opponent with the rear end of a broken spear in vase illustrations, relief carvings or statuary. There are, however, numerous depictions of hoplites fighting with swords, but none of these are represented as being the result of necessity due to a spear breaking in combat. Within the archaeological record, Snodgrass and Matthews claim that the square holes in some pieces of armour in the collection of Olympia are proof of combative impacts made with the *sauroter*.[17] Out of the 150 helmets examined by Blyth at Olympia, nine had square holes, which he states may have been made with a *sauroter*.[18]

Blyth suggests that the shape of the spearhead is indicative of its use to penetrate soft targets such as flesh while the shape of the *sauroter* demonstrates that it was designed to penetrate armour.[19] However, the spearhead was quite capable of piercing the armour worn by the hoplite depending upon the spear's method of delivery (see Chapter 9, The Penetration Power of the Hoplite Spear). When the penetrative abilities of the *sauroter* were tested, it was found that a 'long point' *sauroter* was unable to penetrate a flat target plate 1mm thick. The target plate was mounted on a supporting stack of hay bales at chest height and was struck with the *sauroter* with attacks made from the underarm position. Several of the strikes that impacted at an angle to the surface of the target simply glanced off the plate, leaving a rough graze on its surface. None of the strikes that hit the plate at roughly ninety degrees could create more than a small dent in the plate approximately 10mm across and only a few millimetres deep.

The failure of the *sauroter* to penetrate the target plate was no doubt due to the larger impacting area of the point (4mm) compared with that of the spearhead (0.7mm). While it must be considered that a full, rigid, breastplate may have provided greater resistance to the impact, and therefore may have been more susceptible to penetration, it must also be considered that the majority of surface features of both the helmet and breastplate worn by the hoplite are not flat and that the curvature of the armour will decrease the ability of any impact to pierce it (see Chapter 9, The Penetration Power of the Hoplite Spear). Consequently, a ninety-degree impact against a flat plate can be considered the 'best-case scenario' for an attack delivered with the *sauroter*. Yet even under these conditions the *sauroter* is incapable of piercing the armour plate. This suggests that, if it was employed as a secondary weapon, it would have been rather ineffective.

Blyth estimates that for a *sauroter* to penetrate to a depth capable of causing serious injury it would leave a hole at least 9×9mm in size.[20] However, the square holes he examined at Olympia measure 5–8mm in size, also suggesting that, even if they had somehow been created by a *sauroter* used in an offensive capacity, it was incapable of inflicting serious harm. A more recent survey of armour at Olympia found few holes in the plate larger than 10mm in size and no evidence at all of any impacts made with the *sauroter*. Interestingly, the majority of the holes in the helmets are located either on the lower rim at the back of the helmet or on the cheek flange. Some are also punched from the inside of the helmet out.[21]

The regularity of the size and location of these holes, and the absence of any dramatic buckling of the plate that would be caused by an impact with a relatively blunt instrument like a *sauroter*, suggests that they were not made by hits from a *sauroter* but are from where the helmets and armour have been nailed to posts as battlefield trophies or to the walls of treasuries and sanctuaries. It would be against all probability for impacts made at different times by different individuals and with different weapons to impact, more or less, all in the same place and to a depth that has resulted in damage of such a uniform size and shape. Damage such as this can only be the result of a commonly used manner of presenting the armour as a dedication. Additionally, the amount of flex available within the cheek flange of the helmet itself (not to mention the neck of the person wearing it – which would snap the head backwards with any impact) would negate much of the impact energy of a hit with the *sauroter*. Hoffmann and Raubitschek state that holes in the earlier 'Crowe Corslet' from Olympia were made with a chisel when it was set up as a trophy.[22] Some pieces of Classical Era armour have clearly suffered similar damage (in particular B1621, the right cheek guard from a Thracian helmet (c.450BC) at Olympia).[23]

It must also be considered that the *sauroter* became more rounded in the late fifth century BC and throughout the fourth; with some possessing square or rounded cross-sections over one square centimetre in size or even small, rounded, knobs (see page 5). A large or rounded tip would have made the *sauroter* an even less effective piercing weapon than the elongated spike and it is highly unlikely that these variants of the *sauroter* would penetrate plate or composite armour either. This begs the obvious question: why would the *sauroter* develop in such a fashion if it was meant to be commonly used as a secondary weapon? It can only be concluded that it was not designed to be used in such a manner.[24] Similarly, it can also be concluded that the smaller *styrakion* was not designed to be used as a secondary weapon in any capacity due to its small spike; and that it merely provided a central point of balance to the javelin, protected the end of the shaft from the elements and allowed the javelin to be thrust into the ground when not in use. If the *sauroter* was designed to penetrate armour as Blyth suggests, it is also curious that the spearhead was not also designed as a similar, elongated, spike considering how well covered the hoplite was by his shield, helmet, cuirass and greaves (see Chapter 7, The 'Kill Shot' of Hoplite Combat).

Breaking the hoplite spear

Theories that propose an offensive use of the *sauroter* in the event of a hoplite's spear breaking are reliant upon the assumption that the hoplite's spear would regularly break during the trials of combat. Diodorus' reference to hoplites reverting to the sword as a secondary weapon, and the use of swords at Thermopylae and Coronea, clearly demonstrate that the hoplite spear could break. However, under what conditions, and how regularly, would this have occurred?

Blyth generally states that the hoplite spear could be easily broken but does not outline under what circumstances he considered that this would occur.[25] Hanson states that most spears belonging to the front ranks of a phalanx would break upon the initial contact of two opposing formations due to the momentum of the charge.[26] Any conclusion that the spears of the first ranks would break with the clash of two formations is in itself reliant upon the assumption that all hoplite combat involved the violent collision of two opposing phalanxes. However, this occurred only under specific conditions uncommon to the engagements of the Classical hoplite (see Chapter 13, The Hoplite Battle: Contact, *Othismos*, Breakthrough and Rout). During the opening stages of the battle of Coronea for example, the two sides closed to 'within spear thrust of the enemy' (εἰς δόρυ ἀφικόμενοι ἔτρεψαν τὸ καθ᾽ αὑτούς) indicating that there was no collision of the phalanxes and, subsequently, the spears belonging to the front ranks of both sides are unlikely to have broken due to the momentum of the charge as Hanson would suggest.[27] Plutarch describes the moment of contact between the two formations as being 'without struggle' (οὐκ ἔσχεν ὠθισμὸν), also indicating a lack of collision.[28] Similarly, the Spartans at Mantinea are described as marching slowly into battle to the sound of flutes to keep their battle-line in order.[29] As a result, the Spartan phalanx would not have had a very high level of momentum behind it when it came into contact with the opposing Argive formation and, consequently, their spears are unlikely to have all broken on impact. Spears could also be dedicated to temples as offerings after a battle; again indicating that at least some weapons survived the fighting.[30]

In some, rarer, instances the course of an engagement allowed for the two sides to collide heavily. During the later stages of Coronea, the Theban and Spartan formations crashed headlong into each other at the run; resulting in a violent collision that may have broken some of the front rank weapons. Xenophon's description of the aftermath of the engagement specifically lists broken spears among the detritus of the confrontation.[31] Some of these weapons may have broken during the collision of the two formations. Thus not every encounter created an environment in which the hoplite spear may have been broken as the result of the momentum of a charge. Even when a charge did take place, it is unlikely that every spear belonging to those in the front ranks was broken in the collision. Consequently, Hanson's statement can only be regarded as 'conditionally' correct; reliant upon the actual conditions of each hoplite engagement.

However, the rare collision of two charging phalanxes was not the only way in which a hoplite spear could be broken in combat. Herodotus states that the Persians at Plataea rendered the Greek spears ineffective by grabbing them and snapping the heads off (τὰ γὰρ δόρατα ἐπιλαμβανόμενοι κατέκλων οἱ βάρβαροι).[32] Herodotus additionally states that the Persians at Plataea had constructed a wicker barricade with their shields.[33] This suggests that some form of weapon may have still been wielded in the right hand; which would leave only the left hand free to perform the breakage of the Greek spears.

To test if it is in any way possible for an individual to grab a spear as it is thrust towards them and snap the end off as per Herodotus' account of Plataea, a series of simple experiments were conducted using a 'dummy spear' of an oak wood shaft with a length of 250cm and a diameter of 2.5cm.[34] One participant (representing a Greek hoplite at Plataea) held the 'dummy spear' in an extended position from the underarm posture (simulating a spear thrust) while another participant (representing a Persian) gripped the forward end of the shaft and attempted to break it.

Two tests were conducted with the 'Persian' gripping the shaft with the left hand near its forward tip in both an overhand and underhand manner. The tests were then repeated with the 'Persian' using the right hand (this assumes that the Persians were either not wielding a weapon of any kind or had transferred it to their left hand). Finally, the tests were repeated with the 'Persian' using both hands while standing on either side of the shaft. These last two scenarios could only have occurred if the Persians behind the wicker barricade at Plataea were not wielding a shield or weapon of any kind.

It was found that it was impossible to break a 2.5cm diameter shaft using any of these methods. A single hand alone does not possess enough strength to simply break the end off the shaft, or even bend it significantly, using only the natural flex of the wrist. Blyth estimates that for a shaft to be broken even with both hands, up to four times the amount of energy needs to be applied by the hand closest to the centre of the shaft than needs to be applied by the hand gripping it near the tip.[35] However, any form of pressure exerted by the 'Persian', regardless of its measure, was easily compensated for by a corresponding counter-move by the 'Greek', which simply negated the majority of the applied energy. For example, downward pressure applied by the 'Persian' was negated by the 'Greek' simply allowing the spearhead to be pushed down. Similarly, the 'Greek' could allow the spear tip to rise in response to upward pressure exerted by the 'Persian'. This available movement in the weapon both removed any resistance to the applied pressure that may have caused the shaft to fracture and also caused the 'Persian' to overbalance due to his own actions on a number of occasions. Any grip on a spear supported solely by the wrist (such as the low and overhead stances of current convention) would provide even more movement to the weapon and subsequently even less resistance to any force applied by the 'Persian'. Even when the tests were repeated with the spear held in the well-supported underarm 'ready' position, there was still enough available movement in the posture to negate any external pressures.

The breaking strain of the shaft was also tested by the 'Persian' forcing the weapon downwards and then trying to break it with their foot and the application of their body weight; although this method is unlikely to have been attempted by the Persians at Plataea due to the presence of the wicker barricade.

When the tests were repeated using a thinner 1.9cm shaft, it was found that the 'Persian' was able to cause significant flex in the thinner shaft but could still not get enough leverage to effect a break when using only one hand. However, when using two hands, the combined leverage made it possible for the end of the shaft to be broken. The extensive flex in the thinner shaft, and the ease with which it could be broken, demonstrates the unsuitability of a thinner shaft to withstand the rigours of hand-to-hand combat. It is unlikely that a weapon with such a low breaking strain would have been able to probe shields and armour without breaking and so cannot account for the descriptions of wounds and fatalities found in the ancient literary sources. The fact that the shafts of the spears used by the Greeks at Thermopylae were not all broken until the third day of fighting further indicates the durability of the weapon and suggests that thin shafts (and possibly even tapered shafts) may not have been used in their construction. As a result, it can be concluded that the shaft of the hoplite spear generally had a uniform thickness of around 2.5cm in diameter (see pages 9–10 for how the head and *sauroter* could have been mounted onto a shaft of this diameter).

It can thus be ruled out that the Persians at Plataea simply grabbed the Greek spears and snapped them with their bare hands. The word ἐπιλαμβανόμενοι ('to sieze') used by Herodotus clearly demonstrates that the Persians grabbed the Greek spears, but the word κατέκλων ('to snap in two') additionally shows that some form of severing or breaking was central to the actions of the Persians, rather than them simply seizing the spears and taking them away from the Greeks. It can only be concluded that the Persians managed to break or hack through the Greek spears using a weapon wielded in the right hand.

It is unlikely that the Persians grabbed the Greek weapons while they were held in their 'ready' position as this would have brought any grappling Persian dangerously within range of the spears of the second rank of the Greek phalanx. Nor is it likely that the Spartans merely held their weapons outstretched as the test participants did; they would have been jabbing and probing with their weapons, at chest height over the top of the wicker barricade, right across the Persian line. The Persians could only have attempted to grab the Greek spears at the moment when a hoplite of the front rank had extended their spear into the attack and before they withdrew it again (which would have pulled any Persian holding it onto the spears of the second rank). Consequently, any severing of the Greek spears would need to have been accomplished rapidly; again suggesting the use of a weapon to break the end off.

Herodotus outlines Persian contingents at Thermopylae armed with swords, axes and clubs; weapons well suited to the severing or breaking of spear shafts.[36] Due to the construction of the wicker barricade at Plataea, any Persian so armed would have been able to quickly grab at any extended Greek spear with their free left hand and then, pivoting in on the spear, bring down their sword or axe to sever up to a metre from the end of the weapon. Diodorus describes the same effect resulting from a blow to a Macedonian cavalry lance.[37] That the Persians at Thermopylae did not break the Greek spears in a similar way is indicative of the shields that they bore in their left hands; they had no way of grabbing the Greek spears to try and sever them. This combined grabbing and severing of the Greek spears with a weapon is most likely to be what Herodotus is describing in his description of the battle of Plataea.

However, this can in no way be interpreted as the breaking of *all* of the Greek spears by the Persians at Plataea and many of the Spartan hoplites would have been able to continue to fight with their spears intact. The fact that the Spartans and Athenians were later able to storm the Persian camp, and that the Persians eventually lost the engagement, indicates that the Greek forces had not lost all of their offensive capabilities.[38] As such, Herodotus' description of the events at Plataea must be taken as a case of literary exaggeration. It is quite plausible that the Persians were able to hack through only some of the Greek weapons during the engagement. Importantly though, once the Greek spears were broken, there is no reference to the use of the *sauroter* as a replacement means of offence.

The ancient texts also state that a spear could break simply as a result of the actions of fighting. Euripides, states that spears could break as a result of a powerful thrust (ἀπὸ δ᾽ ἔθραυσ᾽ ἄκρον δόρυ).[39] The Greeks at Thermopylae also resorted to using their swords only once their spears had been broken during the combat of the preceding two days.[40] Diodorus states that the tip of the spear that pierced Epaminondas' chest at Mantinea broke off after it had entered his body.[41] Aeschylus' *Agamemnon* contains a passage that is interpreted by Smyth as 'spears being shivered in the onset' of a hoplite engagement (διακναιομένης τ᾽ ἐν προτελείοις κάμακος).[42] However, the word διακναιομένης would be better translated as 'grated' or 'scraped' instead of 'shivered', and the word κάμακος is only a reference to the spear shafts, not to the spears as a whole as per Smyth's interpretation. As such, Aeschylus' passage may be better translated as 'the spear shafts scrape/grate [against each other] at the onset'. This is most likely a reference to the shafts of spears belonging to the first two ranks of confronting formations sliding along each other as the two phalanxes interlock at spear length; but does not necessarily indicate the breaking or 'shivering' of the weapons. The 'scraping' suggests that a large amount of shaft is projecting forward of the bearer; indicating a weapon held by its correct point of balance towards the rear of the shaft, probably in the underarm position. Similarly, Diodorus states that 'when the spears first hit each other, they rub together due to the density of the blows' (καὶ τὸ μὲν πρῶτον τύπτοντες ἀλλήλους τοῖς δόρασι, καὶ διὰ τὴν πυκνότητα τῶν πληγῶν τὰ πλεῖσψα συντρίψαντες) in another likely reference to the spears of two sides connecting as the phalanxes interlock at spear length.[43]

In the accounts of battle by Herodotus, Euripides and Diodorus, it is interesting that the spears are broken during the course of the fighting and not during any initial collision of the formations involved. Neither passage refers to momentum as an influencing factor in the breaking of the weapon; only the actions of combat. Either passage runs counter to any model for the spear commonly breaking during the clash of two formations. What these passages do suggest is that a strong spear thrust, probably impacting with a hard surface such as the shield or armour of an opponent, was capable of creating enough force to break the spear if the resistance to penetration was high enough. What these passages do not detail, unfortunately, is the manner in which the spear was broken. A spear may have splintered at a weak point that had developed in the wooden shaft, or any rivet or adhesive holding the head in place may have weakened or broken resulting in the head simply falling off. Blyth estimates that, if the head was held in place (such as by penetrating a shield or body) a lateral force of only 119fpds of pressure would wrench the shaft from the socket.[44] The spearhead itself may have also broken at a weak point where the blade of the head meets the socket.[45] Finds from Olympia contain several spearheads broken in just such a manner, suggesting that this was a common weak point in the design of many spearheads and may be what both Herodotus and Euripides are referring to.[46]

If these passages that mention the breaking of the spear (either by severing, as the result of a rare collision of formations or through simple breakage) are accepted as accurate descriptions of a characteristic of hoplite warfare (and there is little reason to suggest that they are not) it seems that, under certain conditions during the trials of close combat, the spear of the hoplite could actually break, or be broken, in his hand. This, however, does not mean that once his spear had broken the hoplite would resort to fighting with the *sauroter* even if he did not possess a sword. In fact, the consideration of how a broken spear could be used in the environment of the hoplite battlefield further indicates that it is highly unlikely that the hoplite would have done so.

The offensive capabilities of a broken hoplite spear

Would a broken spear have been of any use in the massed combat of the phalanx? Could the *sauroter* actually be brought to bear against a target? And could it have reached that target? Due to the varied nature of how a hoplite spear could break or be broken, the remaining weapon could be of any length. Weapons that merely lost the head, either through it breaking or falling off, would lose between 20 and 30cm of their overall length. If the spear fractured at a weak point in the wood, the amount of remaining weapon would be dictated by the location of that weak point anywhere along the shaft. In the case of the spears hacked through by the Persians at Plataea, the length of the weapon may have been reduced by as much as a metre.

For the spears broken at Plataea, the remaining weapon would have been approximately 155cm in length, 30cm of which would be the length of the *sauroter* itself. The removal of the head and around 70cm of shaft dramatically alters the balance of the remaining section of the weapon, which would weigh in the vicinity of 960g. If this broken weapon was turned around so that the *sauroter* acted as the impacting tip, the shortened shaft and missing head relocate the point of balance to 60cm behind the new forward tip of the weapon; a shift of 30cm back towards the *sauroter* (figure 18).

A weapon such as this, if it were wielded by its correct point of balance, leaves nearly a metre of shaft projecting behind the bearer and only half a metre to their front. Due to the large weight of the *sauroter*, it is almost impossible to wield a broken spear by gripping it further rearward than its new point of balance; the muscular stresses placed on the arm caused by the pressure required to keep the weapon level for a protracted period of time are simply too great. Thus even a spear that had only lost its head could not be held much further back than 60–70cm from the tip of the *sauroter*.

It is almost impossible to reposition a weapon balanced in this way so that the *sauroter* can be used offensively when deployed in a phalanx. Regardless of where and how the spear breaks, and regardless of the posture in which it is held, the *sauroter* will be pointing towards the rear when the weapon fractures. The weapon hand, holding the spear at its correct point of balance, will be approximately 90cm forward of the tip of the *sauroter*. In order for the *sauroter* to be brought to bear against a target as a secondary weapon, the broken spear has to be spun around 180 degrees in the hand and the grip repositioned by up to 30cm. It would require a considerable amount of room for a hoplite to rotate a broken weapon 155cm in length, or longer, without it becoming entangled

D1: 20cm   D2: 92.5cm

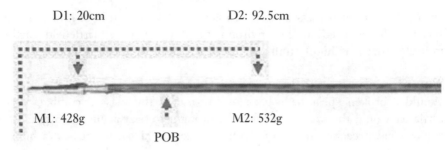

M1: 428g   M2: 532g

POB

Datum

Point of Balance (POB) = (M1 × D1) + (M2 × D2)/(M1 + M2)
Where:
M1 = the mass of the *sauroter*
M2 = the mass of the shaft
D1 = the distance from the datum (the end of the weapon) to the point of balance of the *sauroter*
D2 = the distance from the datum to the point of balance of the shaft
Thus:
POB = (428 × 20) + (532 × 92.5)/(428 + 532)
    = 8,560 + 49,210/960
    = 57,770/960
    = 60 (cm from the datum)

Figure 18: The calculation of the point of balance for a broken spear.

with his own equipment or the other members of the phalanx; more space than is available in either a close or intermediate-order formation. Nor could the broken weapon be reversed using any version of the models proposed for altering the grip on the hoplite spear as any such action with a broken weapon would incur all of the same impediments to movement as those performed with an intact spear (see Chapter 5, Repositioning the Spear in 'Hoplite Drill'). In the confines of a compressed phalanx there is simply no way in which the hoplite would be able to bring the *sauroter* to bear against a target. Hanson's suggestion that the *sauroter* was used to 'get off a few more thrusts' in a phalanx that had collided with that of its opposition is completely untenable.

Even if a hoplite engaged 'at spear length' from his opponent was able to somehow reposition his shattered weapon so that he could strike with the *sauroter*, a broken weapon 155cm in length wielded in the underarm posture and gripped at its forward point of balance affords a *combat range* of only 96cm and an *effective range* of only 115cm when used in an intermediate-order formation. This is over a metre and a half shorter than the reach of a full spear used in the same order (266cm). Thus a hoplite would not even be able to reach an opponent with his broken weapon unless he broke ranks and advanced into the 'no man's land' between the formations to get off 'a few more thrusts' as Hanson suggests (figure 19).

However, it seems unlikely that a hoplite would have advanced forward of his position in the phalanx to attack. Herodotus relates the story of Aristodemus of Sparta who was praised for his bravery for advancing forward of the formation, and simultaneously vilified for leaving his place in the line.[47] Leaving your place in formation was contrary to both Spartan law and Spartan ideals.[48] The Athenian *Ephebic Oath* also declared the intent to remain in position.[49] The amount of broken shaft that projects behind the bearer, with its jagged end, also makes wielding a broken weapon in any formation both dangerous to surrounding hoplites and liable to entanglement with equipment, particularly the overlying spear of the second rank.

At this distance a broken spear could only have been used in a defensive capacity to fend off attacks made by an opponent. The spear could be held in place with the jagged end of the shaft thrust towards an opponent simply to keep him at bay while he was engaged by members of the second rank. In doing

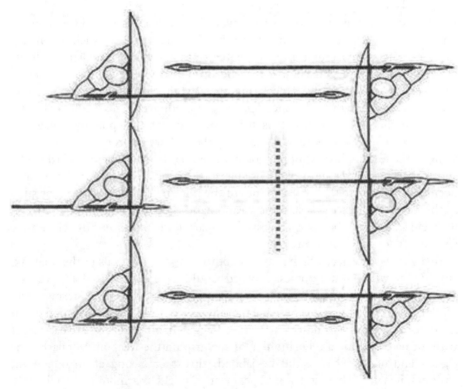

Figure 19: The reduced *effective range* of underarm thrusts made with a broken spear (dotted line).

so the spear does not have to be rotated and only a minor adjustment to where it is held made to compensate for the altered point of balance. If the wooden shaft of the spear had fractured too close to the *sauroter* to make the weapon of any use in this capacity, it would have simply been abandoned on the field. In this case a sword may have been drawn if the hoplite possessed one; although he would be similarly unlikely to reach his opponent with this weapon either, or be able to even swing it without becoming entangled in the weapons of the second rank. It is more likely that a hoplite in this situation simply stood his ground and absorbed any opponent's attacks with his shield while that opponent was engaged by the man in the second rank.

This raises the question: why would a secondary weapon be needed in hoplite combat at all? When the Athenian state began to provide arms and armour to its citizens, the sword was not among the issued equipment.[50] This suggests that the sword was not a vital part of the hoplite's panoply or of hoplite warfare in general. This could only be due to the spear regularly standing up to the toils of combat and an infrequent collision of the formations which may have broken many of the weapons and created an environment in which a short-reach weapon such as a sword would have been useful. Occasionally, hoplite combat 'devolved' into a fierce hand-to-hand melee, such as on day three at Thermopylae or during the later stages at Coronea, where a short-reach secondary weapon could easily be brought to bear against an enemy. Plutarch's repeated passages declaring that 'while Spartan swords are short they get close enough to use them' are undoubtedly references, albeit slightly tongue-in-cheek, to the Spartans being unafraid of this potential phase of hoplite combat.[51] The Spartans, carrying their short swords, may have been some of the few hoplites equipped for any eventuality on the field of battle. The short Spartan swords, most likely used as a thrusting weapon, would have also been better suited to the close confines of the phalanx than larger weapons such as the *falcata*, which was a slashing weapon and therefore required more room to wield. This may be another basis for Spartan claims as to how close they had to get to use their swords.

In a confused melee, which may not conform to the intervals of the phalanx, any hoplite who did not possess a sword would have clearly used any weapon available to defend himself; just as the Spartans had done at Thermopylae. Under these conditions it is possible that the *sauroter* of a broken weapon could have been used to stab downwards, in a dagger-like fashion, at a close target without necessitating a repositioning of the grip on the weapon. Similarly, the jagged end of the shaft could be jabbed, thrust or swung at an opponent; although it is unlikely that it would penetrate a shield or armour and could only have been used against unprotected areas of an opponent's body; in the same way that Diodorus describes Alexander's actions at the Granicus.[52] In such a frenzied environment anything is possible. However, these would have been acts of desperation rather than a standard battlefield use of the *sauroter* as a secondary weapon.

There is no basis of support for theories that propose a use for the *sauroter* as an alternative weapon. If the hoplite's spear broke during combat there would be little reason to retain the broken section except for the possible eventuality that the combat may develop into a situation where a secondary weapon was necessary. If that did not occur, the *sauroter* on the end of a broken spear could not have been brought to bear against a target 'at spear length' in the confines of the phalanx, and could not have reached a target even if it was done so. In these instances, any spear that broke would most likely have been kept in place and used to fend off an attacker while the battle was continued by those whose spears were still intact. Even in a close combat environment, it is unlikely that the *sauroter* would have been able to pierce an opponent's armour and the sword would have been a more suitable weapon in this situation. It is the combination of these factors that make it unlikely that the *sauroter* was used as, or even designed to be, a secondary weapon.

The use of the *sauroter* to attack backwards

Hanson also suggests that a *sauroter*-equipped spear allowed the hoplite to 'thrust backwards at any opponent that came upon him from the side or rear'.[53] This seems highly unlikely within the context of the phalanx. The construction of the arm and shoulder give such an action only a limited amount of reach, regardless of what posture is being used to wield the weapon. An arm wielding a spear in the overhead position of current convention cannot bend in a way that will deliver anything other than a blind swatting action with the end of the spear. Nor can the spear be effectively thrust backwards when wielded in the underarm position. The *sauroter* can be thrust backwards relatively effectively from the low position, and the body can be rotated with the action to allow the strike to be aligned with its target, but the intervals of the phalanx make the deployment of the spear in this position by men in the rear rank (those who would have been vulnerable to the flanking attack suggested by Hanson) unlikely. Thus Hanson's model does not comply with even the current two-stance model of hoplite warfare upon which his own research is based.

For a hoplite to strike to the side as per Hanson's suggestion (it is assumed that Hanson is referring only to the right side; the side that the weapon is on) the spear of the hoplite would have to be extended across the front of several other members of the phalanx in order to bring it into a position to strike laterally at an opponent with the *sauroter*. This would both impede and endanger other members of the formation as it was moved into position and entangle the actions of numerous weapons; making such an action also unlikely.

It would have only been possible for a hoplite to strike backwards with the *sauroter* during a rout. A fleeing hoplite would most likely adopt a low posture to carry his spear as this is the easiest to run with (assuming that he did not just simply abandon the weapon in his panic) and there would be adequate space around each man as the formation broke up during the flight. Should a pursuing enemy come suddenly upon him from behind, the fleeing hoplite may have simply lashed out backwards with his *sauroter* in a desperate attempt to fend off the attacker. The ancient evidence contains no reference to this sort of usage of an infantry weapon by a hoplite in combat and Hanson's theory can only be regarded as speculative within this context.

The use of the *sauroter* to dispatch a fallen opponent

The third proposed offensive use of the *sauroter* is for the dispatching of a fallen opponent who lay prone at a hoplite's feet.[54] Unlike the proposed use of the *sauroter* as a secondary weapon, there are visual representations of the *sauroter* being used in this manner, although they are rare. One illustration (NY 07.286.8.4) clearly shows a hoplite striking an opponent with the rear end of the spear shaft, although no *sauroter* is depicted in the image. Another scene (Louvre S 1677) depicts Athena striking a prone giant with the clearly depicted *sauroter* on the rear end of her spear. In both images, the spears are unbroken and can in no way be taken as the use of the rear end of a broken spear as a secondary weapon. Anderson also suggests that the image on an Attic grave *stele* depicts the slaying of a fallen Spartan hoplite with the *sauroter*. Unfortunately, the top of the *stele* is broken and it cannot be determined with any certainty whether the weapon borne by the figure standing astride the fallen opponent is a spearhead, a *sauroter* or even a dagger. The attribution of this image with the use of the *sauroter* to dispatch a fallen opponent can only be regarded as inconclusive.

Despite these few artistic representations, could a *sauroter* actually be used to dispatch an opponent who was lying prone at a hoplite's feet? To do so, the spear has to be moved into a position where the *sauroter* can be thrust downwards at the target. However, the spear cannot be moved into this position from the overhead position of current convention. The spear would need to be spun 180 degrees in the hand in order to deliver such a blow from the overhead posture. Due to the limitations of spacing within the phalanx (in any order), the length of the spear, the restrictions imposed by the panoply and the inability to move from the overhead posture to another position using any of the proposed methods of doing so, such an action cannot be accomplished.

It is only spears that are wielded in the low and underarm positions that could be used to deliver a downward strike with the *sauroter*. Due to the way the spear is held in these positions, with thumb and forefinger at the front of the grip, the spear could be raised into a vertical position without the requirement of any alteration to the hand. The image of Athena mentioned above clearly shows a spear raised from the underarm position; the spear still runs along the right forearm as it would have when held in its horizontal position and it is gripped by its correct point of balance near the rear end of the shaft. Both the arm and the spear have simply been raised into a vertical position in order to effect the strike.[55]

However, the serried layers of spears belonging to the first two ranks of a close-order formation would not permit a spear borne by members of these ranks to be moved easily into such a position without the risk of impediment, entanglement or the endangering of other members of the phalanx. It is only the weapons belonging to hoplites in intermediate or open-order phalanxes, or those in the third and subsequent ranks of a close-order formation (who would not have been holding their spears horizontally during the initial action to begin with) that could be raised vertically. From a vertical position enough of the spear has to then be allowed to slip through the hand to allow the *sauroter* to reach the ground/target. From here the spear can be easily brought down, through the gap between each man created by the adoption of an oblique body posture, against a target at the feet while the phalanx advanced with the front ranks continuing to project their spears forward at any remaining enemy.

It is unlikely that any *sauroter* that possessed an end with a large cross section or rounded knob would be capable of penetrating armour when used in a downward manner. Thrusts brought directly downwards can generate a great deal of force, but the size and shape of the cross section of the *sauroter* will dictate whether it would be able to penetrate armour or not. When tested against a 12cm thick block of ballistics gelatine (simulating an area of the body without numerous internal bones such as the abdomen) a long-point *sauroter* penetrated the block to a depth of 13cm with very little effort; it went right through the block and was only stopped by the base that the gel was sitting on (plate 23.2).

Clearly, this style of *sauroter* could do considerable damage against an unprotected area of the human body; enough to easily kill or severely injure. However, when the same *sauroter* was tested against a 1mm thick armour plate mounted on a horizontal platform at a height of 12cm above the ground (simulating the height of a body laying prone), the spike was incapable of piercing it. Impacts that hit perpendicular to the plate resulted in a significant buckling of the metal, due to the force of the downward strike, but failed to pierce it. The level of buckling suggests that such an impact may have been able to penetrate a larger, more rigid, target such as a cuirass. However, any impact that hit the plate at an angle simply glanced off; leaving a graze on the surface of the plate. This suggests that the *sauroter* would have been incapable of penetrating the curved surfaces found on most hoplite armour. The inability of the *sauroter* to penetrate plate armour correlates with the one recorded account that may describe the use of a *sauroter* to dispatch an opponent: the death of the Persian commander Masistius at the battle of Plataea in 479BC.

Plutarch and Herodotus state that the death of Masistius was the result of receiving an injury through the eyehole of his helmet after he had been forced from his horse and was on the ground being attacked by numerous Greeks whose spears could not penetrate his armour.[56] The word used by Plutarch to describe the weapon with which Masistius was eventually killed is *styraki* (στύρακι), the dative case of the noun *styrax* (στύραξ). While *styrax* is generally translated to mean the butt-spike of a spear, it can also be used to describe the spear itself.[57] Consequently, this passage can be read as Masistius being killed either by a spear or a spear-butt as the word *styrax* can refer to either. Some translations of Plutarch's account of this incident state that Masistius was killed by a javelin spike.[58] However, the dative case of the term *styrakion* (στυράκιον) is *styrakiōi* (στυρακίῳ), which is not the word that Plutarch uses.[59]

Due to the interchangable interpretative possibilities of the word στύρακι, it cannot be confirmed in what actual manner Masistius was killed. If Plutarch's use of the word *styrax* is interpreted as synonymous with *sauroter*, it is interesting that he can only be injured through the eyehole of his helmet. From this several conclusions can be drawn:

1. The *sauroter* was incapable of penetrating the scale armour that Masistius' is described as wearing but was able to penetrate the soft tissue of the eye and the thin layer of bone at the back of the orbital socket.[60]
2. The choice to use a *sauroter* may have been due to the fact that it would more easily fit through the aperture of the helmet than the wider spearhead.
3. The Greeks would have been standing almost directly over Masistius, striking downwards with the rear ends of their spears.
4. Plutarch states that Masistius was unable to stand back up once he had been thrown from his horse due to the weight of his armour. However, Masistius is unlikely to have been lying still on the ground but rolling about trying to ward off his attackers.[61] The Greeks, once they realized that their spears would not penetrate the armour (and presumably his helmet also), must have consciously aimed blows with the *sauroter* at the opening of the helmet until one strike reached its target.

If Plutarch is referring to the use of the *sauroter* against a prone opponent, it is the only passage that specifically refers to its use by infantry as an offensive weapon. Yet even here it seems to have been a battlefield necessity to circumvent Masistius' armour rather than a standard practice.

If Plutarch is referring to the use of the spear, this also allows certain conclusions to be drawn:

1. Herodotus implies that the Greeks had broken formation in order to slay Masistius and as such the hoplites were not bound by the limitations of any formation.[62] As such, Masistius would have most likely been attacked with blows delivered from the low position; although under-arm strikes cannot be ruled out.
2. In either case the Greeks would have to have been standing back from Masistius; attacking at up to the *effective range* of their spear thrusts at his body while he writhed on the ground fending off attacks.
3. The fact that the Greek spears cannot penetrate Masistius' armour indicates that either insufficient energy could be produced by a thrust delivered to pierce it or that the characteristics of the scale armour prevented penetration.
4. As with the butt-spike interpretation, the strikes made by the Greeks must have been consciously aimed at the openings in Masistius' helmet until one strike was oriented in such a way that the head of the spear passed through the eyehole of the helmet.

Due to the possibility that either of the interpretations for the term στύρακι is correct, the theory for the use of the *sauroter* to dispatch a fallen opponent can neither be confirmed nor dismissed by this passage. However, the main consideration that would suggest that its use in this manner was not a common practice is the fact that, in both Plutarch's account and in the physical testing, the *sauroter* was incapable of penetrating armour. Thus there is no clear evidence that would suggest that the *sauroter* could be effectively used against a prone adversary or that doing so was even a common battlefield practice.

Following Sekunda's lead, modern theories relating to the use of the *sauroter* as an offensive weapon are not supportable. The mechanics behind the use of the *sauroter* as a weapon conflict with all models of hoplite combat. A broken weapon could not be reoriented to use the *sauroter* as the point of impact in most cases. It also seems unlikely that a thrust made with the *sauroter* would penetrate armour in a way that would make it an effective piercing weapon. A broken spear, with a *sauroter* still attached, may have been used to parry blows under the most dire of close-combat conditions, but is unlikely to have been consciously regarded as an alternative weapon or as a means of delivering a rearward attack. Similarly, there is little evidence to support claims that the spike could be used to finish off a fallen adversary. It can therefore only be concluded that modern models for the use of the *sauroter* as an offensive weapon are predominantly incorrect. It can also be concluded that the *sauroter* was only designed to function in its other capacities: to protect the end of the shaft from the elements; to balance the spear correctly; to allow the spear to be thrust upright into the ground and to add weight to the mass of the weapon.

Chapter 11

Conclusion: The Individual Hoplite

Previous scholarship has been mistaken in the conclusions it has made as to how the hoplite functioned and behaved on the battlefields of antiquity. This is due to an often incorrect, incomplete and/or selective use of the source material to formulate and justify particular models of hoplite combat. Through a more comprehensive examination of the available evidence, and by putting both ancient depictions and modern models of hoplite warfare into practice via the processes of physical re-creation and experimentation, a new model for the behaviour of the individual hoplite can be formulated; a model that vastly differs from all preceding theories.

Contrary to many models, the hoplite cannot have adopted either a front-on or a side-on posture to bear his panoply. The limitations of these stances make them too restrictive to be of any value in hand–to–hand combat. The only way that a hoplite could have borne his equipment effectively would have been with the adoption of an oblique posture; with his left leg forward and the upper body rotated to the right by approximately forty-five degrees. Adopting this position allowed for the weight of the large, bowl-shaped, Argive shield to be partially borne by the left shoulder, and be braced in position by the left knee and lower thigh, all while maintaining its defensive position across the front of the body. Positioning the shield in such a manner covered the hoplite from the jaw–line to the knee, while additional protection was provided by the cuirass, helmet and any greaves the hoplite possessed. The oblique posture also allowed the hoplite to move across the battlefield while maintaining this strong body posture with relatively stable footing, and conform to any size variance within the interval of the phalanx. Most importantly, the oblique posture provided each hoplite with sufficient room to engage in fighting with his primary weapon: the thrusting spear.

The hoplite spear was approximately 255cm in length and comprised a shaft 2.5cm in diameter to which an iron head was attached to the forward tip and a weighty *sauroter* attached to the rear end. Due to the difference in the weight of the spear's constituent parts, the point of balance for the weapon was approximately 90cm from the rearward tip. Depending upon the size of both the head and the *sauroter* that were affixed to the shaft, the overall weight of the weapon would have been around 1.4kg.

In the artistic record, shafted weapons are shown being wielded in a variety of postures. The incomplete examination, and selective usage, of the artistic record is the most fundamental area of error in all previous models of hoplite warfare. The failure to both recognize and incorporate the underarm and reverse techniques into their models means that all previous scholarship on the performance of the hoplite in battle cannot be regarded as complete. Furthermore, the overhead stance upon which every previous model of hoplite warfare is based is not a depiction of the hoplite in the thrusting combat of the phalanx but in the missile warfare of an earlier, more heroic, age. Subsequently, the basis for every previous model of hoplite warfare is grounded upon an incorrect interpretation of the available evidence.

With the identification of the overhead technique as the use of the javelin, we are left with a model of hoplite warfare that incorporates the low, the underarm and the reverse techniques; with the hereto unidentified underarm technique being the predominant way a hoplite wielded his weapon. This low/ underarm/reverse model complies with the literary passages that describe hoplite manoeuvres and highlights further areas of inaccuracy within previous models. One of the best examples of this is in the modern theories of 'hoplite drill'. Not one of the proposed methods for how a hoplite could move from the low to the overhead position is physically achievable within the confines of the phalanx or complies with passages such as the order given to Xenophon's Greek mercenaries to 'lower spears'.[1] However, by placing a hoplite using a combination of the low and underarm techniques to wield his weapon within these same contexts, all detailed drill movements and methods of deployment can be accomplished.

The use of the underarm and low stances, and rearward balance of the weapon, also gave the hoplite the greatest reach with his spear and allowed him to fight for longer than if he had been using any other technique. The inability for the overhead position to be maintained for anything more than a few minutes highlights the unlikelihood of this method of attack being used in hoplite combat and further highlights one of the main deficiencies in all previous scholarship.

The adoption of an oblique body posture additionally allowed the hoplite to visually align the tip of his spear with his intended target. This combination of greater reach, stable posture, alignment of weapon to target and the high level of protection given to the hoplite by his panoply, meant that the heavy infantryman of ancient Greece greatly outclassed any opponent that he faced on the battlefields of the Classical Period. This is no more apparent than in engagements where hoplites fought against lightly armed opponents ill-suited to close hand-to-hand fighting, such as the Persians. The high number of casualties that the Greeks were able to inflict upon their Persian adversaries at Marathon, Thermopylae and Plataea, against the comparatively low numbers of Greek losses, are a testament to the superiority of the Greek way of war in such an environment.

With the spear held in the underarm position, the hoplite would have primarily struck directly towards the enemy, taking full advantage of the flat trajectory and reach of the weapon. When engaged against other hoplites, this meant that strikes would be naturally directed against the shield carried by an opponent or the upper parts of the helmet until an exploitable 'opportunity shot' presented itself during the trials of combat. When this sort of target did present itself, it was only a strong committed thrust delivered from either the low or underarm position that would have been capable of producing enough energy to penetrate the bronze plate armour of the day to a 'killing depth' of several inches. It is this aspect alone that demonstrates that the reliance of previous scholars upon the overhead stance as a means of explaining the mechanics of hoplite warfare is in error; strikes made from this position are incapable of accounting for the deaths and injuries that are described in the ancient sources and can, therefore, not be the way in which a hoplite fought. Similarly, previous scholarship has suggested that the *sauroter* on the rear end of the spear was used in a variety of offensive guises. All of these theories can be considered incorrect as they do not stand up to physical experimentation, have sufficient evidence to support their conclusions, or comply with other pieces of evidence.

The very basis of hoplite warfare was founded upon the effective use of both the defensive aspects of the panoply and the hoplite's primary offensive weapon: the thrusting spear. The understanding of how the behaviour of the individual hoplite was both dictated and governed by the necessity to bear and use his panoply correctly in battle allows for the nature of the individual hoplite to be applied to the very environment in which the hoplite functioned: the massed combat of the phalanx. This allows for the dynamics of the broader context of hoplite warfare to be understood to a level far beyond both previous models and the limited accounts available in the ancient source material.

Chapter 12

Phalanxes, Shield Walls and Other Formations

Unlike many of the heroes of earlier ages, the Greek hoplite of the Classical Period did not fight as an individual. Hoplite warfare was a combative style based upon the effective deployment of masses of men in the ordered structure of the phalanx. The phalanx was fundamental to hoplite warfare as the deployment of the formation dictated how the subsequent combat would ensue. An analysis of how the phalanx was formed, and maintained, has been an aspect of hoplite warfare seldom examined by modern scholars to any significant level. By examining the accounts of hoplite deployments and their reported purposes in the ancient texts, combined with an analysis of how many of these deployments were dictated by the very nature of the hoplite's panoply and how it was carried, it becomes clear that the hoplite phalanx was adaptive to varying tactical purposes on the battlefield.

The majority of modern works on hoplite warfare contain only a rudimentary analysis of the formations used in this style of fighting. Many modern works generally omit any analysis of how various hoplite formations were constructed, or the reasons why. For most scholars, hoplite warfare appears to have been limited to a 'block' of ranks and files of men arranged in a rectangular formation we know as the phalanx.[1] Ancient writers on both Classical and Hellenistic formations also use the 'block' phalanx as the basis for any subsequent elaboration on the characteristics of both hoplite and phalangite formations.[2] When the ancient sources merely state that an army 'deployed for battle', it is apparent that some type of standard formation, one that was commonly understood and warranted no detailed explanation to a relatively contemporary audience, is being referred to in the narrative. This is most likely a reference to the 'block' phalanx, unless another formation is otherwise stated. Consequently, any examination of the dynamics of the hoplite phalanx must begin with the structure of the 'block' formation.

Of the sources contemporary with the Classical Period, the works of Xenophon and Thucydides contain the most detailed descriptions of the structure of the 'block' phalanx, particularly that of the Spartans. Thucydides describes the

Spartan army at Mantinea in 418BC (not including 600 *sciritae*) as divided into seven divisions or *morai* (μόραι), each under the command of a *polemarch* (πολέμαρχος). Each *mora* was subdivided into four companies known as a *lochos* (λόχος), each commanded by a *lochagos* (λοχαγός).[3] Each company was further divided into a number of platoon-sized units called an *enomotia* (ἐλωμοτία) led by an *enomotarch* (ἐνωμοτάρχης). A rearward officer, known as an *ouragos* (οὐραγός), was positioned in the rear rank of the unit.[4] At Mantinea, each *enomotia* was deployed in four files (στοῖχος) eight men deep.[5] In a fragmented passage, Xenophon states that the *enomotia* could also be deployed three or six men abreast.[6] A lacuna in the passage has unfortunately removed additional information as to whether it could deploy one (i.e. in single file) or two abreast as well.[7] It has been suggested that the files could also be divided into half-files.[8] When two *enomotiai* were combined, they formed a tactical and administrative unit known as a *pentykostys* (πεντηκοστύς), commanded by a *pentekonter* (πεντηκοντήρ).[9]

Each officer was positioned at the head of the front-right file of the unit he commanded (except for the file-closing *ouragos*), unless that position was occupied by an officer of superior rank. As such, each *enomotarch* was positioned at the front-right of his respective *enomotia*, unless that *enomotia* was the very right-hand platoon of a company, which would then fall under the command of a *lochagos*. A *pentekonter* would be stationed at the front right of a combined group of two platoons unless that position was likewise taken by a superior officer.[10] Xenophon states that the entire front rank of a phalanx was made up of officers.[11] Thus the positioning of a single rearward *ouragos* in early *enomotiai* may have been reconfigured in later formations to create an entire line of *ouragoi*.[12] Xenophon describes the deployment of the phalanx as being like the structure of a house; with the strongest elements making up the roof and the foundations (i.e. the front and rear ranks respectively) in a reference to the positioning of officers across the front and back of the line.[13] In a passage that suggests the use of massed, phalanx-like, formations in the Archaic Period, Nestor is described as deploying his forces in a similar fashion in the *Iliad*.[14] Arrian states that the file commander 'tempers' the file into an effective unit while the *ouragos* should be chosen for his intelligence and experience.[15] According to Xenophon, the correct position for the Spartan king when in the presence of the enemy was at the front-right of the second *mora* so that he was stationed in between the first and second divisions of the phalanx.[16] Thucydides states that the Spartan formation at Mantinea had a frontage of 448 men.[17] This means that each of the 112 *enomotia* was positioned one beside the other in an extended line (figure 20).[18]

Aristotle states that the Athenians divided their hoplite forces by the ten tribes that made up the Athenian populace, each commanded by a *taxiarch*

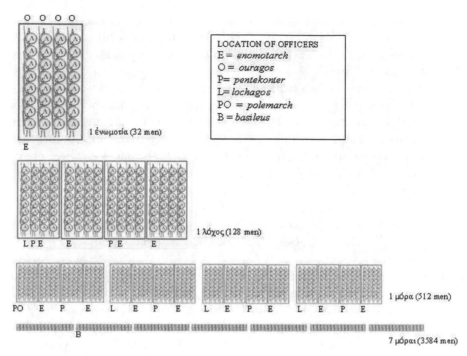

Figure 20: The deployment of the Spartan phalanx at Mantinea (418BC).

(ταξίαρχος). The office of *polemarch* existed but overall command was later given to members of an annually elected board of generals (στρατηγόι).[19] In Boeotia, eleven *boeotarchs* (βοιωτάρχος) were elected from across a confederacy of Boeotian city-states to command divisions (μέρος), each containing one thousand hoplites and one hundred cavalry supplied by the various states on a *pro rata* basis.[20] It can only be assumed that the deployments for other city-states, for which we have far fewer details, followed some similar form of one of the above practices.[21] This explains why many polyglot armies, composed of units from various city-states, are described as deployed in their separate native contingents across the line. Not only may these units have been based around different command structures, but each unit would have acted in the same capacity as the *lochos* or *mora* of a Spartan army.

In the *Cyropaedia* Xenophon describes the fictional army of Cyrus as structured on a basis much more elaborate than the structure he ascribes to the Spartans.[22] It has been suggested by some scholars that Xenophon's description of Cyrus' army is allegorical with that of Sparta.[23] However, it seems unclear how this could be the case when the structures of the two military institutions, described by the same author in different works, are so significantly different.

Similarly, the later military writers describe the elaborate command structure of the Hellenistic Macedonians based upon files of sixteen men. This base unit is subsequently doubled through each of the succeeding ten enlarged units to ultimately form a quadruple phalanx of 16,384 men.[24] Clearly, this aspect of the later military treatises cannot be applied to a Classical hoplite army but merely illustrates how the structure and organization of the phalanx changed in later periods.

Deploying the phalanx

The 'block' phalanx was probably the most commonly used hoplite battle formation as it easily facilitated the redeployment of an army marching in column (ἐπαγωγή or κέρας) into a battle array (παραγωγή or τάξις) when they had arrived on the field.[25] Xenophon describes a marching *lochos* as arranged with each *enomotia* following one behind the other.[26] When moving into line, the column would halt and the second *enomotia* would move forward and take up a position to the left (παρ' ἀσπίδα) of the unit before it. The third and fourth *enomotiai* would follow behind and then they too would redeploy to the left of the unit ahead of it (figure 21).[27]

Connolly and Sekunda use a variation of this method in their analysis of how hoplite armies moved from column into line, basing their models on an *enomotia* of three files of twelve as per Xenophon's description of the battle of Leuctra.[28] Both state that each of the three files of the *enomotia* marched one behind the other in a long column. Sekunda connects this with the 'single file' information missing from the lacuna in Xenophon's *Lacedaemonians*.[29] When forming into line, Connolly and Sekunda state that the successive files, not each *enomotia*, would redeploy to the left of the one before it.[30] Sekunda associates the deployment of three files of the *enomotia* beside each other with Xenophon's description of an *enomotia* deployed 'three abreast'.[31] To create an *enomotia* 'six abreast' as per Xenophon's passage, Sekunda offers that the rear half of each file moved forward into the interval between, thus creating a square formation six men across and six deep.[32] The later military writers refer to the Macedonian

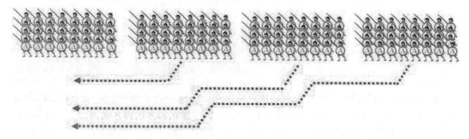

Figure 21: The redeployment of a Spartan *lochos* from column into line.

phalangite performing just such a manouevre, which is referred to as 'doubling' (διπλασιάζμος).[33] Warry also uses the 'doubling' of half-files in his model for the deployment of the Classical phalanx.[34] However, while it appears that some Macedonian contingents were armed as hoplites, this process is not attributed to the hoplite armies of the Classical Age.[35] Indeed, the literary evidence would suggest otherwise. At Cunaxa, for example, the Greek forces opened the files of their phalanx to allow Persian chariots to pass through.[36] Similarly, the Spartans are said to have opened their phalanx at Coronea as a means of breaking up the attacking Theban formation.[37] This suggests that hoplite forces were accustomed to opening and closing the order of their phalanx by moving their files left and right, not by using the process of 'doubling'. There is also no reference to a hoplite formation six ranks deep (other than Xenophon's suggested possibility of deployment – see following), which would be the result of a 'doubling' of the phalanx if its standard deployment was twelve deep.

What the different models for how a hoplite army could have moved from column into line do highlight is the level of flexibility that was available to the deployment of hoplite formations. Due to the structured nature of the phalanx into units and sub-units, any manoeuvre from column into line could be performed at any level, by units of any size or arranged into any depth or width, so long as sufficient space was left by each leading unit for those following in the column to redeploy. For example, if two *lochoi* were in a marching column with the *enomotiai* of each *lochos* arranged one behind the other, as the last *enomotia* of the leading *lochos* took up its position in the line, the second *lochos* could simply continue the procedure and take up a position to the left of first *lochos*, as long as sufficient room had been left for it to deploy. Subsequent units in the second *lochos* could then follow the same process until the entire column had deployed into line (figure 22).

If the marching column contained more than two *lochoi*, the same procedure could be followed with the third *lochos* following behind the second, and so on, until the deployment into line had been accomplished. The differences in the size of the file in these modern models highlight one of the main areas of contention in modern research into hoplite warfare: the depth of the phalanx.

The depth of the phalanx

Hoplite formations of different depths are well attested in the ancient texts (table 17).

Similarly, Asclepiodotus states that the depth of the Macedonian phalanx varied between eight, ten, twelve, sixteen and thirty-two men; with sixteen deep being the standard in his time.[38] As if to clarify any confusion on the part of his audience, Asclepiodotus further states that an eight-deep phalanx used to be the standard; in a probable reference to the depth of earlier hoplite formations.[39]

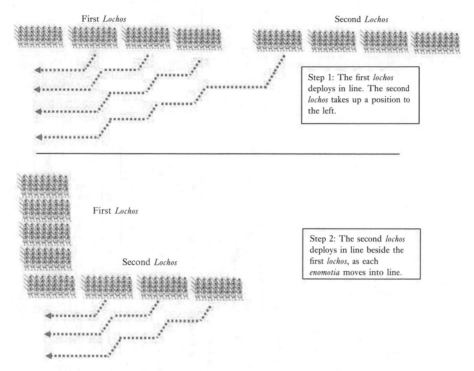

First *Lochos*   Second *Lochos*

Step 1: The first *lochos* deploys in line. The second *lochos* takes up a position to the left.

First *Lochos*

Step 2: The second *lochos* deploys in line beside the first *lochos*, as each *enomotia* moves into line.

Second *Lochos*

Figure 22: The redeployment of two *lochoi* from column into line.

The various depths attributed to hoplite deployments by the ancient authors have led to many different interpretations by modern scholars attempting to determine a standardized depth for the phalanx. Connolly, for example, states that the Archaic *enomotia* comprised three files of eight men, with the rearward *ouragos* positioned behind the unit; giving a base strength of twenty-five men.[40] Thus the combined Archaic *pentekostys* would possess a strength of fifty men, as its name would imply, and each *lochos* would possess a strength of one hundred. Connolly continues to state that by Xenophon's time, the Spartan army was based upon an *enomotia* of thirty-six men deployed in three files of twelve due to an increasing trend towards deep formations (and apparently despite Xenophon's various references to deployments of between eight and ten ranks in depth), while up until the late fifth century the Spartan army had been based upon a depth of eight.[41]

Connolly states that between Xenophon's description of a twelve-deep phalanx at Leuctra and Thucydides' reference to an eight-deep formation at Mantinea, Xenophon's is more likely to be correct as Thucydides himself states that he had difficulty obtaining information on the Spartan deployment.[42] However, both writers were military men and the deployments described by

Table 17: Examples of hoplite formations of various depths.

Depth	Source and details
1 deep	Isocrates, *Archidamus*, 99 – Spartans at Dipaea (c.471BC)
2 deep	Polyaenus, *Stratagems*, 2.1.24 – Spartans at Thebes (c.394BC)
'A few ranks' deep	Herodotus, 6.111 – Greeks at Marathon (490BC) (ἐπὶ τάξιας ὀλίγας)
4 deep	Diodorus 13.72.5 – Spartans at Athens (408BC) Xenophon, *Anabasis*, 1.2.15 – The *possible* deployment during a Greek parade in Asia Minor (401BC) – (see following)
8 deep	Thucydides 4.94 – Athenians at Delium (424BC) Thucydides 5.68 – Spartans at Mantinea (418BC) Thucydides 6.67 – Athenians at Syracuse (415BC) Xenophon, *Hellenica*, 2.4.34 – Athenians at Piraeus (404BC) Polyaenus, *Stratagems*, 2.2.9 – Spartans in Thrace (402BC) Leo the Emperor, *Stratagems*, 19.1 – Hoplites of Iphicrates engaging cavalry Xenophon, *Anabasis*, 7.1.22-23 – Referred to as 'proper' order (400BC) Polyaenus, *Excerpts*, 37.3 – Hoplites of Clearchus engaging cavalry Xenophon, *Hellenica*, 3.2.16 – Spartans at Maeander (399BC) Xenophon, *Hellenica* 6.2.21 – Spartans at Corcyra (373BC)
9–10 deep	Xenophon, *Hellenica*, 2.4.12 – Athenians at Piraeus (404BC) ('not more than ten') Xenophon, *Hellenica* 6.5.19 – Spartans at Mantinea (370BC) ('nine or ten shields deep')
12 deep	Xenophon, *Hellenica*, 6.4.12 – Spartans at Leuctra (371BC) ('not more than twelve')
16 deep	Thucydides 6.67 – Syracusans at Syracuse (415BC) Xenophon, *Hellenica*, 4.2.18 – Ordered deployment at Nemea (394BC)
25 deep	Thucydides 4.93 – Thebans at Delium (424BC)
50 deep	Xenophon, *Hellenica*, 2.4.11 – Athenians marching on Piraeus (404BC) Xenophon, *Hellenica*, 6.4.12 – Thebans at Leuctra (371BC) ('at least fifty shields deep')
'Deep'/'Exceedingly deep'/ 'To great depth'	Thucydides, 7.78–79 – Syracusans at Syracuse (415BC) (πολλοί) Xenophon, *Hellenica*, 2.4.34 – Spartans at Piraeus (404BC) (παντελῶς βαθεῖαν φάλαγγα) Xenophon, *Hellenica*, 4.2.18 – Boeotians at Nemea (394BC) (βαθεῖαν παντελῶς ἐποιήσαντο την φάλαγγα) Diodorus, 17.26.4 – Greeks at Halicarnassus (334BC) (ἐν βαθείᾳ φάλαγγι)

both can be considered plausible hoplite formations.[43] Xenophon himself refers to eight-deep formations at Maeander and Corcyra, and describes eight deep as the 'proper formation'. A deployment twelve ranks deep is only referred to once (see table 17). From this evidence it is unclear how a twelve-deep formation can be considered the standard of Xenophon's time. Although it is possible that Thucydides may not be correct in his attribution of an eight-deep phalanx to the Spartans at Mantinea, and may just be extrapolating using personal experience from other engagements, an eight-deep phalanx was no doubt something witnessed by Thucydides himself. The two accounts may not be in total agreement in terms of numbers and structure, but one cannot be given precedence over the other in respect to a standard battlefield practice.

In a series of confusing passages, Sekunda bases his examination of how a hoplite army could have moved from column into line on an *enomotia* of three files of twelve (based upon Xenophon's description of the Spartans at Leuctra).[44] Earlier in the same work, Sekunda states that sixteen deep was the standard hoplite formation due to the ordered deployment for the battle of Nemea.[45] Based upon the diversity of examples within the literary evidence, neither of Xenophon's descriptions can be considered a standard deployment for the Spartans or the forces from any other city-state.

Pritchett concludes in favour of a standard depth of eight for the hoplite phalanx; a position shared by some other scholars.[46] In seeming contrast to Asclepiodotus and Arrian, Pritchett also concludes that eight deep was the standard for the Macedonian phalanx up to the battle of Issus.[47] This would seem to support Markle's theory for the use of hoplite equipment by elements of the Macedonian army until the battle of Gaugamela and may be what Asclepiodotus is referring to in the stated use of ranks between eight and twelve deep.[48] Pritchett states that references to a sixteen-deep Macedonian phalanx are descriptions of two eight-man files positioned one behind the other.[49] It is also theorized that those in the rear ranks may have been those who could not afford to supply their own equipment.[50] Pritchett also argues that the files were divided into half-files and quarter-files, and interprets Polyaenus' description of a two-deep phalanx as a reference to a deployment by the quarter sections of a standard eight-deep file.[51] Pritchett further rejects Isocrates' reference to a one-deep phalanx as 'unthinkable' and merely dismisses it on the basis that it is the only reference to a formation of that depth.[52] However, if this criteria for selective dismissal is followed, other singular references to depth, including that of the twelve-deep Spartan deployment at Leuctra and the twenty-five-deep Theban position at Delium, should also have been dismissed. Isocrates' statement, while both curious and singular, cannot simply be dismissed in such an offhanded manner while retaining other singular references to depth.

Cawkwell suggests that Isocrates is referring to a single line of Spartans fronting a standard formation comprising men from many different allied states.[53]

This illustrates one problem faced when attempting to compartmentalize the depth of the phalanx into variants of a standard eight-deep file: not all of the deployments cited by ancient authors are readily divisible either by a standard file of eight or a half-file of four. Pritchett attempts to rectify this paradox by postulating that the officers positioned before the file were not always incorporated into the figures given in the ancient texts. Thus he concludes that the Spartan deployment at Mantinea to 'nine or ten shields deep' (ἐλλέα ἤ δέκα ... ἀσπίδων) was the result of standard files of eight hoplites, some with one officer at the head (making a file of nine), and others with two officers (making a file of ten).[54] Pritchett further concludes that the twenty-five-deep Theban position at Delium was the deployment of three standard eight-man files one behind each other with one officer at the head.[55] Similarly, the fifty-deep Theban phalanx at Leuctra is said to have been made from two *enomotiai*, each containing three standard files of eight, with all of the files deployed in column, plus two additional officers.[56]

Pritchett's theory, while numerically expedient and allowing for a standardized file depth, does present a major hazard to the interpretation of the depth of the phalanx. It is curious that the supposed omission of officers occurs only in select passages (i.e. those not divisible by eight) coming from two different authors. If Pritchett's theory is assumed to be correct, how are other passages from these same authors to be interpreted? For example, should the eight-deep Spartan deployment at Mantinea, which is held by Lendon as 'the basis for modern understanding of the methods and customs of hoplite fighting', in fact be re-read as a deployment of nine or ten deep with the officers omitted from the text by Thucydides?[57] Pritchett's model raises more problems and more questions than it solves; problems and questions Pritchett fails to address. Based upon other passages in the ancient sources, it seems more likely that the depth of the phalanx was variable. It may be the case that there was a 'commonly used' depth of deployment rather than a 'standard' depth. The ancient texts show that the depth to which the phalanx was arrayed depended upon several factors influencing its deployment.

Both Thucydides and Xenophon state that the depth of the line could be adjusted to either deep or shallow, depending upon the orders given and the way the line was formed when the army was deployed.[58] This suggests that both writers were aware that formations of varying depths could be, and were, commonly used. It appears that the decision as to what configuration to deploy was left, in some cases, to individual unit commanders rather than the *strategos*. At Thermopylae, for example, the contingents from each city-state were under the command of their own officers with Leonidas in overall command of the army.[59] At both Delium and Leuctra, different contingents deployed at different depths.[60] This suggests a certain level of autonomy in deployment, the absence of a standard depth of the phalanx and possibly different command structures among the forces from different city-states. The hoplites at the Maeander River were 'ordered' to deploy eight deep, further suggesting a lack of an eight-deep standard formation and that they awaited instructions regarding at what depth to deploy.[61] Independent decisions relating to deployment also account for the debate on the subject held by hoplite commanders prior to the battle of Nemea.[62] Interestingly, Xenophon's mercenaries, when ordered to deploy 'in line of battle' (ἐν τάξει), arrange themselves eight deep without further instruction.[63] This suggests that eight deep was the commonly used deployment for members of this contingent, but cannot be interpreted as a standard depth of hoplite formations from all city-states or at every engagement.

It seems clear that hoplite commanders possessed a substantial degree of latitude when it came to the deployment of their forces. Eight seems to have been the most commonly used depth, and could possibly be referred to as a 'standard' deployment, but attestations to the use of other depths imply that hoplite warfare was not limited to one type of formation. As there is no ancient reference to a phalanx six deep, nor evidence to suggest that a sixteen-deep formation was the military standard of the time, models for the redeployment of a marching column into *enomotiai* six abreast, a six-deep close-order formation created by 'doubling' a file of twelve, and the theory of a sixteen-rank standard depth all appear to be unfounded. Yet the question remains as to why a particular depth of the phalanx would be preferred over others under certain conditions.

The benefits of formations of different depths are varied and contested, even among the ancient authors. Arrian, for example, states that deep formations provide density and impetus, characteristics no doubt important to any formation bearing the unwieldy Macedonian *sarissa*. Arrian cites the deployment of the Thebans at Leuctra and the Boeotians at Mantinea as further examples of a formation gaining impetus through density and depth.[64] Diodorus also describes the use of a deep formation to gain impetus.[65] Cawkwell, Pritchett and Adcock offer that the purpose of deep formations was to provide reserves to the front ranks, a suggestion dismissed by Lazenby, Goldsworthy, How and Luginbill.[66] Krentz similarly suggests that hoplite formations had to be deep enough to be able to sustain front-line casualties (i.e. possess sufficient reserves), yet be wide enough to avoid encirclement.[67] This principle can be seen at the battle of Nemea where the Corinthian and Allied contingents were ordered not to make their formations too narrow and weak, or conversely too deep, to avoid being encircled.[68] It has also been suggested that deep formations lent moral support to those who lacked confidence.[69] Arrian further states that deep formations could also be used to solidly receive an attack.[70]

On the other hand, Xenophon, who would have been familiar with formations armed with the shorter hoplite spear, comments that formations that are too deep for the majority of their members to reach their opponents neither harm their enemies nor aid their allies.[71] Xenophon goes on to say that shallow formations are tactically superior as they allow more men to engage at any one time.[72] According to Diodorus, large formations were often the cause of their own undoing (apparently despite any gained impetus) as their size restricted the timely passage of commands, and so could be out-manoeuvred by shallower formations.[73] Wide, shallow formations could also be used to outflank and encircle an opponent.[74] Herodotus states that the Greek deployment at Marathon was designed to create just such an opportunity, but that the centre of the Greek position was weakened as a result of the thinning of the line.[75] At Delium, the outnumbered Athenians specifically deployed eight deep so that they could cover the same frontage as the opposing Thebans.[76] The Messenians deployed similarly for the battle of Ithome.[77] At a battle near Mantinea, the Spartans extended their close-order formation in order to cover the same frontage as the opposing Arcadians and their allies.[78] Thus in these instances, a wide, shallow phalanx was a tactical necessity. This need to cover the same frontage as the opposing formation may also account for deployments shallower than the commonly used eight-man file. It is also offered that a shallow phalanx would make the contingent appear bigger and that its adoption was to intimidate the opposition through the impression of size.[79] Deep phalanxes could similarly be used to hide the size of an army.[80] Arrian states that a depthless formation is good for deception but useless in long engagements.[81] Thus Xenophon's description of the Greek mercenaries parading in 'fours' (τεττάρων) may simply be a ruse to impress onlookers rather than deploying in their standard eight-deep arrangement.[82] A deployment in 'fours' may also be a reference to deploying in four files. The Spartans had deployed in four files of eight at Mantinea less than two decades earlier.[83] As there were many Spartans among the mercenary contingent, an arrangement in four files of eight during the parade can not be discounted.[84]

It is also interesting that most of the references to formations of a depth less than eight pertain to the Spartans who commonly took contingents of Helots on campaign with them. It is possible that what these passages refer to is the number of hoplites across the front of some Spartan phalanxes while the remainder of the file was made up of armed Helots. For example, at Plataea, the Spartan contingent consisted of 5,000 hoplites and 35,000 Helots with seven Helots assigned to each hoplite.[85] All of these Helots were equipped as fighting men.[86] As such the Spartans, had they wished, could have deployed in a common eight-deep phalanx with a single rank of hoplites across the front of the formation (i.e. a depth of one as per Isocrates) with the remainder of each file made up of seven Helots.[87] Similarly, both Isocrates and Diodorus state that there were 1,000 Lacedaemonian fighting men at Thermopylae; a number that must include a contingent of Helots.[88] At the battle of Ithome, a formation of armed Helots occupied the centre position of the Laconian line with the Spartan hoplites positioned on the wings.[89] Thus the presence and role of troops other than hoplites, while often stigmatized and even omitted from ancient texts, may have been a requirement to ensure that a deployment with an adequate frontage was possible. This partially follows Pritchett's theory that the rear ranks of some formations may have held those without hoplite equipment.

The other factor that could influence the depth of a phalanx was terrain. The fifty-deep Athenian formation marching on the Piraeus in 404BC, for example, was no doubt due to the formation advancing down a road.[90] At the Anapus River, the Syracusans were deployed 'many shields deep' because the place where they had deployed was also narrow.[91] At Mantinea, the Spartans were deployed eighteen to twenty deep as they advanced onto the field but, as the terrain widened, they halved the size of their files and opened their phalanx to the eventual arrangement of nine to ten deep.[92] Similarly, shallow deployments may have been used to occupy all of the available terrain.

The interval of the phalanx

As well as different depths, the phalanx could be deployed with varying orders of interval between each man. The sources covering the Classical Period provide no direct figure for the intervals used in different hoplite formations. The main source for the description of intervals is provided by Asclepiodotus. As noted, Asclepiodotus states that hoplite formations could be deployed in one of three orders: a close-order, with interlocked shields, of 45cm per man; an intermediate-order with each man separated by 90cm on all sides; and an open-order with each man spearated by 180cm by width and depth.[93] As previously demonstrated, a hoplite bearing his panoply in an oblique body posture, and wielding his spear in an underarm fashion, could easily conform to any of the intervals detailed by Asclepiodotus in relation to the phalanx (see Chapter 4, Bearing the Hoplite Panoply). In agreement with this conclusion and Asclepiodotus' descriptions, the Classical authors describe hoplite formations deployed in the same three intervals. The manner in which the Greek formations are used also commonly bears a strong resemblance to the purpose of each interval stated by Asclepiodotus (table 18).

The number of occurrences in the ancient texts suggests that the most common hoplite deployment (but not necessarily the 'standard' hoplite deployment) was a close-order formation, probably eight ranks deep. Plutarch

Table 18: Examples of the use of formations of various orders by Greek hoplites.

Order	Source and details
Close-order	Asclepiodotus 3.6 (συνασπισμοῖς), 4.1 (τὸ πυκνότατον καθ᾽ ὃ συνηπιστικός) – Interval of 45cm used to receive an attack with locked shields. Herodotus 9.18 (πυκνόσαντες) – Phocians at Plataea (479BC). To receive an attack. Thucydides, 1.63 (ἐς ἐλάχιστον χωρίον) – Corinthians at Potidaea (432BC). To punch through an enemy line. Thucydides, 2.4 (ξυνεστρέφοντό) – Thebans at Plataea (431BC). To receive an attack. Thucydides, 5.10 (ξυστραφέντες) – Athenians at Amphipolis (422BC). To receive an attack. Xenophon, *Hellenica*, 4.3.18 (συσπειραθέντες ἐχώρουν ἐρρωμένως) – Thebans at Coronea (394BC). To punch through an enemy line. Plutarch, *Pelopidas*, 17 (συνήγαγεν) – Thebans at Tegyra (375BC). To punch through an enemy line. Plutarch, *Pelopidas*, 23 (συναγαγεῖν … συναρμόττειν) – General reference to the Spartans' use of close-order to resist an attack (see also Xenophon, *Agesilaus*, 6.7). Xenophon, *Hellenica*, 7.4.22 (συντεταγμένοι) – Arcadians at Cromnus (365BC). To receive an attack. Xenophon, *Agesilaus*, 6.7 (συντεταγμένον) – Advises to adopt a close-order formation whenever threatened (i.e. to receive an attack). Diodorus, 15.86.4 (συντάγματος) – Thebans at Mantinea (363BC). To punch through an enemy line. Diodorus, 16.3.2 – Macedonians under Philip (360BC) adopt the close-order formation (φάλαγγος πυκνότητα) imitating the close-order formation with overlapping shields (συνασπισμόν) used by the warriors at Troy. Plutarch, *Timoleon*, 27 (πυκνώσας τῷ συνασπισμῷ) – Greeks in Sicily (341BC). To punch through an enemy line. Diodorus, 17.26.4 (φάλαγγι πεπυκνωμένον) – Greeks at Hallicarnassus (334BC). To punch through an enemy line. Plutarch, *Philopoemen*, 9 (ὀπίκνωμα) – Achaeans at Mantinea (207BC). Drilled in close-order formations because of their security. Plutarch, *Philopoemen*, 10 (συνεστηκός) – Achaeans at Mantinea (207BC). To attack an enemy formation.
Intermediate-order	Asclepiodotus 4.1 (τὸ μέσον) – Interval of 90cm to advance into the attack. Thucydides, 4.96 – Thebans and Athenians at Delium (424BC). Attack made at the run (προσέμειξαν δρόμῳ) and would be in intermediate-order at least (see following). Xenophon, *Hellenica*, 4.3.19 – Spartans and Thebans at Coronea (394BC). Attack made at the run (ερρομένος) and clash 'head on' (ἀντιμέτωπος συνέρραξε) and would be in intermediate-order at least (see following). Xenophon, *Hellenica*, 6.2.20 – Corcyreans at Corcyra (373BC). Sally out *en masse* (ἀθρόοι) to punch through an enemy line and would be in intermediate-order at least. Xenophon, *Hellenica*, 6.4.13 – Leuctra (371BC). Thebans attack at the run (ἔτι δὲ ἐνέβαλλον οἱ τῶν Θηβαίων λόχοι) while the Spartans are out of order and both would be in intermediate-order at least (see following). See also Plut. *Pel.* 23 who says the Thebans attacked at the run (δρόμῳ).
Open-order	Asclepiodotus 4.1 (τὸ ἀραιότατον) – Interval of 180cm for normal movement. Xenophon, *Hellenica*, 4.5.15 (ἅτε διώξαντες ὡς τάχους ἕκαστος εἶχεν) – Spartans at Corinth (390BC). Used to pursue routed troops.

states that the Spartan army was trained to close their ranks whenever they were threatened in what must be a practised Spartan tactical defensive manoeuvre.[94] Plutarch also refers to what he calls both 'open' and 'regular' formations (ἐμφανῆ κατάστασιν ἐχούσης καὶ νόμιμον), suggesting that the close-order phalanx was the common deployment for hoplites.[95]

Modern scholarship, similar to its search for a standard depth for the phalanx, is divided amongst those who argue that the phalanx also possessed a standard order or interval. Adcock describes the phalanx as 'a body of infantry in close-order in several ranks that are also in close-order' without detailing what interval he supposed they used.[96] How states that 'the Greeks fought in compact masses without marked intervals'.[97] Krentz states that the 'orthodox' view of spacing is one of 3ft (90cm) per man in close-order and 6ft (180cm) per man in loose-order.[98] Matthews states that the preferred interval for the phalanx was 80cm per man.[99] Connor uses an interval of 180cm per man in a calculation of the area needed to deploy a phalanx of 10,000 men.[100] In Sekunda's model for doubling, also based upon a 90cm interval, when the unit moved to six abreast it would automatically create the close-order formation of Asclepiodotus of 45cm per man by inserting the rear half-files into the intervals. Sekunda, however, does not connect the insertion of troops with the adoption of a completely different order. Warry, in his model for the creation of a close-order formation by 'doubling', states that before any insertion took place, the files of hoplites were separated by 200–250cm per man.[101] This is much greater than even the open-order described by Asclepiodotus. The diagram accompanying Warry's model suggests that, once the 'doubling' process had been completed, the shields of the 'doubled' formation would be interlocked.[102] Due to the spacing upon which Warry's model is based, this could only be accomplished if the hoplite shield had a diameter of over 1.5 metres; a size for which there is no evidence in the archaeological record and that would be far too large to wield effectively.

Similar to the debate over depth, none of the current theories consider that there may not have been a 'standard' order of deployment. The evidence suggests that the hoplite phalanx was deployed, not just in different depths, but also in different orders to suit specific tactical purposes on the battlefield. As indicated by the ancient texts, a close-order formation of hoplites could be used to receive an enemy attack (as per Asclepiodotus), but was also mobile enough to be able to attack an enemy position (see table 18). Some scholars dismiss the association of the close-order interval with the 45cm interval described by Asclepiodotus due to the constraints to movement that they perceive this small a space would impose.[103] However, apart from the ability for the second rank to reach the enemy only while deployed in such an arrangement, the strongest indication that the close-order formation used by hoplite armies was only 45cm per man is that it is the only interval that would allow for the creation of the strongest aspect of the phalanx: the shield wall.

The shield wall

The shield wall was exactly what its name implies: a strong 'wall' of interlocked shields positioned across the front of the phalanx. Some of the earliest clear references to a formation of interlocking shields can be found in the works of the Archaic Period. In the *Iliad*, Homer describes an unengaged Greek forma-tion as waiting with 'shield pressed against shield (ἀσπὶς ἄρ᾿ ἀσπίδ᾿ ἔπειδε), helmet by helmet, man by man'.[104] Similarly, a passage of Tyrtaeus describes a formation of men as 'setting foot beside foot, resting shield against shield (ἀσπίδος ἀσπίδ᾿ ἐρείσας), crest beside crest, helmet beside helmet'.[105] These descriptions of men pressing 'shield against shield' (the way in which these passages are often translated) indicates that the shields being referred to are overlapping and pressing against each other. The passages cannot be descriptions of the contact between two opposing phalanxes as the sides in both passages are not yet engaged in any form of combat.

Tyrtaeus' passage is often taken to be a reference to a more open style of warfare in the Archaic Period. In later lines Tyrtaeus extols the lightly armed skirmishers to 'crouch *on either hand beneath the shield* and fling your great hurl-stones, and throw your smooth javelins against them, in your place *beside* the men of heavier armament'.[106] The terms 'on either hand beneath the shield' and 'beside' have been interpreted by some as references to the light armed troops being dispersed 'in between' the files of the hoplites; protected by the section of the hoplite's shield extending to his left.[107] This would necessitate a deployment of the hoplites in some form of open-order. However, the earlier lines of the same passage describe the hoplites as standing 'shield against shield' in a close-order formation.[108] The more likely interpretation of this whole passage is that the terms 'on either hand' and 'beside' are descriptions of the positioning of the skirmishers on both sides of the entire close-order phalanx of hoplites (i.e. on the wings), in just the way that cavalry and light troops were positioned for the battles of the First Messenian War.[109] Their protection is most likely to have come from their own shields, not from those carried by the hoplites.[110] A depiction of such a 'rock-thrower' can be clearly seen on a fifth century attic *oinchoe* in the Museo Archeologico Pontecagnano (T1240).[111] The figure in this image, while stylized in heroic nudity, none-theless still wears a Corinthian-style helmet fully on his head and carries the large *aspis* of the hoplite while brandishing a large stone in his right hand. Due to the odd way in which the figure is clad, it is impossible to determine whether this image is mythological or contemporary in theme. Regardless, the depiction of this 'rock-thrower' closely follows the description of such troops by Tyrtaeus.

If the 'rock-throwers' of Tyrtaeus' poem were similarly armed, there would be no need for them to crouch behind the shields of the hoplites in the phalanx. This would allow them to be positioned 'beside the men of heavy armament' on the wings while the phalanx was drawn up in the centre in close-order with 'shield against shield' as Tyrtaeus describes it. Diodorus additionally states that one of the reforms made to the Macedonian army by Philip in 360BC was the adoption of the close-order formation (φάλαγγος πυκνότητα) 'imitating the close-order (συνασπισμόν) fighting style with overlapping shields used by the warriors at Troy'.[112] This correlates with Homer's description of the Greeks at Troy adopting close-order formations.[113] Consequently, it can be concluded that the shield wall was a tactical formation known to the Greeks in the eighth century BC at least and possibly much earlier.[114]

Thucydides states that the hoplite shield covered both the bearer and the man to his left.[115] Like Tyrtaeus and Homer before him, Thucydides' passage can only be a reference to shields that overlap the intervals occupied by two adjacent men. Diodorus, in a passage that can in no way be interpreted as anything other than a reference to a shield wall, describes the Spartan formation at Thermopylae as 'standing with closed ranks, making their formation *like a wall*' (τείχει παραπλησίαν).[116] The description of the shield wall by Tyrtaeus in the seventh century BC and Plutarch's later description of the Archaeans using a close-order formation at Mantinea in 207BC (see table 18) demonstrate that this method of hoplite deployment was in use for at least four centuries.[117]

Unfortunately, no contemporary visual representation of the phalanx as a whole survives from the Classical Period.[118] There have been suggestions by various scholars that certain reliefs and/or vase illustrations, the images on the Chigi Vase and the Nereid Monument in particular, are representations of the Classical phalanx in one of its many guises.[119] However, as has been demonstrated, the majority of these depictions reflect the more open missile-based warfare of an earlier age, not the ordered structure of the Classical phalanx. Even if these sources were meant by the artist to be a representation of the phalanx, they are regularly shown in profile and their accuracy is limited by the artistic ability of the craftsman and the conventions of his time. Clearly, the tendency for early Greek art to display the shield beside the body of the hoplite rather than across his front, and the lack of a representation of multiple ranks of men, has a great impact on the ability to determine how the phalanx was formed based solely upon artistic data. As such, no vase illustration, relief or other artwork can be considered an accurate depiction of the phalanx.

A clear example of the inability to rely solely upon artistic representation can be found in the case of a fragmented Archaic Cypriot statue of the three-headed giant Geryon in the New York Metropolitan Museum of Art. Sekunda claims that this statue 'gives an idea of how hoplites locked shields'; suggesting that hoplites interlocked their shields with every second *aspis* positioned behind those on either side in an alternating fashion.[120] However, while it may have been possible, even discounting the artist's ability to correctly proportion the limbs and other body parts, for a mythological three-headed giant to wield his shields in this manner, an analysis of how this would translate to a hoplite phalanx indicates that it would have been impractical to form a close-order shield wall using this method.

To examine the pros and cons of shield walls of various configurations, different formations were created using re-enactors from the Sydney Ancients. Adopting differently configured shield walls allowed observations to be made on how the disposition of the shields affected the defensive and offensive characteristics of the formation, as well as its method of deployment. It was found that it would have been possible for hoplites in a close-order phalanx to position their shields in the same alternating manner as the Geryon statue while still conforming to the 45cm interval for the formation outlined by Asclepiodotus. However, to do so each hoplite would need to hold his shield parallel to the front, also as per the Geryon statue (figure 23).

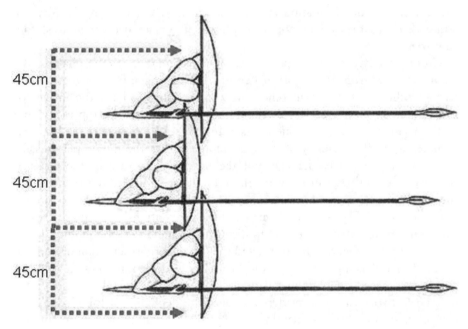

Figure 23: Three hoplites arranged as per the Geryon statue showing the interval per man.

With the adoption of such a deployment, every alternate man across the line would be positioned further forward than those beside them to accommodate the depth of the *aspis*. This creates a disparity of up to 10cm between the front of one hoplite's shield and that of the man next to him, and forms weak points in the line; the very thing the shield wall was designed to negate.

Another aspect highlighted by the re-creations was that any hoplite who had his shield positioned behind those to either side had nothing locking it in place other than his own body and the strength of the posture he had adopted. Thus not all of the shields are 'interlocked'. However, two-thirds of the rearward positioned shields are protected by the overlapping sections of the shields on either side. Shields positioned in the front are supported on either side by those behind, which effectively hold the front shields in place. These supportive and/or protective characteristics are true for all shields across the line except for those borne by the unit commander and his file on the right flank of the formation, which are only supported or protected on the left side depending upon their positioning. If a unit commander's shield was positioned to the front (as per the bottom hoplite in figure 23) strong impacts against the right side of the surface would force it backwards, pivoting at the elbow, which both inhibits the use of the weapon arm and exposes the left side of the body to attack. Similarly, a strong impact against a rearward positioned shield could drive the entire unsupported hoplite backwards or move the shield out of position, also opening potentially dangerous holes in the line. Shields positioned behind those on either side are also prevented from being used to parry any oncoming attack as movement of the *aspis* is checked by the shields overlapping across its front; a hoplite in this position would have had little choice but to accept the blow and hope it did not penetrate his shield.

If a hoplite holding his shield in front of those beside him fell in battle, it would be almost impossible for a member of the second rank to move sufficiently forward enough to be able to slot his shield through the gap between the shields on either side and then reposition it across his front so that it overlapped in the same configuration as that of the man he was replacing. Replacements would only be able to keep their shield across their front and take up a position behind those of the men on either side. This means that where the first rank hoplite had initially been stationed ahead of those on either side of him, his replacement would now be behind them. This would begin to alter the structure and integrity of the shield wall as members of the front rank fell sporadically across the front line during fighting and reserves were unable to effectively replace them.

An alternating shield wall also poses several problems with deployment. Whether moving from a column into line of battle, or shifting files to the right to create a close-order formation, it is unlikely that each individual file would have known in advance whether their shields were meant to be positioned ahead of, or behind, those of the men to their right. The resultant shield wall would have been confused, irregular in its disposition and mutually unsupported across the entire line. It seems improbable that hoplites would have adopted a deployment such as an alternating shield wall, which provided so few defensive benefits, in a formation that the ancient texts state was primarily designed to receive an enemy attack. As such, it can only be assumed that the Geryon statue is the result of an artistic convention of some kind, or the ability of the artist himself. Clearly, the character of the statue cannot possess three left arms to support the three shields, as those supported by three individual hoplites in a phalanx would have been, and the shields may be depicted in an alternating manner due to one being supported by the right arm. Consequently, Sekunda's model of the way that hoplites locked their shields cannot be considered correct.

Thucydides' passage that each man in the phalanx sought protection behind the overlapping section of the shield belonging to the man to his right initially appears to provide a clue to the construction of the shield wall; each man standing with his own shield tucked behind the overlapping section of that to the right.[121] However, the characteristics of the *aspis*, and of a phalanx formed in this manner, also indicate that this was not how the shield wall was constructed.

When this method of deployment was re-created, if each hoplite held his shield parallel to the front as per the Geryon statue, but behind that of the man to his right as per the interpretation of Thucydides, the very depth of the shield, even near its outer edge, positioned each hoplite approximately 10cm behind the front of the man to his right, forming a somewhat oblique line without a parallel frontage (figure 24).

As the line extended across a larger phalanx, this difference would compound. The tenth man in the line, for example, would be approximately one metre behind the frontage of the unit commander at the head of the right-hand file. When this difference is transposed upon the seven *morai* deployment of the Spartans at Mantinea, the hoplite at the head of the far left file would be over ten metres behind the *polemarch* on the right-hand side of the formation (assuming that each unit is not separated from those adjacent to it and that the army was deployed in one long line). This equates to a difference of over three file lengths and suggests that this was an unlikely method of hoplite deployment.

To allow the phalanx to deploy with a flat frontage, yet still present a shield wall formed as per this interpretation of Thucydides' description, the shield borne by each hoplite would have been rotated further around to the right; so that it was beyond parallel to the front by a few degrees. This would allow

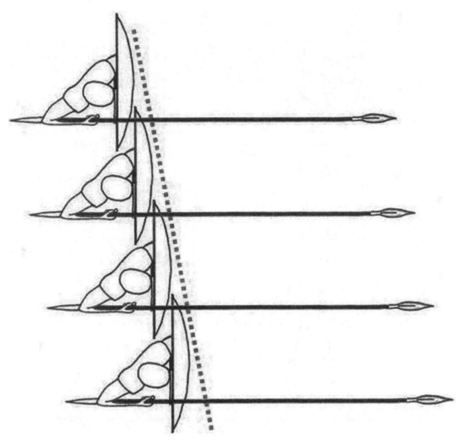

Figure 24: An oblique frontage resulting from shields being held parallel to each other.

the shields of subsequent members of the line to slot in behind that of the man to the right (figure 25).

However, this method of constructing a shield wall also poses problems with defence, offence and deployment. In this method the shields are strongly interlocked and mutually support each other (covered on the right by the one overlapping across it, and supported on the left by the one behind it), yet none but that belonging to the unit commander could be used to parry an attack as the remainder are locked in place by the shield to the right. Offensively, rotating the arm and body to position the shield in such a posture places the torso at a more acute angle to the front, which inhibits the use of the weapon arm, particularly when wearing rigid metal armour. Having the shield positioned further around to the right also brings the rim of the *aspis* closer to the weapon-bearing hand, which similarly inhibits offensive actions.

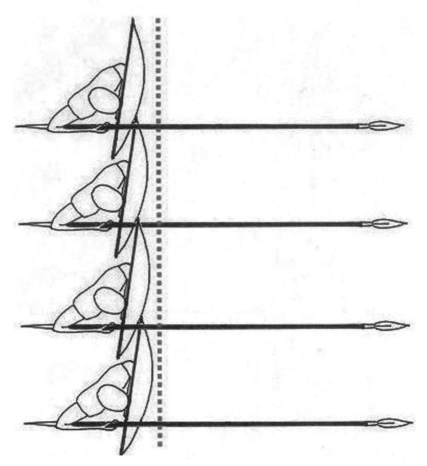

Figure 25: A flat frontage resultant from shields being rotated further to the right.

Like the alternating method, it would have been difficult for a hoplite from the second rank to move forward to replace a fallen comrade and somehow reposition his shield behind that of the man to his right and in front of that of the man to his left. When deploying from marching column, or when creating a close-order formation, each hoplite would, if using this method, have known that his shield was meant to go behind that of the man to his right; but it is difficult to achieve such a position without forming a phalanx with an oblique frontage (figure 24), unless drawn up on a line marked on the ground.

The most likely way that a shield wall was formed would have been by having the shield of each man overlap that of the man to his right instead of being placed behind it as per the initial interpretation of the passage of Thucydides (figure 26).

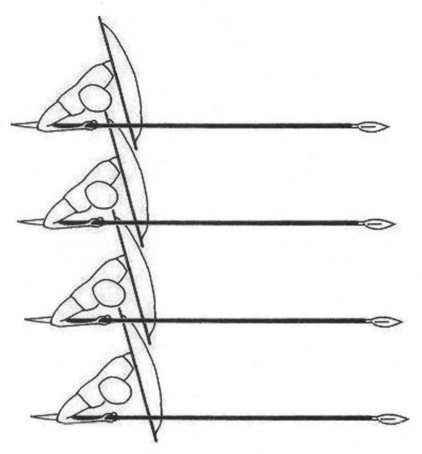

Figure 26: Hoplites forming a shield wall by overlapping their shields from the left.

When arrayed in this position, the phalanx presents a level front, as do those of the second and subsequent ranks, and each man conforms to the 45cm interval detailed by Asclepiodotus for the close-order formation. The shield of each hoplite is also locked in place; supported from behind by the shield to the right and additionally protected by the overlapping section of the shield to the left. The overlapping sections on both sides are approximately one-quarter of the diameter of the shield (around 23cm). Thus each shield is overlapped by one quarter of that to the left and overlaps the one to the right by a quarter of its own diameter. This results in equal support for the shield wall across the entire front of the phalanx, leaving minimal gaps for penetration.[122] Cawkwell states that a spear thrust could slide off the rounded surface of the hoplite shield, even when deployed in a shield wall, and hit the bearer.[123] However, due to the level of protection provided by the large diameter of the *aspis*, the helmet and greaves, and the manner in which the shield interlocks into the shield wall, it is uncertain how this could occur except for a strike that was deflected by the curvature of the shield up into the helmet or down into the legs.

A shield interlocking over that of the man to the right also allows for a close-order formation to be created by files deployed in intermediate-order side-stepping to the right.[124] When moving from column into line, or forming a close-order formation, it is quite easy to extend the right hand rim of the shield slightly forward as two hoplites converge and then pull it back into position as the shields overlap. Similarly, replacements in battle could easily move forward into the gap left by the fallen with their shield slightly 'open' to the front-right and then pull the leading edge back into place to overlap with the shield on the right side rather than attempting to slot in behind it (see Figure 27). In doing so the left hand side of the *aspis* naturally positions itself behind the shield of the man to the left with very little effort, conscious thought or need to visually align the shield, which would necessitate removing one's gaze from the enemy to the front. Holding the shield-bearing arm at a slightly forward-right angle also is a more natural position for the arm to be in than holding it across the front of the body when in an oblique body posture due to the slight rotation of the torso. This places less muscular stress on the shield-bearing arm and sits the inner rim of the *aspis* firmly on the shoulder to support its weight. The left hand does not become dangerously sandwiched between the two overlapping shields as it is encased within the concave bowl of the *aspis*. Interestingly, this method of arrangement still agrees with Thucydides' description of the mechanics of the phalanx. The body of each man is partially situated behind the shield of the man to his right, even though his own shield overlaps it from the front. This is most likely what Thucydides is referring to in his narrative.

Defensively, the interlocking of shields would occur naturally within every rank of the formation when each hoplite conforms to the 45cm interval of Asclepiodotus' close-order. This would have made the close-order formation mutually supporting from within, as well as across the line, and extremely strong. Any attack against the front rank, whether from spear or collision, would be at pains to try and force the creation of any gap in the line. Additionally, the shield belonging to the man on the far right is difficult to budge. The left-hand side of this shield is protected by the overlapping *aspis* of the man beside him and prevents any unit commander's shield from being forced out of position. The strength of this kind of shield wall would have been the primary requirement of a formation regularly used for defensive purposes.

Offensively, having the shield inclined slightly to the front-right provides the weapon-bearing arm with more room to move than when the shield is held across the front of the body. A shield wall created in this manner can be temporarily 'opened' by individual hoplites, momentarily foregoing some of its defence, to allow an attack to be delivered against a low 'opportune target' such as the legs or groin, or for an incoming attack to be parried. The shield can then be returned to its defensive position without necessitating the movement of any of the other shields or overly compromising the integrity of the formation. These strong defensive and offensive abilities are only possible when using a shield wall of this configuration and when using a combination of the low and underarm stances to wield the spear (figure 27).

Through re-creation it was also found that if the hoplites moved closer to each other (only possible when the shield wall is used as a static defensive formation that does not require room for movement) the left-hand section of the shield belonging to the man on the right can be further locked in place between the chest and left arm of the adjacent man. This would have made a static shield wall almost impossible to break, but limits the amount of room for the use of the weapon arm.

Thus what made a shield wall both possible and effective were the physical characteristics of the hoplite shield itself. Pritchett admits that he is unable to see how a 90cm diameter shield could fit into an interval less than 50cm. He states that the archaeological evidence fails to support the interval provided

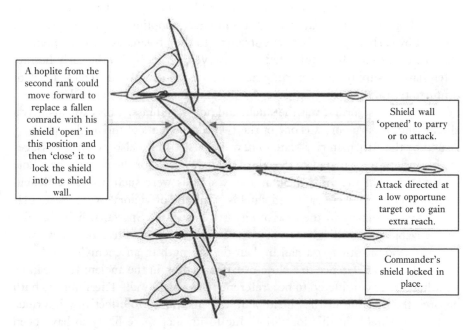

Figure 27: Offensive and defensive characteristics of a shield wall.

by Asclepiodotus, and that the interval of the hoplite phalanx must have therefore been 90cm per man.[125] This position clearly requires revision. It is the 90cm diameter of the shield that makes the close-order shield wall possible. There is simply no way that members of a phalanx carrying shields of this size can stand within 45–50cm intervals and not create a wall of interlocking shields while keeping their shield in a protective position across their front. Conversely, there is no way that a phalanx can create an inter-locking shield wall without each man conforming to the 45cm interval provided by Asclepiodotus. For the shields to effectively overlap, the interval occupied by each man cannot be more than half of the diameter of the shield he is carrying. This creates a condition in which both the left and right edges of the shield extend into to interval occupied by an adjacent man, thereby creating the interlocking shield wall. As the *aspis* had an average diameter of 90cm, the interval of the close-order formation can only have been around 45–50cm, complying with the figure given by Asclepiodotus.

If the *aspis* had possessed a smaller diameter, there would not have been enough of the shield to effectively interlock with others. Had the shield not possessed the concave curvature of its bowl-shaped surface nor the double *porpax/antilabe* grip system, which allowed the shield to be supported on the shoulder and braced into position while the left hand is protected inside the curvature of the shield, the shield wall could similarly not have been maintained. Lorimer states that it was the universal adoption of the bronze plate corselet by early hoplites that gave strength to the phalanx as no weak point in the line could have been tolerated.[126] However, not only did the early hoplite often have to supply his own equipment, which in itself would suggest a lack of uniformity, but clearly what gave the phalanx its strength, particularly when deployed in close-order, was the shield and not the cuirass. This explains why a shield, and not armour, was one of the two components of the hoplite panoply issued by the Athenian city-state to new *ephebes*.[127] This also explains passages in the ancient texts that state that the shield was used for the sake of the whole line, not just for the individual, and why shields were such prized battlefield trophies; not only were captured shields symbolic of victory over a particular adversary, especially in the case of city-states such as Sparta, which placed a recognizable 'national' blazon on the shields of its hoplites, but they were material evidence that you had broken the strength of an enemy's line.[128]

As such, any reference to a close-order formation in the ancient texts can be simultaneously considered to be a reference to a shield wall. The ability to both enforce the creation of the shield wall, and its ability to effectively interlock with other shields in this formation due to its shape, are likely to have been conscious design considerations in the development of the *aspis*, although due to the limited amount of source material available for Archaic Era Greece, there is no way to be certain which came first: the shield or the shield wall.

Hanson claims that a round shield gave few advantages over squarer types of shields other than removing the corners of the square shield itself, which he says did not really offer any protection to the body anyway, thus making the shield lighter.[129] However, it was the very fact that the hoplite shield was round that allowed it to effectively interlock into the shield wall. When two hoplite shields are positioned one behind the other, the overlapping sections create an even, elliptical, shape (figure 28).

Had the *aspis* been square, the overlapping section would still have been even, but rectangular in shape (figure 29).

While shields of both shapes interlock firmly with one another, the difference between the two styles becomes apparent when the hoplite becomes fatigued. When this occurred, the hoplite's shield-bearing arm would droop, pivoting at the elbow, with the forearm moving from a horizontal position into a more vertical one. However, due to the round shape of the hoplite shield, the shape of the interlocking section remains unchanged and thus the integrity of the formation remains uncompromised (figure 30).

However, the cross-section of two interlocking square shields vastly alters when the forearm is repositioned to the same fatigued angle, compromising the structure of the shield wall, highlighting weak points in the formation to an observant enemy, risking injury to the adjacent man on the corner of the shield and potentially exposing areas of the bearer to attack (figure 31).

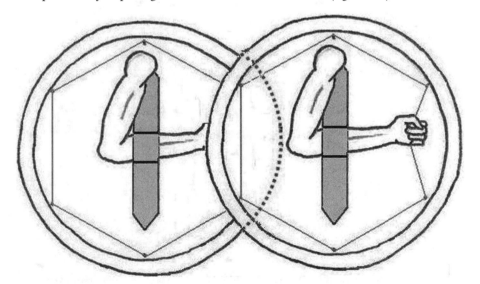

Figure 28: How two hoplite shields interlock.

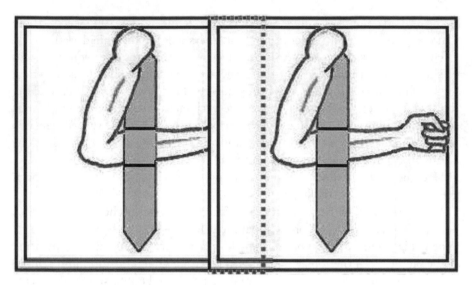

Figure 29: How two square shields interlock.

Round shields are the only ones that also create a 'cradle' for spears deployed in the underarm position. Importantly, this cradle does not disappear when the shield moves due to the fatigue of the arm. A spear held in the underarm position could be rested on the upper rim of a row of interlocked square

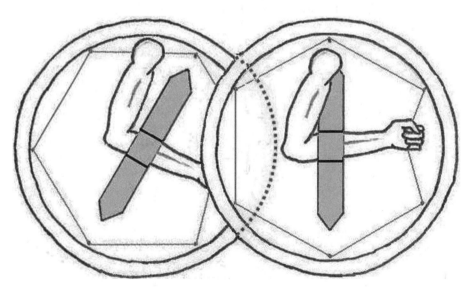

Figure 30: How two hoplite shields will still interlock even when one hoplite (on left) becomes fatigued.

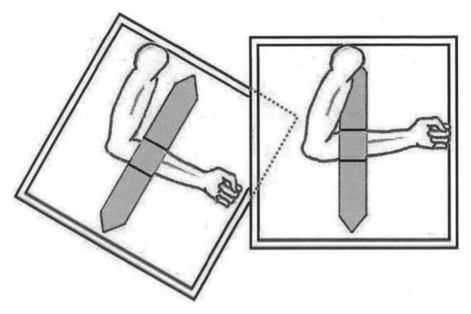

Figure 31: How two square shields do not effectively interlock when one hoplite (on left) becomes fatigued.

shields, but once those shields begin to move with fatigue, the line of the upper rims becomes disjointed and angular with little way of supporting any weapon.

As such, the shield wall could only be formed when the phalanx was deployed in a close-order formation with the men separated by less than the diameter of the shield. The larger intervals of the intermediate- and open-order formations detailed by Asclepiodotus provide no means for the shields to effectively interlock. Hoplites deployed in intermediate-order formations are more likely to have held their shields parallel to the front with their rims touching those on either side, as there was no requirement for the shields to interlock, while still giving a flat frontage to the formation (figure 32).

The order in which a phalanx was deployed allows for what Pritchett refers to as 'topographical determinations': the order and depth will dictate the area that a phalanx will occupy.[130] Snodgrass, for example, states that the three hundred Spartans at Thermopylae could have occupied the fifty foot wide pass at twice their normal depth.[131] However, he does not state what he considers their normal depth to have been. If Snodgrass has based this conclusion upon a standard depth of eight ranks, then twice normal depth would be sixteen deep. A sixteen-deep phalanx would mean that the Spartans could only deploy around nineteen files ($300/16 = 18.75$). Fifty feet (15.3m) divided amongst nineteen files gives an interval of 80cm per man; smaller than the intermediate-order

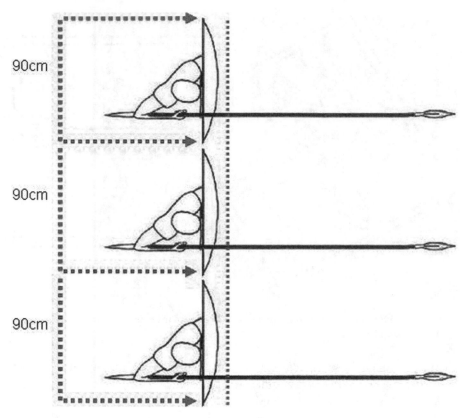

Figure 32: Three hoplites in an intermediate-order with their shields creating a flat frontage.

detailed by Asclepiodotus, but much bigger than that for the close-order formation of 45cm per man. However, it seems unlikely that the Spartans would have adopted an intermediate-order formation to defend the pass as not only would a static close-order formation have given them a greater tactical advantage, but Plutarch states that the Spartan deployment to face danger was the close-order phalanx and Diodorus specifically describes the formation at Thermopylae as being 'like a wall'; also suggesting a close-order deployment.[132] If the Spartan deployment is recalculated using a close-order formation, the Spartans could have adopted a line thirty-four men across and between eight and nine ranks deep, which would only require an area 15.3 metres wide (the stated width of the pass) and 4 metres deep. Snodgrass, therefore, appears to be incorrect in his assumption of a double-depth Spartan deployment at Thermopylae.

Other hoplite formations

The phalanx could also be rearranged into variants of the common 'block' formation. Xenophon states that the Thebans at Mantinea deployed in a wedge-shaped formation (τὸ ἔμβολον) to punch through the enemy line.[133] Plutarch and Diodorus state that the Theban contingent at Leuctra formed an oblique line (λοξὴ φάλαγξ) designed to draw the opposing wing forward.[134] Plutarch also refers to a deployment of a hoplite army into three columns so that an enemy position could be attacked on multiple fronts.[135] Xenophon's mercenaries formed a defensive circle (κύκλος) while effecting a river crossing.[136] The defensive square (τετράγωνος or πλαίσιον) was also a common deployment for hoplite armies.[137] Many of these formations are also echoed in the sources for the Macedonian phalanx, providing a further similarity between the Classical phalanx and its Hellenistic successor.[138] The later military works also contain several other types of 'irregular' formation. Some of these include the concave and convex crescent-shaped line, with both wings swept forward or back respectively, and the open-ended square.[139] These works also contain a vast array of possible configurations for the marching column, depending upon the level of a perceived threat and the direction from which it was expected.[140] While many of these 'irregular' deployments are not detailed in the Classical texts as being commonly used by hoplite armies, the structured nature of the hoplite phalanx into units and sub-units would not preclude a hoplite army from the adoption of such a disposition should the tactical and/or strategic necessities of the moment require it.

Moving the phalanx

Unlike the singular defensive purpose for the close-order formation ascribed by Asclepiodotus, the Greek close-order phalanx was used both defensively and offensively. The order in which the phalanx was deployed dictated the ease in which the formation could move and subsequently the manner in which it could be used for defence or attack.

It was vital for the hoplite to maintain his position in line and hence the structure of the formation; particularly for the close-order shield wall. There are numerous passages in the ancient texts attesting to the importance of maintaining the cohesion of the phalanx and the consequences that befall troops who do not keep order in the ranks.[141] The Greek word for discipline (εὐταξία) literally translates as 'arranged well'. According to Herodotus, keeping one's place in line was Spartan law.[142] McDermott, in his computer modelling of hoplite warfare, showed that without effective cohesion on the battlefield a phalanx was finished.[143] For a close-order phalanx that was used to receive an enemy attack, the maintenance of the formation was somewhat easier so long as the hoplite's morale held firm. If each man maintained his position in line, the structure of the phalanx would hold. The maintenance of the structure of the phalanx became more difficult when the formation was used to attack.

Arrian states that once deployed in a close-order formation, movement for the Macedonian phalanx was all but impossible.[144] Sekunda further echoes this sentiment stating that, once deployed in the six-by-six close-order *enomotia* of his model, movement for the hoplite phalanx would have also been impossible, and that this formation was only used to receive an enemy attack as per Asclepiodotus.[145] However, the literary evidence demonstrates that the close-order hoplite formation was capable of movement and offence.

When re-enactors from the Sydney Ancients were arranged in a close-order shield wall formation and instructed to advance at different paces, it was observed that, in order to keep the shield wall from breaking, the movement of the close-order formation had to be conducted at nothing more than a moderate walking pace. If a faster advance was attempted, the individual members of the formation could not keep pace with each other and the line began to break. Even at the slowest pace, it was almost impossible for each member of the line to strictly maintain his 45cm interval. However, the 23cm section of overlapping shield to either side allowed for some expansion or compression of the intervals between the files during movement without significantly compromising the integrity of the shield wall itself. It was also found that the spears of the second rank, extending to either side of the man in front when held in their underarm 'ready' position, acted as a rough guide for the spacing of the phalanx and limited how far the interval would open as it moved.

It was also found that the integrity of a moving shield wall was almost impossible to maintain when the line was arranged in the 'alternating' fashion proposed by Sekunda. Hoplites with their shields behind those on either side of them had little way of gauging whether they were maintaining their correct spacing as the line advanced. As a result, the intervals between each man became greatly disjointed, shields began to overlap in the wrong manner and gaps began to form in the line. This further suggests that Sekunda's 'alternating' method of deploying a shield wall was not commonly used by hoplite armies.

The ancient sources demonstrate that one method of keeping the shield wall together as it moved was with the use of some form of cadence. Krentz states that the marching to music was only for the purpose of encouragement.[146] However, the use of a cadence would also dictate the pace of the advance, and would keep the formation moving at a speed where the shield wall could be maintained. Thucydides states that the Spartans advanced into battle at Mantinea to the sound of flutes in order to keep in step and prevent the formation from breaking, an outcome that he says large armies were prone to do as they advanced.[147] Polyaenus states that the sound of pipes is useful in battle as it makes it possible to keep the phalanx unbroken and well organized.[148] The

Cretans are said to have marched to the sounds of the lyre and the Lydians used both the pan pipes and the flute.[149] The Mantineans and Arcadians are also said to have used marching to music as a form of dance.[150] The only reason why marching to music and/or keeping in step would have been necessary would be if the hoplites were advancing in close-order. A slow pace of advance would also allow infirm, injured or elderly hoplites to stay in formation regardless of their physical condition.[151] The larger intervals of the open and intermediate-orders do not require each hoplite to remain in step in order to maintain the shape of the formation. However, the close-order shield wall is much more easily maintained when each individual steps in time with the others.

The singing of the *paean*, or war song, by hoplite formations as they advanced into battle would have worked in a similar capacity.[152] Plutarch calls the Spartan *paean* a 'marching song' (ἐμβατήριος παιάν), stressing how they marched in time to the music and the rhythm of the hymn, while drawing encouragement from its lyrics at the same time.[153] Sung or spoken cadences are still used in most modern armies to keep soldiers marching together and in step. Interestingly, the use of the *paean* as a 'marching song' is only attributed to those of Dorian backgrounds by Thucydides and is not associated with the Athenians until the later works of Xenophon.[154] At Nemea, the Spartan formation halted their advance when the two sides had closed to only 200m apart so that a sacrifice could be made before the battle.[155] This demonstrates that the movement of the Spartan formation, if not also that of the opposing Athenians, was conducted in a manner both slow enough, and orderly enough, to allow the commander to halt the advance of the phalanx in order to conduct the ritual. The lack of a use of a cadence also partially explains why at Potidaea, the Corinthians concentrated their troops into 'as small a space as possible' (ὡς ἐς ἐλάχιστον χωρίον) to force their way back into the city; without a cadence of some form they would not have been able to retain a proper close-order formation once it began to move.[156] At Amphipolis, the Spartan general Brasidas inferred from the ungainly step of the approaching Athenians, that they would not be able to resist an attack in a further reference to the importance of cohesion and marching in step.[157] Heracles was similarly able to 'take the measure of a company of the enemy as it advanced'.[158] The regular use of a cadence to maintain a close-order formation would have been a contributing factor to the longevity of Spartan military dominance, particularly in the time before a cadence was commonly used by the troops of other city-states. Interestingly, Polyaenus attributes the Spartan defeat at Leuctra to an absence of flute players in the Spartan phalanx, which meant that the formation could not maintain its cohesion.[159]

If the close-order formation necessitated the creation of the shield wall and slow movement of the phalanx across the field of battle, the intermediate and open-orders, if anything, were the complete opposite. Asclepiodotus' specified uses of these formations both indicate the facilitation of movement.[160] This was no doubt due to the lack of a restrictive interlocking shield wall and the increased intervals of these orders; each hoplite needed only to maintain his position in the line for the formation to maintain its rudimentary structure, even while moving. The larger intervals of the open and intermediate orders also allow for the easier adoption of the low stance by the front ranks, which further facilitates rapid movement.

Asclepiodotus states that the intermediate-order was used to advance into the attack. As Greek hoplites also used the close-order formation to advance, the adoption of an intermediate-order would only have been necessary when a more rapid form of advance, such as a charge, was required. At Marathon, the Greeks charged the Persian position at the run.[161] Similarly, both the Athenians and Thebans ran into the attack at Delium, both the Spartan and Theban contingents advanced upon one another at the run at Coronea, and the Athenians and Syracusans also engaged each other at the run in Sicily.[162]

Via re-creative experiments, Donlan and Thompson proved relatively conclusively that Herodotus' statement that the Greeks charged over a mile at Marathon to engage the Persians was literary embellishment.[163] The results of their tests demonstrated that modern athletes in simulated hoplite armour could only run for approximately 180 metres before being overcome with fatigue.[164] This demonstrates how rapidly physical exertion taxes the energy of an individual wearing hoplite armour and how short most rapid charges across the battlefields of ancient Greece must have been. Conversely, these 'charges' may have been conducted at a slower pace to prevent the hoplites from becoming too fatigued or were conducted slowly with a rapid charge occurring only over the last few metres of the advance to both preserve the hoplite's levels of energy and help maintain the cohesion of the formation.[165]

It would have been impossible for a phalanx to run over any distance while in a close-order formation and maintain its structure at the same time. The only way that a formation could run forward and continue to present some form of secure frontage would be if the men were deployed in an intermediate-order. As such any passage in the ancient texts that refers to a phalanx 'charging' into the attack at anything more than a moderate pace must also be considered to be a reference to an attack conducted by hoplites in intermediate-order at best.[166] Similarly, in passages referring to how depth adds to the impetus of a charge, the deep formation must also be considered to be in intermediate or open-order at best. Donlan and Thompson's conclusion that hoplites could not have run more than 200 metres before becoming overcome with fatigue, suggests that any 'charge' that the ancient sources say was conducted over a greater distance is either literary embellishment or may have been done at nothing more than a brisk trot.[167] Additionally, Hanson's theory that armour could only be penetrated when combined with the momentum of a charge, can only be considered valid in relation to actions conducted by an intermediate- or open-order formation and not as part of the common close-order deployment.[168] The regular offensive use of the slow close-order phalanx makes the validity of Hanson's theory unlikely.

At Mantinea, while the Spartans are described as advancing slowly, the opposing Argives contrastingly attacked with 'violence and fury' (ἐντόνως καὶ ὀργῇ).[169] It seems likely that during this engagement the Spartans maintained their close-order formation while the Argives charged against them in an intermediate or open-order formation. During the second major battle of the First Messenian War, the Messenians similarly charged recklessly while the Spartans advanced slowly so as not to break ranks.[170] At the battle of Cunaxa, the Greeks are said to have clashed their spears against their shields to frighten the Persian cavalry as they charged forward.[171] Croesus' hoplites are said to have acted similarly.[172] Not only does this suggest that the hoplites were deployed in at least an intermediate-order, but it also demonstrates that they were not using the overhead posture of current convention as there is no way to clash a spear held in this position against the shield. Xenophon's hoplites must have been wielding their weapon vertically to clash it against the shield. From such a position, the weapon could only be moved into either the low or underarm posture to actually engage the enemy.

The open and intermediate orders could also be used when an even more rapid advance was required, such as to pursue a routed opponent. If a threat remained on the field, a pursuit could be conducted in what must have been an intermediate-order but the pace would have been much slower and the distance of the pursuit considerably less. Pausanias states that Spartan tradition was to pursue a routed enemy in formation even if security of the formation meant that the occasional enemy evaded them.[173] At Syracuse, Athenian hoplites conducted a pursuit in compact bodies to counter the threat of Syracusan cavalry.[174] The Eleans did not pursue the Arcadians at Olympia, but stood firm to meet a new Argive threat.[175] This suggests that the Eleans had maintained their formation once the Arcadian line had broken. The Greek wings at Marathon halted their pursuit of the routed Persian wings and wheeled in on the centre.[176] This also suggests that the Greek wings had maintained some form of cohesive formation. The hoplites at Cunaxa halted their pursuit and reformed so that they could continue without breaking ranks.[177] This indicates that the Greek line, probably in an intermediate-order, had fragmented somewhat during the pursuit.

A broken formation was easily set upon by an opponent that had not been fully routed from the field, a lesson harshly learnt by some Greek contingents at

Plataea.[178] It must also be considered that a formation that made a charge over a large distance, even if initially conducted in an intermediate-order, might degrade into an open-order or no order at all. As such, it can not be ruled out that the clash between the Thebans and Spartans at Coronea, for example, was the collision of two disorderly masses of heavily armed men.[179] Xenophon states that the Spartans were trained in the use of speed for when it was necessary.[180] As it appears that the Spartans regularly used the close-order formation in battle, this speed could only have been of use during a pursuit or an uncommonly conducted Spartan charge.

The 'shift' of the phalanx

Thucydides' states that the phalanx regularly shifted to the right as it advanced, as each man sought protection behind the shield of the man to his right.[181] Thucydides lays the blame for this shift on the right-hand file who had no extra protection on their right-hand side and equates the drift of the formation with fear. Thucydides further states that this phenomenon affected all armies. However, it may not have affected all armies to the same extent. Being mostly experienced veterans, it would have been less likely for the Spartan officers, positioned at the head of the right-hand file of their respective units, to have been affected by fear, influenced by any sideways pressure exerted by the man beside them or to march at a pace quicker or slower than was required to maintain the integrity of the line. As such, the Spartan officer needed to have only held his position, and keep in time to the cadence, to limit the lateral drift of the formation. Phalanxes from other city-states, having fewer officers and more inexperienced hoplites in their files, may have been more prone to this shift than the Spartans or other 'professional' units. McDermott demonstrated through his computer modelling that hoplites with the discipline to maintain their position in line limited the amount of distance that the formation shifted to the right.[182] However, even amongst the experienced Spartan phalanx, the physical characteristics of the formation itself would have created even a marginal shift to the right.[183]

When deployed in a close-order formation, the limited interval, and the diameter of the *aspis*, meant that each man would have been unable to shift much further to the right than he already was without physically pushing the man beside him as he sought further protection behind his shield. This would have forced the adjacent man (any officers possibly included) to the right. Due to the slow advance of a close-order formation, this shift would have been negligible over short distances of under fifty metres; as was observed in the members of the Sydney Ancients. Over greater distances the shift becomes considerably more apparent. The stationary defensive use of the close-order phalanx would have involved no shift of the files to the right due to the static nature of the formation.

If moving in the more open intermediate-order, the larger spacing of the interval allows for a compression of the files and a more dramatic shift of the phalanx to the right. As the formation advanced, hoplites would have been able to move behind the shield belonging to the man to their right as they sought additional protection as per Thucydides' statement. In effect, this begins a process of decreasing the interval of an intermediate-order formation into something akin to a close-order as each man shifts to the right. This compression would either physically push adjoining men (resulting in a right shift of the phalanx) or the right-hand file would attempt to maintain its intermediate-order interval by additionally side-stepping to the right (which also results in a shift of the entire phalanx). Any man to the left of someone shifting to the right would also have no choice but to shift as well in order to maintain the formation; otherwise dangerous gaps would begin to form in the line. McDermott's computer modelling suggested that if each man did not seek further protection behind the shield of his neighbour, the phalanx would not shift to the right at all.[184]

However, a phalanx could also drift if if its members moved at varying paces. If those on the right side of the formation moved at a pace quicker than those on the left, the line would shift as the slower members strived to catch up. If those on the left of a close-order formation moved at a quicker pace, the way in which the shields are interlocked physically pushes the adjacent man to the right. This demonstrates the importance that a cadence and a slow pace of advance had in the maintenance of the shield wall. Additionally, if one slotted his own shield behind that of the man to his right as he sought extra protection rather than in front of it, this would create a line with an oblique frontage (see figure 24), which would also contribute to the right shift of the formation.

The very posture used to bear the panoply also plays a part in the drift. With the adoption of an oblique body posture, a hoplite would have had a tendency to walk slightly off centre to the right. This slight variance, while again not extensive over a short distance, when carried over more than fifty metres translates to a potentially substantial right-shift of the line. This further indicates that both front-on and side-on postures were not used to carry the hoplite panoply; and highlights why the Greeks placed so much emphasis on hoplites maintaining their position in the formation. During some engagements, the phalanx was purposefully moved to the right in an attempt to outflank an opposing formation.[185] Lendon states that this was the cause of the right-shift.[186] However, this type of battlefield manouevring should in no way be confused with the unconscious right shift of an advancing formation.

The manner in which a hoplite phalanx was deployed could vary greatly and, contrary to modern scholarship, there does not appear to have been a 'standard' method of hoplite deployment. The most 'common' deployment was that of an eight-deep phalanx with a close-order interval of 45cm per man. However, this can in no way be considered the 'standard' deployment for the troops from all city-states or at every confrontation. The phalanx could be set at a number of intervals, and arranged in different configurations, depending upon the tactical requirements of the engagement. Considerations such as shape, depth, order and movement were vital to the outcome of a hoplite engagement, as they would dictate what occurred when two opposing formations clashed on the field of battle.

Chapter 13

The Hoplite Battle: Contact, *Othismos*, Breakthrough and Rout

Once either, or both, of the opposing phalanxes had begun to advance across the battlefield, a contest of arms was almost inevitable. However, what happened when the two formations met and fought is the most disputed aspect of any relating to hoplite warfare. The debate is predominantly focused around the interpretation of the word *othismos* (ὠθισμός), and its variants, which are used by many ancient writers in their descriptions of different hoplite engagements. The *othismos* is generally interpreted in connection with the action of one group of hoplites physically pushing against another. Modern scholarship is divided into two camps relating to how the pushing context of this interpretation should be applied to the descriptions given in the ancient texts and, subsequently, is divided about how it is believed a hoplite engagement actually took place. An examination of the literary evidence used to support these differing models, combined with an analysis of the physical characteristics of the hoplites and formations involved, indicates that neither side of this debate is fully correct.

One side of the *othismos* debate (called the 'orthodox view' by some, and hereafter referred to as the 'literal model') believes that the term *othismos*, and its 'pushing' context, are meant to be taken literally. Scholars adhering to this position state that hoplite warfare involved a violent collision of two opposing forces, generally considered to have been charging upon one another. The momentum of the charge and collision would force the opposing front ranks together where the weight of the formations physically pushed each other 'shield against shield' in a concerted effort to try and break the enemy's line and drive them from the field. The rear ranks are believed to have supported the front ranks by pressing their shields into the back of the man in front of them and driving them forward. In these models the collision and push are often compared to a scrum in a game of rugby, a scrimmage in a game of American football or a tug-o-war in reverse.[1]

The other side of the debate (referred to in some works as the 'heretical view' and hereafter referred to as the 'figurative model') interprets the context of the word *othismos*, and its usage by ancient sources, in a more metaphorical sense. Scholars adhering to this view claim that hoplite warfare did not involve an immediate collision of the formations at the onset, that fighting was conducted at a distance and that the 'pushing' was a figurative expression used by the ancient authors to describe how one side was forced from the field by another during this period of combat.[2] There are some scholars who hold to a variation, known as the 'final phase theory', suggesting that a hoplite engagement could, after a period of combat, develop into a situation where a physical pushing occurred, but suggest that this was uncommon.[3]

These models are all vastly different from each other. Both sides of the debate hold that their position is the correct interpretation of how hoplite warfare was conducted and cite a variety of reasons as to why the other model is incorrect. What neither side of this debate appears to have considered is the possibility that hoplite warfare was much more dynamic and variable than the predictable engagements that either of these two theories would suggest. Yet this is exactly what the available evidence indicates; not that one model was more likely than the other, but that hoplite warfare could have occurred in a manner that conformed to either, and occasionally both, of these models depending upon the circumstances of the individual engagement. The varied nature of hoplite warfare becomes evident from an analysis of two main areas of evidence: the literary texts, and the physical characteristics of the hoplite and the phalanx.

The literary basis of the *othismos*

Literary evidence that supports the concept of a collision and push is not extensive. Fraser argues that the entire 'literal model' is based upon only three passages.[4] Goldsworthy highlights the fact that no ancient author says that the *othismos* was a push by all of ranks of the phalanx.[5] An examination of the literary usage of certain terminology in connection with the description of hoplite battles indicates that some terms clearly describe a physical collision and push of two opposing sides, others are meant to convey the concept of fighting while separated by a distance that has involved no collision, and others are ambiguous in their context.

For example, terms that are often interpreted as 'shield against shield' by modern scholars, and that regularly form the basis of theories forwarded by adherents of the 'literal model', have two descriptive uses in the ancient texts.[6] The first is to describe the close-order shield wall. Examples of this description of the shield wall are found in the works of Homer, Tyrtaeus, and Xenophon where formations of hoplites are described as being 'shield pressed against shield', yet are not engaged with any opponent.[7] As such, these passages cannot be the description of two formations that have collided during the course of an engagement. This descriptive terminology can only be a reference to the shields of each hoplite pressing against those of the men beside them in the close-order formation.[8]

There are also four instances of the use of the term 'shield against shield' being used to describe two formations that have collided. Both sides at Delium are said to have collided at the run and fought 'with a pushing of shields' (ὠθισμῷ ἀσπίδων ξυνειστήκει), with one side charging downhill into the attack.[9] Similarly, during the later phases of the battle of Coronea, the Theban and Spartan phalanxes collided head-on and were pressed 'shield against shield' (σμυβαλόντες τὰς ἀσπίδας).[10] Aristophanes also refers to a meeting of shields in combat (ἔβαλον ῥινούς τε καὶ ἀσπίδας ὀμφαλοέσσας) in a likely reference to a collision of two formations, although no attribution to a specific battle is attached to the passage.[11] Similarly, Tyrtaeus also describes a collision of two phalanxes and the terrible din that was caused by the two sides clashing 'shield against rounded shield' (ἀσπίδας εὐκύκλους ἀσπίσι τυπτομένας).[12] However, no attribution to a specific battle is mentioned here either.[13] These four passages all support the 'literal model's' concept of a collision of the phalanxes.

In seeming conflict with this are passages that describe hoplite combat as being conducted 'at spear length' from the enemy. Tyrtaeus' suggestion to 'stand near [rather than next to or against] and reach forth and strike the foe', the swift conclusion of the 'Tearless Battle' when the Argives had received their first casualties within range of the Spartan spears, the 'non violent' clash of the phalanxes at the opening of the battle of Coronea and the Carthaginians withstanding the 'spear thrusts' of the Greeks in Sicily before closing for hand-to-hand combat with swords all describe battles that appear not to have involved the violent collision of the formations that the 'literal model' holds true.[14] Homer describes the use of the spear to parry or defend against attacks (φράξαντες δόρυ δουρι); a technique that is unlikely to have been performed in the confines of two compressed phalanxes.[15] Interestingly Aeschylus, who would have had first-hand experience of hoplite warfare against the Persians, describes combat as 'a contest of the spear' (ἐν μάχῃ δορὸς) not 'a contest of the push' or 'where shield meets shield'.[16] These contradicting passages suggest that both the opening and combative phases of a hoplite battle could be greatly varied and could conform to either the 'literal' or 'figurative' model based conditionally upon the circumstances of each encounter.

The term *othismos* (and its equivalents) is commonly used to describe the actions of a hoplite engagement. At Delium, the Thebans pushed the Athenians back 'step by step' (ὠσάμενοι κατὰ βραχὺ) after fighting 'shield pressed against shield', which suggests the continuous pressure of a mass push.[17] Thus the use of a variant of the term *othismos* in this case should most likely be taken literally. Similarly, the hoplites during the later stages of Coronea are said to have 'pushed' (ἐωθοῦντο) after clashing 'shield against shield'.[18] This can also be considered a literal use of the word *othismos* as a reference to a pushing action. There was a 'great deal of pushing' (πολὺς ἦν ὠθισμὸς) at the gates of Drilae as some of Xenophon's mercenaries tried to force their way in while others tried to force their way out; again the term *othismos* is meant to convey the idea of a physical push.[19] Interestingly, Plutarch uses the negative of the term *othismos* (οὐκ ἔσχεν ὠθισμὸν) to describe the opening clash of Coronea as being 'without struggle', an event that Xenophon describes as combat at spear length.[20] In this case the term *othismos* should also be taken in its literal, albeit negative, context of a physical push. However, the word *othismos*, while possessing the definitions of 'to push with the body' or 'to push with the shield' used by some scholars, does have other meanings.[21] Thus it cannot be automatically concluded that the term *othismos* will exclusively mean only one of many possible interpretations but must be dependent upon the context of the passage in which it is used.

The context of the four passages cited above appears relatively clear. However, these are the only examples of such a clear definition of the concept of the *othismos* in the ancient texts. Others uses of the term are much more ambiguous, without a greater understanding of the engagements that are being described. At Plataea, for example, the Persians 'pressed hardest' (μάλιστα ... ἐπίεσαν) at the point where their commander was stationed.[22] On Sphacteria the Athenians attempted to 'push back' (ὤσασθαι) the Spartans by frontal assault.[23] At Mantinea, the Argives 'pushed back' (ἐξέωσαν) part of the Spartan line after charging into gaps that had formed in the formation.[24] In Sicily, an Athenian breakthrough occurred only after the Syracusans had been 'pushed back' (ὠσαμένων).[25] At the Piraeus, the Spartans 'pushed' (ἐξεώσθησαν) the Athenians into the marsh of Halae.[26] Thebans attacking the city of Sparta were 'pushed back forcefully' (ἐξώσθησαν μετὰ βίας) by the Spartans.[27] Many of these passages are used by proponents of the 'literal model' as evidence of a physical push.[28] However, none of them are conclusive proof of such an action. All of these passages would make sense if the 'push' was given a more figurative definition. For example, the Spartans could have 'driven' the Athenians into the marsh of Halae at spear-point, but not necessarily physically pushed them 'shield against shield' as per the 'literal model'. At Plataea, the Spartans fought over a defensive wicker barricade that the Persians had constructed from their shields, which would have prevented any collision of the two sides.[29] Fighting here must have also been initially at spear length and is most likely to have continued that way even once the barricade had been thrown down. The later fighting is said to have involved only small groups of Persians and is unlikely to have involved any 'mass shoving'.[30] Despite this, Cartledge uses the battle of

Plataea to support the model of a hoplite *othismos* akin to a rugby scrum.[31] Luginbill claims that the *othismos* was a vital element of the battle of Plataea but inadvertently contradicts himself by citing how, according to Herodotus, the Persians were able to blunt the Greek attack by snapping the heads off their spears.[32] This suggests both that the fighting was conducted at spear length and that it was the Greek's weapons, and not any physical push, that were vital to the Greek's offensive capabilities. Thus the association of the term *othismos* with this battle must be taken in its figurative context to mean forced or driven back. Similarly, on Sphacteria the Athenians engaged the Spartans with skirmishers and *peltasts*, which, we are told, the heavier Spartan hoplites were unable to come to grips with.[33] Consequently, the use of the term *othismos* in this instance must also be taken in its figurative context. The difference between the two readings is a matter of interpretation: 'push' suggests something physical, while 'drive' suggests something less tactile. For example, the 'great *othismos*' (ὀθισμὸς ... πολλός) over the body of Leonidas at Thermopylae cannot be used as evidence of a mass push as the term may simply mean 'great struggle'; an interpretation adopted in both De Sélincourt's and Godley's translations.[34]

There are several other uses of the term *othismos* in ancient texts that could also have either a literal or figurative meaning. Xenophon describes the Eleans 'pushing' (ἐώθουν) their opponents towards the altar of Hestia in Olympia.[35] In the *Iliad*, Hector is said to have been eager to 'push back' (ὤσαιτ') the Argives.[36] Teucer exclaims how the Greeks were able to 'push' (ὠσάμεθ') the Trojans back into the city.[37] The Trojans were later able to 'push back' (ὦσαν) the Greeks.[38] During an attack on the Greek encampment, the Lycians were similarly 'pushed back' (ὤσασθαι).[39] Zeus later ponders whether he should allow Sarpedon to 'push' (ὤσαιτο) the Trojans back to the city yet again.[40] All of these passages are unclear in the context of the pushing action and they may be references to a physical shoving or may be metaphorical. Ajax 'pushed back' (ὦσε) Hector by thrusting the tip of his spear against Hector's shield.[41] This is a clear reference to a combat taking place at spear length. While there is little doubt that this 'push' contains physical contact between the two protagonists, it is not in the same context as the 'shield against shield' pushing of the 'literal model' and the term *othismos* must be read as 'to push with a weapon' rather than 'to push with the body' or 'to push with the shield'.

In other passages, the term *othismos* is clearly meant to be taken figuratively. At Plataea the Greeks 'pushed back' (τήν ἵππον ὤσαντο) a charge by Persian cavalry.[42] At the 'Tearless Battle' the Spartans 'pushed forward' (ὠθεῖσθαι εἰς τὸ πρόσθεν) into the attack.[43] In this instance, the term *othismos* is synonymous with the concept of advancing (i.e. to 'push forward') rather than a physical pushing action. Herodotus uses the term ὠθισμὸς λόγων to describe verbal disputes.[44] Variants of the term *othismos* are also used to describe naval engagements, which must be a use of the term in its figurative context to mean 'forced' or 'driven' back.[45]

Other passages that use the term *othismos*, but that are not direct descriptions of combat, are also used to support the concept of a mass push. Here too, the context of these passages is not conclusive. Xenophon states that weaker hoplites were positioned in the middle ranks of the phalanx so that they could be led from the front and 'pushed' (ὠθῶνται) by those behind.[46] Hanson cites this as further evidence of a mass pushing by the whole phalanx.[47] Yet again, the meaning of the terminology is ambiguous. The passage still makes sense with the figurative connotation of being 'driven' or 'supported' from behind without necessitating any physical contact between the men. Passages by Polybius, Asclepiodotus and Arrian that describe how the rear ranks of the Macedonian phalanx 'pressed forward' to add to the attack and to prevent the front ranks from routing have similarly been used to support the concept of the mass push.[48] Yet these passages are also uncertain. Xenophon describes how experienced men formed the front and rear ranks of the Greek phalanx in order to prevent routs but does not connect this deployment with the act of pushing.[49] Interestingly Arrian, despite being cited as evidence of the push, states that the *ouragos* positioned to the rear of the file was selected for his experience and intelligence, rather than his strength.[50] Similarly, Epaminondas is said to have trained himself in agility rather than strength as the former was necessary for war whereas the latter was useful only in athletics.[51] These claims are at odds with the concept of a mass push by the phalanx; if such a concept is meant to be applied to all hoplite engagements as per the 'literal model'. This suggests that the 'pressing forward' by the rear ranks described by Arrian and other authors may be figurative rather than literal.

Hanson, in a rebuttal against claims made by proponents of the 'figurative model', states that:

> Some recent scholars have branded the image of the mass shoving contest as ridiculous and absurd. Yet careful compilation of ancient descriptions of Greek warfare makes it certain beyond doubt that this was precisely what happened in hoplite battle.[52]

Hanson is clearly mistaken. While there are passages that do indicate that a mass collision and push between hoplite formations did occur, there are other passages that show that the contrary also took place. Many of the passages cited by Hanson and other scholars are clearly inconclusive in their context and are in no way confirmation that a mass push was a regular occurrence on the hoplite battlefield. It can only be concluded that these different terms and contexts are meant to describe different aspects of the varied environment of hoplite combat. Thus the term *othismos*, although central to the scholarly debate that bears its name, is far from clear in its meaning. The only clue as to how it should be interpreted comes from further details of the individual engagement and a consideration of the physical characteristics of the hoplites and the formations involved in the encounter; a consideration that, unfortunately, many proponents of both sides of the debate have failed to undertake.

The physical basis of the *othismos*

Both sides of the *othismos* debate use a variety of passages to justify their positions but have incorporated little physical analysis into their theories. Neither side has conducted significant research into whether the attributes of the hoplite's panoply (the length and balance of the spear, or the size of the shield), how it was carried (posture) or the characteristics of the phalanx itself allow for their conclusions to be achieved in physical reality, and yet the very order of the phalanx is what will dictate whether a collision with opposing forces was possible or not.

Many hoplite battles involved at least one side deployed in a close–order formation, or something as close to it as possible (see Chapter 12, Phalanxes, Shield Walls and Other Formations). However, the physical characteristics of the close–order formation would have made it almost impossible for an opposing phalanx to collide with its front rank as per the 'literal model', regardless of the order in which the opposing force had deployed, and regard-less of whether the close–order formation was stationary or simultaneously advancing upon the enemy. At Mantinea in 418BC, for example, the slowly advancing Spartan close–order shield wall was met by the charging loose-order phalanx of the Argives.[53] As a result of the two different orders used, the interval between the files of the phalanxes, and subsequently their offensive and defensive characteristics, would have been vastly different. The Spartan spears, for example, would have been separated by an interval of around 45–50cm as each man attempted to maintain the spacing of the close–order shield wall while the formation advanced. Additionally, the spears of the first two Spartan ranks would have extended well forward of the front of the formation. The Argive phalanx would have charged against this strong position in an order of around 90cm per man at best (figure 33).

The different spacing between the files of the two phalanxes means that some men across the front of the Argive formation would have faced at least fours spears of the opposing Spartan phalanx; two from the front rank and two from the second rank (bottom right in figure 33). Even if it is assumed that the Spartans kept their weapons parallel and pointing directly ahead, and did

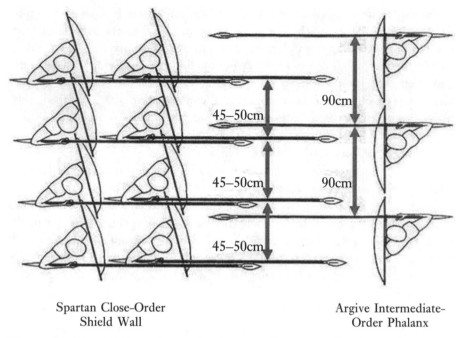

Spartan Close-Order
Shield Wall

Argive Intermediate-
Order Phalanx

Figure 33: The difference in spacing between the spears of a close-order and an intermediate-order phalanx.

not aim them at an oncoming opponent, scholars adherring exclusively to the 'literal model' would have it believed that a hoplite, bearing a shield 90cm in diameter, would have been able to force his way between two pair of spears, which are separated by a distance half the size of the shield he is carrying, and then force the interval of the opposing line apart so that he could physically collide against the shield of his opponent. This can only be considered an impossibility, both for the hoplites at Mantinea and for any other engagement that involved at least one close-order formation.

An impact against four spears would have undoubtedly stopped an attacking hoplite in his tracks. The attacking hoplite is unlikely to have been able to apply a sufficient amount of body mass behind the impact with the weapons in order to create enough force to break all four weapons and so be able to advance any further. Even if the close-order formation was advancing, the slow pace of the march would have added little momentum to the combined impetus of the collision of the two phalanxes.

If an attacking hoplite used his shield to parry one pair of spears to either side in order to widen the gap, not only would this leave him exposed to attack by the other pair of spears, but the man beside him in the attacking phalanx would then have to overcome two additional spears, and would encounter further problems with trying to close with his opponent. Similarly, an attacking hoplite could not simply parry the spears of the first rank without leaving himself vulnerable to those of the second. Hoplites attacking a close-order shield wall could have only penetrated the gap by moving their shield out of its protective position and trying to slide 'shoulder first' between the spears. This would leave them exceptionally vulnerable to attack, and lacking the cover of their shield, and seems unlikely to have occurred. Advancing in this manner would also prevent them from colliding 'shield against shield' with an opponent as per some of the ancient descriptions that support the 'literal model'.

Due to the interval of the intermediate-order formation, some of the attacking hoplites may have faced only one pair of spears (top right in figure 33). However, these spears would have undoubtedly been pointed directly at the centre of their shield (or head). As such, attacking hoplites in this position would have been able to get more of their body mass behind the impact with an opponent's weapon. This may have caused some spears to break upon impact, although it is unlikely that this would have occurred right across the line. Placing substantial body mass behind the impact with an opponent's weapon may have also simply aided that weapon in piercing the shield, armour and flesh of the attacker, thus killing the charging hoplite in the initial clash.

Charging onto the closely arrayed spears of a shield wall with the momentum of their own advance would have resulted in not every man across the front of the attacking line physically closing with his opponent; either due to men hesitating at the last moment, being stopped by the enemy spears or by simply being slain at the moment of impact. As a consequence of the small gap between the spears of the close-order formation, none of the attacking hoplites would have been capable of physically closing with their opponent beyond a 'spear length' of about two metres. This could still be described as a physical collision of the two formations, but it is not in the same manner as that proposed by adherents of the 'literal model' and involves no bodily contact between the opposing hoplites or a pressing of 'shield against shield'. Consequently, any account in the ancient sources that refers to a battle involving at least one close-order phalanx is unlikely to have begun with a physical collision of the front ranks as per the 'literal model'; it was simply not physically possible for the two formations to close to that proximity.

The inability to physically close with an opponent deployed in a close-order formation beyond a distance of about two metres explains the passages in the ancient texts that describe encounters conducted 'at spear length'. Tyrtaeus' suggestion to 'reach forth and strike the foe', the account of the Tearless Battle, and the Carthaginians withstanding the 'spear thrusts' of the Greeks in Sicily all describe engagements involving close-order formations and the cause of the fighting at weapon range can be attributed to the inability to overcome the closely spaced weapons of the close-order phalanx. Hanson cites Tyrtaeus' description of men fighting 'chest to chest' (στέρνον στέρνῳ) as further evidence of a collision of formations.[54] However, Tyrtaeus' passage describes the characteristics of a close-order shield wall and is therefore not likely to be a description of a collision of two opposing sides. Tyrtaeus' passage must therefore be a reference to standing up to, and facing, one's enemy rather than a description of a physical connection between the men.

The opening clash at the battle of Coronea is also described as being 'at spear length' even though both sides are described as charging against each other, which would suggest a use of loose order formations.[55] However, the Spartans initially advanced slowly and only charged once the distance to the enemy had closed to 100 metres.[56] With the other side rapidly charging against them, the Spartans would have only needed to cover a distance of perhaps 20 metres once their charge gained its momentum. Consequently, well drilled hoplites such as the Spartans may have been able to maintain a close-order formation over a charge of such a short distance, particularly if it was conducted only at a moderate pace. The fact that the ancient writers state that there was no opening collision in this battle certainly suggests the presence of at least one close-order formation. Anderson suggests that it was only the Spartan allies who charged, and the regular Spartans advanced slowly as they had done at Mantinea.[57] Plutarch's description of the clash being 'without struggle' seems to confirm the lack of a collision, even though Hanson uses the description of this encounter as proof of the 'literal model'.[58] These passages alone indicate that the 'literal model' cannot be applied to every hoplite engagement.

Not only did the use of the underarm posture and the adoption of a close-order formation prevent a charging opponent from physically colliding with the phalanx, it also meant that any body of hoplites drawn up in close-order possessed a vastly superior advantage on the battlefield over those deployed in a looser order. In terms of both defence and offence, the close-order formation greatly outclassed any open variant of the phalanx during the initial clash. However, once the phalanxes had met, the front ranks of the charging intermediate-order formation would have been brought to an abrupt halt by the closely arrayed spears of the opposing shield wall. This abrupt halt of the front line would result in the interval between each rank of the intermediate-order formation compressing as the momentum of the charge drove each man forward to collide with the back of the man in front of him (possibly forcing the front rank onto the spear tips of the enemy, resulting in further casualties to the attacking side). Once this had occurred, the hoplites in the second rank of the intermediate-order phalanx would find themselves in a position where they too could engage the enemy due to the reduced distance between each rank (which would become similar to that of the opposing close-order formation). However, where the close-order formation retained an advantage was in the fact that the men in this formation, and more importantly their weapons, were separated by half the distance of those belonging to the intermediate-order formation across the front of the line.[59] As such, each member of the front rank of the intermediate-order phalanx faced the attacks of twice as many opponents as did the members of the shield wall. Additionally, the attacking formation may have also lost a substantial number of its experienced front-rank fighters in the inital clash. Furthermore, the larger interval between each file of the intermediate-order formation meant that the attacking phalanx would be lacking the defensive benefits of the interlocking shield wall while facing up to four enemy spears.

The strength of the close-order shield wall on the battlefield is demonstrated by the accounts of battles that involve close-order formations. In every case, when a close-order phalanx fought against one in intermediate-order, or even against cavalry, the hoplites deployed in close-order were always victorious. In the comparatively rare engagement of two sides both deployed in close-order, the contest came down to other factors such as experience, morale, armament, terrain or the simple luck of the day (table 19).

The advantage of the close-order formation over the intermediate partially explains why the deployment for battle, including the depth and interval of the phalanx, was often left to the decision of the individual commander. Varying depths and orders would have been used depending upon the type of attack that was going to be made or received.[60] This raises the obvious question: if the forces of a city-state experienced such a disadvantage by attacking in an intermediate-order during a particular battle, why would they deploy in a similar manner again at a later engagement? For city-states who did not regularly use a cadence or other means to help them maintain a close-order formation with mainly inexperienced hoplites, it would have been not so much a matter of them not learning from past engagements but more of them not being able to maintain any method of attack other than the intermediate-order formation. Had the forces of a city-state always fought against opponents who had also used intermediate-order deployments, they would not have any first-hand knowledge of the superiority of the close-order formation and would only learn so when they actually fought against one; by which time it was too late. Terrain and/or a need for rapid movement may have also necessitated the adoption of an intermediate-order formation. Such reasons explain why the Corinthians at Potidaea deployed in a body 'as compact as possible': they understood the benefits of a close-order formation but could not effectively maintain it in battle, particularly at the run, and so stayed as close together as they were able.[61] The differences between the capabilities of the two formations also

Table 19: Examples of the results of engagements where at least one side was deployed in a close-order formation.

Source	Engagement	Deployment	Result
Herodotus, 7.176–7.231	Thermopylae 480BC	Greeks in close-order vs Persians forced into a compressed mass by the terrain.	Greeks hold Persians for two days until their spears break and the position is flanked.
Herodotus, 9.18	Plataea 479BC	Phocians in close-order vs Persian cavalry.	Persian cavalry withdraws after observing the strength of the Phocian position.
Thucydides, 1.63	Potidaea 432BC	Corinthians in 'as close an order as possible' vs Athenians (order unknown).	Allows Corinthians to force their way back into the town with minimal losses.
Thucydides, 2.4	Plataea 431BC	Thebans in close-order vs a sally made by the Plataeans (intermediate-order at best).	Plataeans are unable to break the Theban line.
Thucydides, 5.70–72	Mantinea 418BC	Argives charge in intermediate-order vs Spartans advancing slowly in close-order.	Argives break Spartan line only where a gap has opened during the advance. Elsewhere the Argives rout after first contact with the Spartans.
Thucydides, 6.97	Syracuse 415BC	Syracusans charge Athenians positioned on the Epipolae heights at the run (intermediate-order at best).	The Syracusans attack in disorder due to running and are easily defeated.
Xenophon, *Hellenica*, 6.2.20	Corcyra 373BC	Corcyreans in close-order attack a Spartan line.	Spartans consider their line too weak to resist the attack and try to withdraw.
Xenophon, *Hellenica*, 7.1.29	'Tearless Battle' 368BC	Argives and Arcadians vs Spartans in close-order.	Argive/Arcadian line breaks after suffering first casualties 'at spear length'.
Xenophon, *Hellenica*, 7.4.22	Crommus 365BC	Arcadians in close-order vs Lacedaemonians.	Arcadians are able to repel charges by *peltasts*, cavalry and Spartan hoplites.
Plutarch, *Timoleon*, 27–28	Sicily 341BC	Greeks in close-order vs Carthaginians (order unknown).	Carthaginians initially resist the Greek spear thrusts but then draw their swords and close for hand-to-hand fighting. The Carthaginian line eventually breaks.
Diodorus, 17.26.4–27.4	Halicarnassus 334BC	Greeks in close-order vs Macedonians in close-order.	Greeks engage in close-order and are successful until counter-attacked by Macedonian veterans in a formation with interlocked shields. Greek line breaks.

explains passages in the ancient texts that state that frequent campaigning against the Thebans by the Spartans taught the Thebans how to fight.[62] Clearly, what these passages are referring to is not that the Spartans actually taught the Thebans how to fight as hoplites; but more that the Thebans, through numerous engagements with the Spartans, learnt the benefits of the regular Spartan close-order shield wall (i.e. to fight like Spartans). The regular Spartan use of the close-order shield wall, and their extensive training, also partially explains the longevity of their dominance on the battlefield and why the very presence of the Spartans caused such fear among opposing hoplite formations.[63]

The deployment of Chabrias

The strength of the close-order formation also explains the 'unorthodox' deployment of the Athenian commander Chabrias. Nepos, in describing the event, states that Chabrias:

> ... forbade the rest of the phalanx to quit their ground but instructed them to receive an attack of the enemy with the knee placed firmly against the shield and the spear stretched out. When Agsesilaus saw this new sight he did not dare to advance but recalled his men.[64]

The interpretation of this passage has caused much debate among scholars. The subsequent statue of Chabrias, erected in the Athenian agora to commemorate the event, is generally believed to have shown him kneeling down with his shield resting against his knee as per one interpretation of Nepos' passage; an interpretation dismissed by Anderson and Buckler.[65] Interestingly, both Diodorus and Polyaenus describe the event with slight variations. Diodorus states that Chabrias' men were deployed with their shield on their knee and with their spears inclined upwards (καὶ τὰς ἀσπίδας πρὸς τὸ γόνυ κλίναντας ὀρθῷ τῷ δόρατι).[66] Polyaenus describes the positioning of the spears as angled upwards and forwards δόρατα ὀρθὰ προτειναμένους).[67] Polyaenus additionally describes Chabris' deployment as a stationary battle formation (στάσιμον σχῆμα τῆς μάχης).[68] In a similar account, Xenophon relates how the troops of Clearchus remained in 'immediate readiness to support' by standing with their shields 'placed against their knees' (ἀσπίδας πρὸς τὰ γόνατα θέντας).[69]

Anderson interprets the use of the term 'upright' (ὀρθὰ) by Diodorus and Polyaenus to describe the spears of Chabrias' men as a description of the hoplites standing at attention with the shield resting on the ground, but leaning against the left knee, while the spear is held vertically.[70] Buckler similarly suggests that Chabrias' hoplites were standing in an 'at ease' position with the spear thrust vertically into the ground and the shield resting against the leg.[71] Anderson further discounts Nepos' use of the term 'extended' (*proiecta*) to describe the positioning of the spears as a mistranslation of *ortha* on his part.[72] However, the word *ortha* can also mean 'to stick straight out'; a term more consistent with a description of the underarm position to wield the spear and a term that would correlate with Nepos' use of the term *proiecta*. Additionally, Anderson's interpretations ignore the descriptions of the weapons being angled or inclined forward instead of just being held vertically. It is more likely that what Nepos, Diodorus and Polyaenus are describing is the weapon being held in a way that it projected upwards and forwards at an angle; with those of the rear ranks extending above the heads of the men in front of them – a formation later adopted by the *sarissa*-wielding Macedonian phalangite.[73]

Anderson also erroneously uses another passage of Polyaenus' to support his 'attention' interpretation, which demonstrates the lack of consideration for the physical characteristics of the panoply on his part. Prior to the battle of Leuctra, Epaminondas is said to have had a statue of Athena secretly altered in order to encourage his troops. The statue, which had had its shield lying on the ground before it, was altered so that the goddess' arm was through the *porpax*, and the soldiers were heartened to see that the goddess, who had been 'at ease', was now 'on guard'.[74] Anderson equates this 'on guard' position with the 'attention' posture of his model. However, when a shield is placed on the ground and rested against the knees as per Anderson's 'attention' position, the left arm can in no way be inserted through the *porpax* as per Polyaenus' description of the statue of Athena. The shield on the statue must have been in its proper defensive position on the left shoulder, and braced in place by the left thigh and knee (i.e. 'with the knee placed firmly against the shield' as per Nepos' description of Chabrias' men), to be in a protective 'on guard' position.

Had Chabrias' troops merely been standing at attention or 'at ease' as per Anderson and Buckler, there would have been no reason for the Spartans to call off their attack. To bring a shield from a position on the ground resting against the knees up and onto the left shoulder, the right hand must first be freed (one method is by thrusting the *sauroter* of the spear into the ground) so that the shield can be lifted and the left arm inserted through the *porpax*. Another way is for the hoplite to bend down and slot his left arm through the armband before standing erect again. Both moves would have to be conducted in unison by all members of the phalanx if any form of entanglement was to be avoided, and both moves momentarily leave each hoplite without any offensive or defensive capabilities. Thus a phalanx standing at attention is defensively very weak and there would have been little reason for the Spartans to call off an attack against such a formation. Lendon says Chabrias' men were in a posture of contempt (Diodorus uses the term καταφράνησιν to describe it) and that the Spartans called off their attack because they expected some kind of ruse.[75] Anderson suggests Chabrias' men were not attacked simply because they looked well disciplined.[76]

Had Chabrias' men been kneeling as per Burnett and Edmonson, there would have similarly been little reason for the Spartans for call off their attack. If Chabrias' men chose to receive the initial attack kneeling down, any strike made from this position would have been weak, and with a reduced reach, directed towards the Spartan shields and therefore easy to deflect. However, the heads of Chabrias' men would have been a prime target for Spartan spears held in the underarm position. This would make fighting while in a kneeling position both dangerous and highly unlikely. Had Chabrias' men been ordered to stand prior to the moment of the meeting of the two formations, this would have given the Spartans an exploitable advantage while the opposing formation was slightly 'out of order' as each individual stood and adjusted his position in line. Even if only slightly weakened by such a move, Chabrias' formation is unlikely to have withstood an attack by an experienced Spartan phalanx.

What is most likely being described in the ancient passages is Chabrias' men adopting a stationary Athenian close-order shield wall; standing 'on guard' with their shield on their left shoulder and braced in position by their left knee, and with their spears angled upwards and forwards. From this position the weapons of the front two ranks could be easily lowered into the underarm 'ready' position to receive the attack. A similar order was issued to Xenophon's mercenaries.[77] Nepos' description of the spears being 'extended' could either be a reference to this angled positioning of the spears prior to engagement, or may be a description of weapons already lowered into the underarm position extending beyond the front of the shield wall. A posture with the spear either angled forward while the shield is on the left shoulder, or with the spear held in the underarm 'ready' position, is the most likely pose for the later statue of Chabrias in the Athenian *agora* (marketplace).

If the description of Chabrias' troops is interpreted in this manner, this not only accounts for the posture that his hoplites adopted, but also for the subsequent actions of the attacking Spartans. The word used by Nepos to describe the Spartan advance (*incurrentes*) can mean either 'to rush/charge at' or simply 'to attack'.[78] As such, the Spartans may have been in either a close or intermediate-order formation. Regardless, as the Spartans advanced Agesilaus would have observed the static shield wall formed by Chabrias' men in Polyaenus' account; the 'new sight' of Nepos' version as it was not the standard deployment for hoplites from many city-states. Being experienced in the use of the close-order formation, Agesilaus would have recognized the strength of Chabrias' position, and subsequently called off the assault.[79]

The panoply and the *othismos*

Hanson states that the size of the hoplite shield is evidence that a collision and push were a common aspect of hoplite warfare.[80] Similarly, Bardunias states that the curvature of the shield allowed it to withstand the pressures experienced in the compression of the phalanxes and that the bowl-like cavity of the shield is what provided the hoplite with enough space to breathe and avoid succumbing to constrictive asphyxia in the crush of two collided formations.[81] However, as Pritchett points out, if hoplite warfare was always decided by a mass pushing of the phalanxes, it is curious that the Greeks adopted the round and concave *aspis* rather than the large rectangular shield of the Egyptians that Xenophon states was perfectly suited to such an action.[82]

Additionally, the forces exerted by a surging crowd with a density of more than five people per square metre can reach 12.3 kilo-neutons (2,460fpds) per metre; enough to collapse steel railings, crush people, and in some cases horses, to death, and lift other people off their feet and project them several metres into the air. At the same time, the overcrowding of the mass results in a breakdown of internal communication and a loss of individual control over movement.[83] Two crowds pushing against each other would create even more pressure in the area of contact. Contrary to Bardunias' conclusions, the bulk of the *aspis* would make it impossible for the members of a phalanx to crowd each other to the extent that these characteristics would manifest themselves; and both the shield and the individual would be unlikely to withstand such pressures even if they could. Xenophon, in his description of the aftermath of the battle of Coronea (one of the few instances where pushing 'shield against shield' did occur – see following) lists shattered shields among the debris littering the field; suggesting that the hoplite shield could not stand up to the pressures of a mass push.[84] Additionally, the casualty rates for victorious hoplite armies are relatively low, and references to crushing or asphyxiating deaths during fighting are non-existent.[85] This, contrary to Bardunias' claims, suggests that a massed, crowded, push was not a common aspect of a hoplite engagement, nor was the hoplite shield designed to be the instrument of such a mass push.

It seems more likely that the *aspis* was designed to be supported by the shoulder and to lock into the shield wall. Luginbill suggests that the hoplite extended his left arm forward and struck the opponent with the outer edge of his shield; transferring the energy of those pushing from behind.[86] This is also unlikely. Not only would this remove much of the protective covering that the shield was designed to give, but to do so would require the shield to be taken off the shoulder, which would place considerable muscular strain on the extended left arm. Additionally, this move could not be made if both sides were abutted against each other 'shield against shield' as per the literal model, nor would a shield reach an opponent who was engaged at 'spear length'.

Some proponents of the 'figurative model' state that the confined nature of two compressed and pushing phalanxes would only prevent a hoplite from using his weapons.[87] This is certainly true of the hoplite spear. A spear with a rearward point of balance, if it did not break during any initial collision, would be completely redundant as a thrusting weapon in the compressed mass of phalanxes of the 'literal model'.[88] Sophocles' generalization of hoplite combat being a 'storm of spears' (δορός ... ἐν χειμῶνι) rather than a 'mass push' can only be a reference to the regular hoplite battle occurring in a way in which weapons were the primary form of offence (i.e. while the two sides were separated at 'spear length' from each other).[89]

Even when the formations were engaged at spear length, a man in the second rank can only push against the right arm and *sauroter* of the man in front of him with his shield when that man is in an oblique body posture. This would greatly reduce the effectiveness of the hoplite's weapon. Even allowing for the posture to be altered by a charge or collision of two phalanxes into something more akin to a front-on stance, pushing someone squarely in the back with the large *aspis*, would still prevent movement of the weapon arm. The members of the front rank would also have no way of knowing when a push from the men behind them was coming, and so could not prepare for it accordingly. If the push from the rear or the momentum of the charge was too forceful, the front rank would be unbalanced and simply forced onto the spears of their opposition.

The violent and unpredictable nature of a mass collision would also make the *sauroter* dangerous to members of the rear ranks. However, there are no literary references to injuries sustained in such an environment and the sharp point on some examples of the *sauroter* suggests that hoplite warfare was not commonly of a style where it would endanger those to the rear. If the massed push was the way of all hoplite battles, it is uncertain why hoplites would even be armed with such a weapon as a spear equipped with a *sauroter*. The only condition in which the pushing of the second rank would be beneficial would be if the phalanx was stationary and waiting to receive an enemy charge. In this case, by pressing their shield hard up against the arm and *sauroter* of the man in front, the second rank would brace the first rank's weapon in position. If the front rank did not thrust their weapon forward to meet the attack but simply held it in place, the support from the second rank would prevent the spear from being forced back by any impact with a charging opponent and would have aided the penetration of his shield, armour and/or flesh. The *sauroter* would be pressed into the shield of the man behind and this would prevent it from sliding off the surface of the *aspis* and so keep the spear in position.

Mitchell and Goldsworthy state that swords were the Greeks' close quarters weapon and this is supported by accounts of battles such as Thermopylae, Coronea and Mantinea.[90] Lorimer argues that hoplite fighting was conducted at a distance close enough for the two front lines to grab each other.[91] However, these conclusions fail to consider the obvious question: if hoplites were already equipped with swords for close-quarters combat, and fought in close proximity to each other as per the 'literal model' of the *othismos*, why wield a long spear if the concept of a mass collision is to be applied to every hoplite engagement? If the whole concept of hoplite warfare was to use the weight of the phalanx to push, this also fails to explain what modern scholarship perceives to have been a reduction in the weight of hoplite armour.[92] Heavier armour would have added more mass behind any collision and subsequent push.

The confines of two compressed and pushing phalanxes can also not account for many of the descriptions of wounds and fatalities that are found in the ancient sources. If the 'literal model' is to be taken as the standard, then every description of spears penetrating shields, armour and bodies must be assumed to have occurred during the initial collision of the phalanxes as there would have been little room for weapon usage once the formations had compressed. Descriptions of the dead littering the field in piles in the aftermath of battle are clearly references to casualties sustained as two phalanxes fought separated by the deadly 'no man's land' of spear range, into which the bodies of the slain front ranks fell and piled up as the fighting continued and those of the rear ranks stepped forward to replace them.[93] Clearly the hoplite panoply demonstrates that a violent collision of the phalanxes resulting in one side pushing 'shield against shield' against another was not the standard course of hoplite warfare.

The collision of loose-order formations

The inability to physically collide with a shield wall does not mean that the collision of the 'literal model' should be dismissed altogether. As noted, there are descriptions of battles in the ancient texts that indicate that a collision of the phalanxes did occur. In a generalization, Hanson states that the charge usually resulted in one phalanx smashing into the other.[94] However, accounts of engagements that possessed the conditions necessary for two phalanxes to collide 'shield against shield' as per the 'literal model' are relatively rare in the literary record.

Interestingly, the use of the term 'shield against shield' (or one of its variants) to describe the collision of two formations (see pages 206–207) is never used in conjunction with a battle involving a close-order shield wall. The terminology is only used in connection with phalanxes that have charged over large distances and where *both* formations would have been in at least an intermediate-order.

The fragmentation of the phalanxes into ones with larger intervals during a charge would negate many of the obstacles associated with trying to collide with a shield wall: the larger space between the spears of the enemy would allow the charging hoplites to close with their opponent as per the 'literal model'. This is an indication that a collision that would allow for pushing 'shield against shield' could not have occurred when a close-order formation was involved in the engagement. McDermott estimates that a formation could lose as much as 35 per cent of the cohesion of its lines prior to any clash due to conducting a charge.[95] The terrain and rapid advance of both sides at Delium, for example, would have made the maintenance of any close-order formation almost impossible.[96] Similarly, during the later phases of the battle of Coronea, the Thebans are said to have deployed in close-order but then advanced furiously, which would have made their formation impossible to maintain. No formation is given for the Spartans, but even if they were still in their regular close-order formation, the distance covered during the charge and the detritus of earlier fighting, which it would have been nescessary to cross, would have broken up this formation. Aristotle states that even a minor obstacle could disrupt the phalanx.[97] As such, when the two sides collided they would have both been in an intermediate-order at best, if not something more akin to a general rabble, and this would have allowed them to collide 'shield against shield'.

The Thebans also charged against a Spartan phalanx, which was not in its regular close-order deployment, at the battle of Leuctra 'with the force of a breaking wave'.[98] In Plutarch's account of the battle the Spartan line was disorderly due to it moving to outflank the Thebans. In Xenophon's, the Spartan line was fouled by their own retreating cavalry. Polyaenus offers that they were out of order due to not marching to music.[99] Regardless of the cause, the Spartans were clearly not in their regular close-order formation and both sides may have met while in a looser order. As such, the initial meeting of the phalanxes at Leuctra is an example of the rare meeting of a relatively stationary loose-order formation and a charging one, and must have also involved a collision of the front ranks even though no reference to the hoplites being pressed 'shield against shield' is used in connection with the encounter. Thus there are only three clear references to a collision of the phalanxes in all of the accounts of hoplite versus hoplite battles: Delium, the later phase of Coronea and Leuctra.[100] This demonstrates that, while a collision occurred during these engagements, the collision of the 'literal model' cannot be applied to all hoplite battles.

In the cases where two fragmented formations charged upon one another, a violent collision was almost unavoidable. Keegan states that masses of troops generally do not smash into each other, but that one side usually gives way at the critical moment.[101] This notion is dismissed by Hanson who states that men in this position would not possess the rational level of thought required to halt their charge at the moment of impact.[102] However, it was probably not a frenzied or irrational mindset that prevented a hoplite from arresting his charge, but more the pace at which that charge was conducted. The slow advance of the close-order formation would have provided ample opportunity for the formation to halt; as indicated by the ability for the Spartans to stop their advance at Nemea in order to conduct a sacrifice.[103] However, once charging at speed, the forward motion of the mass would simply carry any hoplite of the front ranks along with it regardless of whether he was hesitant to attack or not. Placed in this situation the front rank hoplite would have had little choice but to place his shield in a strong defensive position on his shoulder, extend his spear forward, and await the impact of the two rapidly closing forces. Two charging sides pulling back before the collision and engaging only at weapon range must have been rare. This explains why Plutarch goes to such lengths to describe the first clash at Coronea as 'without struggle' as it directly contrasts against the later phase of the battle where the collision between the Spartans and Thebans is described as 'shield against shield'.[104] Contrary to Hanson, the battle of Coronea provides evidence of the ability of two advancing formations to arrest their charge prior to the moment of collision. Additionally, and contrary to Keegan, the later phase of the same battle indicates that mass formations of hoplites did occasionally smash into each other under certain battlefield conditions.

However, even though spatially possible, it is unlikely that the members of each front rank would have simply allowed the opposing hoplites to pass between their spears and close with them in such a manner. Each front rank must have aimed their spears at the oncoming enemy (there is no point carrying a spear if you are not going to point it at your foe) and used their weapons to the best of their ability to either kill their opponent or to prevent any collision by directing it at the shield of the closing hoplite; just as Ajax did to Hector in the *Iliad*.[105] Plutarch recounts how the Macedonians purposefully created this exact same effect at the battle of Pydna. He states that the Macedonians 'placed the tips of their *sarissae* against the shields of the Romans, who were thus prevented from reaching them with their swords'.[106] Similarly, the hoplite spear could have been used to keep an opponent at bay as well as to attack. Interestingly, the ability to hold an opponent at bay with the hoplite spear in this manner can only be accomplished through the use of the underarm and low techniques to wield the weapon; further indicating that this was how the spear was held to engage in hoplite combat.

With weapons positioned in such a way, the collision of the charging phalanxes would have been violent, and its outcome varied, right across both front lines. Some spears would have penetrated shields, armour and flesh, instantly killing or wounding hoplites in both front ranks who would have undoubtedly not collided with their opposition. Other spears may have broken with the impetus of the charge and the force of the impact, the momentum of the advance driving the hoplite onwards to collide against the shield of his opponent. Yet other spears would have neither broken nor penetrated the shields of the enemy. In this case both hoplites would be stopped in their tracks as each would be prevented from closing with their opponent by the spear pressed against his shield. In some instances a hoplite may have lost his grip on a weapon that failed to penetrate his opponent's armour if the momentum of the charge carried him forward to collide against the shield of his enemy while the resistance against the spear forced the weapon back and out of his hand (see pages 142–143). This would have been one of the few conditions under which the *sauroter* became extremely dangerous to those in the rearward ranks. Other (lucky?) hoplites may have been entirely missed by the spears of the opposition in the confusion of the collision. These men would have also been carried forward by the impetus of the charge to collide with their opponent. Thus any semblance of order within the front ranks that may have remained after the charge would have shattered at the moment of impact. Perhaps only a third of the men would have instantly collided with the man in front of them. In this moment, the force of the advance, and abrupt halt by those in the front ranks, would have caused the phalanx to further fragment as men were forced into the gaps left vacant by the fallen as the intervals between the ranks compressed.

The purpose of the 'charge' and the 'push'

Some scholars consider that the purpose of the charge was to break the enemy line on contact.[107] However, in the three accounts of engagements that clearly allow for a violent collision of two loose-order formations (Delium, Coronea and Leuctra) it is interesting that in every instance the charge fails to break the opposing phalanx at the moment of collision (as also occurs in every account when a loose order formation charges against a close-order shield wall). All three engagements involve further fighting or pushing after the collision has occurred.[108] It therefore seems that the charge was not designed to break an enemy phalanx through the momentum of the attack or, if it was, it can only be concluded that it was a tactic that failed to achieve its goal every time it was attempted. The concept of the mass push after the collision is the very foundation of the 'literal model'.[109] Yet the characteristics of the phalanx show that the collision, which would have placed the hoplites of the front ranks in a position where they would have been able to physically push against their opponent, could only have occurred during the uncommon clash of two charging loose-order formations. It is in the moments after these two formations had collided, and were pressed 'shield against shield', that the physical pushing action of the literal interpretation of the term *othismos* could have taken place.

The purpose of any push would have been to dislodge the opposing phalanx once two loose-order formations had collided. This cannot have been a tactical consideration of the charge but can only have been a combined offensive and defensive default due to no other action being possible in the confines of the compressed phalanxes. At Delium the Thebans were able to push the Athenians back. However, it was not only the strength of the Theban push that resulted in the Athenian rout, but also a panic that spread through the Athenian line when enemy cavalry appeared behind them.[110] Thus a failure of Athenian morale was a contributing factor in the breaking of their line.

However, what happened if the morale of neither side failed during the push? Cawkwell offers that a physical pushing action could not have been maintained for a considerable period of time by any one group of hoplites.[111] If the pressure of those in a position to push did not cause the other side to flee, there would have been no choice but to attempt to revert to some form of weapon combat.[112] Those pressed against the enemy would have had no choice but to try and step back in order to create enough space to bring their weapons to bear in the confines of the compressed phalanx. This separation would have occurred on an individual basis as each man struggled to disengage from the man to his front and to use his weapons.[113] This may be the basis of techniques such as the Thessalian Feint, where hoplites stepped back and allowed those pressed against them to stumble forward so that they could be attacked while they were off balance; and for the Theban training in grappling and throwing techniques, which could be used to open a gap between combatants.[114] As Krentz points out, the word used by Plutarch to describe the wrestling at Leuctra (ὠθισμοῖς) is the plural of the term *othismos* and therefore cannot be a reference to a single mass push, but is a description of many individual contests.[115] The hoplite's secondary weapon, the sword, would have also been more useful under these confined circumstances than the lengthy spear. The use of the sword during the phases incorporating the push and subsequent separation of the phalanxes is attested to by Xenophon's description of the fallen after the battle of Coronea still clutching their swords in their hands.[116]

Thus the separation of the phalanxes would have been gradual, probably begun by a relaxing of any pressure exerted by the rear ranks to provide the front ranks with limited room to attempt to disengage. Eventually, some semblance of the lines would reform and weapon combat would continue right across the front. At Olynthus (382BC) the Spartans and Olynthians 'drew apart after an even contest' (καὶ τὸ μὲν πρῶτον ἰσορρόπου τοῦ κινδύνου γενομένου διεχωρίσθσαν), only to later re-engage.[117] Diodorus does not elaborate on whether the initial combat occurred 'at spear length' or involved a violent collision of the two opposing formations; or whether the second clash occurred immediately after the separation of the lines. Regardless, there was clearly the means and opportunity for the two sides to cease fighting and separate.[118] At a battle near Mantinea, the Arcadians are said to have purposefully feigned a retreat by the centre of their line, thus creating a concave crescent, in order to draw in the opposing Spartans so that they could be attacked by the encircling wings.[119] It is unlikely that the Arcadian centre would have been able to perform this manouevre while the opposing Spartans were abutted against them as per the 'literal model'; the preceeding combat must have either been conducted at spear length or the two sides had separated, which would have given the Arcadians room to move.

The Spartans also performed feigned retreats at Thermopylae (480BC) in order to draw the Persians forward, only to then about-face and begin the contest afresh.[120] Here, too, it is unlikely that the Persian mass would have been pressed up against the Spartan line on account of the smaller interval between the Greek spears due to their adoption of the shield wall (see pages 89–90). The most likely purpose of the Spartan feint at Thermopylae would have been to provide the Greeks with a new 'killing field'. As the Persian dead piled up before their original position, the Persians would find it difficult to advance to a point where the Greeks could have effectively engaged them due to the numerous bodies the Persians would have had to have crossed. Additionally, by crossing piles of their own dead, any Persian armed with a missile weapon would have momentarily held the 'high ground'.[121] By withdrawing slightly and then returning to the fight, the Spartans forced the Persians to cross the mound of their own dead, further disrupting their formation, before once again engaging the strong Greek position on a relatively level field where the advantages of the Greek panoply could be fully brought to bear.[122]

The waxing and waning of the push is also evidenced by the account of the battle of Leuctra. The Theban charge did not break the Spartan line and the two sides were most likely pressed against each other after the collision.[123] Those pressed against the Spartan front would have pushed forward to try and break the line, but the Spartans were able to hold. As the Theban push was unable to break through, and the Spartans were unable to drive the deep Theban phalanx back, there would have been little choice but to separate the phalanxes and continue fighting with weapons. We are told that in this phase of the battle the Spartans initially had the better of things, no doubt due to their experienced weapon-handling skills.[124] The separation of the lines is also evidenced by the fact that Cleombrotus was able to be removed from the Spartan front lines after he was wounded.[125] This indicates that the ranks and files of the Spartan phalanx at least were not compressed and that there was enough room for wounded men to be extracted during the weapon combat phase. Similarly, Sphodrias, was knocked down three times but managed to regain his feet each time and keep fighting.[126] It is uncertain how he could have accomplished this act if the front ranks of the phalanxes were vigorously pressed together, with each trying to surge forward under a concerted push. If hoplite warfare was consistently a contest of compressed formations and mass pushing, passages such as these would have seemed incredulous to a contemporary audience who would have known differently.

During the subsequent combat at Leuctra, members of the Spartan front ranks began to fall, some individually named by Xenophon, and the Spartan line broke only after this period of combat, which followed the separation of the compressed lines, had reduced the Spartan numbers. According to Polyaenus, Epaminondas exhorted his men, asking them 'as a favour, to give me [Epaminondas] one more step' and thus secured victory (ἐν βῆμα χαρίσασθέ μοι, καὶ τὴν νίκην ἕξομεν).[127] Despite this anecdote being absent from the accounts of Xenophon, Diodorus and Plutarch (and the lack of any reference to 'pushing') Luginbill interprets this passage as evidence of a mass push giving the Thebans victory.[128] However, the Theban victory was gained only after the lines had separated and weapon combat had taken place. Thus Epaminondas' command is most likely a figurative exhortation.[129] Had the Thebans gained victory during the pushing phase immediately after the collision of the two formations, Polyaenus' passage could be interpreted as a refernce to a literal push. As it is associated with the later phase of weapons combat, in which the Theban phalanx actually gained victory, Polyaenus' passage can only be a reference to a figurative expression given by Epaminondas to encourage his men to maintain the pressure of their attack. A similar order is said to have been issued by Iphicrates with a similar result.[130] Yet again, the context of these passages cannot be used to support the concept of a mass push.

The separation of compressed phalanxes is also evident in the account of the later stages of Coronea. The two sides met at the run and were pressed 'shield against shield'. The hoplites are then said to have 'pushed, fought, killed and been killed' (ἐωθοῦτο ἐμάχοντο ἀπέκτεινον ἀπέθνῃσκον).[131] The *othismos* could be a reference to a push by those in contact with their opponent or could just be a figurative expression for 'struggling', which could pertain to any part of the contest. As neither side was able to break the opposing line with a collision or push, the hoplites separated to fight with weapons (to fight, kill and be killed). Xenophon's description may not be a list of concurrently occurring activities, but a chronological description of the progress of the battle (i.e. [collision], push/struggle, [separate], fight, kill and be killed), defining two distinctly different phases of the encounter. As Goldsworthy points out, the pushing action of the compressed formations and the killing of the weapons combat cannot have been occurring at the same time.[132] Agesilaus is said to have received many wounds from swords and spears that penetrated his armour and it is unlikely that all of these were inflicted in the initial collision or the pushing phase.[133] Many had to have been received during a later period of weapon combat once the lines had separated. This clearly shows that not all hoplite spears would break during the collision of the formations. Weapon combat is evident from the description of bodies still clutching weapons as they littered the field in the aftermath of the engagement.[134] The separation of the lines is further indicated by the ability of the Spartans to expand the intervals of their files to allow the Thebans to pass through as a means of disrupting their formation.[135] Agesilaus is said to have ordered the phalanx to 'cease the desperate fight and open the intervals' (παυσάμενοι τῆς θυμομαχίας διαστῶμεν).[136] Clearly, by this stage neither side was ardently pushing against the other.

Similarly, in a detailed description of the second major battle of the First Messenian War, Pausanias describes the Messenians as charging recklessly into the attack while the Spartans advanced slowly so as not to break ranks.[137] This suggests that the Messenians were in an intermediate-order formation at best, while the Spartans may have maintained a close-order shield wall. The two sides clashed with 'mass pushing against mass, and man against man' (ἀθρόοι τε πρὸς ἀθρόους ὠθισμῷ ... καὶ ἀνὴρ ἀνδρὶ ἐπιόντες).[138] The description of this phase of the battle, and the use of the term *othismos*, suggests a collision 'shield against shield' and a mass pushing of the phalanx in line with the 'literal model'; although the slow advance of the Spartans, and the possible involvement of a close-order shield wall in the encounter, would suggest otherwise. However, if the Spartans were not in a close-order formation, and a violent collision and mass push did occur, the subsequent events of the battle demonstrate a separation of the phalanxes for the resumption of weapon combat. The Messenian charge did not break the Spartan line, which the Spartans are said to have maintained as they expected the Messenians to succumb to their wounds, and become fatigued by the fighting, more quickly than they did.[139] At this point the phalanxes must have separated (or were only ever engaged at spear length) as some of the Messenians are said to have advanced forward of their ranks to fight and die in individual duels and bouts of personal glory.[140] Other hoplites advanced to try and strip the dead of their armour.[141] Even both kings advanced to fight an individual duel.[142] After a brief respite (possibly another separation of the lines) the fighting began afresh only to be stopped by the setting of the sun.[143] Clearly, a large portion of this battle was fought with both phalanxes separated from each other. Whether this occured from the onset, or was the result of the failure of either side to break their opponent's formation with a mass push, is uncertain.

Some scholars have suggested that a hoplite engagement may have developed into a pushing match after a period of spear combat.[144] When the Carthaginians closed with the Greeks in Sicily to fight with swords, this is likely to have been the case. When engaged at spear length, there can clearly have been no collision or pushing between the front ranks. Once the Carthaginians closed to engage with their swords, Plutarch states that the contest was more one of strength rather than one of skill, and it can be concluded that a certain amount of physical pushing occurred (either with the shield or with weapons or with both).[145] This aspect agrees with the 'literal model' interpretation of the *othismos*. However, as the opening stages of the engagement involved combat with no collision of forces, this stage of the battle is more consistent with the 'figurative model' and the whole engagement is more compliant with the 'final phase' theory. In engagements involving the collision of two formations, it is more likely this development occurred in the reverse order with the pushing resultant from the collision evolving into weapon combat if neither line was broken by the force of the opposing push. As such, the nature of some engagements clearly altered from one model to another during the course of the battle.

An engagement involving a close-order phalanx could also develop into a pushing match when one side began to break. It is unlikely that an entire phalanx would have simply 'about faced' and fled. It is more likely that the rout happened in stages with the men from the rear and sides of the phalanx fleeing while those at the front were still engaged.[146] Krentz suggests that once the rear ranks had broken, those in the middle, even if not yet engaged, would have been tempted to follow suit due to the lack of perceived support.[147] As this occurred, the attacking phalanx could advance as resistance to their front lessened (the 'one more step' of Epaminondas' exhortation at Leuctra) and 'push' the breaking phalanx back at spear point until the remaining hoplites also turned their back and fled. The break of the Argive line at the opening of Coronea, for example, is most likely to have begun in the rear ranks while the Spartans were still advancing. This left only the front ranks to resist the first spear thrusts of the Spartans before they too broke and fled. Whether this should be interpreted as a literal or figurative collision and pushing action is a matter of semantics.

Phalanx depth and the *othismos*

This returns us to the debate over the depth of the phalanx (see Chapter 12, Phalanxes, Shield Walls and Other Formations). The question is not if there was a standard depth or, if so, what that was, but more what the tactical benefits of a deep phalanx may have been. For those adhering to the 'literal model', the purpose of the rear ranks was to push into the back of the man in front and so drive the phalanx forward. It is assumed that the greater the depth of the phalanx, the greater the impact of the clash and that the weight of the charge and subsequent push would decide the outcome of the battle.[148] Contrary to this, Anderson states that a deep phalanx, such as the fifty-deep Theban deployment at Leuctra, would add no weight at all to the front lines of the formation.[149] This certainly makes sense. A formation does not impact with an enemy line in what Goldsworthy refers to as a 'solid, human battering-ram', regardless of deployment.[150] When advancing, either slowly or at a run, the individual members of the phalanx would be separated by the interval of the order used or by the fragmentation of the formation. Thus the force of any collision would only be exerted by the front rank at the moment of contact, and even then only on an individual by individual basis. Once contact had been made, the remaining ranks would simply compress the phalanx as momentum carried them forward, without adding to the force of the initial collision. So regardless of the depth of deployment, the force of any charge could only be expelled by the front ranks and a deep formation has no bearing upon the weight of the collision whatsoever. Unlike the rugby scrum used in the 'literal model's' comparison to the phalanx, hoplites did not hold onto each other while they advanced and so gained no advantage, balance or support from acting in concert with each other.[151] This explains why the deep Theban phalanxes at Delium and Leuctra failed to break the shallower opposing formations.[152] The deep deployment at Leuctra is said to have been adopted for the specific purpose of crushing the opposing line.[153] However, this cannot be taken as a reference to the use of a deep phalanx to smash an enemy position through the force of its collision. If it is interpreted in this way, then it must be concluded that this was also a failed tactical aspect of the manouevre as it did not achieve its immediate goal and the outcome of the engagement was only decided once battle had been joined.[154] Diodorus states that valour and experience will make up for numbers in war; a lesson harshly learnt by the Persians at Thermopylae in 480BC and at Cunaxa in 401BC.[155] These are clear references to the advantages of skill and discipline in weapon combat, which was a common element of all hoplite engagements regardless of whether there was a collision or not.

Even once compressed, it is difficult to comprehend how a deep phalanx could aid any push. A hoplite pushing from the fiftieth rank would in no manner influence those at the front and any force that he exerted through pushing would simply be diffused and absorbed by the ranks before him in the phalanx. Anderson and Bardunias state that this would not occur if the pushing action was coordinated.[156] However, it is uncertain how this co-ordination could be achieved if overcrowding results in a breakdown of internal communications and a lack of individual control over movement; particularly in a formation containing multiple ranks and potentially thousands of men.

Similarly, the man in the front rank of one phalanx would in no way be able to drive back a man in the rear rank of an opposing phalanx simply by pressing against the man in front of him. It is most likely that any influence to brace the front ranks in position, or to push them forward, could only be exerted by members of the first few ranks of the phalanx. This explains why a common hoplite deployment was to a depth of eight ranks. The first rank would be the point of contact: either through collision or at spear length. The second rank could also engage when deployed in close-order and could brace the front rank in position if the formation was being used defensively. Ranks three to seven would further brace the front lines in place and provide enough density to prevent the front lines from immediately breaking under the ferocity of an enemy charge or attack. The *ouragoi* in rank eight would be there to ensure the middle ranks supported the front. This explains why the *ouragos* was chosen for his intelligence and experience rather than his strength.

Why then would the Thebans have deployed to a depth of twenty-five men at Delium and fifty at Leuctra? What purpose did the deeper formation have that outweighed the possibility of deploying shallower but wider and outflanking the opposition with superior numbers as the Peloponnesian army had done at Olpe in 426BC?[157] The Corinthian and Allied units at Nemea were specifically ordered not to deploy too deep to avoid such encirclement, which suggests that it was a common battlefield possibility.[158] The Athenians at Delium deployed eight deep so that they could cover the same frontage as the deeper-deployed Theban phalanx, no doubt also to avoid encirclement.[159] The use of the rear ranks to provide reserves, encouragement and security have been individually proposed by some scholars and summarily dismissed by others (see Chapter 12, Phalanxes, Shield Walls and Other Formations). However the combination of these factors, coupled with the offensive abilities of the different formations, allowed the phalanx to comply with the one basic requirement of all hoplite warfare: the need to adequately resist the strength of your opponent. Luginbill states that only a formation willing to stand up to the attack of another phalanx could hope to oppose it effectively.[160] This, and not a mass push by the rear ranks, is the very essence of hoplite combat. Computer simulations have shown that phalanxes that do not resist the attack of their opponent, for whatever reason, are readily put to flight.[161] Luginbill further states, somewhat contradictorily, that the proof that the rear ranks were not reserves comes from the fact that hoplite battles were not wars of attrition; one side always broke and fled.[162] However, one side could have in no way known exactly when another side would break. Hoplite warfare was not so formalized that it could be assumed that one side would break at a particular moment in time, under a specific condition or when it had suffered a certain number of casualties. In the case of the Spartans, who were forbidden to withdraw by law, the chances of their line breaking would have been remote.[163] As a consequence, one way to improve the chances of victory would have been to ensure that your phalanx was able to outlast that of your enemy.

One way that a hoplite commander could ensure that his phalanx would outlast that of his opponent would be to deploy it deeper than the formation he was facing. If two sides met in battle in the same order and depth, the contest would come down to the skill, discipline and morale of the two sides. If these skill sets were relatively equal, neither side would hold an offensive or defensive advantage. Conversely, any side with more weapon-handling skill, such as the Spartans, could possibly expect to inflict casualties at greater rate among the enemy hoplites than it would sustain itself.[164] Thus the numbers of the less experienced side would decrease at a more substantial rate than those of their enemy. This loss through death and injury would continue until a point of critical mass was reached when the morale of those in the rear ranks, who had been slowly advancing to replace the fallen, failed and the phalanx began to break.

This is where deploying in a deeper phalanx would have provided an advantage; not from being able to add weight to a collision or physical push, but by simply being able to sustain more casualties than the opposition before it reached the point of critical mass where the line would break. The rear ranks of the deep phalanx, unable to directly observe how the battle was progressing due to noise, dust, distance and other environmental conditions would have simply held their position and, in doing so, prevented the phalanx from breaking. The front ranks would suffer casualties, but so too would the front ranks of their opposition. If no other factors were involved to cause a break in the line (such as low morale or a flank attack), as the fighting continued, the rear ranks of both sides would have to advance to replace the fallen.[165] However, a shallow formation could only count on possibly eight rows of replacements, and that was only if they fought to the very last man. The deeper phalanx, on the other hand, could rely on many more rows of reserves, many of whom (those at the far back) would have had little idea of the progress of the engagement and merely held the formation in place. Eventually, the shallower line would have reached the point where it gave way long before the deep phalanx had begun to waver. As such, the deep phalanx would have secured its victory through mere weight of numbers.

Deep phalanxes were generally adopted by one side only when they faced an opponent of superior skill and experience. At Syracuse for example, the relatively inexperienced Syracusans deployed sixteen deep to face the more experienced eight-deep Athenians.[166] At Nemea, the Athenians and their allies deployed at least sixteen ranks deep to face the Spartans.[167] Goldsworthy and Krentz offer that the members of a shallow formation, seeing the numerous ranks of a deep phalanx with which they were about to be engaged, may have been psychologically overwhelmed (although this is unlikely to have occurred to the Spartans).[168]

The Thebans had lost every major confrontation they had been involved in since the time of the Persian Wars (where they were on the losing side at Plataea) and for nearly a century they had been continuously beaten by the Athenians except when fighting as allies of Sparta.[169] Thus at Delium, the twenty-five-deep deployment would have allowed the Thebans to fight longer than the superior force of eight-deep Athenians. The charge and depth of the phalanx did not break the thinner Athenian line and so cannot be considered the designed purpose of the deployment. Once the pushing phase began after the collision of the formations, the rear ranks of the deep Theban phalanx would have had little to do but keep the formation in place while the front ranks pushed. If neither side was dislodged by the push of the other side, in the weapon fighting that would have developed as the lines separated, the deep Theban phalanx would have held the advantage due to their lines of reserves. However, the Athenian line wavered at the sight of enemy cavalry to their rear and the Thebans were able to drive them back with their push. As the lines did not separate for weapon combat, the tactical advantage of the deep deployment was not required.

At Leuctra the Thebans deployed fifty deep: twice the depth of their deployment at Delium. The reasons for this deployment can be attributed to several factors: the hoplites the Thebans faced at Leuctra were Spartans – much more experienced than the Athenians they faced at Delium; the Spartan line was unlikely to break easily (if at all) as they were prohibited to do so by Spartan law; the Thebans did not gain any advantage from charging downhill as they had at Delium; the Spartans were deployed twelve deep – four ranks deeper than the Athenians at Delium; and the regular Spartan deployment was the close-order shield wall, which was both defensively and offensively very strong. At Leuctra the overall advantage in numbers also rested with the Spartans and their allies, although the numbers in both the Theban and Spartan contingents may have been equal.[170] To meet such an opponent, the Theban phalanx had to be deployed to such a depth that they could sustain massive casualties, retain their formation and still fight until the last Spartan had been slain or routed. At both Delium and Leuctra the Thebans deployed roughly four times deeper than their opponents. These deep Theban deployments may be an indication that the Theban commanders had estimated that they could, or would, suffer almost four times as many casualties as their opponents and that by deploying deep the phalanx could suffer such losses and still retain the integrity of the formation.[171]

If the numbers of both the Theban and Spartan contingents at Leuctra were equal, this would mean that the Theban formation on the left wing, while four times deeper than that of the Spartans, would also have been four times narrower across its frontage.[172] The elite Sacred Band would have been positioned at the head of this formation.[173] The Thebans are said to have directed their attack directly against the position of Cleombrotus.[174] For the Spartans, the proper position for their king was between the first and second *morai.*[175] Thus the deep Theban phalanx would have struck the Spartan line at a point where almost an entire division of Spartans extended beyond their left flank but in a manner that allowed them to concentrate the force of their attack at what they perceived to be a vital point in the Spartan line. Goldsworthy suggests that the thin, deep formation would have also encountered fewer obstacles during the advance and would thus have been easier to maintain.[176]

It must be considered why the Spartan line did not simply fold around this attack and encircle the Thebans.[177] Firstly, Plutarch tells us that the entire Boeotian phalanx advanced obliquely against the Spartans, not just the Theban contingent (although not all of the allies would have engaged the Spartans directly but must have engaged some of the allies on the Spartan left wing).[178] One thousand Spartans died in the battle, including four hundred of the seven hundred officers (who would have made up the bulk of the front rank).[179] This loss of two-thirds of the front rank indicates that more than just those around Cleombrotus were engaged in the fighting and many of these casualties must have been incurred at the hands of the Theban allies. Therefore, the right flank of the narrow Theban contingent was protected by the presence of these allied units. The left side of the formation, while not covered by a contingent of allied hoplites, is the side upon which the hoplite shield is located and is thus defensively stronger against any flanking attack. Additionally, the Boeotian cavalry, after routing the Spartan cavalry prior to the advance of the infantry, would have been in a position to also cover this side of the phalanx.[180] Furthermore, most of the Spartan *morai* would have had a frontage of around forty-eight men.[181] Those on the left of the first *mora*, close to Cleombrotus, would have been engaged against some of the Sacred Band. Thus the remaining Spartans on the right could not have simply swung around to engage the fifty-deep Theban flank without thinning their line in order to cover the depth of the new frontage and expose themselves to attacks by the Boeotian cavalry in doing so.[182] As a consequence, the Spartans would have been unable to envelop the Theban formation on either side and those around Cleombrotus would have had to engage the deep Theban phalanx on their own.

This explains the purpose of the charge (both at Leuctra and elsewhere). As Matthews points out, any flanking manoeuvre requires precision timing to execute it effectively. If the manoeuvre is made too early, the opposing side can simply extend their line and meet the flanking units head on. If the move is made too late, the battle may well be over before the manoeuvre could have any effect on the outcome.[183] Additionally, as occurred at Leuctra, the place where the brunt of an attack strikes the opposing line may have also prevented any flanking movement by that opponent. Thus what charging into the attack achieves is limiting the amount of time an opposing side has to react to, and possibly out-manoeuvre, that attack.[184]

Pelopidas and the Sacred Band are said to have charged into the attack at the head of the Theban formation.[185] The fouling of the Spartan lines negated the advantage of their shield wall and so the two formations would have collided violently together. With the failure of the Theban charge and push to break the enemy line, the formations would have separated for weapon combat where the experience of the Spartans is said to have given them the initial advantage.[186] Both lines would have been sustaining casualties in this action, the Thebans most likely at a faster rate than the Spartans. However, the thinner Spartan line could ill afford to lose many hoplites and once the members of their front ranks had fallen, the Spartan line was 'pushed back (ὠθούμενοι) before the Theban masses' in a figurative reference to victory gained through the numbers of the deep phalanx.[187] A similar use of a deep formation to gain victory over a thinner one can also be seen in the confrontation between the Spartans and the Athenians at the Piraeus where the deep Spartan formation was able to drive the shallower Athenian formation into the marsh of Halae.[188]

Once one side had begun to break, the engagement was all but concluded. These later phases of hoplite battles are well attested to in the ancient literature and have been covered extensively by modern scholars; particularly by Pritchett. As the morale of one side began to waver, its phalanx would fragment and its hoplites scatter and flee. If the broken side did not rally, reform and counter-attack, the other side would be left in possession of the field. The victorious army could pursue the routing troops, or not, depending upon their will and the availability of troops suitable for the pursuit such as cavalry, peltasts or young hoplites. Commonly, envoys were sent to the victors with a formal request to recover the bodies of the dead under the terms of a truce. Spoils were stripped from the bodies of the fallen and a battlefield trophy was erected at the site where the losing side had broken. Other spoils were given as offerings to the gods or sent to cult centres such as Delphi or Olympia. The formal request for the recovery of the dead and the erection of the trophy generally marked the conclusion of the battle.[189]

Based upon both the physical and literary evidence it can be concluded that there were two very dynamic and different types of hoplite engagement, each agreeing with one side of the *othismos* debate. The more common form of battle, containing at least one close-order phalanx, did not involve a collision of the two formations. This resulted in the majority of the fighting being conducted at weapons range where characteristics such as skill, discipline and morale were deciding factors in the outcome of the engagement. This type of hoplite battle closely follows the principles of the 'figurative model'. The other, rarer, type of hoplite engagement involved the rapid, violent collision of two disorderly masses of heavily armed hoplites as per the 'literal model'. The momentum of the charge and the depth of the phalanxes involved would have played little part in deciding such an encounter. Once compressed, the men of both sides would have physically pushed against each other using their shields to try and dislodge their opponent. Further to the 'literal model' of the collision and push, if the pushing action was unable to break the enemy's line, the phalanxes would have had little choice but to gradually separate to a distance, where weapon combat could be conducted, and revert to the style of fighting where the skill and morale of both sides would decide the outcome. It is only in the context of this fighting 'at spear length' (regardless of whether there had been a charge and collision or not) that the depth of the phalanxes involved truly came into play, as a deep formation allowed for greater casualties to be sustained before the integrity of the phalanx would be compromised. Even against technically superior opponents, the deep phalanx allowed for greater numbers of casualties to be sustained while the more experienced side was worn down by weight of numbers. Eventually, one side would reach a critical point where its morale failed, either through sustained losses or through general panic, and that side would break, leaving the victorious side in possession of the field.

Chapter 14

Conclusion: The Nature of Hoplite Combat

It has been suggested that 'you must understand the armies before you can understand the wars'.[1] However, in relation to the conflicts of the Classical Greeks, previous scholarship cannot be further from understanding how the functionality of the hoplite affected the nature of warfare within the broader context of the phalanx and the engagements of the Classical world. The majority of work that has been conducted on hoplite warfare so far has primarily concentrated on the 'who', the 'when', the 'where' and the 'why' of hoplite wars and engagements. It has been only recently that scholarship's focus has expanded to incorporate the 'how'. Yet this final element is essential to the comprehension of how the hoplites of ancient Greece fought the battles they were involved in. It is only by comprehending the basic principles of hoplite warfare, gained through physical re-creation, experimental archaeology and ballistics testing, and then analyzing the results of these tests in conjunction with the literary, artistic and archaeological evidence, that scholarship begins to approach the concept of 'understanding' both the armies and the warfare of Classical Greece.

For more than a century and a half scholarship into the wars of the ancient Greeks has been based upon an incorrect interpretation of the available evidence. Often the literary evidence alone does not comply with the models of hoplite warfare forwarded by previous scholars. However this inconsistency has, for the most part, been ignored in the light of no other means of explaining the mechanics of hoplite warfare. The numerous debates among scholars demonstrate that, until now, the full nature of hoplite warfare has been far from fully understood. The reappraisal of the available artistic, literary and archaeological records, combined with physical re-creation and experimental archaeology, allows for the nature of hoplite warfare to be understood in a way never before explored and demonstrates that there was more to hoplite warfare than was previously imagined.

Hoplite warfare was far more than the frenzied, chaotic and disorganized brawl between two masses of heavily armed men bearing spears that it has commonly believed to have been. The elaborate organization of the phalanx into units and sub-units, combined with at least an elementary command structure, made hoplite warfare much more orderly and adaptable to the changing tactical conditions of the ancient battlefield. Hoplite armies could deploy at different depths, with the most common formation being that of eight ranks deep, depending upon the amount of terrain that was available for the army to be deployed in and the tactical requirements of the situation. Deeper formations were also used to provide rows of reserves should a hoplite army face a superior opponent.

Similarly, the interval between the ranks and files was also varied. The close-order formation of 45cm per man (or something akin to it) was the most common form of hoplite deployment. This order allowed the first two ranks of a phalanx to engage an enemy while being supported by the rows of reserves behind them. The close-order formation also allowed for the creation of the 'shield wall': an interlocking row of shields overlapping each other from the left, which left little part of the hoplite, or his formation, exposed to attack. However, these benefits came at a cost. The close-order shield wall could only be maintained at a slow pace by experienced hoplites when it was on the move, and even then only through the use of a cadence and/or a sung *paean* to keep the members of the phalanx in step. The offensive and defensive benefits of the shield wall came at the sacrifice of mobility. Less experienced hoplite forces could only maintain a semblance of the close-order formation due to their limited training.

The more open intermediate-order formation of 90cm per man facilitated movement but came at the cost of a weaker frontage across the formation and the inability of members of the second rank to reach the enemy with their weapons upon initial contact between the two sides. For many hoplite forces, this was the best type of formation they could hope to maintain and the decision as to what depth, and to what interval, a contingent of hoplites would be deployed was often left to the individual unit commander rather than to the *strategos*. However, hoplite formations were not merely limited to a simple block of ranks and files. Depending upon the tactical situation, hoplite formations could assume a variety of shapes so as to best utilize the terrain, a preconceived strategy and/or the perceived level, and expected direction, of any threat.

Fighting between two groups of hoplites was normally conducted with both sides 'at spear length' from each other as the nature of the common close-order phalanx prevented the formations from getting any closer. Examples of this style of fighting can be seen during the opening stages of the battle of Coronea (394BC), in the 'Tearless Battle' (368BC) and in Sicily (341BC).[2] At this range the hoplites of the front ranks would have jabbed and probed their spears at their opponents from the underarm position; directing their attacks at the shield and upper regions of the helmet until a committed blow could be delivered against an opportune target, which may have either injured or slayed the opponent. This style of fighting would continue until one side broke and ran. The cause of this flight could be varied. Flanking attacks by other units could cause an opposing formation to scatter; a loss of a significant number of its members could also cause a phalanx to break; as could a generally low level of morale. In some instances, a combination of all of these elements was the contributing factor in the rout of one side or another.

On rarer occasions the characteristics of a hoplite battle were such that they allowed for the two sides to heavily collide against each other in a manner similar to that generally thought to have been the common form of hoplite warfare by modern scholars. When both sides were in a loose-order formation, either through deployment or due to the formation fragmenting during the course of a battle, the larger interval between the men of the phalanx allowed for a rapid massed charge to be conducted. When two formations clashed in such a manner, parts of the front ranks would become pressed against each other and a fierce contest of pushing and close-quarters combat would ensue as each side tried to drive the other from the field. This frenzied style of fighting can be seen in the accounts of the battles of Delium (424BC), Leuctra (371BC) and the later stages of the battle of Coronea (394BC).[3] If neither side was able to break the opposing line, the formations would gradually separate to a distance where any weapons that had not been broken in the collision of the phalanxes could be employed to better use. The encounter would then 'evolve' into a contest 'at spear length' where factors such as the skill and morale of each side would determine the subsequent outcome of the battle. These two styles of hoplite combat, one involving close-order formations engaged 'at spear length' and the other involving loose-order formations colliding, pushing, separating and then fighting can be found in every literary account of a hoplite battle from the late eighth century BC to the third.

This is not to say that the methods of employing hoplite armies were static across the period in question. Rather, the tactics and strategies of the broader hoplite battle continually developed and evolved throughout the Classical Age from their Archaic origins. By the fourth century BC, as Cawkwell points out: 'the art of war was developing so fast that every battle was in some sense novel'.[4] The period of the Peloponnesian War, for example, witnessed an increase in the use of peltasts, cavalry, missile troops and other light skirmishers to directly engage hoplites, often from a distance where the offensive and defensive advantages of the phalanx could not be brought to bear.[5] The most infamous uses of this style of fighting were on the island of Sphacteria in 425BC where harassing attacks by peltasts and archers resulted in the unprecedented surrender of Spartan hoplites, and in the loss of an entire *mora* of Spartiates to peltasts at Lechaeum in 390BC.[6]

The increase in the use of missiles and other troops also resulted in a change in the overall nature of hoplite battles; from previously where two lines of hoplites had confronted each other to decide the outcome of an engagement, to a style of fighting where the phalanx was often used to keep the opposing lines at bay while skirmishers and mounted troops delivered the *coup de grâce* on the flanks. At Sardis in 395BC for example, the Spartan king Agesilaus attacked a formation of Persian cavalry with coordinated sorties by his own cavalry, peltasts and the phalanx.[7] No longer was the morale of the hoplite, and his willingness to hold his place in line for an indeterminable length of time, of paramount concern to the outcome of a battle. The effective positioning and use of ranged weapons, light troops and cavalry often became the deciding factor in battles of the late Classical Age. The hoplite need to have only held his position long enough for these troops to make their attack and rout the foe.

The Peloponnesian War also saw an increase in the use of mercenaries and standing units, which allowed for protracted campaigns to be undertaken by men not beholden to an agricultural livelihood.[8] Hoplite combat, for many, became a year-round profession. The rise of professional units contributed to the decline of Spartan military dominance on the battlefields of ancient Greece as other 'standing' armies, troops of mercenaries and commanders gained the experience, innovation and tactical adaptability to effectively counter any threat posed by the Spartan war machine.

However, many of these aspects belong to the broader realm of hoplite generalship, not to the narrower focus of hoplite combat. From the perspective of the individual hoplite, the techniques of fighting remained relatively unchanged throughout the entire Classical Period. The effective use of his weapons in the underarm and low stances, his ability to conform to any desired formation and the major offensive and defensive benefits that these characteristics bestowed, warranted no need to alter the way in which the individual hoplite fought within the confines of the phalanx. The Greek way of warfare, while later incorporating the use of other arms, remained based upon the use of the hoplite and the phalanx. However, like all styles of warfare throughout history, the fighting techniques of the hoplite were eventually outclassed; signalling the demise of the Classical Period. The age of the hoplite was superseded by the adoption of a new style of fighting, and the rise of a new military power, which adopted, adapted and refined the principles of warfare laid down by the Classical Greek hoplite: the *sarissa*-wielding phalanxes of Macedon.

Notes

Preface

1. V.D. Hanson, *The Western Way of War* (Berkeley, University of California Press, 1989), p. 22.
2. Mitchell argues differently, stating that 'the primary evidence for ancient Greek warfare is both familiar and well-stated'. However, of all of the works he cites, none deal with the combative techniques of the hoplite. See S. Mitchell. 'Hoplite Warfare in Ancient Greece' in A.B. Lloyd (ed.), *Battle in Antiquity* (London, Duckworth, 1996), pp. 87–88.
3. For example, in his modelling of ancient warfare, Philip Sabin uses a number of 'common denominators' or generalizations to formulate a standardized overview of an ancient battle. Such conclusions include the assumption that a 'safe generalization is that the frontage of armies did not vary with the number of troops in a linear fashion. Larger armies seem to have formed up instead in significantly greater depth' (see: P. Sabin, *Lost Battles – Reconstructing the Great Clashes of the Ancient World* (London, Continuum, 2009), pp. 31). In relation to hoplite warfare, Sabin further concludes (p. 49) that 'hoplites must always launch all-out attacks whenever possible [in his model] because of the ferocity with which they charged in an attempt to reach a rapid result'. Due to this assumption that all hoplite combat sought a quick conclusion, Sabin further generalizes that 'cavalry combats tended to be decided a lot quicker than contests between heavy infantry other than hoplites'. However, the charge was not a common element of hoplite combat, and failed to accomplish anything even when it was conducted. Additionally, the duration of hoplite engagements greatly varied (from less than an hour to most of a day) as did the way in which the armies were deployed (see Chapter 13 The Hoplite Battle: Contact, *Othismos*, Breakthrough and Rout). Furthermore, Sabin often omits or 'down-sizes' units that he perceives had no direct bearing on the actual fighting. For example, the 10,000-strong unit of Boeotian light-infantry at Delium mentioned by Thucydides (4.93) is diminished in Sabin's reconstruction into a 'token' unit of around 1,000 as he concludes that they 'do not seem to have contributed anything significant during the battle' (p. 99). However, the mere presence of such a large body of troops on the battlefield would greatly influence how both sides deployed and manoeuvred. It is unlikely that the Athenians would have deployed or moved in a way that left their flanks vulnerable to such a large body of light infantry, and the Boeotians must have taken the size of this contingent into account when forming up for battle. Consequently, the removal of such a large contingent of men will greatly alter the way any model recreates the battle. If only the units involved in the actual fighting are used (as in Sabin's reconstructions), and no other variables are brought into play (such as other bodies of troops), then it is hardly surprising that the results of these 'replays' are exactly the same as what the ancient sources tell us. Indeed, the system has been tweaked so

that another outcome is all but impossible. As a result, it is unlikely that any model incorporating factors such as these would be able to accurately replicate the variable nature of any or all hoplite engagements. For a use of computer modelling to examine specific aspects of hoplite combat see: R. McDermott, *Modelling Hoplite Battle in SWARM* (New Zealand, Massey University, 2004 (unpublished thesis)).

4. For an overview of how re-enactment and physical re-creation has enhanced the understanding of many aspects of Roman warfare see: W.B. Griffiths, 'Re-enactment as Research: Towards a Set of Guidelines for Re-enactors and Academics', *JRMES* 11 (2000), pp. 135–139; For other examples of the use of re-enactment and physical re-creation as a research tool see: M.M. Markle III, 'The Macedonian *Sarissa*, Spear and Related Armour', *AJA* 8:3 (Summer 1977), pp. 323–339; R.E. Dickinson, 'Length Isn't Everything – Use of the Macedonian *Sarissa* in the Time of Alexander the Great', *JBT* 3:3 (November 2000), pp. 51–62; W. Donlan and J. Thompson, 'The Charge at Marathon: Herodotus 6.112', *Classical Journal* 71:4 (Apr–May 1976), pp. 339–343; P. Connolly 'Experiments with the *Sarissa* – the Macedonian Pike and Cavalry Lance – a Functional View', *JRMES* 11 (2000), pp. 103–112; although a relatively recent practice as a research tool, the possession of a practical knowledge of military techniques as an essential part of writing valid history is not a modern concept. Polybius (12.25e–28a) declares that any history written solely on the review of memoirs and prior historical writings is completely without value (ὠφελεῖ δ᾿ οὐδέν) for its readers.

Chapter 1 – The Hoplite Spear

1. Eur. *HF* 189–193.
2. For example, see: J.K. Anderson, *Military Theory and Practice in the Age of Xenophon* (Berkeley, University of California Press, 1970), p. 37; J.K. Anderson, 'Hoplite Weapons and Offensive Arms' in V.D. Hanson (ed.), *Hoplites – The Classical Greek Battle Experience* (London, Routledge, 2004), p. 22; E. Bradford, *Thermopylae – The Battle for the West* (U.S.A., Da Capo Press, 1993), p. 71; P. Connolly, *Greece and Rome at War* (London, Greenhill Books, 1998), p. 63; D. Featherstone, *Warriors and Warfare in Ancient and Medieval Times* (London, Constable, 1988), p. 44; V.D. Hanson, *The Western Way of War* (Berkeley, University of California Press, 1989), p. 84; V.D. Hanson, *Wars of the Ancient Greeks* (London, Cassell, 1999), p. 61; M.M. Markle III, 'The Macedonian *Sarissa*, Spear and Related Armour' *AJA* 8:3 (Summer 1977), p. 325; A.M. Snodgrass, *Arms and Armour of the Greeks* (Baltimore, Johns Hopkins University Press, 1999), p. 53; H. van Wees, *Greek Warfare – Myths and Realities* (London, Duckworth, 2004), p. 48; J. Warry, *Warfare in the Classical World* (Norman, University of Oklahoma Press, 1995), pp. 35, 37; R. Gabriel and K. Metz, *From Sumer to Rome – The Military Capabilities of Ancient Armies* (Connecticut, Greenwood Press, 1991), p. 94; F.E. Adcock, *The Greek and Macedonian Art of War* (Berkeley, University of California Press, 1957), p. 3; A.K. Goldsworthy, 'The *Othismos*, Myths and Heresies: The Nature of Hoplite Battle', *War in History* 4:1 (1997) p. 6; P. Cartledge, *Thermopylae – The Battle that Changed the World* (London, Pan Books, 2007), p. 144; R. Matthews, *The Battle of Thermopylae – A Campaign in Context* (Gloucestershire, Spellmount, 2006), p. 56.
3. Ascl. *Tact.*, 2.1–5.2; Polyb. 6.19–42.
4. Nep. *Iphicrates*, 1.4; Diod. Sic. 15.44.3; the word used by Diodorus to describe the size of the new weapon is ἡμιολίῳ (from ἡμιόλιος) meaning 'one and a half'; 'half as much'; or, in agreement with Nepos, 'as large again' (i.e. doubled). See also: L. Ueda-Sarson, 'The Evolution of Hellenistic Infantry (Part 1): The Reforms of Iphikrates', *Slingshot* 222 (May

2002), pp. 30–36; H.L. Lorimer, 'The Hoplite Phalanx with Special Reference to the Poems of Archilochus and Tyrtaeus', *ABSA* 42 (1947), p. 124.

5. N. Whatley, 'On the Possibility of Reconstructing Marathon and Other Ancient Battles', *JHS* 94 (1964), p. 123; P. Cartledge, 'Hoplites and Heroes: Sparta's Contribution to the Technique of Ancient Warfare', *JHS*, Vol. 97 (1977), p. 12; van Wees, *Greek Warfare*, p. 152; R. McDermott, *Modelling Hoplite Battle in SWARM* (New Zealand, Massey University, 2004 (unpublished thesis)), pp. 12, 16; F.M. Combellack, 'Achilles – Bare of Foot?', *Classical Journal*, 41:5 (Feb 1946), p. 197; Anderson, *Military Theory*, p. 9.

6. *Sauroter*: Hdt. 7.41; Hom. *Il.* 10.153; *Anth. Pal*, 6.110; Polyb., 6.25.6, 11.18.4; Plut. *Mor.* 183A; Hsch. 4.280 s.v. 'σαυρωτήρ'; *styrax*: Pl. *Lach.* 184a, Xen. *Hell.* 6.2.19; Aen. Tact. 18.10; Hsch. 4.2029 s.v. 'Στύραξ'; *ouriachos*: Hom. *Il.* 13.443, 16.612, 17.528; *Anth. Pal.* 6.111; Ap. Rhod. *Argon.* 3.1253, Hsch. 3.1860 s.v. 'οὐρίαχον'. Many functions have been ascribed to the *sauroter* by modern scholarship: to protect the end of the shaft against the elements: Snodgrass, *Arms and Armour*, p. 80, Cartledge, 'Hoplites and Heroes', p. 15; to allow the weapon to be thrust into the ground when not in use: Hom. *Il.* 10.153; Arist. *Poet.* 25.14; see also: J. McK. Camp II, 'A Spear Butt from the Lesbians', *Hesperia*, 47:2 (Apr–Jun 1978), p. 192, Cartledge, 'Hoplites and Heroes', p. 15; as a tool for altering the grip on the weapon: J. Lazenby, 'The Killing Zone' in Hanson (ed.), *Hoplites*, p. 93; to act as a counterweight against the weight of the spearhead: Snodgrass, *Arms and Armour*, p. 80, Camp, 'Spear Butt', p. 192; van Wees, *Greek Warfare*, p. 48; G.M.A. Richter, 'Greek Bronzes Recently Acquired by the Metropolitan Museum of Art', *AJA* 43:2 (Apr–Jun 1939), p. 196; as a tool to help the hoplite brace himself in battle: P. Bardunias, 'The Aspis – Surviving Hoplite Battle', *Ancient Warfare* 1:3 (2007), p. 14; to use as a weapon: Camp, 'Spear Butt', p. 192; Snodgrass, *Arms and Armour*, pp. 56, 80; V.D. Hanson, 'Hoplite Technology in Phalanx Battle' in Hanson (ed.), *Hoplites*, pp. 71–72; Warry, *Warfare*, p. 35; Hanson, *Western*, pp. 85, 164; S. Mitchell. 'Hoplite Warfare in Ancient Greece' in A.B. Lloyd (ed.), *Battle in Antiquity* (London, Duckworth, 1996), p. 90; Cartledge, 'Hoplites and Heroes', p. 15; Hanson, *Wars*, pp. 51, 53, 58, 62; Goldsworthy, '*Othismos*', p. 2; Anderson, *Military Theory*, p. 37; Richter, 'Greek Bronzes', p. 195.

7. A.M. Snodgrass, *Early Greek Armour and Weapons* (Edinburgh, Edinburgh University Press, 1964), pp. 116–133.

8. Snodgrass, *Early Greek*, p. 123.

9. Snodgrass, *Early Greek*, pp. 123–126.

10. This is based upon the average dimensions and weights given for 'J style' spearheads found at Olympia. See H. Baitinger, *Die Angriffswaffen aus Olympia* (Berlin, De Gruyter, 2001), pp. 142–219.

11. M.M. Markle III, 'Use of the *Sarissa* by Philip and Alexander of Macedon', *AJA* 82:4 (Autumn 1978), p. 487; Markle, 'Spear', p. 325; Snodgrass, *Arms and Armour*, p. 80; Connolly, *Greece and Rome*, p. 63; Snodgrass (*Arms and Armour*, p. 38) states that Dark Age spearheads averaged '37 inches' (93cm) in length.

12. G.R. Davidson, *Corinth: Results of Excavations Conducted by the American School of Classical Studies at Athens – Vol. XII – The Minor Objects* (Princeton, American School of Classical Studies at Athens, 1952), p. 200.

13. Markle, 'Philip', p. 487; Markle, 'Spear', pp. 323–339.

14. D.M. Robinson, *Excavations at Olynthus, Part X – Metal and Minor Miscellaneous Finds* (Baltimore, Johns Hopkins University Press, 1941), pp. 412–414.

15. Grattius (*Hunting*, pp. 117–120) warns of the long Macedonian pikes with their 'small teeth' (*Macetum immensos libeat si dicere contos. Quam longa exigui spicant hastilia dentes*).

This suggests that the head of the Macedonian *sarissa* was recognizably smaller than the head of the hoplite spear. A *sarissa* head recovered from the so-called 'Tomb of Philip II' at Vergina weighed only 97g (Connolly, *Greece and Rome*, p. 77); see also: Markle, 'Philip', p. 487.

16. N. Sekunda, *Greek Hoplite 480–323BC* (Oxford, Osprey Publishing, 2004), p. 14; Matthews (*Thermopylae*, p. 56) simply says the head was attached with 'glue'.
17. Anderson, 'Hoplite Offensive Arms' in Hanson (ed.), *Hoplites*, p. 23.
18. T. Everson, *Warfare in Ancient Greece* (Stroud, Sutton Publishing, 2004), p. 113.
19. Everson, *Warfare*, p. 163.
20. Hanson, 'Hoplite Technology' in Hanson (ed.), *Hoplites*, p. 71.
21. Anderson, 'Hoplite Offensive Arms' in Hanson (ed.), *Hoplites*, p. 24.
22. Snodgrass, *Early Greek*, p. 153.
23. Camp, 'Spear Butt', p. 192.
24. Snodgrass, *Arms and Armour*, p. 80.
25. Richter, 'Greek Bronzes', p. 194.
26. Robinson, *Olynthus X*, pp. 416–418.
27. Markle, 'Spear', p. 325.
28. See H. Baitinger, *Die Angriffswaffen aus Olympia* (Berlin, Walter de Gruyter, 2000), pp. 224–231, plates 59–62.
29. E. Kunze and H. Schleif, *Olympische Forschungen* (Berlin, Verlag Walter de Gruyter and Co., 1944), pp. 158–160, plate 68; see also Baitinger, *Die Angriffswaffen*, pp. 224–231, plates 59–62.
30. Thuc. 2.4.3.
31. Images taken from: Baitinger, *Die Angriffswaffen aus Olympia*, plates 44, 50, 54, 59.
32. Tyrt. 1; Hom. *Il.* 4.47, 19.390; Pliny the Elder (*HN* 16.228) states that ash was a good wood for a spear shaft as it is lighter than that of the Cornelian cherry and is more pliant that that of the 'service-tree'. See also Sekunda, *Greek Hoplite*, p. 13.
33. Xen. *Eq.* 12.12; *AP* 6.122, 6.123; some modern authors also cite Strabo 12.7.3; Hdt. 7.92, Xen. *Hell.* 3.4.14, Xen. *Cyr.* 7.1.2; Theoph. *Caus. pl.* 3.12; and Arr. *Anab.* 1.15.5 as references to the use of Cornelian cherry (see: Markle, 'Spear', p. 324; Hanson, *Western*, p. 84; Hanson, *Wars*, p. 58; Anderson, *Military Theory*, p. 37). However, many of these passages detail the use of this wood only in the manufacture of bows, javelins and other weapons, predominantly used by non-Greeks.
34. Anderson, 'Hoplite Offensive Arms' in Hanson (ed.), *Hoplites*, p. 23; Bradford, *Thermopylae*, p. 71.
35. Xen. *Cyr.* 6.2.32.
36. Xen. *Cyr.* 6.2.32.
37. Markle, 'Spear', p. 324.
38. Hanson, *Wars*, p. 61.
39. Markle, 'Spear', p. 324.
40. See Appendix II; see also: Markle, 'Spear', p. 324; Camp, 'Spear Butt', p. 192.
41. Sekunda, *Greek Hoplite*, p. 14.
42. Matthews, *Thermopylae*, p. 56.
43. Xen. *Cyr.* 6.2.32.
44. Xen. *Lac.* 11.2; see also Xen. *Cyr.* 6.2.37.
45. Spear makers: Ar. *Pax* 1164–1166; see also Xen. *Hell.* 3.4.17; shield makers: Lys. 12.19, 14.6.
46. Strabo 4.1.5.

47. Diod. Sic. 14.41.4–5.
48. Nep. *Agesilaus* 3.2–3.
49. How a Greek city-state was able to procure sufficient numbers of straight pieces of timber to adequately fashion the hundreds or thousands of spear shafts used by their forces is somewhat of a mystery. There was clearly a preference as to the type of wood used in shield construction (see: Theophr. *Caus. pl.* 5.3.4; Plin. (E) *HN* 16.77) but whether this wood was cultivated specifically for this purpose or merely obtained by other means is not outlined. Nor is there clear evidence for the cultivation of trees for weapon manufacture. One method of obtaining mass quantities of spear shafts would have been by splitting larger logs lengthways into sections that could then be shaped into a spear shaft. Another method would have been by simply using the trunk of a young sapling to fashion a single shaft (as the spoke-shave bearing troops described by Xenophon are likely to have done in the field). This would suggest that city-states had access to large numbers of cultivated trees that may have been specifically grown for the purpose of weapon making, and would indicate that some sort of specialized industry, possibly on a massed scale, for the manufacture of weapons was in effect. Yet another way of obtaining this timber would have been through the process of 'coppicing' existing trees. Coppicing is the process whereby numerous shoots of new growth grow from the trunk of an existing tree when it is felled. Depending upon the species of tree, these shoots may grow long and straight. In some instances (again depending upon the species of tree and for how long the new shoots are left to grow before being cut themselves) the shoot may have a uniform thickness along its entire length or a slight taper. This may account for some of the differences in spear shafts seen in the artistic record. The growth of such shoots from the trunks of felled trees was a phenomenon not unknown to the Greeks (see: Theophr. *Caus. pl.* 2.7.2, 3.7.1–2, 4.16.1–4). However, there is no reference to this (or any other) kind of specialized agricultural technique being used on a mass scale for the production of weaponry. As such, any suggested means for the procurement of wood by the city-state for the manufacture of spears and other weapons can only be considered speculative.
50. J. Kromayer and G. Veith, *Heerwesen und Kriegführung der Griechen und Romer* (Munchen, 1928), p. 51.
51. Hanson, *Wars*, p. 59.
52. W. Donlan and J. Thompson, 'The Charge at Marathon: Herodotus 6.112', *Classical Journal* 71:4 (Apr–May 1976), p. 341; Gabriel and Metz, *Sumer to Rome*, p. 71.
53. Personal correspondence with J. Stroszeck of the Deutsches Archäologisches Institut 1–4 March 2008; see also: J. Stroszeck, '*Lakonisch-rotfigurige Keramik aus den Lakedaimonier-gräbern am Kerameikos von Athen*', *AA* 2 (2006), pp. 101–120; van Wees, *Greek Warfare*, pp. 146–147; C.F. Salazar, *The Treatment of War Wounds in Greco-Roman Antiquity* (Leiden, Brill, 2000), pp. 233–234; W.K. Pritchett, *The Greek State at War – Part IV* (Berkeley, University of California Press, 1985), pp. 133–134; L. van Hook, 'On the Lacedaemonians Buried in the Kerameikos', *AJA* 36:3 (Jul–Sep 1932), pp. 290–292.
54. Salazar, *War Wounds*, pp. 233–234; Pritchett, *Greek State IV*, p. 136; E. Kastorchis, 'ΠΕΡΙ ΤΟΥ ΕΝ ΧΑΙΡΩΝΕΙΑ ΑΕΟΝΤΟΣ', *Athenaion* 8 (1879), pp. 486–491; L Phytalis, 'ΕΡΕΥΝΑΙ ΕΝ ΤΩ ΠΟΛΥΑΝΔΡΙΩ ΧΑΙΠΩΝΕΙΑΣ', *Athenaion* 9 (1880), pp. 347- 352, plate 1.
55. Veg. *Mil.* 1.5.
56. Markle, 'Spear', p. 324.
57. Markle, 'Spear', p. 334; Biton's (third century BC) treatise on siege warfare states that oak or ash should be used for the construction of the wheels and axles of war machines and artillery due to the strength of the wood. It is further recommended that fir or pine should

be used for the structure of these machines also due to the strength of the wood (52); see E.W. Marsden, *Greek and Roman Artillery Vol. II – Technical Treatises* (Oxford, Clarendon Press, 1971), p. 71. Theophrastus (*Caus. pl.* 3.16.1–3, 5.6.2, 5.7.6) additionally outlines the strength and lightness of oak. It seems unlikely that woods that were known for being both strong and light would not be used in the manufacture of weaponry. In his study of the use of timber by ancient armies, Meiggs only concentrates on the use of wood in the construction of fleets, fortifications, buildings and siege equipment; with the omission of the use of timber in weapon manufacture. Similarly, his examination of the species of tree accessible to the inhabitants of Attica also fails to include any analysis of weapon making in their uses. See R. Meiggs, *Trees and Timber in the Ancient Mediterranean World* (Oxford, Clarendon Press, 1982), pp. 154–217.

58. Markle, 'Spear', p. 324.
59. Markle, 'Spear', p. 324; see also Connolly, *Greece and Rome*, p. 63.
60. Snodgrass, *Arms and Armour*, p. 80; Camp, 'Spear Butt', p. 192; van Wees, *Greek Warfare*, p. 48; Richter, 'Greek Bronzes', p. 196.
61. Matthews (*Thermopylae* p. 56) states that the head of the hoplite spear was only 15cm long and that the *sauroter* was even smaller; but may have had an extra lead weight attached to it. Despite these inconsistencies with the archaeological record, Matthews somehow still estimated a point of balance for the hoplite spear 80cm from the rear end of the shaft. This may have been due to his assumption that all hoplite weapons possessed tapered shafts.
62. Sekunda, *Greek Hoplite*, pp. 52–53; Warry (*Warfare* p. 35) offers that the grip on the hoplite spear was made from leather thonging but provides no supporting reference.
63. Interestingly, the head on the weapon shown on the Achilles Amphora is much smaller than the *sauroter* that is attached to the weapon; thus further accentuating the rearward shift of the weapon's point of balance.
64. Due to the lack of any standardized set of weights and measures across the ancient Greek world, it is difficult to correlate the average characteristics of the hoplite spear to anything the ancient Greeks would have used. The smallest Attic unit of length was the *daktylos* (δάκτυλος); a unit representing the thickness of the finger and measuring 1.85cm. The *Olympian dactylos* measured 2.00cm. *Dactyloi* from other regions measured 1.93cm. Thus an average spear length of 253cm equates to around 132 *dactyloi*; an average length for the spearhead of 27.9cm equates to 15 *dactyloi*; and an average length for the *sauroter* of 25.9cm equates to 14 *dactyloi*. One *dactylos* is also the likely standard measurement for the inner diameter of the socket for both the spearhead and the *sauroter*, as well as for the thickness of the shaft for the javelin. The smallest Attic/Euboian units for measuring weight were based upon coinage. These were the *obol* (ὀβολός) weighing 0.72g and the *drachma* (δραχμή) equivalent to six *obols* and weighing 4.33g. Thus an average total weight for the spear of 1,332g equates to 1,850 *Attic obol* (308 *Attic drachmae*); the average weight of 153g for the spearhead equates to approximately 212 *Attic obols* (35 *Attic drachmae*); and the average weight of 329g for the *sauroter* equates to around 457 *Attic obols* (76 *Attic drachmae*). In the larger Aeginetian standard (based upon an *obol* weighing 1.05g and a *drachma* of 6.3g) the average weights for the hoplite spear and its individual constituent parts would equate to smaller amounts of comparative coinage. This apparent lack of a closely regulated standard for coinage may possibly be one reason for the variance in weight among examples of the spearhead and *sauroter* found in the archaeological record. For details of the units for weight and measurement used in ancient Greece see: W.F. Richardson, *Numbering and Measuring in the Classical World* (Bristol, Bristol Phoenix Press, 2004), pp. 29–32, 37–39; F. Hultsch, *Greichische und Römische Metrologie* (Berlin, Weidmannsche Buchhandlung,

1882), pp. 28–34, 697. For the details of the weights of some examples of the *Attic obol* and *drachma*, see: C.G. Starr, *Athenian Coinage 480–447BC* (Oxford, Clarendon Press, 1970), pp. 15–16, 25–26, 30, 36–38, 46–47, 52–53, 61–62.

Chapter 2 – Wielding the Hoplite Spear

1. Tyrt. 12.
2. Xen. *Hell.* 4.3.17; see also Xen. *Hell.* 7.1.31; Xen. *Ages.* 2.10–11; Plut. *Ages.* 18.
3. Eur. *HF* 121–123.
4. G.L. Cawkwell, 'Orthodoxy and Hoplites' in *CQ* Vol. 39, No. 2 (1989), p. 381, 385; P. Cartledge, 'Hoplites and Heroes: Sparta's Contribution to the Technique of Ancient Warfare', *JHS*, p. 97 (1977), p. 15; V.D. Hanson, *Wars of the Ancient Greeks* (London, Cassell, 1999), pp. 48, 132; P. Connolly, *Greece and Rome at War* (London, Greenhill Books, 1998), pp. 41–42; J. Warry, *Warfare in the Classical World* (Norman, University of Oklahoma Press, 1995), pp. 34–35; M.M. Markle III, 'The Macedonian *Sarissa*, Spear and Related Armour', *AJA* 8:3 (Summer 1977), pp. 334–336; J.K. Anderson, 'Hoplite Weapons and Offensive Arms' in V.D. Hanson (ed.), *Hoplites – The Classical Greek Battle Experience* (London, Routledge, 2004), p. 31; V.D. Hanson, *The Western Way of War* (Berkeley, University of California Press, 1989), p. 84; J. Lazenby, 'The Killing Zone' in Hanson (ed.), *Hoplites*, pp. 92–93; H. van Wees, *Greek Warfare – Myths and Realities* (London, Duckworth, 2004), p. 189; F.E. Adcock, *The Greek and Macedonian Art of War* (Berkeley, University of California Press, 1957), p. 3; J.E. Lendon, *Soldiers and Ghosts – A History of Battle in Classical Antiquity* (New Haven, Yale University Press, 2005), p. 54; W.K. Pritchett, *The Greek State at War – Vol. IV* (Berkeley, University of California Press, 1985), p. 60; J.K. Anderson, *Military Theory and Practice in the Age of Xenophon* (Berkeley, University of California Press, 1970), p. 88.
5. One exception is I.P Stephenson, *Roman Infantry Equipment – The Later Empire* (Stroud, Tempus, 1991), pp. 58–60, although this is in relation to Roman warfare and not that of the hoplite.

Chapter 3 – Spears, Javelins and the Hoplite in Greek Art

1. B.A. Sparkes, *The Red and The Black: Studies in Greek Pottery* (London, Routledge, 1996), p. 114.
2. For the balance of thrown spears see: B. Cotterrell and J. Kamminga, *Mechanics of Pre-Industrial Technology: An Introduction to the Mechanics of Ancient and Traditional Material* (Melbourne, Cambridge University Press, 1990), pp. 163–175.
3. Cotterrell and Kamminga, *Pre-Industrial Technology*, p. 172.
4. *Styrakion* (Thuc. 2.4) translated as javelin spike: R. Warner, 1972; C.F. Smith, 1969; R.B. Strassler (ed.), 1996; as a javelin head: The Hobbes Translation, 1989; as a spear butt: W. Blanco, 1998; J.P. Rhodes, 1988; H, Dale, 1849.
5. J. Kromayer and G. Veith, *Heerwesen und Kriegführung der Griechen und Romer* (Munich, 1928), p. 51.
6. See: G.M.A. Richter, *Perspective in Greek and Roman Art* (London, Phaidon Press Ltd), pp. 14–48.
7. T. Everson, *Warfare in Ancient Greece* (Stroud, Sutton Publishing, 2004), p. 63; H.L. Lorimer, *Homer and the Monuments* (London, MacMillan, 1950), pp. 258–259.
8. A.M. Snodgrass, *Arms and Armour of the Greeks* (Baltimore, Johns Hopkins University Press, 1999), pp. 57–58.

9. A.M. Snodgrass, *Early Greek Armour and Weapons* (Edinburgh, Edinburgh University Press, 1964), p. 136–137.
10. Snodgrass, *Early Greek*, p. 136–137.
11. Everson, *Warfare*, p. 123.
12. J.M. Hurwitt, 'Reading the Chigi Vase', *Hesperia* 71:1 (Jan–Mar 2002), p. 14.
13. H.L. Lorimer, 'The Hoplite Phalanx with Special Reference to the Poems of Archilochus and Tyrtaeus', *ABSA* 42 (1947), p. 83; Snodgrass, *Early Greek*, p. 138.
14. Lorimer, 'Hoplite Phalanx', p. 107; S. Mitchell. 'Hoplite Warfare in Ancient Greece' in A.B. Lloyd (ed.), *Battle in Antiquity* (London, Duckworth, 1996), p. 90.
15. For examples of Homeric missile warfare see: Hom. *Il.* 3.356, 5.292, 11.232, 13.506, 13.586, 16.612, 17.525, 22.325, 23.821; see also A.M. Snodgrass, 'The Hoplite Reform and History', *JHS* 85 (1965), p. 111; H. van Wees, *Greek Warfare – Myths and Realities* (London, Duckworth, 2004), p. 171; Hurwitt, 'Reading Chigi', p. 19; J.K. Anderson, 'Hoplite Weapons and Offensive Arms' in V.D. Hanson (ed.), *Hoplites – The Classical Greek Battle Experience* (London, Routledge, 2004), p. 16; Everson, *Warfare*, p. 71; Lorimer, 'Hoplite Phalanx', p. 118; H. van Wees, 'The Development of the Hoplite Phalanx – Iconography and Reality in the Seventh Century' in H. van Wees (ed.), *War and Violence in Ancient Greece* (London, Duckworth, 2000), pp. 134–146.
16. Van Wees, *Greek Warfare*, pp. 50, 169, 172; H. van Wees 'The Homeric Way of War: The 'Iliad' and the Hoplite Phalanx (II)', *Greece and Rome*, 2nd Series 41:2 (Oct 1994), pp. 145–146; Snodgrass, *Arms and Armour*, p. 57.
17. Everson, *Warfare*, p. 123.
18. Van Wees, *Greek Warfare*, p. 177; see also van Wees, 'Development of the Hoplite Phalanx' in van Wees (ed.) *War and Violence*, pp. 136, 142, 147–148.
19. Van Wees, *Greek Warfare*, p. 177; see also van Wees, 'Development of the Hoplite Phalanx' in van Wees (ed.) *War and Violence*, pp. 136, 142, 147–148.
20. E.N. Gardiner, 'Throwing the Javelin', *JHS* 27 (1907), pp. 249–251; E.C. Curwen, 'Spear-Throwing with a Cord', *Man* 34 (Jul 1934), pp. 105–106.
21. Archil. 114.3; Diod. Sic. 14.27.6.
22. Gardiner, 'Javelin', p. 251; van Wees, *Greek Warfare*, p. 170; Cotterrell and Kamminga, *Pre-Industrial Technology*, pp. 163–175.
23. Snodgrass, *Early Greek*, p. 138, plate 33.
24. The small 'blobs' on the rear end of these depicted weapons may also be a rudimentary attempt to show the smaller *styrakion*, which would also distinguish these weapons as javelins. See also: C.A. Matthew, 'When Push Comes to Shove: What was the *Othismos* of Hoplite Combat?' *Historia* 58:4 (2009), p. 404.
25. Van Wees, *Greek Warfare*, pp. 170–172; van Wees, 'Development of the Hoplite Phalanx' in van Wees (ed.) *War and Violence*, p. 136–139; P. Krentz, 'Fighting by the Rules: The Invention of the Hoplite *Agon*', *Hesperia* 71:1 (Jan–Mar 2002), p. 29.
26. Lorimer, 'Hoplite Phalanx', p. 83; J. Salmon, 'Political Hoplites?' *JHS* 97 (1977), p. 90; Snodgrass, *Early Greek*, p. 138.
27. J. Boardman, *Athenian Red Figure Vases – The Archaic Period* (London, Thames and Hudson, 1983), p. 218; J. Boardman, *Athenian Red Figure Vases – The Classical Period* (London, Thames and Hudson, 1989), p. 220.
28. V.D. Hanson, *Wars of the Ancient Greeks* (London, Cassell, 1999), p. 63.
29. E. Jarva, *Archaiologia on Archaic Greek Body Armour* (Studia Archaeologica Septentrionalia 3), (Rovaniemi: Pohjois-Suomen Historiallinen Yhdistys, Societas Historica Finlandiae Septentrionalis, 1995), p. 123.

30. N. Sekunda, *The Spartan Army* (Oxford, Osprey Publishing, 1998), pp. 52–53.
31. Everson, *Warfare*, p. 71.
32. Everson, *Warfare*, p. 71.
33. Everson, *Warfare*, p. 71, 123.
34. Krentz, 'Fighting by the Rules', p. 35; see also van Wees, 'Development of the Hoplite Phalanx' in van Wees (ed.), *War and Violence*, p. 139; Trundle argues similarly for the works of Tyrtaeus. See: M. Trundle, 'The Spartan Revolution: Hoplite Warfare in the late Archaic Period' in *War and Society* 19:10 (Oct 2001), p. 13.
35. Salmon, 'Political Hoplites?' p. 90.
36. Hurwitt, 'Reading Chigi', p. 14; Anderson, 'Hoplite Offensive Arms' in Hanson (ed.), *Hoplites*, pp. 18–19; G.L. Cawkwell, 'Orthodoxy and Hoplites' in *CQ* Vol. 39, No. 2 (1989), p. 385; Snodgrass, *Arms and Armour*, p. 58; Snodgrass, *Early Greek Armour*, p. 138; Lorimer, 'Hoplite Phalanx', pp. 81–95; Trundle, 'Spartan Revolution', p. 11; Salmon, 'Political Hoplites?', pp. 87–88; Everson, *Warfare*, p. 71; J. Lendon, *Soldiers and Ghosts – A History of Battle in Classical Antiquity* (New Haven, Yale University Press, 2005), p. 48; W.K. Pritchett, *The Greek State at War – Vol. IV* (Berkeley, University of California Press, 1985), p. 72; Jarva, *Archaiologia*, p. 119; P. Ducrey, *Warfare in Ancient Greece* (New York, Schocken Books, 1986), pp. 63, 75.
37. Xen. *Eq.* 12.13.
38. Gardiner, 'Javelin', pp. 258–273; see also: Pind. *Pyth.* 1.43–45; Antiph. *Tetr.* 2.
39. Veg. *Mil.* 1.20.
40. M.M. Markle III, 'The Macedonian *Sarissa*, Spear and Related Armour', *AJA* 8:3 (Summer 1977), p. 327.
41. See: G.M.A. Richter, *Red-Figured Athenian Vases in the Metropolitan Museum of Art Vol. I* (New Haven, Yale University Press, 1936), p. 57.
42. Everson, *Warfare*, p. 129.
43. Everson, *Warfare*, p. 129.
44. J.L. Benson, 'Human Figures and Narrative in Later Protocorinthian Vase Painting', *Hesperia*, 64:2 (Apr–Jun 1995), pp. 163, 175; S. Lowenstam, 'Talking Vases: The Relationship between the Homeric Poems and Archaic Representation of Epic Myth', *Transactions of the American Philological Society (1974–)* 127 (1997), pp. 21-76.
45. Boardman, *Red Figure – Archaic*, pp. 223, 230–231; J. Onians, *Classical Art and the Cultures of Greece and Rome* (New Haven, Yale University Press, 1999), pp. 16–18, 73, 75; see also: Lowenstam, 'Talking Vases', pp. 21–76.
46. Snodgrass, 'Hoplite Reform', p. 112; see also: J. Boardman, 'Nudity in Art' in D. Kurtz (ed.), *Reception of Classical Art, an Introduction* (BAR International Series 1295, 2004), p. 49; Benson, 'Protocorinthian', pp. 170, 175; Sparkes, *Red and Black*, p. 133; Lendon, *Soldiers and Ghosts*, pp. 11, 45, 66.
47. Lorimer, 'Hoplite Phalanx', p. 104.
48. J.K. Anderson, *Military Theory and Practice in the Age of Xenophon* (Berkeley, University of California Press, 1970), pp. 87–89; B.F. Cook, 'Footwork in Ancient Greek Swordsmanship', *MMJ* 24 (1989), pp. 57–62; Onians, *Art and Cultures*, p. 73.
49. Anderson, *Military Theory*, pp. 14, 87; Lorimer, *Homer and the Monuments*, p. 167; see also: Everson, *Warfare*, p. 190 for the possibility of the use of props by the sculptor of the fourth century BC 'Alexander Sarcophagus'.
50. Xen. *Mem.* 3.11.1–2.
51. Lowenstam, 'Talking Vases', p. 25.

52. Snodgrass, *Arms and Armour*, p. 55; Boardman, *Red Figure – Archaic*, p. 218; Hurwitt, 'Reading Chigi', p. 19; Anderson, *Military Theory*, pp. 14; Lorimer, 'Hoplite Phalanx', pp. 89, 95, 124; Everson, *Warfare*, p. 119.

53. In another stylistic convention, the victor is also generally (but not always) positioned on the left-hand side of the image facing to the right.

54. G.H. Chase, *The Shield Devices of the Greeks in Art and Literature* (Chicago, Ares Publishers, 1979), pp. 10–11; see also: J.D. Beazley and B. Ashmole, *Greek Sculpture and Painting to the End of the Hellenistic Period* (Cambridge, Cambridge University Press, 1966), p. 5.

55. Everson, *Warfare*, pp. 73–76.

56. J. Boardman, *The Greeks Overseas* (London, Thames and Hudson, 1999), pp. 54–84, 141–153; W. Burkert, *The Orientalizing Revolution: Near Eastern Influence on Greek Culture in the Early Archaic Age* (Cambridge, Harvard University Press, 1992), pp. 9–25; G. Markoe, 'The Emergence of Orientalizing in Greek Art: Some Observations on the Interchange between Greeks and Phoenicians in the Eighth and Seventh Centuries B.C.', *Bulletin of the American Schools of Oriental Research* 301 (Feb. 1996), pp. 47, 52–54; see also: Hom. *Od.* 13.272–277, 15.403–484; Hdt. 1.1; Thuc. 6.2.6; Plato, *Epin.* 987E.

57. Burkert, *Orientalizing Revolution*, pp. 19–20; Markoe, 'Emergence of Orientalizing', pp. 59–50.

58. Everson, *Warfare*, p. 63, 69.

59. Lorimer, 'Hoplite Phalanx', p. 110; L. Bonfante, 'Nudity as a Costume in Classical Art', *AJA* Vol. 93, No. 4 (Oct. 1989), p. 549; see also Anderson, *Military Theory*, pp. 20, 24–25.

60. Plin. (E) *HN* 34.57–58, 34.65; Quint. *Inst.* 5.12.21, 12.10.7–9; see also: Onians, *Art and Cultures*, pp. 35–41; Boardman 'Nudity' in Kurtz (ed.), *Reception of Classical Art*, p. 50 plate 41; Snodgrass, *Arms and Armour*, p. 57; Bonfante, 'Nudity', pp. 544, 558.

61. Pind. *Isthm.* 5.22–29, 1.50–51; Pind. *Ol.* 6.9–11. For importance of nudity in art see: J. Boardman, *Greek Art* (London, Thames and Hudson, 1996), pp. 158, 272–273; parallels between sport and war: Isoc. *Antid.* 15.184–185; D. Pritchard, 'Athletics, War and Democracy in Classical Athens', *Teaching History* 39:4 (Term 4, 2005), pp. 6–7; Bonfante, 'Nudity', pp. 543–558.

62. Pausanias (5.8.10) suggests that the race in armour was introduced into the Olympic programme for the sake of military training. See also: N.B. Reed, *More Than Just a Game: The Military Nature of Greek Athletic Contests* (Chicago, Ares Publishers, 1998), pp. 1–8; Lendon, *Soldiers and Ghosts*, p. 56.

63. Courage: Pind. *Isthm.* 1.15–28, 3.13–14; Pind. *Ol.* 6.9–10, 10.20–21; Pind. *Nem.* 6.23–24; Thuc. 2.42.4; toils and dangers: Pind. *Isthm.* 5.22–25, 4.47; Pind. *Ol.* 5.7–8, 6.9–11, 10.22–23; Thuc. 2.39.1, 2.43.4, 2.62.1; esteem: Pind. *Isthm.* 1.50–51, Pind. *Pyth.* 9.97–103, 10.55–59; Hdt. 8.17, 8.93, 9.74, 9.104.

64. M. Golden, *Sport and Society in Ancient Greece* (Cambridge, Cambridge University Press, 1998), p. 27.

65. Reed, *More Than Just a Game*, pp. 36, 42–43; H.W. Parke, 'Festivals of the Athenians' in H.H. Scullard (ed.), *Aspects of Greek and Roman Life* (Ithaca, Cornell University Press, 1977), p. 43.

66. So little is known about how the event was conducted. It is possible that the 'combatants' in the *hoplomachia* fought in 'Archaic style' with shield and javelin, which would explain the depictions on the prize amphorae.

67. Everson, *Warfare*, pp. 132–134.

68. Everson, *Warfare*, p. 132.

69. Bonfante, 'Nudity', p. 555; see also: Xen. *Ages.* 1.28; Hdt. 1.10.3; Thuc. 1.5–6; Pl. *Resp.* 5.452a–e; Polyaenus, *Strat.* 2.1.6.

70. Hom. *Il.* 3.189, 6.186; in the fifth century BC, Proclus (*Chrestomathia* 2) wrote a review and summary of the *Aethiopis:* the 'sequel' to the *Iliad* written by Arctinus of Miletus in the eighth century BC (c.775BC). In the summary Penthesilea, queen of the Amazons, is killed by Achilles 'after showing great prowess' (κτείνει αὐτὴν ἀριστεύουσαν Ἀχιλλεύς). Scholia (*On Iliad* 24.804) describes Penthesilea as 'the daughter of great-souled Ares: the slayer of men' (Ἄρηος θυγάτηρ μεγαλήτοπος ἀνδροφόνοιο). Like the description in Homer, both of these passages hardly make the Amazons appear effeminate. As such, any comparison of the Persians to the Amazons is likely to have been designed to make the Persians appear as formidable and foreign adversaries thus heightening the glory of the victory over them.

71. See: Plut. *Thes.* 26–27; Diod. Sic. 4.28.1–4; Aesch. *Eum.* 680–695.

72. Aristotle (*Pol.* 7.2.5) states that military strength was held in high honour by the Persians. Interestingly, Hippocrates (*Aer.* 16.3–8, 16.14–42) states that the reason why Asiatics [i.e. Persians] are less warlike and more gentle in character is the uniformity of the seasons in Persian regions and suggests that it is partially for this reason, and partially due to the Persians being ruled by kings and despots (rather than any effeminate nature) that the Persians are feeble and more inclined to 'appear warlike' rather than actually be militarily efficient.

73. Contrasts between Greek and Persian cultural practices can also be found in other examples of Greek literature. See: Aech. *Pers.* 230–245; Polyaenus. *Strat.* 7.6.4. Arr. *Anab.* 2.8. See also: S. Goldhill, 'Battle Narrative and Politics in Aeschylus' Persae', *JHS* 108 (1988), pp. 189–193; A. Stewart, 'Imag(in)ing the Other: Amazons and Ethnicity in Fifth-Century Athens', *Poetics Today* 16:4 (1995), p. 584.

74. Boardman, *Red Figure – Classical*, p. 220; Boardman 'Nudity' in Kurtz (ed.), *Reception of Classical Art*, pp. 48–51; E. Buschor, *Greek Vase Painting* (New York, Hacker Art Books, 1978), pp. 20–21; Everson, *Warfare*, p. 158–159; Sekunda, *Spartan Army*, pp. 20, 28; for a counter argument see: Snodgrass, 'Hoplite Reform' p. 110; van Wees, 'Homeric II', p. 138.

75. Even a cursory glance through a Greek lexicon at words like χιτών (tunic), ἱμάτιον (cloak), μέδιλον (sandal) and περόνη (brooch – an adornment that would have to have been attached to an item of clothing) should be sufficient to demonstrate that the ancient Greeks, whether male or female, hoplite or civilian, were neither regularly naked nor barefoot. Bonfante, 'Nudity', p. 549 suggests that nudity in art 'was not necessarily a depiction of reality'.

76. See A.G. Geddes, 'Rags and Riches: The Costume of Athenian Men in the Fifth Century', *CQ* 37:2 (1987), pp. 307–331.

77. For example see Xen. *An.* 4.2.28, 6.1.5.

78. Aesch. *Ag.* 562.

79. Plut. *Mor.* 245A.

80. Plut. *Mor.* 238F.

81. Plut. *Pel.* 9; Paus. 7.1.5.

82. Polyaenus, *Strat.* 3.13.2.

83. Plut. *Pho.* 4.2.

84. Polyaenus, *Strat.* 3.9.34; Polyaenus, *Excerpts*, 1.1; Leonis Imp. *Strat.* 3.1.

85. Paus. 5.5.2, 6.25.5, 6.26.6–8, 8.4.1; Theoc. *Epigr.* 2.73; Strabo 15.1.20; Philostr. *VA* 2.20; see also: Aesch. *Supp.* 121, 132; Ar. *Ran.* 1347; *AP* 6.231; Hom. *Il.* 9.661; Pausanias (5.5.2) states that *Byssos* (βύσσος) grew exclusively in Elis. Jones and Ormerod translate the word *Byssos* in this passage as meaning 'fine flax' (Cambridge, Harvard University Press – Loeb Classical Library, 1966). Levi translates the same passage as 'fine linen' (which is made from flax) but suggests in a footnote that what Pausanias may be describing is actually

cotton (London, Penguin Books, 1971 – p. 206 n.32). Wild flax/linen (*Linum bienne*) was quite common in early Europe and Pausanias may be distinguishing the difference between this plant and cultivated linen/flax (*Linum usitatissium*). Edmonds translates Theocritus' use of *Byssos* (2.73) to mean 'silk' (*Greek Bucolic Poets* – Cambridge, Harvard University Press – Loeb Classical Library, 1960). Jones similarly states that Strabo (15.1.20) is referring to silk in his use of the term *Byssos* (*Geography Vol. VII* – Cambridge, Harvard University Press – Loeb Classical Library, 1961). Conybeare says that Philostratus (*VA* 2.20) is referring to cotton (*Life of Apollonius of Tyana* – Cambridge, Harvard University Press – Loeb Classical Library, 1969). Wright translates Empedocles' use of *Byssos* (93) as simply 'linen' (*Empedocles: The Extant Fragments* (New Haven, Yale University Press, 1981)). The word *linon* (λίνον) is used by many other ancient authors to describe articles of clothing and is usually also translated as 'linen'; see: Aesch. *Supp.* 121, 132; Ar. *Ran.* 1347; *AP* 6.231; Hom. *Il.* 9.661; Philostr. *VA* 2.20. Regardless of what plant the word *Byssos* is actually referring to, it is clear that the Greeks had access to at least one cultivatable plant (and possibly more) that would produce fibres that could be spun into cloth for the production of clothing.

86. Diod. Sic. 9.4.1, 9.20.1, 11.63.6.
87. For example see: Thuc. 5.74 (προθέμενοι τῶν πολεμίων). If the hoplite was commonly naked as has been suggested, it is uncertain what the bodies of the dead were actually stripped of in order to adorn the trophy.
88. Ar. *Ach.* 279, 1133; Ar. *Pax* 1224–1283.
89. Alc. 19.
90. Plut. *Pel.* 9, 18, 33; Plut. *Dion*, 28; Plut. *Tim.* 4; Dion is said to have gathered 5,000 suits of armour (πανοπλίας) in order to equip his troops for the invasion of Syracuse – Diod. Sic. 16.6.5, 16.9.5, 16.10.3. This indicates that it was not just the higher ranks who wore armour, but the common soldiery as well. Similarly, Timaenetus collected suits of armour to equip his troops when he wanted to establish himself as tyrant of Corinth in 346BC – Diod. Sic. 16.65.3.
91. Plut. *Ages.* 34.
92. For armour dedicated at Olympia see: Paus. 6.19.7.
93. F.M. Combellack, 'Achilles – Bare of Foot?' *Classical Journal* 41:5 (Feb 1946), pp. 193–198; A.A. Bryant, 'Greek Shoes in the Classical Period', *Harvard Studies in Classical Philology* 10 (1899), pp. 57–102; see also Jarva, *Archaiologia*, p. 106.
94. Jarva, *Archaiologia*, p. 106–109; for example, a terracotta flask in the shape of a boot (c.1300–1250BC) was found in House II on the Panagia Ridge at Mycenae and is now on display in the museum at the site. Similarly, boot-shaped *rhytons* (c.1300BC) were found in Attic chamber tombs and are now on display in the National Archaeological Museum in Athens (#8557 and #15879); clay representations of boots, possibly women's, were found in the Athenian agora (c.900BC); footwear-shaped flasks were also found at Olympia (c.525BC), the Kerameikos (c.500BC) and are all on display in the associated museums. The remains of 'Simon's Shoestore' in the Athenian *agora*, home of the famous philosopher-cobbler of the fifth century BC, contained the remnants of leather soles, collections of hobnails and bone eyelets used for the lacing of shoes; clear indicators of the mass production of footwear in fifth century Athens. See: H.A. Thompson and R.E. Wycherley, *The Athenian Agora Vol. XIV – The Agora of Athens* (Glückstadt, J.J. Augustin, 1972), p. 174; D.B. Thompson, *The Athenian Agora – An Ancient Shopping Centre* (Vermont, The Stinehour Press, 1993), pp. 13–14; for visits by Socrates to Simon's establishment and the titles of some of Simon's philosophical treatises see: Diog. Laert. 2.13.122–123.

95. Combellack, 'Achilles', p. 197; See also Xen. *Lac.* 2.1, 2.3–4.
96. Everson, *Warfare*, pp. 104, 114; Anderson, *Military Theory*, pp. 26–28 also claims that hoplites were not totally naked but may have worn light armour or just their tunic.
97. Some armour was handed down through the generations. See: Plut. *Mor.* 241F.
98. Arist. *Ath. Pol.* 42.4; Lycurg. *Leoc.* 76–78, 80–82; Isoc. 8.82; Aeschin. 3.154; Bertosa ('The Supply of Hoplite Equipment by the Athenian State down to the Lamian War', *Journal of Military History* 67:2 (2003), pp. 361–379) suggests that while the spear and shield may have been adequate for garrison duty on the frontiers of Attica, the remainder of the panoply would have been required for battle. Bertosa further suggests, following Kromayer and Veith (*Heerwesen und Kriegführung der Griechen und Romer*, p. 50), that Athens only issued the shield and spear due to the cost and numbers involved in the issue. However the *ephebe*, regardless of the class from which he had come, had to provide the remainder of the panoply at his own expense.
99. Skarmintzos suggests, in an unreferenced passage, that marines wore the full hoplite panoply and that by running the extra risk of drowning if they fell overboard due to wearing all of the heavy armour, the marines therefore considered themselves elite troops (see: S. Skarmintzos, 'Armed Passengers – Hoplite Marines', *Ancient Warfare* 2:3 (2008), pp. 18).
100. For sculpture see: Boardman, *Greek Art*, pp. 160, 230–231.
101. Xenophanes, 14, 15.

Chapter 4 – Bearing the Hoplite Panoply

1. *Aspis*: Xen. *An.* 2.1.6; Xen. *Mem.* 3.9.2; Ar. *Pax* 1274–1275; Plut. *Tim.* 28; Arr. *Tact.* 3.2; *hoplon*: Thuc. 7.75; Diod. Sic. 17.55.4, 17.57.2, 17.106.7.
2. E. Kunze, *Bericht Über die Ausgrabungen in Olympia – Vol. V* (Berlin, Verlag Walter de Gruyter and Co., 1956), pp. 35–68, plates 11–33; E. Kunze, *Bericht Über die Ausgrabungen in Olympia – Vol. VI* (Berlin, Verlag Walter de Gruyter and Co., 1958), pp. 74–117, plates 13–32; M. Andronicos, *Olympia* (Athens, Ekdotike Athenon, 1999), pp. 31–32, 70, 76; M.T. Homolle, *Fouilles de Delphes – Tome V* (Paris, Ancienne Librairie Thorin et Fils, 1908), pp. 103–106; P. Connolly, *Greece and Rome at War* (London, Greenhill Books, 1998), p. 53; T. Everson, *Warfare in Ancient Greece* (Stroud, Sutton Publishing, 2004), p. 121–122, 161; P. Cartledge, 'Hoplites and Heroes: Sparta's Contribution to the Technique of Ancient Warfare', *JHS* 97 (1977), p. 13; Sekunda, *Greek Hoplite*, p. 10, 50.
3. L. Ueda-Sarson, 'The Evolution of Hellenistic Infantry (Part 2): Infantry of the Successors', *Slingshot*, 223 (July 2002), p. 24; Cartledge, 'Hoplites and Heroes', p. 13; E. Bradford, *Thermopylae – The Battle for the West* (USA, Da Capo Press, 1993), p. 71; H.L. Lorimer, 'The Hoplite Phalanx with Special Reference to the Poems of Archilochus and Tyrtaeus', *ABSA* 42 (1947), p. 76; W.K. Pritchett, *The Greek State at War – Vol. I* (Berkeley, University of California Press, 1974), p. 148; J.K. Anderson, *Military Theory and Practice in the Age of Xenophon* (Berkeley, University of California Press, 1970), p. 17.
4. Tyrt. 1; Ar. *Av.* 484; Xen. *Hell.* 5.4.18; see also P.C. Bol, *Argivische Schilde* (Berlin, Walter de Gruyter, 1989), pp. 106–117; Homolle, *Delphes V*, p. 103, D.M. Robinson, *Excavations at Olynthus, Part X – Metal and Minor Miscellaneous Finds* (Blatimore, Johns Hopkins University Press, 1941), p. 443; T.L Shear 'The Campaign of 1936', *Hesperia #6 – The American Excavations in the Athenian Agora: 12th Report* 6:3 (1937), p. 347; M.M. Markle III, 'The Macedonian *Sarissa*, Spear and Related Armour', *AJA* 8:3 (Summer 1977), p. 326; Connolly, *Greece and Rome*, p. 53; H. van Wees, *Greek Warfare – Myths and Realities* (London, Duckworth, 2004), p. 48, A.M. Snodgrass, *Arms and Armour of the*

Greeks (Baltimore, Johns Hopkins University Press, 1999), p. 53; N. Sekunda, *Greek Hoplite 480–323BC* (Oxford, Osprey Publishing, 2004), pp. 10, 50; D. Featherstone, *Warriors and Warfare in Ancient and Medieval Times* (London, Constable, 1988), p. 44; Bradford, *Thermopylae*, p. 71; V.D. Hanson, *Wars of the Ancient Greeks* (London, Cassell, 1999), pp. 57–60, 122; Lorimer, 'The Hoplite Phalanx', p. 77; S. Mitchell, 'Hoplite Warfare in Ancient Greece' in A.B. Lloyd (ed.), *Battle in Antiquity* (London, Duckworth, 1996), p. 89; P. Krentz, 'The Nature of Hoplite Battle', *Classical Antiquity* 16 (1985), p. 55; F.E. Adcock, *The Greek and Macedonian Art of War* (Berkeley, University of California Press, 1957), p. 3; Pritchett, *Greek State at War I*, pp. 146–151; Anderson, *Military Theory*, p. 15, 17; H. van Wees, 'The Development of the Hoplite Phalanx – Iconography and Reality in the Seventh Century' in van Wees (ed.) *War and Violence in Ancient Greece* (London, Duckworth, 2000), p. 126; L. Rawlings, 'Alternative Agonies – Hoplite Martial and Combat Experiences Beyond the Phalanx' in van Wees (ed.), *War and Violence*, p. 247; E. Jarva, *Archaiologia on Archaic Greek Body Armour* (Studia Archaeologica Septentrionalia 3), (Rovaniemi: Pohjois-Suomen Historiallinen Yhdistys, Societas Historica Finlandiae Septentrionalis, 1995), p. 134; V.D. Hanson, *The Western Way of War* (Berkeley, University of California Press, 1989), p. 84; W. Donlan and J. Thompson, 'The Charge at Marathon: Herodotus 6.112', *Classical Journal* 71:4 (Apr–May 1976), p. 341; P. Ducrey, *Warfare in Ancient Greece* (New York, Schocken Books, 1986), p. 47.

5. *Porpax*: Eur. *Hel.* 1376; Eur. *Phoen.* 1127; Eur. *Tro.* 1196; Soph. *Aj.* 576; Strabo 3.3.6; Plut. *Mor.* 193E; *antilabe*: Thuc. 7.65; Strabo 3.3.6.

6. N. Sekunda, *The Spartan Army* (Oxford, Osprey Publishing, 1998), p. 26.

7. Van Wees, *Greek Warfare*, pp. 48, 167; Connolly, *Greece and Rome*, p. 54; Hanson, *Western*, pp. 65–71; Everson, *Warfare*, p. 120; for a counter argument see: R.D. Luginbill, 'Othismos: The Importance of the Mass-Shove in Hoplite Warfare', *Phoenix* 48:1 (Spring 1994), p. 54; Mitchell, 'Hoplite Warfare' in Lloyd (ed.), *Battle in Antiquity*, p. 89; J.E. Lendon, *Soldiers and Ghosts – A History of Battle in Classical Antiquity* (New Haven, Yale University Press, 2005), p. 8; W.K. Pritchett, *The Greek State at War – Vol. IV* (Berkeley, University of California Press, 1985), p. 60; van Wees, 'Development of the Hoplite Phalanx' in van Wees (ed.) *War and Violence*, p. 126; Rawlings, 'Alternative Agonies' in van Wees (ed.) *War and Violence*, p. 247.

8. Philostr. *Gym.* 33.

9. Theoc. 24.125.

10. Eur. *Tro.* 1197–1199; this assumes that Euripides is using a contemporary *aspis* in his description of Homeric Age combat. Herodotus (6.117) similarly describes how the beard of a large individual at Marathon overshadowed his shield. However, it is not stated how this individual is armed (i.e. as a Persian or as a hoplite).

11. Everson, *Warfare*, p. 122.

12. Bardunias, 'The Aspis', *Ancient Warfare* 1:3 (2007), p. 13; see: Pl. *Resp.* 616C.

13. Bradford, *Thermopylae*, p. 71; Anderson, *Military Theory*, p. 16.

14. R. Matthews, *The Battle of Thermopylae – A Campaign in Context* (Gloucestershire, Spellmount, 2006), p. 54.

15. An effective shoulder strap, or *telamon* (τελαμών) can be created by simply tying a loop of cord or strap through the *porpax*. The cord can then be looped over the head to rest on the right shoulder. The left arm can be easily inserted through the *porpax* while the cord is in place, with little discomfort, allowing the shield to be supported simultaneously by both the left shoulder and the *telemon;* thus causing little stress on the muscles of the left arm and allowing the shield to be carried almost indefinitely. Importantly, inserting a *telamon*

256 A Storm of Spears

through the *porpax* does not require the adjustment of the length of the *antilabe*. The presence of such a shoulder strap in no way inhibits movement of the shield for any form of action. The use of a *telamon* in the Archaic Age is quite well attested in the literary record (see: Hom. *Il.* 2.388, 5.796, 11.38, 12.401, 14.404, 16.803, 17.290, 18.480; Hdt. 1.171) and it is suggested that the small *peltē* carried by the later Macedonian phalangite was also equipped with a shoulder strap (see: S. English, 'Hoplite or Peltast? – Macedonian 'Heavy' Infantry', *Ancient Warfare* 2:1 (2008), p. 35, W. Heckel and R. Jones, *Macedonian Warrior: Alexander's Elite Infantryman* (Oxford, Osprey, 2006), p. 14; Everson, *Warfare*, p. 178; Snodgrass, *Arms and Armour*, p. 118). While there is little evidence for the use of a *telamon* by the Classical hoplite, experimentation with this kind of configuration for the *aspis* found a shoulder strap to be very effective for long marches, and under combat conditions, and the continued use of a *telamon* by hoplites from the Archaic Age to the Classical Age should not be fully discounted.

16. See: M. Andronicos, *Delphi* (Athens, Ekdotike Athenon, 2000), p. 59; Pausanias (5.26.3) compares the shape of jumping weights to the grip of a shield by stating that both are elliptical in shape rather than semi-circular (κύκλου παραμηκεστέρου κὰι οὐκ ἐς τὸ ἀκριβέστατον περιφεροῦς εἰσὶν ἥμισυ, πεποίηται δὲ ὡς καὶ τοὺς δακτύλους τῶν χειρῶν διιέναι καθάπερ δὶ ὀχάνων ἀσπίδος). This also suggests that, in some cases, the hand grip of the *aspis* may have been some form of handle rather than a cord that ran around the inner rim.

17. See: J. Boldsen, 'A Statistical Evaluation of the Basis for Predicting Stature from the Lengths of Long Bones in European Populations', *AJPA* 65 (1984), pp. 305–311; J.K. Lundy, 'Regression Equations for Estimating Living Stature from Long Limb Bones in South African Negro', *SAJS* 79 (1983), pp. 337–338; G. Oliver, C. Aaron, G. Fully and G. Tisser, 'New Estimations of Stature and Cranial Capacity in Modern Man', *JHE* 7 (1978), pp. 513–518.

18. Van Wees, *Greek Warfare*, p. 167; see also van Wees, 'Development of the Hoplite Phalanx' in van Wees (ed.) *War and Violence*, p. 128.

19. Van Wees, *Greek Warfare*, p. 168.

20. Luginbill, 'Othismos', p. 54.

21. Van Wees, *Greek Warfare*, pp. 167–168; see also van Wees, 'Development of the Hoplite Phalanx' in van Wees (ed.) *War and Violence*, p. 129–130.

22. Van Wees, *Greek Warfare*, plate IV; see also Everson, *Warfare*, pp. 119–120.

23. Sekunda, *Greek Hoplite*, p. 26.

24. Matthews, *Thermopylae*, pp. 52, 58.

25. For example, see the figures using the underarm stance on pages 29 and 45; for the new trends of the Classical Age see: G.M.A. Richter, *Perspective in Greek and Roman Art* (London, Phaidon Press Ltd.), pp. 14–17, 21–26, 30–32; J. Onians, *Classical Art and the Cultures of Greece and Rome* (New Haven, Yale University Press, 1999), p. 84.

26. Eur. *Phoen.* 1404–1415.

27. Theoc. 24.125.

28. Xen. *Cyn.* 10.11–12.

29. Arr. *Tact* 3.5. This practice may have begun in the Mycenaean Age. See: D. Fortenberry, 'Single Greaves in the Late Helladic Period', *AJA* 94:4 (Oct. 1991), pp. 623–627.

30. Everson, *Warfare*, p. 22.

31. Everson, *Warfare*, pp. 54, 56–57; see also Fortenberry, 'Single greaves', pp. 623–627; P. Schauer, 'Die Beinschienen der Späten Bronzen und Frühen Eisenzeit', *Römisch-Germanisches Zentralmuseums* 29 (1982), p. 149.

32. Luginbill, 'Othismos', p. 53.
33. Xen. *An.* 4.1.18.
34. These locations of damage to hoplite armour were identified during a forensic examination of hoplite helmets, shields and armour belonging to the Deutsche Archaeological Institute housed at Olympia in Greece made in 2008.
35. Xen. *An.* 4.4.11; Xen. *Lac.* 11.9; Thuc. 5.10, 5.71.
36. E.L. Wheeler, 'The General as Hoplite' in V.D. Hanson (ed.), *Hoplites – The Classical Greek Battle Experience* (London, Routledge, 2004), p. 129; Lorimer, 'Hoplite Phalanx', p. 77; Krentz, 'Nature of Hoplite Battle', p. 53; Anderson, *Military Theory*, p. 16.
37. Van Wees, *Greek Warfare*, pp. 168–169.
38. Van Wees, *Greek Warfare*, p. 169; see also Snodgrass, *Arms and Armour*, p. 54.
39. Tyrt. 10, 11.
40. Veg. *Mil.* 1.20.
41. Arr. *Tact.* 16.13.
42. Ascl. *Tact.* 4.1.
43. Polyb. 18.29; Arr. *Tact.* 11.3.
44. For the differences in the size of the cubit and a claim that Polybius used the Macedonian cubit see: R.E. Dickinson, 'Length Isn't Everything – Use of the Macedonian *Sarissa* in the Time of Alexander the Great', *JBT* 3:3 (November 2000), pp. 51–62.
45. G. Cawkwell, 'Orthodoxy and Hoplites', *CQ* 39:2 (1989), p. 383; see also P. Krentz, 'Continuing the Othismos on Othismos', *AHB* 8:2 (1994), p. 47.
46. Markle ('Use of the *Sarissa* by Philip and Alexander of Macedon', *AJA*, 82:4 (Autumn 1978), pp. 483–497; 'A Shield Monument from Veria and the Chronology of Macedonian Shield Types', *Hesperia* 68:2 (April–June 1999), pp. 219–254) suggests that the *sarissa* was not used in the army of Alexander the Great until the battle of Gaugamela in 331BC.
47. Diod. Sic. 17.27.2; Asclepiodotus (3.6) and Plutarch (*Tim.* 27; *Phil.* 9) also uses variants of the word (συνασπίσαντες) to describe Macedonian formations with 'interlocked shields'.
48. Diameter of the Macedonian shield: Ascl. *Tact.* 5.1; the weapons of the first five ranks: Polyb. 18.29; Ascl. *Tact.* 5.1.
49. It is interesting that the root of the word used to describe these formations (συνασπίσαντες) is *aspis* rather than *peltē*; further suggesting the use of the larger hoplite shield by some elements of the Macedonian infantry.
50. Polyaenus, *Strat.* 4.4.1.
51. Everson, *Warfare*, p. 177; N. Sekunda, *The Army of Alexander the Great* (Oxford, Osprey Publishing, 1999), p. 30.
52. Tyre: Arr. *An.* 2.23; Diod. Sic. 17.46.1–2; Curt. 4.4.10–12; Plut. *Alex.* 25; Gaza: Arr. *An.* 2.27; Diod. Sic. 17.46.1–3; Curt. 4.6.21–26; Aornus: Arr. *An.* 4.28-30, Diod. Sic. 17.85.2–7; Curt. 8.11.2-25; for more recent accounts of the difficult ascent of Aornus see: A. Stein, *On Alexander's Track to the Indus* (New Delhi, Asian Publications, 1985), pp. 113–154; M. Wood, *In the Footsteps of Alexander the Great* (London, BBC Worldwide, 2001), pp. 178–181.
53. Arr. *An.* 2.23; Diod. Sic. 17.46.1–2.
54. Macedonian troops bearing the *aspis* can also be seen on the Monument of Aemelius Paulus at Delphi; built to commemorate the Roman victory over the Macedonians at Pydna in 168BC.
55. M. Park, 'The Silver Shields – Philip's and Alexander's Hypaspists', *Ancient Warfare* 1:3 (2007), p. 28.
56. Krentz, 'Nature of Hoplite Battle', p. 55.

57. Thuc. 5.71.
58. Interestingly, a *pēchus* was measured as the distance between the tip of the elbow and the tip of the middle finger. A hoplite standing in an oblique posture, and with his shield supported on his left shoulder, has his left forearm positioned in such a way that this exact same method of measuring the interval is stretched across the front of the space he occupies. The smallest distance between two men in a close-order formation is the distance between one man's left elbow to the other man's left elbow; the exact same distance and further confirmation that Asclepiodotus is referring to men equipped as Classical hoplites and not Macedonian phalangites.
59. The facilitation of movement is one of the traits of the intermediate-order formation specified by Asclepiodotus (3.6).
60. Troops armed as phalangites can only conform to the intermediate and open-orders outlined by Asclepiodotus as the small diameter of the *peltē*, and the weapons of the first five ranks projecting between the files, prevent the adoption of a close-order deployment. This further indicates that the intervals outlined by Asclepiodotus are for both hoplites and phalangites.
61. Tyrt. 10, 11.

Chapter 5 – Repositioning the Spear in 'Hoplite Drill'

1. Pl. *Lach.* 179e–184c.
2. P. Connolly, *Greece and Rome at War* (London, Greenhill Books, 1998), pp. 41–42; V.D. Hanson, *Wars of the Ancient Greeks* (London, Cassell, 1999), p. 63.
3. J. Lazenby, 'The Killing Zone' in V.D. Hanson (ed.), *Hoplites – The Classical Greek Battle Experience* (London, Routledge, 2004), p. 93.
4. Connolly, *Greece and Rome*, p. 41; H.L. Lorimer, 'The Hoplite Phalanx with Special Reference to the Poems of Archilochus and Tyrtaeus', *ABSA* 42 (1947), p. 114; J.K. Anderson, *Military Theory and Practice in the Age of Xenophon* (Berkeley, University of California Press, 1970), p. 87; H. van Wees, 'The Development of the Hoplite Phalanx – Iconography and Reality in the Seventh Century' in H. van Wees (ed.), *War and Violence in Ancient Greece* (London, Duckworth, 2000), p. 138; Matthews (*The Battle of Thermopylae – A Campaign in Context* (Gloucestershire, Spellmount, 2006), p. 58) states that the spear was carried into battle sloped over the shoulder and then raised directly into the overhead position. Such a move would still encounter all of the problems outlined here.
5. Hanson, *Wars*, p. 132; V.D. Hanson, *The Western Way of War* (Berkeley, University of California Press, 1989), p. 84; see also: Lazenby, 'Killing Zone' in Hanson (ed.), *Hoplites*, pp. 92–93; J.K. Anderson, 'Hoplite Weapons and Offensive Arms' in Hanson (ed.), *Hoplites*, p. 31; Connolly, *Greece and Rome*, pp. 41–42.
6. Polyb. 18.30.
7. Lazenby, 'Killing Zone' in Hanson (ed.), *Hoplites*, p. 93.
8. M.M. Markle III, 'The Macedonian *Sarissa*, Spear and Related Armour', *AJA* 8:3 (Summer 1977), p. 334.
9. Anderson, 'Hoplite Offensive Arms' in Hanson (ed.), *Hoplites*, p. 31; see also: Anderson, *Military Theory*, p. 88; Lazenby, 'Killing Zone' in Hanson (ed.), *Hoplites*, p. 93.
10. Anderson, 'Hoplite Offensive Arms' in Hanson (ed.), *Hoplites*, p. 31; Anderson, *Military Theory*, p. 88.
11. Based on observations of, and participation with, re-enactors from the Sydney Ancients May 2006–June 2007.

12. Lazenby, 'Killing Zone' in Hanson (ed.), *Hoplites*, p. 93.
13. Xen. *An.* 1.2.17.
14. Xen. *An.* 6.5.25; Anderson, *Military Theory*, p. 87 interprets these descriptions as a move only to the low position. However, a similar move to the underarm position cannot be ruled out.
15. Polyaenus, *Strat.* 3.9.8.
16. Theoc. 24.125. Oenomaus is additionally described as holding his spear in a couched position (Οἰνόμαος προτενὲς δόρυ χειρὶ) while fighting from a chariot (Ap. Rhod. *Argon.* 1.756).
17. Hom. *Il.* 11.594, 15.298, 17.234; Tyrt. 1.
18. Lorimer, 'Hoplite Phalanx', p. 114.

Chapter 6 – The Reach and Trajectory of Attacks made with the Hoplite Spear
1. J. Chananie, 'The Physics of Karate Strikes', *Journal of How Things Work* 1 (Fall 1999), p. 3.
2. Chananie, 'Karate Strikes', p. 3.
3. Tyrt. 12 (δηίων ὀρέγοιτ᾽ ἐγγύθεν ἱστάμενος); Xen. *Hell.* 4.3.17 (εἰς δόρυ ἀφικόμενοι ἔτρεψαν τὸ καθ᾽ αὑτούς); see also: Xen. *Hell.* 7.1; Xen. *Ages.* 2.10–11; Plut. *Ages.* 18; Plut. *Tim.* 27–28.
4. H. van Wees, *Greek Warfare – Myths and Realities* (London, Duckworth, 2004), p. 189.
5. A.M. Snodgrass, *Arms and Armour of the Greeks* (Baltimore, Johns Hopkins University Press, 1999), p. 53.
6. Arr. *Tact.* 12.3; Ael. Tact. *Tact*13.3; see also G.L. Cawkwell, 'Orthodoxy and Hoplites', *CQ* 39:2 (1989), p. 385. Hammond claims that only the front rank of a hoplite formation could engage. See N.G.L. Hammond, 'Casualties and Reinforcements of Citizen Soldiers in Greece and Macedonia', *JHS* 109 (1989), p. 60.
7. V.D. Hanson, *Wars of the Ancient Greeks* (London, Cassell, 1999), p. 51; R. Matthews, *The Battle of Thermopylae – A Campaign in Context* (Gloucestershire, Spellmount, 2006), p. 59; In the Byzantine abridgement of the *Stratagems of War* (referred to in translation as the 'Excerpts'), Polyaenus recommends that the spears belonging to the members of the first three ranks of a phalanx should be of different lengths so that, when they are lowered, they will present a level frontage (18.8). However, it is uncertain whether this passage should be attributed to a Greek, Macedonian or later formation of spearmen; and there is no reference to a historical individual to place the passage in its correct context. That it does not agree with other references to the spears of the first two ranks of a Greek phalanx reaching the enemy (Arr. *Tact.* 12.3; Ael. Tact. *Tact.* 13.3), or the weapons of the first five ranks projecting beyond the front of a Macedonian phalanx (Polyb. 18.29; Ascl. *Tact.* 5.1), suggests that this passage should not be attributed to either of these formations, or that it is merely a recommendation rather than a description of a used practice.
8. J. Warry, *Warfare in the Classical World* (Norman, University of Oklahoma Press, 1995), p. 37.
9. P.H. Blyth, *The Effectiveness of Greek Armour against Arrows in the Persian Wars (490–479B.C.): An Interdisciplinary Enquiry* (London, British Library Lending Division (unpublished thesis – University of Reading, 1977)), pp. 177–178.
10. Tyrt. 12 (δηίων ὀρέγοιτ᾽ ἐγγύθεν ἱστάμενος); Tearless Battle: Xen. *Hell.* 7.1.31 (εἰς δόρυ); Coronea: Plut. *Ages.* 18 (οὐκ ἔσχεν ὠθισμὸν) see also Xen. *Hell.* 4.3.17 (εἰς δόρυ ἀφικόμενοι ἔτρεψαν τὸ καθ᾽ αὑτούς); Sicily: Plut. *Tim.* 27–28 (διεκπούοντο τὸν δορατισμόν); see also: Chapter 13, The Hoplite Battle: Contact, *Othismos*, Breakthrough and Rout.

11. Even in a more open-order formation, the spear can still be rested on the rim of the shield when using the underarm technique.
12. Hom. *Il.* 13.130–135.
13. Hom. *Il.* 13.134–135 (trans. M. Hammond).
14. J.K. Anderson, 'Hoplites and Heresies: A Note', *JHS* 104 (1984), p. 152; Cawkwell, 'Orthodoxy and Hoplites', p. 381. See also: A.D. Fraser, 'Myth of the Phalanx-scrimmage', *Classical Weekly* 36 (Oct 1942-Jun 1943), p. 15.
15. R. Gabriel and K. Metz, *From Sumer to Rome – The Military Capabilities of Ancient Armies* (Connecticut, Greenwood Press, 1991), p. 83.
16. V.D. Hanson, *The Western Way of War* (Berkeley, University of California Press, 1989), pp. 162, 189; V.D. Hanson, 'Hoplite Technology in Phalanx Battle' in V.D. Hanson (ed.), *Hoplites – The Classical Greek Battle Experience* (London, Routledge, 2004), pp. 71–72; Hanson, *Wars*, pp. 52–53.
17. P. Connolly, *Greece and Rome at War* (London, Greenhill Books, 1998), p. 42.
18. See: W.K. Pritchett, 'New Light on Thermopylai', *AJA* 62:2 (Apr. 1958), p. 203.
19. Hdt. 7.211. See also: W.W. How, 'Arms, Tactics and Strategy in the Persian War', *JHS* 43:2 (1923), pp. 123–124.
20. Aesch. *Pers.* 817; Hdt. 9.62.
21. Xen. *Hell.* 7.6.1.
22. Hdt. 7.176–177, 7.200; see also Diod. Sic. 11.6.4; Pausanias (10.21.2) describes Thermopylae as 'a narrow pass with broken and slippery ground; a continuous series of rivulets among rocky outcrops'.
23. Pritchett, 'Thermopylai', p. 211; W.K. Pritchett, 'New light on Plataia', *AJA* 61:1 (Jan. 957), pp. 9–28; W.K. Pritchett, 'Xerxes' Route over Mount Olympus', *AJA* 65:4 (Oct. 1961), pp. 369–375; Kromayer and Veiths' topographical map of the battle site (Map 3 – *Die Thermopylen*) gives a width of around 25m. See: Kromayer, J. and Veith, G., *Schlachten-Atlas zur Antiken Kriegsgeschichte* (revised by R. Gabriel (ed.) and re-released as *The Battle Atlas of Ancient Military History* (Ontario, Canadian Defence Academy Press, 2008), p. 4; geophysical surveys of the ancient coastline at Thermopylae confirm the accuracy of Herodotus' descriptions of the terrain; particularly the width of the battle-field. See: J.C. Kraft, G. Rapp, J.G. Szemler, C. Tziavos and E.W. Kase, 'The Pass at Thermopylae, Greece', *Journal of Field Archaeology* 14:2 (1987), pp. 187–195.
24. Polyaenus, *Strat.* 7.15.5; Polyaenus, *Excerpts*, 13.2; the narrow strip of the Thermopylae pass certainly meant that the Persians could not bring the full force of their numbers to bear against the Greek position and this was exactly why such a narrow field of battle was chosen by the Greeks for the defence (Hdt. 7.177; Lys. 1.30).
25. Diod. Sic. 11.7.2–3, 11.8.1.
26. Diod. Sic. 11.7.2.
27. Connolly, *Greece and Rome*, p. 13; Matthews, *Thermopylae*, pp. 19, 146, 170; Warry, *Warfare*, pp. 38–39; D. Featherstone, *Warriors and Warfare in Ancient and Medieval Times* (London, Constable, 1988), p. 41; see also: E. Bradford, *Thermopylae – The Battle for the West* (USA, Da Capo Press, 1993), p. 127.
28. In an unreferenced passage, Matthews (*Thermopylae* p. 19) states that the ball on the end of the Persian spear was 'heavy' but provides no figures for its weight.
29. Hdt. 7.61–80; Xen. *Anab.* 1.5.15, 1.8.3; Xen. *Cyr.* 7.1.2; Matthews (*Thermopylae* p. 19) states that the Persian spear was only for thrusting.
30. Xen. *Cyr.* 4.3.9.
31. Aesch. *Pers.* 240.

32. Nep. *Datames* 9.3–5.
33. Hdt. 8.55.
34. Diod. Sic. 11.6.3, 11.7.2; Hdt. 7.61–62, 7.64.
35. It is possible that the axe-wielding contingent of the third assault was sent in to hack through the Greek spears, as was later done at Plataea (see Chapter 10, The Use of the *Sauroter* as a Weapon), after the Persians had lost substantial numbers to the Greek spears in the first two attacks.
36. Diod. Sic. 11.7.3.
37. Hdt. 7.224–225.
38. Hdt. 7.229–231.
39. Matthews (*Thermopylae* p. 151) suggests that the difference in reach between the Greek and Persian spears may have only been 20cm which, again, hardly seems noteworthy.
40. Hdt. 7.61–80.
41. Hdt. 7.224.
42. Hdt. 8.24, Diod. Sic. 11.7.4; Polyaenus, *Strat.* 7.15.4–5.
43. Thuc. 5.70.
44. See examples in: Thuc. 3.108; Plut. *Mor.* 211F; Diod. Sic. 12.79.4. For the disparity in casualties between victors and vanquished see: P. Krentz, 'Casualties in Hoplite Battles', *GRBS* 26 (1985), pp. 13–20; Gabriel and Metz, *Sumer to Rome*, pp. 84–87; Hammond, 'Casualties and Reinforcements', p. 60. For an anlysis of the estimation and/or rounding of casualty figures by Thucydides see: C. Rubincam, 'Casualty Figures in the Battle Descriptions of Thucydides', *Transactions of the American Philological Society (1974–)* 121 (1991), pp. 181–198.

Chapter 7 – The 'Kill Shot' of Hoplite Combat

1. G.L. Cawkwell, 'Orthodoxy and Hoplites', *CQ* 39:2 (1989), p. 381; P. Cartledge, 'Hoplites and Heroes: Sparta's Contribution to the Technique of Ancient Warfare', *JHS* 97 (1977), p. 15; A.M. Snodgrass, 'The Hoplite Reform and History', *JHS* 85 (1965), p. 115; H.L. Lorimer, 'The Hoplite Phalanx with Special Reference to the Poems of Archilochus and Tyrtaeus', *ABSA* 42 (1947), pp. 83, 94, 99; S. Mitchell. 'Hoplite Warfare in Ancient Greece' in A.B. Lloyd (ed.), *Battle in Antiquity* (London, Duckworth, 1996), p. 89; W.K. Pritchett, *The Greek State at War – Vol. IV* (Berkeley, University of California Press, 1985), p. 60; C.F. Salazar, *The Treatment of War Wounds in Greco-Roman Antiquity* (Leiden, Brill, 2000), pp. 233–234.
2. A.M. Snodgrass, *Arms and Armour of the Greeks* (Baltimore, Johns Hopkins University Press, 1999), p. 56; Lorimer, 'Hoplite Phalanx', pp. 83, 94.
3. V.D. Hanson, *Wars of the Ancient Greeks* (London, Cassell, 1999), pp. 48, 62; T. Everson, *Warfare in Ancient Greece* (Stroud, Sutton Publishing, 2004), pp. 76, 98, 149, 157; R. Gabriel and K. Metz, *From Sumer to Rome – The Military Capabilities of Ancient Armies* (Connecticut, Greenwood Press, 1991), p. 60.
4. N. Sekunda, *Greek Hoplite 480–323BC* (Oxford, Osprey Publishing, 2004), p. 27.
5. E. Bradford, *Thermopylae – The Battle for the West* (USA, Da Capo Press, 1993), pp. 69–70.
6. Snodgrass, *Arms and Armour*, p. 56.
7. J.K. Anderson, *Military Theory and Practice in the Age of Xenophon* (Berkeley, University of California Press, 1970), p. 28; Ducrey (*Warfare in Ancient Greece* (New York, Schocken Books 1986), p. 56) similarly says that the Corinthian helmets covered the top and back of the head as well as the cheeks and the nose but makes no reference to protection for the throat.

8. J.E. Lendon, *Soldiers and Ghosts – A History of Battle in Classical Antiquity* (New Haven, Yale University Press, 2005), p. 53.
9. Everson, *Warfare*, p. 80.
10. Everson, *Warfare*, p. 76.
11. H. van Wees, 'The Homeric Way of War: The 'Iliad' and the Hoplite Phalanx (II)', *Greece and Rome*, 2nd Series, 41:2 (Oct 1994), p. 135.
12. Alc. *Frag.* 19.
13. Everson, *Warfare*, p. 162; Everson also cites one artistic representation of the 'shield apron' dated to c.400BC, which implies that it may have also been used during the Peloponnesian War, but suggests that it may not have been very popular. The lack of depiction of the 'shield apron' in later art seems to confirm this.
14. Lorimer, 'Hoplite Phalanx', p. 126; Tyrt. 8.
15. Large shields like the early 'Figure Eight' or the rectangular 'Tower Shield' (c. 1500BC–1250BC) also provide cover from shoulder to ankle but would not have been in use at the time Tyrtaeus was writing so it is unlikely that this is what he is describing.
16. It is unlikely that any sandal worn would have adequately protected the foot against impacts such as spear thrusts and so the whole surface area of the top of the foot has been included in this calculation.
17. Veg. *Mil.* 1.12.
18. Diod. Sic. 11.7.2–3.
19. Gabriel and Metz, Sumer to Rome, p. 72. Similarly, P.H. Blyth (*The Effectiveness of Greek Armour against Arrows in the Persian Wars (490–479B.C.): An Interdisciplinary Enquiry* (London, British Library Lending Division (unpublished thesis – University of Reading, 1977)), pp. 178–181) estimates that all of the arrows fired by the Persians as part of the opening volleys of the battle of Marathon (approximately 22,000 arrows in all) may have resulted in no more than 175 Greek casualties (an effectiveness of less than 1 per cent). In an experiment conducted at the 15th Australasian Historical Conference (10–13 April 2009), 20 people equipped as hoplites formed a close-order formation five men across and four ranks deep. This formation then slowly advanced over 100m of open field against a rank of 16 archers firing rubber tipped arrows with 30lb bows. Each archer fired six arrows during the time of the advance of the formation (a total of 96 arrows fired). This 'advance' was repeated 7 times (in some cases with the formation halting at a distance of only 20m from the archers to provide them with a static target) resulting in an overall total of 672 arrows fired at the formation during the course of the test. Any 'hit' by an arrow against an unarmoured area of the body was noted. Only three minor 'injuries' were recorded: one hoplite was hit in the right upper arm; another, who was without greaves, was hit in the shin; and another was hit in the right hand. All other arrows struck either the large hoplite *aspis*, glanced off the helmet crest, sides of the helmet or shoulder sections of the breastplate, or failed to hit the formation. The three recorded 'hits' would have been incapacitating to the recipient under real combat conditions, but no fatalities would have been sustained by the formation from the volleys of missiles unless an arrow managed to penetrate the armour it had struck.
20. Arthur Nock curiously suggests that wars between the Greek city-states 'were only slightly more dangerous than American football' (see: D. Grossman, *On Killing* (New York, Back Bay Books, 1996), p. 12). The casualty figures for hoplite battles would suggest that they were substantially more dangerous than this.
21. Everson, *Warfare*, pp. 80, 169.

22. A.K. Goldsworthy, 'The *Othismos*, Myths and Heresies: The Nature of Hoplite Battle', *War in History* 4:1 (1997), p. 23; N. Sekunda, *The Spartan Army* (Oxford, Osprey Publishing, 1998), p. 29; J.K. Anderson, *Military Theory and Practice in the Age of Xenophon* (Berkeley, University of California Press, 1970), p. 28; V.D. Hanson, 'Hoplite Battle' in H. van Wees (ed.), *War and Violence in Ancient Greece* (London, Duckworth, 2000), p. 207; P. Cartledge, *Thermopylae – The Battle that Changed the World* (London, Pan Books, 2007), p. 143; R. Matthews, *The Battle of Thermopylae – A Campaign in Context* (Gloucestershire, Spellmount, 2006), p. 54.
23. Thuc. 7.44.
24. Mitchell, 'Hoplite Warfare' in Lloyd (ed.), *Battle in Antiquity*, p. 89.
25. Blyth, *Effectiveness of Greek Armour*, p. 67.
26. Blyth, *Effectiveness of Greek Armour*, p. 67.
27. This difference in the size of the eyeholes was observed in the helmets housed in the collection of the Deutshce Archaeological Institute at Olympia in Greece. The appertures for the eye in these helmets range between 4.7–8/7cm in width and 2.4–6.0cm in height.
28. D. Grossman and B. Siddle, 'Psychological Effects of Combat' in L.R. Kutz (ed.), *Encyclopedia of Violence, Peace and Conflict* (Orlando, Academic Press, 1999), pp. 139–149; N. Whatley, 'On the Possibility of Reconstructing Marathon and Other Ancient Battles', *JHS* 94 (1964), pp. 120-121; E.C. Godnig, 'Tunnel Vision: Its Causes and Treatment Strategies', *Journal of Behavioral Optometry* 14:4 (2003), pp. 95–97; D. Klinger, *Police Responses to Officer-involved Shootings* (Washington, US Department of Justice, 2002), pp. 3–47.
29. J. Keegan, *The Face of Battle* (London, Penguin Books, 1983), p. 39.
30. Eur. *El.* 377–378.
31. Eur. *Supp.* 846–847, 855–856; S. Hornblower, *A Commentary on Thucydides Vol. II* (Oxford, Clarendon Press, 1996), pp. 308–309 details the possible association of Euripides' play with the clash of the phalanxes at Delium.
32. Hdt 6.117.
33. On 'shell shock' see: D.A. Worcester, 'Shell-Shock in the Battle of Marathon', *Science* 58:1288 (Sept. 1919), p. 230.
34. Von Bothmer, *Amazons in Greek Art*, p. 70, plate LI; J.D. Beazley, *Attic Black-Figure Vase-Painters* (New York, Hacker Art Books, 1978), p. 144; see also: *LIMC Vol. VII* (Zurich, Artemis Verlag, 1994), p. 298.
35. Quint. Smyrn. 1.591–629.
36. Interestingly, in both images, Penthesileia is fleeing to the right of the image but has turned her upper body to face Achilles. Thus she is not the victim of 'face-to-face combat' but is a victim brought down while being pursued. Consequently, even if the signed Exekias vase is meant to be a depition of an impact against the throat, it cannot confirm a throat 'kill shot' in face-to-face hoplite combat.
37. H. van Wees, 'The Homeric Way of War: The 'Iliad' and the Hoplite Phalanx (I)', *Greece and Rome*, 2nd Series, 41:1 (Apr 1994), p. 2; van Wees ('Homeric II', p. 144) states that heroic fiction must have some basis in reality and that Homer should be treated as any other source.
38. Groin: Tyrt. 10; chest: Tyrt. 1, 12, 19; midriff: Tyrt. 11.
39. Adapted from: H. Frolich, *Die Militarmedicin Homers* (Stuttgart, 1879), pp. 56–60 and Gabriel and Metz, *Sumer to Rome*, pp. 91–92.
40. Hom. *Il.* 22.325.
41. Hom. *Il.* 23.821.

42. Hippoc. *Medic.* 220; see also Hippoc. *Epid.* 5.21–5.220.
43. It is possible that wounds to the region of the throat were deemed 'untreatable'. However, it is surprising that wounds to this region are not even mentioned as such within the Hippocratic corpus. This further suggests that the throat was not a regularly targeted, or hit, area of the body.
44. Eur. *Phoen.* 1385, 1397–1398; Eur. *Heracl.* 738.
45. Plut. *Pel.* 4–5; Diodorus (15.87.1) says that Epaminondas received a mortal wound to the chest and that the spearhead broke off and remained embedded in his body. Nepos (*Epam.* 9.1–3) recounts similarly but the weapon that kills Epaminondas is a javelin rather than a spear. Regardless, all of these injuries must have been sustained through the breastplate.
46. Plut. *Pel.* 2.
47. Plut. *Ages.* 18–19; Plut. *Mor.* 212A, 217E; Xen. *Hell.* 4.3.20; Xen. *Ages.* 2.13, 5.2; Nep. *Agesilaus* 4.6; Diod. Sic. 14.84.2.
48. Plut. *Mor.* 190B, 219C.
49. Plut. *Dion* 30; Plut. *Tim.* 4.
50. Plut. *Mor.* 214D.
51. Plut. *Pel.* 18.
52. Plut. *Ages.* 26.2.
53. Alcibaides: Plut. *Alc.* 7.3; Sphodrias: Xen. *Hell.* 5.4.33; Pelopidas: Plut. *Pel.* 4.5.
54. Paus. 4.8.7.
55. Plut. *Mor.* 242A.
56. Hdt. 7.181.
57. See R.H. Sternberg, 'The Transport of Sick and Wounded Soldiers in Classical Greece', *Phoenix* 53:3/4 (Autumn–Winter 1999), pp. 191–205.
58. Thuc. 7.75; Diodorus (13.18.6) says that the Athenian wounded were placed in the centre of the retreating column.
59. Diod. Sic. 13.18.3.
60. Thuc. 8.27.
61. Diod. Sic. 13.66.2.
62. Polyaenus, *Strat.* 2.31.1.
63. Xen. *An.* 3.4.32, 4.5.22, 5.8.6–11.
64. Hom. *Il.* 22.325.
65. Hom. *Il.* 22.328–329.
66. Xen. *Eq.* 12.
67. Hippoc. *VC* 19.
68. Xen. *Hell.* 7.4.32.
69. Plut. *Mor.* 241E, 241F.
70. Ar. *Ach.* 1226. In a previous line (1175) a messenger states that the injury was inflicted by a sharpened stake that Lamachus stepped on while crossing a ditch. If Lamachus was wounded by a 'spear', it may have been a broken shaft (or stake?) lying on the ground as part of the detritus of battle.
71. Plut. *Dion*, 30.6.
72. Salazar, *War Wounds*, pp. 13, 235.
73. See: J. Stroszeck, 'Lakonisch-rotfigurige Keramik aus den Lakedaimoniergräbern am Kerameikos von Athen', *AA* 2 (2006), pp. 101–120; Salazar, *War Wounds*, pp. 233–234; Pritchett, *Greek State IV*, p. 136; E. Kastorchis, 'ΠΕΡΙ ΤΟΥ ΕΝ ΧΑΙΡΩΝΕΙΑ ΛΕΟΝΤΟΣ', *Athenaion* 8 (1879), pp. 486–491; L Phytalis, 'ΕΡΕΥΝΑΙ ΕΝ ΤΩ ΠΟΛΥΑΝΔΡΙΩ ΧΑΙΠΩΝΕΙΑΣ', *Athenaion* 9 (1880), pp. 347–352, plate 1; H. van Wees, *Greek Warfare*

– *Myths and Realities* (London, Duckworth, 2004), pp. 146–147; cremated remains from a recently excavated *polyandreia* in Athens are being forensically tested, which may signal a shift in academic investigations. See: M. Rose, 'Fallen Heroes – Bones of Pericles' Soldiers come to New York for Analysis', *Archaeology* (Mar–Apr 2000), pp. 42–45.

74. See: J. Stroszeck, 'Lakonisch-rotfigurige Keramik aus den Lakedaimoniergräbern am Kerameikos von Athen', *AA* 2 (2006), pp. 101–120; Salazar, *War Wounds*, pp. 233–234; Pritchett, *Greek State IV*, p. 136; Kastorchis, 'ΠΕΡΙ ΤΟΥ ΕΝ ΧΑΙΡΩΝΕΙΑ ΛΕΟΝΤΟΣ', pp. 486–491; Phytalis, 'ΕΡΕΥΝΑΙ ΕΝ ΤΩ ΠΟΛΥΑΝΔΡΙΩ ΧΑΙΠΩΝΕΙΑΣ', pp. 347–352, plate 1; van Wees, *Greek Warfare*, pp. 146–147.

75. Blyth, *Effectiveness of Greek Armour*, pp. 80–84; see also: Salazar, *War Wounds*, pp. 231–232; Snodgrass, *Arms and Armour*, p. 56; A.H. Jackson, 'Hoplites and the Gods: The Dedication of Captured Arms and Armour' in V.D. Hanson (ed.), *Hoplites – The Classical Greek Battle Experience* (London, Routledge, 2004), p. 239.

76. Gabriel and Metz, *Sumer to Rome*, pp. 47–51.

77. Gabriel and Metz, *Sumer to Rome*, p. 49.

78. Hanson, *Wars*, p. 59; Sekunda, *Greek Hoplite*, pp. 51, 59; van Wees, *Greek Warfare*, p. 48; Snodgrass, *Arms and Armour*, pp. 93–94; Connolly, *Greece and Rome*, pp. 60–62; Warry, *Warfare*, pp. 35, 44–45; Everson, *Warfare*, p. 136; Lendon, *Soldiers and Ghosts*, p. 63; Anderson, *Military Theory*, p. 29; Sekunda, *Spartan Army*, pp. 29–30.

79. Blyth, *Effectiveness of Greek Armour*, p. 71, 80.

80. Blyth, *Effectiveness of Greek Armour*, p. 80.

81. Despite all of the examples of battle damaged helemts at Olympia, Everson (*Warfare*, p. 139) states that there is no evidence of any sort of damage to this area of any helmet that would warrant such reinforcing.

82. Gabriel and Metz (*Sumer to Rome*, p. 54) mention this ability of the felt *pilos* in general but do not attribute it its dissipation effects specifically in relation to the Corinthian helmet.

83. Snodgrass, *Arms and Armour*, p. 93; Everson, *Warfare*, pp. 106–108, 112, 129, 146; Anderson, *Military Theory*, p. 24; Sekunda, *Spartan Army*, pp. 30–31.

84. Sekunda, *Spartan Army*, pp. 30–31.

85. As previously noted (p. 262), archery fire against armoured hoplites had an effective rate of fire of less than 1 per cent.

86. Xen. *Eq.* 12.5–8.

87. Veg. *Mil.* 1.12.

88. Matthews (*Thermopylae* p. 55) states that the linen cuirass was lighter and provided less protection than the bronze corslet. However, it has been determined that the linen composite cuirass afforded no better protection or advantage in weight than its bronze equivalent (Jarva, *Archaiologia*, pp. 135–143; see also Everson, *Warfare*, pp. 111, 147 for views on the effectiveness of different types of composite armour over bronze). Re-created examples certainly agree with this conclusion, at least in terms of weight. Nepos (*Iphicrates* 1.4) says that the linen corselet was lighter but gave the same protection as bronze. Pausanias (1.21.8) states that the linen corslet would not protect against spears and was only suitable for hunting. Anderson (*Military Theory*, p. 23) suggests that Pausanias may have had no actual experience with this type of armour.

89. Veg. *Mil.* 1.12.

90. Plut. *Arist.* 18.

91. Blyth, *Effectiveness of Greek Armour*, pp. 81–83; interestingly, all of these injuries are located above the level at which the rim of the shield would have sat.

92. Soph. *Ant.* 670.

Chapter 8 – Endurance and Accuracy when Fighting with the Hoplite Spear
 1. Hom. *Il.* 13.785, 19.160.
 2. Hdt. 5.120, 6.113, 7.167, 7.221; Thuc. 3.109, 5.71; Xen. *Hell.* 1.3.6; Diod. Sic. 13.51.3–4, 14.33.2: see also W.K. Pritchett, *The Greek State at War – Vol. IV* (Berkeley, University of California Press, 1985), pp. 46–51.
 3. R.D. Luginbill, 'Othismos: The Importance of the Mass-Shove in Hoplite Warfare', *Phoenix* 48:1 (Spring 1994), p. 55.
 4. J.A.R. Munro, 'Some Observations on the Persian Wars', *JHS* 19 (1899), p. 196.
 5. Xen. *Hell.* 7.1.28–29; Plut. *Ages.* 33; Diod. Sic. 15.72.3.
 6. Himera: Hdt. 7.167; Thermopylae: Diod. Sic. 11.8.1 (Hdt. 7.212 states that the Greeks fought in relays on day two but even these contingents are unlikely to have fought for only a few minutes each); Sphacteria: Thuc. 4.35: for other references see Pritchett, *Greek State IV*, pp. 47–49.
 7. Xen. *Hell.* 4.3.16–20.
 8. Dem. 9.48; Xen. *Hell.* 5.2.4, 5.3.19, 5.4.47; Plut. *Mor.* 214A. For comments on environmental conditions in hoplite combat see: P. Krentz, 'Fighting by the Rules: The Invention of the Hoplite *Agon*', *Hesperia*, 71:1 (Jan–Mar 2002), p. 27; V.D. Hanson, *The Western Way of War* (Berkeley, University of California Press, 1989), p. 56; A.M. Snodgrass, 'The Hoplite Reform and History', *JHS* 85 (1965), p. 115.
 9. Hdt. 9.10–49.
10. Thuc. 7.75–83.
11. Thuc. 7.84.
12. Paus.4.21.8–9; Diod. Sic. 14.105.1; see also: J. Ramsey, 'Heat and Cold' in R. Hockey (ed.), *Stress and Fatigue in Human Performance* (Chichester, Wiley and Sons, 1983), pp. 33–57.
13. R. Matthews, *The Battle of Thermopylae – A Campaign in Context* (Gloucestershire, Spellmount, 2006), p. 60.
14. T. Everson, *Warfare in Ancient Greece* (Stroud, Sutton Publishing, 2004), p. 91.
15. R. Gabriel and K. Metz, *From Sumer to Rome – The Military Capabilities of Ancient Armies* (Connecticut, Greenwood Press, 1991), p. 42, 83; A. Ferrill, *The Origins of War* (London, Thames and Hudson, 1985), p. 103.
16. Hanson, *Western*, p. 56; Hanson, in 'Hoplite Technology' (V.D. Hanson (ed.), *Hoplites – The Classical Greek Battle Experience* (London, Routledge, 2004), p. 63 note 2), confusingly describes the limits of these same observations as 'only a few minutes'.
17. H. van Wees, 'The Homeric Way of War: The 'Iliad' and the Hoplite Phalanx (II)', *Greece and Rome*, 2nd Series, 41:2 (Oct 1994), p. 137; A.K. Goldsworthy, 'The Othismos, Myths and Heresies: The Nature of Hoplite Battle', *War in History* 4:1 (1997), p. 21.
18. A.D. Fraser, 'Myth of the Phalanx-scrimmage', *Classical Weekly* 36 (Oct 1942–Jun 1943), p. 16.
19. Courage: Pind. *Isthm.* 1.15–28, 3.13–14; Pind. *Ol.* 6.9–10, 10.20–21; Pind. *Nem.* 6.23–24; Thuc. 2.42.4; toils and dangers: Pind. *Isthm.* 5.22–25, 4.47; Pind. *Ol.* 5.7–8, 6.9–11, 10.22–23; Thuc. 2.39.1, 2.43.4, 2.62.1; esteem: Pind. *Isthm.* 1.50–51, Pind. *Pyth.* 9.97–103, 10.55–59; Hdt. 8.17, 8.93, 9.74, 9.104; parallels between sport and war: Isoc. *Antid.* 15.184–185; see also: D. Pritchard, 'Athletics, War and Democracy in Classical Athens', *Teaching History* 39:4 (Term 4, 2005), pp. 6–7; L. Bonfante, 'Nudity as a Costume in Classical Art', *AJA* 93:4 (Oct. 1989), pp. 543–558.
20. D. Holding, 'Fatigue' in Hockey (ed.), *Stress and Fatigue*, pp. 145–164; N. Forestier and V. Nougier, 'The Effects of Muscular Fatigue on the Co-ordination of Multijoint

Movement in Humans', *Neuroscience Letters* 252:3 (August 1998), pp. 187–190; K. Royal, D. Farrow, I. Mujika, S. Hanson, D. Pyne and B. Abernethy, 'The Effects of Fatigue on Decision Making and Shooting Skill in Water Polo Players', *Journal of Sports Sciences* 24:8 (August 2006), pp. 807–815; P.R. Davey, R.D. Thorpe and C. Williams, 'Fatigue Decreases Tennis Performance', *Journal of Sports Sciences* 20:4 (April 2002), pp. 311–318.

21. G.P. Krueger, 'Sustained Work, Fatigue, Sleep Loss and Performance: A Review of the Issues', *Work and Stress* 3:2 (April 1989), pp. 129–141.

22. Xen. *Cyr.* 3.3.59; Xen. (*Hell.* 6.1.5), in an obvious comparison to the Spartan way of training, states that many citizen-based armies contain many who have either passed, or not yet reached, their prime and that there are few in the city who keep themselves in good physical condition.

23. Leonis Imp. *Strat.* 9.4.

24. Pl. *Leg.* 815a; Xen. *An.* 6.1.5–13; Eur. *Andr.* 1129–1141; Ar. *Nub.* 988–989; Ath. 628F; Theoc. 24.125–126; see also: E.L. Wheeler, '*Hoplomachia* and Greek Dances in Arms', *GRBS* 23:3 (Autumn 1982), pp. 223–233.

25. Pl. *Lach.* 179e–184c.

26. Ath. 628F.

27. Nep. *Alcibaides* 11.4.

28. Nep. *Iphicrates* 3.2.

29. Nep. *Epam.* 2.5.

30. Nep. *Epam.* 5.4; Plut. *Mor.* 192D.

31. Pl. *Leg.* 806B.

32. Paus. 4.7.1–3.

33. Arist. *Eth. Nic.* 3.8.7–9.

34. Diod. Sic. 9.2.5.

35. Technical skill/courage: Veg. *Mil.* 1.1, 1.8, 1.13, 2.23–24, 3.9–10; fitness: Veg. *Mil.* 1.1, 1.5–6, 1.9, 1.13, 1.19, 1.27, 2.23, 3.11; Vegetius also states (1.3) that those nurtured by a life of hard work under the sun, with a lack of acquaintance with luxury and bath-houses, toughened by every kind of toil from wielding iron, digging trenches and carrying burdens, and those who are simple souled and content with little are the best in war. For the Greeks, these diametrically opposed lifestyles are nowhere more apparent than in a comparison of the Spartans (with their *agoge*, simple diet, prohibition on art, luxury and commerce and their professional army) to the members of any other city-state (with their theatres, their *symposia*, trade concerns and short term militia). Vegetius specifically states (3.0, 3.10) that the Athenians sought the cultivation of arts other than war, whereas the chief interest of the Spartans was only war itself. Alcibiades is said to have remarked that it is not unexpected that the Spartans die so fearlessly in battle; for they use death as a means of escaping from the harsh lifestyle they left behind in Sparta (Aelian, *VH* 13.38–37).

36. As Vegetius states (*Mil.* 3.11): '...when a man who is tired, or sweating, or has been running enters battle against a man who is rested, alert and has been standing at his post, the two fight on unequal terms.'.

37. Again, as Vegetius states (*Mil.* 3.9): training and long-term service makes for better soldiers 'for men who stopped fighting a long time ago should be treated as recruits'.

38. Xen. *Lac.* 13.5; Arist. *Pol.* 8.3.4; Plut. *Pel.* 18–19; Plut. *Lyc.* 22; Xen. *Mem.* 3.5.15; 3.12.5; Pl. *Lach.* 182A; Thuc. 6.68–69; 6.72; Polyaenus, *Strat.* 2.5.1; see also A.J. Holladay, 'Hoplites and Heresies', *JHS* 102 (1982), p. 95.

39. Thuc. 5.67; Diod. Sic. 12.79.4; Polyaenus (*Strat.* 3.8.1) refers to the manufacture of weapons at the expense of the Argive state but does not attribute this cost to training as

well. See W.K. Pritchett, *The Greek State at War – Vol. II* (Berkeley, University of California Press, 1974), pp. 221–224, for details of other 'elite' hoplite units.

40. For the agricultural nature of most members of the *polis* see: Arist. *Pol.* 1256a7.

41. P. Ducrey, *Warfare in Ancient Greece* (New York, Schocken Books, 1986), pp. 67–70.

42. Plut. *Mor.* 214; Plut. *Ages.* 26; see also Polyaenus, *Strat.* 2.1.7.

43. C. Idzikowski and A. Baddeley, 'Fear and Dangerous Environments' in R. Hockey (ed.), *Stress and Fatigue* (Chichester, Wiley and Sons, 1983), pp. 123–141.

44. Idzikowski and Baddeley, 'Fear and Dangerous Environments' in Hockey (ed.), *Stress and Fatigue*, p. 126.

45. Arist. *Eth. Nic.* 3.8.13.

46. Sen. (Y), *Prov.* 4.12 (*contemptum periculorum adsiduitas periclitandi dabit*).

47. Idzikowski and Baddeley, 'Fear and Dangerous Environments' in Hockey (ed.), *Stress and Fatigue*, p. 127.

48. Nep. *Thrasybulos* 1.4; interestingly, Thucydides (2.87–89) recounts that, during a naval engagement at the mouth of the Gulf of Corinth in 429BC, the commanders of the inexperienced, yet numerically superior, Peloponnesian fleet attempted to bolster the courage of their crews by stating that their lack of experience was made up by their superior daring. Phormio, the commander of the smaller Athenian fleet, bolstered his own men by stating that both sides were as brave as the other, but the confidence of the Peloponnesians came from their land victories; victories that could have no bearing on a naval engagement. Furthermore, Phormio stated, it was the Athenians' experience as sailors that gave them the advantage. In the subsequent battle (2.90–92) the Athenians were victorious after a hard struggle; thus suggesting that, in naval warfare at least, experience and skill could overcome numbers and daring.

49. Pindar (*Frag.* 110) states that war is sweet to those with no familiarity of it, but is frightening to those who have experienced it. Vegetius (*Mil.* 3.12) states that fear in battle is an ordinary reaction. For a broad discussion of the forms and effects of different types of fear, courage and experience in battle, see: Arist. *Eth. Nic.* 3.7.10–3.8.16.

50. Throughout his book *On Killing*, Grossman outlines how many soldiers of the modern era, unconditioned to the turmoils of war, may demonstrate a resistance to killing another human being in combat while those who have been 'conditioned' are more effective killers (see: D. Grossman, *On Killing* (New York, Back Bay Books, 1996), pp. 3, 13–15, 67–73). If this psychology holds as true for the ancient warrior as it does for the modern, then those hoplites who had been 'conditioned' for war, such as the Spartans, may have also been more accepting to killing an opposing man than members of phalanxes from other city-states. It has been suggested that many of the militarily based institutions of Sparta, such as the *agoge*, the *krypteia*, the establishment of a temple to Fear and the absence of walls to fortify the city, were the product of an inherently cowardly people living in a perpetual state of fear (see: P.H. Epps, 'Fear in Spartan Character', *Classical Philology* 28:1 (Jan 1933), pp. 12–29). It is further suggested that this heightened sense of fear is also present in many of the actions of the Spartan phalanx. As evidence, events such as the surrender of the Spartan hoplites on Sphacteria (Thuc. 4.38–41), the failure of the Spartans to fight to the death at Leuctra (Xen. *Hell.* 6.4.14) and the suggested redeployment at Plataea (so that the Athenians would face the Persian infantry while the Spartans faced the Medizing Greeks – Hdt. 9.46; Plut. *Arist.* 16) are cited. However, the surrender on Sphacteria, while notably unprecedented, cannot be solely attributed to fear. The Athenians engaged the Spartans with missiles at long range rather than fight hand-to-hand. Thucydides (4.33–36) relates how the heavier Spartan hoplites were unable to close with the Athenian light

infantry and were penned in from all sides. Consequently, the Spartans were unable to get into a position where they were actually able to fight and may have taken the unprecedented step of surrendering in the hope that they could fight another day (Aristodemus, one of the few Spartans to survive Thermopylae, was condemned as a coward for his actions but was later given a position in the front rank of the Spartan phalanx at Plataea (Hdt 9.71)). Leuctra was a clear defeat but the Spartans only withdrew so that they could reform. According to Diodorus (15.56.2), the initial withdrawal was conducted with the Spartan army still maintaining their formation rather than fleeing in panic. Many wished to counter-attack but those in command decided against it as the Spartans had already suffered many casualties (particularly among the officers of the front ranks) and the *allies* had no heart left for fighting (Xen. *Hell.* 6.4.15, Paus. 9.13.12; see also: G.L. Cawkwell, 'The Decline of Sparta', *CQ* 33:2 (1983), pp. 396–399). In other words, the Spartans had not been overcome with fear but the decision not to continue fighting was made based upon the condition of the entire army. At Plataea, both Herodotus (9.46) and Plutarch (*Arist.* 16) state that Pausanius wished to re-deploy because the Athenians had had more experience in fighting the Persians (there would have undoubtedly been many veterans from Marathon in the Athenian phalanx). Additionally, by facing the Medizing Greeks, the Spartans would have faced other hoplites that would have been a more formidable opponent to engage; hardly the actions of a group of cowards. Thus the decision to redeploy at Plataea is more a result of astute generalship rather than the consequence of fear. When Sparta was in its decline, the effects of fear appear to have been felt more readily by the Spartans to the point that the city was finally walled (for example see: Polyb. 5.18–23, 11.16; Plut. *Mor.* 239F–240B; Just. *Epit.* 14.5). However, the walling of the city may simply have been an acknowledgement by the Spartans of their own waning power – Sparta had not been invaded for centuries prior to the incursion by Epaminondas in 369BC and so needed no walls *per se* (see: Plut. *Mor.* 194B; Plut. *Ages.* 31; Diod. Sic. 15.65.1). Arrian (*Anab.* 1.9) states that the invasion of Laconia in 369BC 'struck terror' into Sparta and her allies. However, the Spartan army at this time contained many allies and emancipated Helots to bolster the numbers lost at engagements like Leuctra. The fear felt by these hoplites, both in battle and at news of Epaminondas' incursion, would have simply been a natural reaction for less experienced soldiers and mirrors that which would have been experienced by the hoplites of every other city-state.

51. Xen. *Cyr.* 2.3.9–10; this is also the fundamental principle behind much of the physical re-creation and experimental archaeology conducted as part of this study.
52. Photius, *Lexicon*, 180 s.v. Ephebes; Hesychius (2.7447 s.v. 'ἔφηβος') merely calls the *ephebes* 'young men in their prime' (παῖς μικρός ἐν τη ἀκμῇ); see also: Arist. *Ath. Pol.* 42.3–4; Pl. *Leg.* 778D–E; Xen. *Mem.* 3.12.5; Aeschin. 2.167; B.F. Cook, 'Footwork in Ancient Greek Swordsmanship', *MMJ* 24 (1989), p. 59; Pritchett, *Greek State II*, p. 211; Pritchett, *Greek State IV*, pp. 63–64; Anderson, *Military Theory*, p. 134–135.
53. Xen. *Lac.* 2.1–4.7; Plut. *Lyc.* 13, 16–25; interestingly, the training of modern combat troops includes 'conditioning' by subjecting them to the exact same privations in order to make them into more effective soldiers (see: Grossman, *On Killing*, pp. 67–73).
54. D. Grossman and B. Siddle, 'Psychological Effects of Combat' in L.R. Kutz (ed.), *Encyclopedia of Violence, Peace and Conflict* (Orlando, Academic Press, 1999), pp. 142–145; Idzikowski and Baddeley, 'Fear and Dangerous Environments' in Hockey (ed.), *Stress and Fatigue*, pp. 123–141; N. Whatley, 'On the Possibility of Reconstructing Marathon and Other Ancient Battles', *JHS* 94 (1964), pp. 120–121; E.C. Godnig, 'Tunnel Vision: Its Causes and Treatment Strategies', *Journal of Behavioral Optometry* 14:4 (2003), pp. 95–97;

D. Klinger, *Police Responses to Officer-involved Shootings* (Washington, US Department of Justice, 2002), pp. 3–47.

55. Ar. *Pax* 240–241.
56. Grossman and Siddle, 'Psychological Effects of Combat' in Kutz (ed.), *Encyclopedia of Violence*, p. 142; Grossman, *On Killing*, pp. 70–71.
57. Grossman and Siddle, 'Psychological Effects of Combat' in Kutz (ed.), *Encyclopedia of Violence*, p. 142; the debilitating effects of fear also caused only 20 per cent of combatants to actually fire their weapons during the course of a battle. See: Idzikowski and Baddeley, 'Fear and Dangerous Environments' in Hockey (ed.), *Stress and Fatigue*, p. 126; Grossman (*On Killing*, pp. 3, 13–15) attributes this phenomena to man's 'innate resistance to killing their fellow human beings' rather than to fear.
58. For comments on fear in hoplite combat see: H. van Wees, *Greek Warfare – Myths and Realities* (London, Duckworth, 2004), pp. 151, 192–194; Hanson, *Western*, pp. 96–104.
59. Plut. *Cleom.* 8–9; there were numerous other 'militaristic' cults in Sparta. Apart from shrines, temples and monuments to Homeric heroes and popular generals (Paus. 3.12.1– 3.17.5, 3.20.8), and a temple to 'wild' Ares (Paus. 3.19.7), there were temples to other deities who had assumed martial characteristics; such as the 'militarized' cult of the 'Aphrodite of War' (Paus. 3.17.5). Armed Aphrodite was also worshipped in Corinth (Paus. 2.4.7) and a statue of 'Armed Aphrodite' was found at the sanctuary of Asclepius at Epidaurus in the Argolid. A copy of the statue now stands in the site's museum while the original stands in the National Archaeological Museum in Athens.
60. Idzikowski and Baddeley, 'Fear and Dangerous Environments' in Hockey (ed.), *Stress and Fatigue*, p. 125.
61. During participation in the filming of battles scenes for a documentary on the Persian Wars, it was observed that the director had quite a lot of trouble controlling many of the extras once the adrenaline of combat conditions took hold. Many takes that were supposed to be only 'light contact' devolved into 'full contact' combat sessions of several minutes in temperatures over 30°C. Despite this, most extras were not overcome with fatigue; even after two days of semi-continuous combat.
62. P.H. Blyth, *The Effectiveness of Greek Armour against Arrows in the Persian Wars (490–479B.C.): An Interdisciplinary Enquiry* (London, British Library Lending Division (unpublished thesis – University of Reading, 1977)), p. 14.
63. Hdt. 8.11, 8.124, 9.81; Thuc. 4.116; Isoc. 16.29; Pl. *Symp.* 220de; Pl. *Leg.* 943c; Plut. *Alc.* 7; Soph. *Phil.* 1425–1431; Diod. Sic. 11.25.1, 13.34.5, 14.53.4; Polyaenus, *Excerpts*, 14.13.
64. Hdt. 8.124; Xen. *Hell.* 6.4.14; Xen. *Lac.* 4.1–6; Plut. *Lyc.* 25; Plut. *Mor.* 191F.
65. Xen. *Hell.* 3.4.16.
66. Arist. *Eth. Nic.* 3.8.1 suggests that 'those races among which cowards are degraded, and brave men held in honour, appear to be the bravest'. According to modern psychological studies with combat soldiers, a 'fear of death or injury' is more prevalent in soldiers with no combat experience. Once battle has been joined, the greatest fear of a modern soldier is of 'letting his comrades down'. Shalit determined that 'even in the face of a society and culture that tells soldiers that selfish fear of death and injury should be their primary concern, it is instead the fear of not being able to meet the terrible obligations of combat that weighs most heavily on the minds of combat soldiers' (see: Grossman, *On Killing*, pp. 52–53). Both of these fears are evident in the accounts of hoplite warfare. Consequently, hoplites conditioned for the horrors of war, such as the Spartans, would be less likely to succumb to the effects of a fear of death or injury, but would be more concerned with the security of the unit and their performance in battle; thus making them more effective

combatants. This also explains why hoplite phalanxes were regularly deployed with experienced men in the front and rear of the formation (Hom. *Il.* 4.297–300; Xen. *Cyr.* 6.3.25; Xen. *Mem.* 3.1.7–8; Arr. *Tact.* 12). Those at the front would perform better under the physical and psychological stresses of combat conditions, while those in the rear would have held the inexperienced men in the centre of the formation in place until they had become accustomed to the turmoils of battle and were thus ready to take their place at the front of the line.

67. Comparative tests against an abdomen level target, which would favour a low thrust, were not conducted as part of this research.
68. See: Veg. *Mil.* 2.2.

Chapter 9 – The Penetration Power of the Hoplite Spear

1. Hdt. 2.152.
2. Epaminondas: Plut. *Pel.* 4.5; Diod. Sic. 15.87.1; Agesilaus: Plut. *Ages.* 18–19; Plut. *Mor.* 212A, 217E; Xen. *Hell.* 4.3.20; Xen. *Ages.* 2.13, 5.2; Nepos, *Agesilaus* 4.6; Brasidas: Plut. *Mor.* 190B, 219C; Chares: Plut. *Pel.* 2; for other examples of attacks directed at the chest or shield see: Tyrt. 1, 11, 12, 19; Eur. *Phoen.* 1385, 1397–1398; Eur. *Heracl.* 738; Plut. *Dion* 30; Plut. *Tim.* 4.
3. P.H. Blyth, *The Effectiveness of Greek Armour against Arrows in the Persian Wars (490–479B.C.): An Interdisciplinary Enquiry* (London, British Library Lending Division (unpublished thesis – University of Reading, 1977)), pp. 81–84.
4. H. van Wees, 'The Homeric Way of War: The 'Iliad' and the Hoplite Phalanx (II)' *Greece and Rome*, 2nd Series, 41:2 (Oct 1994), p. 136.
5. A.M. Snodgrass, *Arms and Armour of the Greeks* (Baltimore, Johns Hopkins University Press, 1999), p. 56.
6. V.D. Hanson, *The Western Way of War* (Berkeley, University of California Press, 1989), pp. 71, 163; V.D. Hanson, *Wars of the Ancient Greeks* (London, Cassell, 1999), p. 62; F.E. Adcock, *The Greek and Macedonian Art of War* (Berkeley, University of California Press, 1957), p. 4 also suggests that momentum increased the impetus of the charge.
7. T. Everson, *Warfare in Ancient Greece* (Stroud, Sutton Publishing, 2004), pp. 145–147.
8. Blyth, *Effectiveness of Greek Armour*, pp. 15–18.
9. Blyth, *Effectiveness of Greek Armour*, p. 85.
10. R. Gabriel and K. Metz, *From Sumer to Rome – The Military Capabilities of Ancient Armies* (Connecticut, Greenwood Press, 1991), p. xix.
11. Gabriel and Metz, *Sumer to Rome*, p. 59; in the text, results are designated simply as 'overhand' and 'underhand'; which suggests only the low/overhead thrusting actions of current convention. Personal correspondence with Gabriel (14 April 2008) confirmed the presence of a test for a thrown weapon. Whether the figures given for the 'overhand' method are for a thrust or for a thrown weapon is not stated but are unlikely to be for both. The high velocity given for the 'overhand' method suggests that this is for a cast, rather than a thrust, weapon (see following). The tests conducted by Gabriel and Metz also do not consider the underarm or reverse postures as combative techniques with the hoplite spear; no doubt due to the lack of analysis of these techniques by previous scholars.
12. Personal correspondence with Professor Jeffery Schnick of St Anselm College (20 July 2007), who assisted Gabriel and Metz with their experiments and calculations, provided details of how many of the tests were conducted.
13. Gabriel and Metz, *Sumer to Rome*, pp. xviii–xix;.
14. Gabriel and Metz, *Sumer to Rome*, p. 59; Blyth, *Effectiveness of Greek Armour*, pp. 15–18.

15. Interestingly, Blyth (*Effectiveness of Greek Armour*, pp. 15–18) states that a weapon will produce twice as much energy (therefore requiring twice as much velocity) when thrown rather than when it is thrust.

16. Gabriel and Metz, *Sumer to Rome*, p. xix.

17. Gabriel and Metz, *Sumer to Rome*, p. xix;.

18. Adapted from Gabriel and Metz, *Sumer to Rome*, p. 59. Metric conversions are the author's.

19. Gabriel and Metz, *Sumer to Rome*, pp. xix–xx.

20. Gabriel and Metz, *Sumer to Rome*, p. xx; Veg. *Mil.* 12; via personal correspondence (01 June 07 – 06 July 07) Gabriel confirmed that Vegetius' description of a 'killing depth' was the basis for their calculations but concedes that in many parts of the body a wound to a depth of only one inch would mostly be fatal; either immediately or through later infection. Similarly, Blyth (*Effectiveness of Greek Armour* p. 24) suggests that to cause serious damage to the head, a spear would only have to penetrate up to 3cm but would have to penetrate deeper, creating a hole almost the entire width of the average spear blade, to seriously damage the chest. Many of the weapon perforations he identified at Olympia (pp. 81–83) are 4–5cm in length; long enough to have been created by a spearhead penetrating to a depth of up to 8cm or more.

21. Gabriel and Metz, *Sumer to Rome*, p. xx; basically the function is that, if the size of the impacting edge is the same, and it requires a certain amount of energy for one weapon to penetrate to a depth of 2 inches (A) resulting in an opening in the target of a certain size (B), then for a different weapon to penetrate to the same depth but create an opening of a different size (C), that weapon must deliver an amount of energy equal to $(A/B) \times C$.

22. Gabriel and Metz, *Sumer to Rome*, pp. 59–60, 63.

23. Gabriel and Metz, *Sumer to Rome*, pp. xix, 57, 60, 95.

24. Gabriel and Metz, *Sumer to Rome*, p. 63.

25. Gabriel and Metz, *Sumer to Rome*, p. 59.

26. Gabriel and Metz, *Sumer to Rome*, p. 91.

27. Hanson, *Wars*, p. 216.

28. Blyth, *Effectiveness of Greek Armour*, p. 71 tabulates the thickness of different parts of the helmet for nine different examples in the collection of Olympia.

29. A. Williams, *The Knight and the Blast Furnace – A History of the Metallurgy of Armour in the Middle Ages and the Early Modern Period* (Leiden, Brill, 2003), pp. 928–929, 936.

30. The calculation for this is: 113.0 (*energy to pierce 2mm*)/2.9 (*2mm 'energy multiplier'*) × 1.0 (*1mm 'energy multiplier'*) = 39.0.

31. Confirmed through personal correspondence with R. Gabriel, 01 June 07 – 06 July 07.

32. Williams, *The Knight and the Blast Furnace*, pp. 929–930; for example, if the weapon impact connects 'square-on' to the centre of a barrel shaped cuirass, it will hit roughly perpendicular to the surface of the armour. However, the further around to either side the weapon strikes, the more curvature of the plate the thrust would have to overcome.

33. Everson, *Warfare*, pp. 91, 145.

34. Williams, *The Knight and the Blast Furnace*, p. 937.

35. Personal correspondence with R. Gabriel, 01 June 07 – 06 July 07.

36. Other proposed uses for the *sauroter* are as follows: as protection from the elements: Snodgrass, *Arms and Armour*, p. 80, Cartledge, 'Hoplites and Heroes', p. 15; to rest upright: Hom. *Il.* 10.153; Arist. *Poet.* 25.14 see also: J. McK. Camp II, 'A Spear Butt from the Lesbians', *Hesperia*, 47:2 (Apr–Jun 1978), p. 192, Cartledge, 'Hoplites and Heroes', p. 15; for altering the grip: J. Lazenby, 'The Killing Zone' in Hanson (ed.), *Hoplites*, p. 93; as a

counterweight: Snodgrass, *Arms and Armour*, p. 80, Camp, 'Spear Butt', p. 192; van Wees, *Greek Warfare*, p. 48; G.M.A. Richter, 'Greek Bronzes Recently Acquired by the Metropolitan Museum of Art', *AJA* 43:2 (Apr–Jun 1939), p. 196; for leverage: P. Bardunias, 'The Aspis – Surviving Hoplite Battle', *Ancient Warfare*, 1:3 (2007), p. 14; as a weapon: Camp, 'Spear Butt', p. 192; Snodgrass, *Arms and Armour*, pp. 56, 80; V.D. Hanson, 'Hoplite Technology in Phalanx Battle' in Hanson (ed.), *Hoplites*, pp. 71–72; Warry, *Warfare*, p. 35; Hanson, *Western*, pp. 85, 164; S. Mitchell. 'Hoplite Warfare in Ancient Greece' in A.B. Lloyd (ed.), *Battle in Antiquity* (London, Duckworth, 1996), p. 90; Cartledge, 'Hoplites and Heroes', p. 15; Hanson, *Wars*, pp. 51, 53, 58, 62; Goldsworthy, 'Othismos', p. 2; Anderson, *Military Theory*, p. 37; Richter, 'Greek Bronzes', p. 195.

37. Personal correspondence with R. Gabriel, 01 June 07 – 06 July 07.
38. In fact, there is no evidence on the artefacts at Olympia for any impact following the downward trajectory of the overhead strike (for example, see plate 9).
39. Personal correspondence with Alex Scheibner of Talerwin Forge who made the spear used in this study based upon a spearhead and *sauroter* found at Olympia (28 January 2008).
40. Blyth, *Effectiveness of Greek Armour*, p. 226.
41. Blyth, *Effectiveness of Greek Armour*, p. 226-229.
42. Personal correspondence with Alex Scheibner of Talerwin Forge (28 January 2008); see also: Blyth, *Effectiveness of Greek Armour*, p. 226.
43. Blyth, *Effectiveness of Greek Armour*, pp. 79–80, 85.
44. Williams, *The Knight and the Blast Furnace*, pp. 931–932.
45. Blyth, *Effectiveness of Greek Armour*, pp. 78–79.
46. Blyth, *Effectiveness of Greek Armour*, p. 72.
47. Hdt. 7.208–209; Xen. *Lac.* 11.3, 13.8; Plut. *Lyc.* 22; Plut. *Mor.* 189E–F; 228F; Cartledge (*Thermopylae – The Battle that Changed the World* (London, Pan Books, 2007), pp. *xi*, 94) suggests that the reason why the Spartans were tending to their hair at Thermopylae was to prepare for a 'beautiful death' (he later (pp. 129–130) compares the Spartan defence of the pass with the actions of Japanese kamikaze pilots of the Second World War). However, the narrative of Herodotus is unclear as to the full purpose of this attention to the hair. Herodotus says that some of the Spartans were exercising and it is possible that their hair was being groomed in preparation for, or after, exercise. Xerxes, upon questioning the scout who had observed this behaviour in the Spartans, was incredulous to what Herodotus later explains was the Spartans preparing to 'die and deliver death with all of their strength' (i.e. to fight). However, does this means a conscious decision to accept death (as in a suicide mission) or was it just the regular Spartan preparation for battle with the acknowledgement that some of them may die in the engagement? It must be remembered that this behaviour in the Spartans was observed before the first day of fighting had commenced and well before the Greek position was outflanked on day three. At this early stage of the confrontation the Greeks, particularly the Spartans, must have felt that they could hold the pass as that was why the location was chosen. When Xerxes enquired of Demaratus as to the meaning of the Spartans' behaviour, Demaratus replied that the Spartans were preparing for the coming struggle; again without being clear about whether this was a regular Spartan custom or a ritual as part of some suicide mission. Interestingly, the scout did not see the rest of the Greek force, who were positioned behind the Phocian Wall, and, at first appearances, it may have looked like there was only 300 men guarding the pass. As such, Xerxes' incredulity may not have been on account of the Spartans tending their hair but to their very presence in the pass itself as it would have seemed incredible that only 300 men were preparing to 'deliver death' to the mighty Persian host. Cartledge (*Thermopylae*

p. 135) also suggests that the Spartans grew their hair long as a 'visible sign of adult male warrior status' because 'real men grow their hair long'. Matthews (*The Battle of Thermopylae – A Campaign in Context* (Gloucestershire, Spellmount, 2006), p. 75) says that, for the Spartans, long hair was a symbol of them being the 'aristocrats of war'. However, despite any cosmetic or social significance, professional soldiers like the Spartans would have also recognized the value of hair acting as an additional layer of padding beneath their helmets.

48. Blyth, *Effectiveness of Greek Armour*, pp. 72–73.
49. Modern motorcycle helmets work on the same principle.
50. Everson, *Warfare*, pp. 145–147.
51. Hanson, *Western*, pp. 71, 163; Hanson, *Wars*, p. 62.
52. Blyth, *Effectiveness of Greek Armour*, p. 13.
53. Blyth, *Effectiveness of Greek Armour*, p. 14.
54. Blyth, *Effectiveness of Greek Armour*, pp. 14, 156.
55. See Blyth, *Effectiveness of Greek Armour*, pp. 13–14; a medieval knight at a joust, keeping his lance couched in his armpit, would gain not only the mass of his own body and armour behind the impact of the weapon but, due to being firmly fixed on the horse via the saddle and stirrups, the mass and momentum of his steed as well. This explains why medieval heavy cavalry was so effective. Without the use of the stirrup, Greek cavalry would not have received this augmentation. During the invasion of Sparta in 272BC, for example, Pyrrhus of Eprius ran through a Spartan with his lance but was knocked from his horse by the force of the blow at the same time (Plut. *Pyrrh.* 30). This was most likely due to the lack of a supportive saddle and stirrups. An infantry weapon gripped with both hands and held at hip level, such as the Macedonian *sarissa*, could deliver a blow with as much as 300.0fpds (406.7joules) behind it due to the strength of the posture used to wield it.
56. Blyth, *Effectiveness of Greek Armour*, p. 14.
57. For the differences in the number of casualties suffered by both victors and vanquished see: P. Krentz, 'Casualties in Hoplite Battles', *GRBS* 26 (1985), pp. 13–20.

Chapter 10 – The Use of the *Sauroter* as a Weapon

1. J. McK. Camp II, 'A Spear Butt from the Lesbians', *Hesperia* 47:2 (Apr–Jun 1978), p. 192; A.M. Snodgrass, *Arms and Armour of the Greeks* (Baltimore, Johns Hopkins University Press, 1999), pp. 56, 80; V.D. Hanson, *Wars of the Ancient Greeks* (London, Cassell, 1999), p. 51; V.D. Hanson, 'Hoplite Technology in Phalanx Battle' in V.D. Hanson (ed.), *Hoplites – The Classical Greek Battle Experience* (London, Routledge, 2004), pp. 71–72; J. Warry, *Warfare in the Classical World* (Norman, University of Oklahoma Press, 1995), p. 35; V.D. Hanson, *The Western Way of War* (Berkeley, University of California Press, 1989), pp. 85, 164; S. Mitchell. 'Hoplite Warfare in Ancient Greece' in A.B. Lloyd (ed.), *Battle in Antiquity* (London, Duckworth, 1996), p. 90; T. Everson, *Warfare in Ancient Greece* (Stroud, Sutton Publishing, 2004), p. 26; R. Matthews, *The Battle of Thermopylae – A Campaign in Context* (Gloucestershire, Spellmount, 2006), pp. 56, 59.
2. Everson, *Warfare*, p. 62.
3. Hanson, *Western*, p. 85.
4. Mitchell, 'Hoplite Warfare', in Lloyd, *Battle in Antiquity*, p. 90.
5. N. Sekunda, *Greek Hoplite 480–323BC* (Oxford, Osprey Publishing, 2004), p. 16.
6. Diod. Sic. 15.86.2; Sekunda (*Greek Hoplite*, p. 28) and Everson (*Warfare*, p. 126) both state that the sword was the hoplite's secondary weapon.
7. Hdt. 7.224–225.

8. Xen. *Ages.* 2.14.
9. Xen. *Hell.* 6.2.19.
10. Polyb. 6.25.9.
11. Hanson, *Western*, p. 85.
12. See: M.M. Markle III, 'The Macedonian *Sarissa*, Spear and Related Armour', *AJA* 8:3 (Summer 1977), pp. 333–339.
13. Arr. *Anab.* 1.15.6; Plut. *Alex.* 16.
14. Diod. Sic. 17.20.4–5.
15. Xen. *Eq.*, 8.10.
16. In 207BC the Spartan Machanidas was slain, first with a blow delivered with a lance head, and then with a secondary strike delivered with a *sauroter* during a cavalry skirmish (Polyb. 11.18 – καὶ πατάξας τῷ δόρατι καιρίως καὶ προσενεγκὼν τῷ σαυρωτῆρι πληγὴν ἄλλην ἐκ διαλήψεως). However: a) The weapon in question had not broken, which suggests that the secondary strike with the *sauroter* was made as an opportune strike, possibly in a rearward direction as the two horsemen passed each other, rather than resorting to the use of the *sauroter* in the event of the weapon breaking; and b) this can in no way be used as confirmation of the use of the *sauroter* as an offensive weapon, in any capacity, by infantry in the confines of a massed phalanx or even as a regular practice of cavalry.
17. Snodgrass, *Arms and Armour*, pp. 56, 80; Matthews, *Thermopylae*, p. 56.
18. P.H. Blyth, *The Effectiveness of Greek Armour against Arrows in the Persian Wars (490–479B.C.): An Interdisciplinary Enquiry* (London, British Library Lending Division (unpublished thesis – University of Reading, 1977)), pp. 29–31, 81–84.
19. Blyth, *Effectiveness of Greek Armour*, p. 21.
20. Blyth, *Effectiveness of Greek Armour*, p. 28.
21. Blyth, *Effectiveness of Greek Armour*, pp. 29–30.
22. H. Hoffmann and A.E. Raubitschek, *Early Cretan Armourers* (Mainz, P. von Zabern, 1972), pp. 52–53.
23. See: E. Kunze, *Bericht über die Ausgrabungen in Olympia IX* (Berlin, Walter de Gruyter, 1994), p. 90, pl.31.2.
24. Similarly, Bardunias' claim that the *sauroter* was thrust into the ground to allow the the upright spear to be used 'as a staff in steadying a man in the rear ranks and allowing him to add the strength of his right arm in pushing' within the confines of two collided formations (see: P. Bardunias, 'The Aspis – Surviving Hoplite Battle', *Ancient Warfare* 1:3 (2007), p. 14) is also without merit as any *sauroter* that possessed only a small rounded knob or large cross-section could not be thrust into the ground to gain such leverage.
25. Blyth, *Effectiveness of Greek Armour*, p. 178.
26. Hanson, *Western*, pp. 85, 164; see also: Everson, *Warfare*, p. 126; Matthews, *Thermopylae*, p. 56, 58–59.
27. Xen. *Hell.* 4.3.17.
28. Plut. *Ages.* 18.
29. Thuc. 5.70; see also Plut. *Mor.* 210F; Ath. *Deip.* 14.627D, Polyaenus, *Strat.* 1.10.1; Paus. 3.17.5.
30. *Anth. Pal.* 6.123.
31. Xen. *Hell.* 4.3.19; Xen. *Ages.* 2.12–14.
32. Hdt. 9.62.
33. Hdt. 9.62.
34. For safety reasons the shaft used in this test was devoid of either a *sauroter* or a spearhead. While this affected the balance of the shaft, it would have had no bearing on the fracture point of the wood.

35. Blyth, *Effectiveness of Greek Armour*, p. 122e.
36. Hdt. 7.61–80.
37. Diod. Sic. 17.100.7.
38. Hdt. 9.67–70.
39. Eur. *Phoen.* 1396–1399.
40. Hdt. 7.224.
41. Diod. Sic. 15.87.1.
42. Aesch. *Ag.* 65–67.
43. Diod. Sic. 15.86.2; Sherman translates this same sentence as: 'at the first exchange of spears in which most were shattered by the very density of the missiles'. However, as the passage describes the clash of two advancing phalanxes, it is unlikely that there would have been an initial exchange of 'missiles' by the hoplites.
44. Blyth, *Effectiveness of Greek Armour*, pp. 22–22e.
45. Blyth, *Effectiveness of Greek Armour*, pp. 22–22e.
46. H. Baitinger, *Die Angriffswaffen aus Olympia* (Berlin, Walter de Gruyter, 2000), plates 14, 17, 19, 20, 40, 41, 42.
47. Hdt. 9.71.
48. Hdt. 7.104; Plut. *Mor.* 191C; *PA* 7.431; during the eighth century BC, advancing forward of the phalanx for the performance of deeds of personal glory seems to have been a more common practice, even for the Spartans (Paus. 4.8.4, 4.8.7–8). However, at this time phalanx tactics would have still been undergoing their formative processes and may have still involved elements of the Heroic style of combat.
49. P. Siewert, 'The Ephebic Oath in Fifth-Century Athens', *JHS* 97 (1977), pp. 102–103; see also Pl. *Ap.* 28d; Soph. *Ant.* 670.
50. Arist. *Ath. Pol.* 42.3–4; Lycurg. *Leoc.* 76–78, 80–82; Isoc. 8.82; Aeschin. 3.154; see also: P.J. Rhodes and R. Osborne (eds), *Greek Historical Inscriptions 404–323BC* (Oxford, Oxford University Press, 2003), #88 pp. 440–449; C.L. Lawton, *Attic Document Reliefs* (Oxford, Clarendon Press, 1995), p. 155, pl.92; for a commentary on the issuance of arms by the Athenian state see B. Bertosa, 'The Supply of Hoplite Equipment by the Athenian State Down to the Lamian War', *Journal of Military History* 67: 2 (Apr 2003), pp. 361–379.
51. Plut. *Mor.* 191E, 216C, 217E; Plut. *Dion* 58; Plut. *Lyc.* 19.
52. Diod. Sic. 17.20.4–5.
53. Hanson, *Western*, p. 85.
54. P. Cartledge, 'Hoplites and Heroes: Sparta's Contribution to the Technique of Ancient Warfare', *JHS* 97 (1977), p. 15; Hanson, *Wars*, pp. 53, 58, 62; Mitchell, 'Hoplite Warfare', in Lloyd (ed.), *Battle in Antiquity*, p. 90; A.K. Goldsworthy, 'The Othismos, Myths and Heresies: The Nature of Hoplite Battle', *War in History* 4:1 (1997), p. 2; J.K. Anderson, *Military Theory and Practice in the Age of Xenophon* (Berkeley, University of California Press, 1970), p. 37.
55. The image of the hoplite in the other figure mentioned is harder to interpret. The weapon is not held by its correct point of balance, but is gripped up near the head, and the arm is more conducive with the overhead posture. It is also unclear why the rear end of a spear that is apparently unadorned with a *sauroter*, and still had its head intact, would be used to attack an opponent. It may simply be that the image is the result of some kind of error by the artist where the *sauroter* should have been depicted on the upper end of the shaft rather than the head as this would at least place the wielding hand at the weapon's correct point of balance.
56. Plut. *Arist.* 14; Hdt. 9.22.

57. Hesychius (4.2029 s.v 'Στύραξ') states that the term *styrax* relates to either the '*sauroter* of the spear' (σαυρωτηρ τοῦ δόρατος) or 'the spearhead' (καὶ λόγχη). Additionally, his definition of the *sauroter* (4.280 s.v. 'σαυρωτήρ') (τὸ ἔσχατον σιδήριον τοῦ δοράτος) can be read as either 'the lowest iron tool of the spear' or 'the lowest iron weapon of the spear'; so an offensive use of the *sauroter/styrax* cannot be confirmed using either definition. The reference to the *sauroter* being made of iron is indicative of the change of the material from which the *sauroter* was constructed from the late Classical Period onwards.

58. Plut. *Arist.* 14 (trans. B. Perrin, 1968; I. Scott-Kilvert, 1960).

59. Onasander (10.4) uses the term *styrax* to describe a javelin shaft, but his may simply be a reference to the type of wood that it is made from.

60. Hdt. 9.22.

61. Plut. *Arist.* 14; Hdt. 9.22.

62. Hdt. 9.22.

Chapter 11 – Conclusion: The Individual Hoplite

1. Xen. *An.* 6.5.25 (παρήγγελτο δὲ τὰ μὲν δόρατα ἐπὶ τὸν δεξιὸν ὦμον ἔχειν ἕως σηναίνοι τῇ σάλπιγγι· ἔπειτα δὲ εἰς προσβολὴν καθέντας ἔπεσθαι βάδην); Polyaenus, *Strat.* 3.9.8 (χλῖναι τὸ δόρυ).

Chapter 12 – Phalanxes, Shield Walls and Other Formations

1. For examples see: P. Connolly, *Greece and Rome at War* (London, Greenhill Books, 1998), pp. 37–40; T. Everson, *Warfare in Ancient Greece* (Stroud, Sutton Publishing, 2004), pp. 69–71; N. Sekunda, *Greek Hoplite 480–323BC* (Oxford, Osprey Publishing, 2004), pp. 21, 60; J. Warry, *Warfare in the Classical World* (Norman, University of Oklahoma Press, 1995), pp. 34, 46–48; J. Lazenby, 'The Killing Zone' in V.D. Hanson (ed.), *Hoplites – The Classical Greek Battle Experience* (London, Routledge, 2004), pp. 89–90; V.D. Hanson, *The Western Way of War* (Berkeley, University of California Press, 1989), p. 28; H. van Wees, *Greek Warfare – Myths and Realities* (London, Duckworth, 2004), pp. 185–187; R. McDermott, *Modelling Hoplite Battle in SWARM* (New Zealand, Massey University, 2004 (unpublished thesis)), p. 11; W.K. Pritchett, *The Greek State at War – Vol. I* (Berkeley, University of California Press, 1974), p. 134; J.E. Lendon, *Soldiers and Ghosts – A History of Battle in Classical Antiquity* (New Haven, Yale University Press, 2005), pp. 9, 16, 41, 98.

2. Thuc. 5.66–68; Xen. *Lac.* 11.4; Xen. *Hell.* 3.4.16; Ascl. *Tact.* 2.1, 10.21; Arr. *Tact.* 2.5–6, 26.1, 29.1; Ael. Tact. *Tact.* 3–7; Polyb. 18.29–30.

3. Thuc. 5.66–68; Xen. *Lac.* 11.4; Xen. *Hell.* 3.4.16.

4. Xen. *An.* 4.3.26; see also: Ascl. *Tact.* 2.2; Ael. Tact. *Tact.* 5; Arr. *Tact.* 5.4.

5. Thuc. 5.66–68; see also: Xen. *Lac.* 11.4.

6. Xen. *Lac.* 11.4.

7. Marchant, in his translation (Harvard University Press – Loeb Classical Library, 2000) states that the missing word is either ἕνα (one) or δύο (two) but inserts two into the text. Anderson (*Military Theory and Practice in the Age of Xenophon* (Berkeley, University of California Press, 1970), p. 74) uses single file.

8. Connolly, *Greece and Rome*, p. 40; Warry, *Warfare*, p. 34.

9. Xen. *Lac.* 11.4; Xen. *Hell.* 3.5.22; 4.5.7.

10. Connolly, *Greece and Rome*, p. 40.

11. Xen. *Lac.* 11.5; Xen. *Cyr.* 2.3.22; 6.3.25; this would suggest that, if an officer's position was taken by a superior, that officer would then take up a position to the left of the superior

within the front rank of the unit. As such, within a *pentykostys*, the right-hand position would be occupied by the *pentekonter*. Next to him would stand the *enomotarch* of the right hand *enomotia* (as his normal position on the front-right was occupied by the *pentekonter*). Next to the *enomotarch* would be a 'file leader' (πρωτοστάτης) at the head of each remaining file of the unit. If the *pentykostys* was at the front right of a *lochos*, the position of the *pentekonter* would be taken by the *lochagos* and each subordinate officer's position would subsequently be shifted to the left (see figure 20).

12. Connolly, *Greece and Rome*, p. 40.
13. Xen. *Cyr.* 6.3.25; Xen. *Mem.* 3.1.7–8.
14. Hom. *Il.* 4.297–300.
15. Arr. *Tact.* 12.
16. Xen. *Lac.* 13.6.
17. Thuc. 5.68.
18. That is: 4 files × 112 *enomotiai* = 448 men. Agesilaus' army of 377BC is similarly described as being made up of five *morai*, each containing 500 men – see: Diod. Sic. 15.32.1.
19. Arist. *Ath. Pol.* 21.1–22.2,42.1–5, 61.1–3; Hdt. 6.109; Nep. *Milt.* 4.4; Plut. *Mor.* 177C. See also: van Wees, *Greek Warfare*, p. 99; Lendon, *Soldiers and Ghosts*, p. 74; Connolly, *Greece and Rome*, p. 38.
20. *Hell. Oxy.* 16.3–4.
21. For example, Strabo (*Geography* 4.1.5) states that the government of the Greek colony of Massilia was made up of a council of 600 members. Fifteen of these members were set above the others to carry on the immediate business of government. Three more councillors presided above the fifteen. How these offices translated into the structure of the Massiliot army in times of war is unknown. Similarly, according to Diodorus (15.59.1), the Arcadian league had a common council of 10,000 men empowered to decide on issues of war and peace. How the structure of this council would have translated to the command of an Arcadian army is also unknown.
22. Xen. *Cyr.* 2.1.22-25, 2.3.21-22, 3.3.11, 6.3.21, 6.3.31.
23. C. Nadon, 'From Republic to Empire: Political Revolution and the Common Good in Xenophon's Education of Cyrus', *American Political Science Review* 90 (June 1996), p. 364; see also the introduction to W. Miller's translation of the *Cyropaedia Vol. I* (Loeb Classical Library, 1968), pp. viii–x; Anderson, *Military Theory*, pp. 62, 84, 96, 140, 165, 170, 175.
24. Ascl. *Tact.* 2.7–2.10; Arr. *Tact.* 8–10; Ael. Tact. *Tact.* 8; Vegetius (*Mil.* 2.2) states that for both the Greeks and Madedonians a phalanx was a unit of 8,000 men.
25. Xen. *Lac.* 11.6–9; Ascl. *Tact.* 11.1; Arr. *Tact.* 20.3; Ael. Tact. *Tact.* 37.
26. Xen. *Lac.* 11.8.
27. Xen. *Lac.* 11.8; Xen. *An.* 4.3.26; see also: Xen. *Cyr.* 2.3.21; Anderson, *Military Theory*, p. 100.
28. Xen. *Hell.* 6.4.12; Connolly, *Greece and Rome*, p. 43; Sekunda, *Greek Hoplite*, p. 60; N. Sekunda, *The Spartan Army* (Oxford, Osprey Publishing, 1998), p. 15.
29. Sekunda, *Greek Hoplite*, p. 60.
30. Connolly, *Greece and Rome*, p. 43; Sekunda, *Greek Hoplite*, p. 60, Plate G.
31. Sekunda, *Greek Hoplite*, p. 60, plate G.
32. Sekunda, *Greek Hoplite*, p. 60, plate G.
33. Ascl. *Tact.* 10.1, 10.17–20; Arr. *Tact.* 25; Ael. Tact. *Tact.* 32.
34. Warry, *Warfare*, pp. 34, 46.
35. Anderson (*Military Theory* p. 101) states that the process of 'doubling' cannot be attributed to hoplite formations as it is not attested in the literary sources. However, he fails to

consider that some units of the later Macedonians may have been equipped as hoplites. Thus Macedonian hoplites may have used the 'doubling' process but it seems that the Classical hoplite did not.

36. Xen. *An.* 1.8.19–20.
37. Plut. *Ages.* 18; Polyaenus, *Strat.* 2.1.19; Frontin. *Str.* 2.6.6.
38. Ascl. *Tact.* 2.1; see also: Ael. Tact. *Tact.* 4; Arr. *Tact.* 5.9.
39. Ascl. *Tact.* 2.9.
40. Connolly, *Greece and Rome*, p. 37.
41. Connolly, *Greece and Rome*, p. 40; see also: H. Droysen, *Heerwesen und Kreigführung der Griechen* (Elibron Classics, 2006), p. 44; Matthews (*The Battle of Thermopylae – A Campaign in Context* (Gloucestershire, Spellmount, 2006), p. 70) says that the 'standard' Spartan phalanx was eight deep but does not elaborate on whether he considers this practice to be unchanging.
42. Connolly, *Greece and Rome*, p. 39; see also: Thuc. 5.68.
43. Warry (*Warfare*, p. 34, 46) uses both an eight- and twelve-deep phalanx in his models but does not distinguish if he felt one was more common than the other.
44. Sekunda, *Greek Hoplite*, p. 60; Xen. *Hell.* 6.4.12.
45. Sekunda, *Greek Hoplite*, p. 9; Xen. *Hell.*, 4.2.18; both Asclepiodotus (2.1) and Arrian (*Tact.* 5,9) state that sixteen deep was the standard of the *sarissa*-wielding Macedonian phalanx. Matthews (*Thermopylae* p. 57) suggests that sixteen-deep formations were only used with hoplites who were inexperienced or had low morale (see following).
46. Pritchett, *The Greek State I*, p. 137; see also: Warry, *Warfare*, pp. 34, 46, van Wees, *Greek Warfare*, p. 185; Hanson, *Western*, p. 28.
47. Pritchett, *Greek State I*, pp. 137–139.
48. M.M. Markle III, 'Use of the *Sarissa* by Philip and Alexander of Macedon', *AJA* 82:4 (Autumn 1978), pp. 483–497; M.M. Markle III, 'A Shield Monument from Veria and the Chronology of Macedonian Shield Types', *Hesperia* 68:2 (April–June 1999), pp. 219–254.
49. Pritchett, *Greek State I*, p. 138.
50. Pritchett, *Greek State I*, p. 138.
51. Pritchett, *Greek State I*, p. 137.
52. Pritchett, *Greek State I*, p. 137.
53. G. Cawkwell, 'The Decline of Sparta', *CQ* 33 (1983), p. 387.
54. Pritchett, *Greek State I*, p. 139; Xen. *Hell.* 6.5.19.
55. Pritchett, *Greek State I*, p. 139; Thuc. 4.93. However, if a deployment to '9 or 10 shields deep' was the result of a single eight-man file with one or two officers attached, a deployment of three files should contain as many as six additional officers; giving a depth of thirty rather than twenty-five. Pritchett does not elaborate on what he thinks has happened to these 'missing' officers.
56. Pritchett, *Greek State I*, p. 139; Xen. *Hell.* 6.4.12; W.W. How, ('Arms, Tactics and Strategy in the Persian War', *JHS* 43:2 (1923), pp. 121–122) suggests that references to formations twenty-five and fifty deep are actually references to formations twenty-four and forty-eight deep respectively with the figures rounded up. How suggests this so that the figures for these formations will comform to what he percieves to be a 'standard multiple' of the phalanx of four or eight.
57. Thuc. 5.68; Lendon, *Soldiers and Ghosts*, p. 91.
58. Xen. *Lac.* 11.6; *Hell.* 3.2.16; *An.* 5.2.8; Thuc. 4.93, 5.68; see also Warry, *Warfare*, pp 36, 63; Anderson, *Military Theory*, p. 73.
59. Hdt. 7.204.

60. Delium: Thuc. 4.93; Leuctra: Xen. *Hell.* 6.4.12; Diod. Sic. 15.55.2–15.56.1; Plut. *Pel.* 23.
61. Xen. *Hell.* 3.2.16.
62. Xen. *Hell.* 4.2.13.
63. Xen. *An.* 7.1.22-23.
64. Arr. *Tact.* 11; See also Pritchett, *Greek State I*, p. 141.
65. Diod. Sic. 17.26.4.
66. G. Cawkwell, *Philip of Macedon* (London, Faber and Faber, 1978), pp. 154–155; F.E. Adcock, *The Greek and Macedonian Art of War* (Berkeley, University of California Press, 1957), p. 4; Lazenby, 'Killing Zone' in Hanson (ed.), *Hoplites*, p. 98; A.K. Goldsworthy, 'The Othismos, Myths and Heresies: The Nature of Hoplite Battle', *War in History* 4:1 (1997), pp. 7, 23; How, 'Arms, Tactics and Strategy', p. 121; R.D. Luginbill, 'Othismos: The Importance of the Mass-Shove in Hoplite Warfare', *Phoenix* 48:1 (Spring 1994), pp. 59–60; Pritchett (*The Greek State at War – Vol. IV* (Berkeley, University of California Press, 1985), p. 59) suggests the purpose of rear ranks was to provide reserves, to help in pushing the phalanx forward and to stop any retreat.
67. P. Krentz, 'The Nature of Hoplite Battle', *Classical Antiquity* 16 (1985), p. 59.
68. Xen. *Hell.* 4.2.13.
69. Pritchett, *Greek State I*, p. 141; Goldsworthy, 'Othismos', pp. 13, 23.
70. Arr. *Tact.* 11.
71. Xen. *Cyr.* 6.3.22.
72. Xen. *Cyr.* 6.3.23.
73. Diod. Sic. 10.34.13.
74. Front. *Strat.* 2.3.12; Polyaenus, *Strat.* 2.10.4; for other examples see: Pritchett, *Greek State IV*, pp. 74–76.
75. Hdt. 6.111.
76. Thuc. 4.94.
77. Paus. 4.11.2.
78. Paus. 8.10.6.
79. Polyaenus, *Strat.* 4.6.20; see also Prtichett, *Greek State I*, pp. 141–142.
80. Polyaenus, *Strat.* 2.10.4; Polyaenus, *Excerpts*, 17.2; Front. *Strat.* 2.3.12.
81. Arr. *Tact.* 18.4.
82. Xen. *An.* 1.2.15; Prtichett, *Greek State I*, p. 141.
83. Thuc. 5.66-68.
84. Xenophon's description of the arrangement for the parade in Asia Minor (*An.* 1.2.15) reads: 'He ordered the Greeks to deploy in the manner they were accustomed to for battle, with each commander seeing to the order of his men. So they deployed by "fours" ' (ἐκέλευσε δὲ τοὺς Ἕλληνας ὡς νόμος αὐτοῖς εἰς μάχην οὕτω ταχθῆναι καὶ στῆναι, συντάξαι δ᾿ ἕκαστον τοὺς ἑαυτοῦ. ἐτάξθησαν οὖν ἐπὶ τεττάρων). From the language of the text it is difficult to ascertain whether the figure of 'fours' is a reference to the depth of the line or the number of files in each *enomotia*. Brownson, in his translation of the text, interprets the lines as being 'four deep'. How ('Arms, Tactics and Strategy', p. 121) similarly states that Xenophon is referring to a formation with 'a depth of four'. However, the word for 'deep' (βαθύς), or one of its variants, is not found in the passage itself. Warner, in his translation, more closely follows the written Greek by simply saying that the hoplites 'stood on parade in "fours" '. See also: Xen. *Lac.* 11.4; for the presence of Spartans among the mercenaries see: Diod. Sic. 14.19.5, 14.21.1.
85. Herodotus 9.10, 9.28, 9.61.

86. Hdt. 9.29; Matthews (*Thermopylae* p. 73) suggests that the Helots were only ever armed as *psiloi* or light infantry.
87. Hunt ('Helots at the Battle of Plataea' *Historia* 46 (1997), pp. 129–144) agrees with the Helots forming the rear seven ranks of the Spartan phalanx at Plataea but does not attribute the single rank of Spartan hoplites with Isocrates' description of the deployment for Dipea. Cornelius ('Pausanius', *Historia* 22 (1973), p. 503) suggests that the Spartan hoplites at Plataea formed the first two ranks of the phalanx. However, if each of the seven Helots allocated to each Spartan were arranged behind the members of the first two ranks, this would give the Spartan phalanx an unlikely, and by Spartan standards unprecedented, depth of sixteen men. Matthews (*Thermopylae*, p. 73) suggests that armed Helots were only ever used to guard camps and mountian passes.
88. Isoc. *Paneg.* 90; Isoc. 6.100; Diod. Sic. 11.4.2; Flower ('Simonides, Ephorus and Herodotus on the Battle of Thermopylae', *CQ* 48:2 (1998), p. 368) suggests that the 700 extra Lacedaemonians were *perioeci* that Herodotus failed to mention because they did not remain to fight on day three of the battle. Cartledge (*Thermopylae – The Battle that Changed the World* (London, Pan Books, 2007), p. 66) similarly suggests that the 'Helots' were actually troops drawn from the *perioeci*. However, as such a large contingent of Helots was present at the later battle of Plataea, the presence of a contingent of armed Helots at Thermopylae cannot be ruled out. Similarly, Helots were used to replace the fallen in hoplite contingents during the Messenian War (Paus. 4.16.6); Helots were used to break the blockade on Sphacteria in 425BC (Thuc. 4.26); Brasidas enrolled non-Spartiates (possibly including Helots) into service in 424BC (Thuc. 4.80); and Helots served in Sicily in 413BC (Thuc. 6.19). Similarly, Athens equipped 1,500 *thetes* as hoplites, initially to serve as ship-board marines, for the Sicilian campaign (Thuc. 6.43). When Sparta was invaded in 369BC, Helots were offered emancipation if they fought in the defence of the city; thousands volunteered (Xen. *Hel.* 6.5.28; Diod. Sic. 15.65.6). On the general absence of casualty figures for troops other than hoplites in the ancient narratives see: C. Rubincam, 'Casualty Figures in the Battle Descriptions of Thucydides', *Transactions of the American Philological Society (1974–)* 121 (1991), pp. 187–188; see also: N. Barley, 'Thucydides on Lightly Armed Troops', *Ancient Warfare* 2:1 (2008), pp. 14–17. Contrary to the statements of Diodorus and Isocrates, Pausanias (10.20.2) states that there was 'not more than three hundred' Spartans at Thermopylae (Λακεδαιμόνιοι οἱ μετὰ Λεωνίδου τριακοσίων οὐ πλείονες) and may not be including armed Helots or *perioeci* in this figure.
89. Paus. 4.11.1.
90. Xen. *Hell.* 2.4.11.
91. Thuc. 7.79.
92. Xen. *Hell.* 6.5.19; Alexander followed a similar method of deployment at the battle of Issus (see: Arr. *Anab.* 2.8–9). However, Alexander lengthened his line by bringing up rearward units into the widening areas on the flanks as he advanced until the whole army was in line (see the redeployment of two *lochoi* on p. 173) rather than 'doubling' the files of his phalanx. As such, the rear half of the deep Spartan 'files' at Mantinea, may have been other units (even as small as another *enomotia*) following in column behind each other as the terrain allowed. The 'halving' of these files that Xenophon describes may have simply been a redeployment into their standard position as the terrain opened.
93. Ascl. *Tact.* 4.1. see also pages 53–57.
94. Plut. *Pel.* 23.
95. Plut. *Pel.* 15.
96. Adcock, *Art of War*, p. 3.

97. How, 'Arms, Tactics and Strategy, p. 121.
98. Krentz, 'Nature of Hoplite Battle', pp. 50, 54; in P. Krentz, 'Continuing the Othismos on Othismos', *AHB* 8:2 (1994), pp. 46–47, intervals of three and six metres per man are given in a likely typographical error; see also Pritchett, *Greek State I*, p. 144; Anderson, *Military Theory*, p. 101; Sekunda, *Greek Hoplite*, p. 60.
99. Matthews, *Thermopylae*, p. 57.
100. W.R. Connor, 'Early Greek Land Warfare as Symbolic Expression', *Past and Present* 119 (May 1988), p. 12.
101. Warry, *Warfare*, pp. 34, 46.
102. Warry, *Warfare*, pp. 34, 46.
103. See: G.L. Cawkwell, 'Orthodoxy and Hoplites', *CQ* 39:2 (1989), p. 283; Pritchett, *Greek State I*, p. 154.
104. Hom. *Il.* 13.133–134.
105. Tyrt. 11.
106. Tyrt. 11 (italics are the emphasis of the author).
107. Van Wees, *Greek Warfare*, p. 173; E.L. Wheeler, 'The General as Hoplite' in Hanson (ed.), *Hoplites*, p. 130; Lendon, *Soldiers and Ghosts*, p. 43; A.M. Snodgrass, *Early Greek Armour and Weapons* (Edinburgh, Edinburgh University Press, 1964), p. 182; H. van Wees, 'The Development of the Hoplite Phalanx – Iconography and Reality in the Seventh Century' in H. van Wees (ed.) *War and Violence in Ancient Greece* (London, Duckworth, 2000), p. 151; the use of a spearman's shield to protect a more vulnerable second warrior who is using a missile weapon can be seen in the account of Teucer and Ajax in the *Iliad* (8.266–272). Teucer, using a bow, was protected behind Ajax's shield. Ajax would move his shield slightly to provide Teucer with a better field of fire. Teucer would then discharge his weapon at a target before returning to the safety behind the shield 'like a child running to its mother'.
108. Tyrt. 11.
109. Paus. 4.7.4–5, 4.8.12. At Ithome (Paus. 4.11.5) the light troops were positioned behind the Messenian line. During the fighting, these light troops moved onto the wings and attacked the Laconian formation in the flank, which eventually caused them to rout.
110. This conclusion is supported by Pritchett, *Greek State IV*, p. 40.
111. For a clear image of the figure see: P. Ducrey, *Warfare in Ancient Greece* (New York, Schocken Books, 1986), p. 121.
112. Diod. Sic. 16.3.2.
113. It also correlates with the conclusion that at least some elements of the Macedonian infantry used the larger hoplite *aspis* and spear.
114. Pausanias' detailed description of the engagements of the First Messenian War also describes the deployment of the heavy infantry in contingents in extended line (and in some instances 'deep and dense'), reminiscent of a Spartan *lochos* or *mora* in close-order, which also indicates the use of massed formations of hoplites at this time. See: Paus. 4.7.7–8, 4.11.1.
115. Thuc. 5.70.
116. Diod. Sic. 11.8.1.
117. Pliny the Elder (*HN* 7.202) claims that military formations were 'invented' by Palamedes during the Trojan War. Homer's *Iliad*, written in the eighth century BC, does contain a reference to a shield wall (13.133–134). However, dating any event based upon the works of Homer is somewhat problematic and will be dependant upon a) what year the Trojan war is dated to; b) when the particular piece of the Homeric narrative may have been composed

before it was written down in the eighth century BC; and c) whether the piece of narrative was based upon ancient techniques or was a more contemporary interpolation. As such, if Homer's narrative is taken as based upon actual Mycenaean-era battle tactics (as per Pliny), then the shield wall can be said to have been used for at least a millennia (c.1,200–200BC). If, on the other hand, Homer's narrative is taken as an eighth century interpolation used to flesh out the story and make it more comprehensible to a contemporary audience, then the shield wall can be said to have been in use for more than five centuries (c.750–200BC).

118. A.D. Fraser, 'Myth of the Phalanx-scrimmage', *Classical Weekly* 36 (Oct 1942–Jun 1943), p. 15; Pritchett, *Greek State IV*, p. 72.

119. J.M. Hurwitt, 'Reading the Chigi Vase', *Hesperia* 71:1 (Jan–Mar 2002), p. 14; J.K. Anderson, 'Hoplite Weapons and Offensive Arms' in Hanson (ed.), *Hoplites*, pp. 18–19; Cawkwell, 'Orthodoxy and Hoplites', p. 385; A.M. Snodgrass, *Arms and Armour of the Greeks* (Baltimore, Johns Hopkins University Press, 1999), p. 58; Snodgrass, *Early Greek*, p. 138; H.L. Lorimer, 'The Hoplite Phalanx with Special Reference to the Poems of Archilochus and Tyrtaeus', *ABSA* 42 (1947), pp. 81–95; M. Trundle, 'The Spartan Revolution: Hoplite Warfare in the late Archaic Period', *War and Society* 19:10 (Oct 2001), p. 11; J. Salmon, 'Political Hoplites?' *JHS* 97 (1977), pp. 87–88; Everson, *Warfare*, p. 71; Pritchett, *Greek State IV*, p. 72.

120. Sekunda, *Greek Hoplite*, p. 26.

121. Thuc. 5.70.

122. Matthews (*Thermopylae* p. 58) says that the shields overlap because the diameter of the shield is around 90cm and the interval of the phalanx is 80cm per man. This would result in a very small amout of overlapping shield to lock them in place; thus resulting in a very weak 'shield wall'.

123. Cawkwell, 'Orthodoxy and Hoplites', p. 385.

124. Ael. Tact. *Tact.* 11.

125. Pritchett, *Greek State I*, p. 154.

126. Lorimer, 'Hoplite Phalanx', p. 108.

127. Arist. *Ath.* Pol. 42.3–4.

128. Sake of the line: Diod. Sic. 12.62.5; Plut. *Pel.* 1; Plut. *Mor.* 220A; trophies: Paus. 1.15.4, 2.21.4, 5.26.11, 6.19.4, 6.19.13; Ar. *Eq.* 850–860; Diod. Sic. 12.70.5; Anac. 158; the 'national' blazon of the Spartans: Paus. 4.28.5; Photius, *Lexicon*, n.v 'lambda'; see also T.L. Shear 'The Campaign of 1936', *Hesperia #6 – The American Excavations in the Athenian Agora: 12th Report* 6:3 (1937), pp. 346–348.

129. V.D. Hanson, 'Hoplite Technology in Phalanx Battle' in Hanson (ed.), *Hoplites*, pp. 69–70.

130. Pritchett, *Greek State I*, p. 144.

131. Snodgrass, *Arms and Armour*, p. 103.

132. Plut. *Pel.* 23; Diod. Sic. 11.8.1.

133. Xen. *Hell.* 7.5.22–23; for a discussion and counter-discussion of the possible configuration of the wedge formation, particularly those that may have been employed by Epaminondas, see: A.M. Devine, 'EMBOLON: A Study in Tactical Terminology', *Phoenix* 37:3 (1983), pp. 201–217; J. Buckler, 'Epameinondas and the Embolon', *Phoenix* 39:2 (1985), pp. 134–143.

134. Plut. *Pel.* 23; Diod. Sic. 15.55.2; see also: Polyaenus, *Strat.* 1.35.1.

135. Plut. *Dion*, 45; Epaminondas is said to have used a similar deployment and tactic so that he could attack the city of Sparta on multiple fronts in 363BC. See: Diod. Sic. 15.83.4. It is uncertain whether these hoplites retained this formation to engage, or redeployed into another formation, such as the 'block', before they closed with the enemy.

136. Xen. *An.* 7.8.18; Brownson (*Anabasis Vol. II* (Cambridge, Harvard University Press – Loeb Classical Library, 1922) interprets the word κύκλος as 'curved line' rather than 'circle'. However, Xenophon states that the hoplite's shields were facing in all directions, so the passage is unlikely to be a reference to a 'curved line'.
137. Thuc. 4.125, 6.67, 7.78; Xen. *Hell.* 4.3.4; Xen. *An.* 3.2.36, 7.8.16; Polyaenus, *Strat.* 2.1.25; Diod. Sic. 14.80.1.
138. Ascl. *Tact.* 11.6; Arr. *Tactics*, 29.6–8; Ael. Tact. *Tact.* 37.
139. At a battle near Mantinea, the Arcadians are said to have purposefully feigned a retreat by the centre of their line, thus creating a concave crescent, in order to draw in the opposing Spartans so that they could be attacked by the encircling wings (Paus. 8.10.7).
140. Ascl. *Tact.* 11.1–5; Arr. *Tact.* 20–29; Ael. Tact. *Tact.* 34–49; see also Polyaenus, *Strat.* 1.49.2.
141. Arist. *Pol.* 1297B; Tyrt. 11; Hdt. 9.67–68, 9.71; Thuc. 3.108, 5.10; Plut. *Mor.* 214B, 217C; Diod. Sic. 5.34.5, 14.104.4, 15.36.2; Pl. *Ap.* 28D; Xen. *Hell.* 4.5.15, 7.5.24; Plut. *Ages.* 30; Plut. *Tim.* 27; Hom. *Il.* 17.364–365; Polyaenus, *Strat.* 1.43.2, 2.3.3, 2.10.2, 3.9.49, 3.9.54, 3.11.6, 5.44.4; Polyaenus, *Excerpts*, 18.2, 31.1, 31.3; Leonis Imp. *Strat.* 12.2, 14.3.
142. Hdt. 7.104.
143. McDermott, *Modelling Hoplite Battle*, p. 62.
144. Arr. *Tact.* 11; F.W. Walbank (*A Historical Commentary on Polybius Vol. I* (Oxford, Clarendon Press, 1967), pp. 286–287) echoes this statement by stating that the phalanx (in this case the *sarissa*-wielding Macedonian phalanx) could not operate with intervals of only 1½ feet per man.
145. Sekunda, *Greek Hoplite*, p. 60.
146. P. Krentz, 'Fighting by the Rules: The Invention of the Hoplite *Agon*', *Hesperia*, 71:1 (Jan–Mar 2002), p. 34.
147. Thuc. 5.70, see also: Plut. *Mor.* 210F; Ath. *Deip.* 14.627D, Polyaenus, *Strat.* 1.10.1; Pausanias (3.17.5) additionally states that the Spartans 'marched into battle, not to the sound of trumpets, but to the sounds of flutes and the striking of lyres and *kitharae.* ' The 'Paeans of Sophocles' (3) also detail marching to the sounds of pipes.
148. Polyaenus, *Excerpts*, 18.1.
149. Ath. *Deip.* 14.627D.
150. Xen. *An.* 6.1.11.
151. Plut. *Ages.* 2; Plut. *Dion*, 30; Plut. *Mor*, 222, 234E, 241F; Hdt. 7.229; Xen. *Hell.* 6.1.5; Tyrt. 10.
152. See: Aesch. *Pers.* 393; Thuc. 1.50, 4.43, 4.96, 5.70; 7.44, 7.83; Xen. *Hell.* 2.4.17, 4.2.19; Xen. *An.* 1.8.17, 1.10.20, 4.3.19–31, 4.8.16, 5.2.14, 6.5.27.
153. Plut. *Lyc.* 21–22; Plut. *Mor.* 238A–B; see also Polyaenus, *Strat.* 1.10.1; Aeneas Tacticus (27.3–4) suggests that, when an army is beset by panic, each man should call out the word 'Paean' right along the line to help settle them and help them stand their ground.
154. See Pritchett, *Greek State I*, p. 107.
155. Xen. *Hell.* 4.2.20.
156. Thuc. 1.63.
157. Thuc. 5.10.
158. Theoc. 24.125.
159. Polyaenus, *Strat.* 1.10.1; Polyaenus, *Excerpts*, 18.1.
160. Ascl. *Tact.* 4.1.
161. Hdt. 6.112.
162. Delium: Thuc. 4.96; Coronea: Xen. *Hell.* 4.3.19; Sicily: Thuc. 6.97–100.

163. Hdt. 6.112.
164. W. Donlan and J. Thompson, 'The Charge at Marathon: Herodotus 6.112', *Classical Journal* 71:4 (Apr–May 1976), pp. 339–341; see also: H, Delbrück, *History of the Art of War Vol. I* (Westport, Greenwood Press, 1975), pp. 82–88; Xenophon states that the Persian bow, while superior to that of the Cretan archer, could be outdistanced by the Rhodian slinger (Xen. *An.* 3.3.7, 3.3.16, 3.4.17). This suggests an effective range of around 200m for the Persian bow. If this is the case, it is uncertain why the Greeks at Marathon would have seen the need to charge for 'not less than a mile'.
165. At Cunaxa, the hoplites began their advance slowly to the chant of a *paean* when the two sides were 600–800m apart. After advancing some distance they then began to charge, not at full speed, but at a moderate pace in order to preserve their formation (Xen. *An.* 1.8.17–20).
166. Hdt. 6.112; Thuc. 4.128, 6.97–98, 6.100; Xen. *Hell.* 2.4.5, 3.4.23, 6.5.31, 7.2.22; Xen. *An.* 1.2.17, 1.8.17–18, 4.3.27–31.
167. Donlan and Thompson, 'The Charge at Marathon', p. 341.
168. Hanson, *Western*, pp. 71, 163; V.D. Hanson, *Wars of the Ancient Greeks* (London, Cassell, 1999), p. 62; see also: Adcock, *Art of War*, p. 4.
169. Thuc. 5.70.
170. Paus. 4.8.1.
171. Xen. *An.* 1.8.18.
172. Polyaenus *Strat.* 7.8.1.
173. Paus. 4.8.11.
174. Thuc. 6.70.
175. Xen. *Hell.* 7.4.30.
176. Hdt. 6.113.
177. Xen. *An.* 1.8.19.
178. Hdt. 9.67–69.
179. Xen. *Hell.* 4.3.19.
180. Xen. *Lac.* 2.
181. Thuc. 5.71.
182. McDermott, *Modelling Hoplite Battle*, p. 62.
183. Thucydides (5.71) blames both men seeking extra protection behind the shield of the man to the right and the man on the far right of the formation trying to protect his 'unprotected side' for the right shift of the phalanx. This shows that there was more than one element at work in the creation of this phenomenon.
184. McDermott, *Modelling Hoplite Battle*, p. 64.
185. Xen. *Hell.* 4.2.18–19.
186. Lendon, *Soldiers and Ghosts*, p. 69.

Chapter 13 – The Hoplite Battle: Contact, *Othismos*, Breakthrough and Rout

1. See: V.D. Hanson, *The Western Way of War* (Berkeley, University of California Press, 1989), pp. 28, 154–159, 174–175; V.D. Hanson, 'Hoplite Technology in Phalanx Battle' in V.D. Hanson (ed.), *Hoplites – The Classical Greek Battle Experience* (London, Routledge, 2004), p. 69; N. Sekunda, *Greek Hoplite 480–323BC* (Oxford, Osprey Publishing, 2004), p. 27; J.K. Anderson, 'Hoplite Weapons and Offensive Arms' in Hanson (ed.), *Hoplites*, p. 15; S. Mitchell. 'Hoplite Warfare in Ancient Greece' in A.B. Lloyd (ed.), *Battle in Antiquity* (London, Duckworth, 1996), p. 90; A.J. Holladay, 'Hoplites and Heresies', *JHS*

102 (1982), pp. 94–97; P. Connolly, *Greece and Rome at War* (London, Greenhill Books, 1998), p. 48; P. Cartledge, 'Hoplites and Heroes: Sparta's Contribution to the Technique of Ancient Warfare', *JHS* 97 (1977), p. 16; R.D. Luginbill, 'Othismos: The Importance of the Mass-Shove in Hoplite Warfare', *Phoenix* 48:1 (Spring 1994), p. 56; F.E. Adcock, *The Greek and Macedonian Art of War* (Berkeley, University of California Press, 1957), p. 4; J.K. Anderson, *Military Theory and Practice in the Age of Xenophon* (Berkeley, University of California Press, 1970), p. 176; J.E. Lendon, *Soldiers and Ghosts – A History of Battle in Classical Antiquity* (New Haven, Yale University Press, 2005), pp. 41, 71; J.M. Hurwitt, 'Reading the Chigi Vase', *Hesperia* 71:1 (Jan–Mar 2002), p. 14; see also P. Krentz, 'The Nature of Hoplite Battle', *Classical Antiquity* 16 (1985), p. 50; A.D. Fraser, 'Myth of the Phalanx-scrimmage', *Classical Weekly* 36 (Oct 1942–Jun 1943), p. 15; J. Lazenby, 'The Killing Zone' in Hanson (ed.), *Hoplites*, p. 97; W.R. Connor, 'Early Greek Land Warfare as Symbolic Expression', *Past and Present* 119 (May 1988), p. 14; W.W. How, 'Arms, Tactics and Strategy in the Persian War', *JHS* 43:2 (1923), pp. 121–122; R. Matthews, *The Battle of Thermopylae – A Campaign in Context* (Gloucestershire, Spellmount, 2006), p. 59.

2. See: Fraser, 'Phalanx-scrimmage', p. 15; Krentz, 'Nature of Hoplite Battle', pp. 50–59; H. van Wees, *Greek Warfare – Myths and Realities* (London, Duckworth, 2004), pp. 52, 185; A.K. Goldsworthy, 'The Othismos, Myths and Heresies: The Nature of Hoplite Battle', *War in History* 4:1 (1997), pp. 1–25; H. van Wees, 'Development of the Hoplite Phalanx' in H. van Wees (ed.), *War and Violence in Ancient Greece* (London, Duckworth, 2000), pp. 131–132.

3. See: J. Warry, *Warfare in the Classical World* (Norman, University of Oklahoma Press, 1995), pp. 37, 63; Krentz, 'Nature of Hoplite Battle', p. 50; G.L. Cawkwell, 'Orthodoxy and Hoplites', *CQ* 39:2 (1989), p. 376; G. Cawkwell, *Philip of Macedon* (London, Faber and Faber, 1978), p. 152.

4. Fraser, 'Phalanx-scrimmage', p. 15; the cited passages are: Thuc. 4.96, 6.70; Polyaenus, *Strat.* 2.3.4;.

5. Goldsworthy, 'Othismos', p. 2.

6. Fraser, ('Phalanx-scrimmage' p. 16) also offers a third interpretation: a description of confusion in the phalanx. However, there are no clear literary uses of the term to describe confusion other than as the result of battle.

7. Hom. *Il.* 13.133–134 (ἀσπὶς ἄρ' ἀσπίδ' ἔρειδε); Tyrt. 11 (ἀσπίδος ἀσπίδ' ἐρείσας); Xen. *Hell.* 7.4.22 (συντεταγμένοι).

8. Hanson, *Western*, p. 155 interprets Tyrtaeus' (11) description of men in ranks standing 'crest beside crest' (ἐν δὲ λόθον τε λόφῳ) as 'crest against crest' citing it as evidence of a collision. However, as the formation being described is not yet engaged, it is more likely to be the description of men standing side-by-side in a close-order phalanx rather than of a collision.

9. Thuc. 4.96.

10. Xen. *Hell.* 4.3.19.

11. Ar. *Pax* 1274.

12. Tyrt. 1.

13. The audience of both Aristophanes and Tyrtaeus would have expected a certain level of realism in their works, particularly in any references to battles or fighting techniques, of which much of their audience would have had first-hand experience. Consequently, the descriptions in both Tyrtaeus and Aristophanes are likely to be accurate descriptions of one element of hoplite combat.

14. Tyrt. 12 (δηίων ὀρέγοιτ᾽ ἐγγύθεν ἱστάμενος); Tearless Battle: Xen. *Hell*. 7.1.31 (εἰς δόρυ); Coronea: Plut. *Ages*. 18 (οὐκ ἔσχεν ὠθισμὸν) see also Xen. *Hell*. 4.3.17 (εἰς δόρυ ἀφικόμενοι ἔτρεψαν τὸ καθ᾽ αὐτούς); Sicily: Plut. *Tim*. 27–28 (διεκρούοντο τὸν δορατισμόν); passages that describe the spears of the first two ranks 'reaching the enemy' (Arr. *Tact*. 12.3; Ael. Tact. *Tact*. 13.3) must also be references to battles conducted at spear length (see pages 83–87). As such, these confrontations would not have involved a collision of the lines nor a subsequent pushing of 'shield against shield'.
15. Hom. *Il*. 13.130.
16. Aesch. *Ag*. 437.
17. Thuc. 4.96.
18. Xen. *Hell*. 4.3.19.
19. Xen. *An*. 5.2.17–18.
20. Plut. *Ages*. 18; Xen. *Hell*. 4.3.17.
21. Under ὠθέω in the Liddell and Scott *Greek-English Lexicon* the following definitions are given: thrust, push (mostly of human force), throw down, push (with weapons), force out, stuff into, force open, non-human forces (e.g. streams or wind), force back in battle, banish, push matters on (i.e. hurry them along), push off from land, throw (as a horse throws a rider), press forward, to fall violently, a crowd, a throng, to jostle. Under ὠθισμός specifically are the following definitions: thrusting, pushing (as of shield against shield), jostling, struggling (as of combatants in a melee). Under ὠθισμός in the *Oxford Classical Greek Dictionary* the following definitions are given: thrusting, pushing, struggling, battle.
22. Hdt. 9.62–63.
23. Thuc. 4.35.
24. Thuc. 5.72.
25. Thuc. 6.70.
26. Xen. *Hell*. 2.4.34.
27. Polyaenus, *Strat*. 2.3.10.
28. Cartledge, 'Hoplites and Heroes', p. 16; Anderson, *Military Theory*, p. 76; Luginbill, 'Othismos', pp. 51, 54–55; see also W.K. Pritchett, *The Greek State at War – Vol. IV* (Berkeley, University of California Press, 1985), pp. 65–66.
29. Hdt. 9.62–63.
30. Hdt. 9.62.
31. Cartledge, 'Hoplites and Heroes', p. 16.
32. Luginbill, 'Othismos', p. 55; Hdt. 9.62.
33. Thuc. 4.32–35.
34. Hdt. 7.225.
35. Xen. *Hell*. 7.4.31.
36. Hom. *Il*. 5.691.
37. Hom. *Il*. 8.295.
38. Hom. *Il*. 8.336.
39. Hom. *Il*. 12.420.
40. Hom. *Il*. 16.655.
41. Hom. *Il*. 13.193.
42. Hdt. 9.25.
43. Xen. *Hell*. 7.1.29.
44. Hdt. 8.78, 9.26.
45. Thuc. 7.36, 7.52, 7.63, 8.104.
46. Xen. *Mem*. 3.1.8.

47. Hanson, *Western*, p. 29.
48. Polyb. 18.30.4; Ascl. *Tact.* 5.5; Arr. *Tact.* 16.–13–14; Anderson, *Military Theory*, p. 176; Luginbill, 'Othismos', p. 52.
49. Xen. *Cyr.* 6.3.25; Xen. *Mem.* 3.1.7–8.
50. Arr. *Tact.* 12; see also Ascl. *Tact.* 3.6 who similarly states that the file closers should 'surpass all others in state of mind' but makes no mention of strength being a requirement as well.
51. Nep. *Epam.* 2.4–5.
52. Hanson, *Western*, 28.
53. Thuc. 5.70; Pausanias (4.8.1), basing his account on the works of Rianos of Bene and Myron of Priene (both third century BC), similarly states that during the second major battle of the First Messenian War (eighth century BC), the Messenians 'charged' recklessly against a Spartan formation moving slowly so as to preserve its ranks. Consequently, the Messenian formation is most likely to have been in an intermediate-order at best while the Spartans are likely to have been in a close-order. As such, many of the characteristics outlined here for the clash at Mantinea can also be attributed to this engagement as well. For comments on the validity of the works of Rianos and Myron see: *FGrHist* 106 T1–15; *FGrHist* 265 T1–3, F1–60; L. Pearson, 'The Pseudo-History of Messenia and its Authors', *Historia* 11:3 (1962), pp. 397–426.
54. Hanson, *Western*, p. 154; Tyrt. 11; see also Goldsworthy, 'Othismos', p. 18.
55. Xen. *Hell.* 4.3.17, Xen. *Ages.* 2.10–11.
56. Xen. *Hell.* 4.3.17; Xen. *Ages.* 2.10–11.
57. Anderson, *Military Theory*, p. 78.
58. Plut. *Ages.* 18 see also: Hanson, *Western*, p. 155, 157.
59. In other words, the members of the close-order formation are separated by 45cm front-to-back and side-to-side, and their spears are separated by around 45–50cm. The members of the intermediate-order formation, on the other hand, once its ranks compress, are separated by around 45cm front-to-back but still by the intermediate interval of 90cm side-to-side. As such, their weapons are also separated by 90cm, even though the compression of the lines places the members of the second rank at a distance from the enemy where they can now reach them with their spears.
60. See: Xen. *An.* 5.2.8.
61. Thuc. 1.63.
62. Plut. *Ages.* 26; Plut. *Pel.* 15; Plut. *Mor.* 189F, 213F, 217E; see also Polyaenus, *Strat.* 1.16.2, Polyaenus, *Excerpts*, 13.1.
63. Xen. *Lac.* 1.1; Plut. *Pel.* 17; Plut. *Mor.* 238F; Lys. 16–17; Thuc 1.10, 4.40; Pausanius (4.29.3) states that the Messenians were afraid to confront the Spartans due to the extensive military training that the Spartans had received. Similarly, Diodorus Siculus (15.23.4) states that the constant attention paid by the Spartans to skill at arms aroused fear in their opponents.
64. Nep. *Chabrias* 1.2 (*reliquam phalangem loco vetuit cedere obnixoque genu scuto, proiecta hastam impetum excipere hostium docuit. Id nouum Agesilaus contuens progredi non est ausus suosque iam ... revocauit*).
65. Diod. Sic. 15.33.4; Nepos, *Chabrias*, 1; see also: A.P. Burnett and C.N. Edmonson, 'The Chabrias Monument in the Athenian Agora', *Hesperia* 30:1 (Jan–Mar 1961), pp. 89–90; J.K. Anderson, 'The Statue of Chabrias', *AJA* 67:4 (Oct. 1963), p. 411; J. Buckler, 'A Second Look at the Monument of Chabrias', *Hesperia* 41:4 (Oct–Dec 1972), pp. 466–474.
66. Diod. Sic. 15.32.5.

67. Polyaenus, *Strat.* 2.1.2.
68. Polyaenus, *Strat.* 2.1.2.
69. Xen. *An.* 1.5.13.
70. Anderson, 'Statue of Chabrias', pp. 412–413; Anderson, 'Hoplite Weapons' in Hanson, *Hoplites*, p. 30.
71. Buckler, 'Monument of Chabrias', p. 471.
72. Anderson, 'Statue of Chabrias', p. 412.
73. Polyb. 18.30.
74. Polyaenus, *Strat.* 2.3.12; Anderson, 'Statue of Chabrias', p. 413.
75. Lendon, *Soldiers and Ghosts*, p. 85.
76. Anderson, *Military Theory*, pp. 89, 134.
77. Xen. *An.* 1.2.17, 6.5.25.
78. The *Oxford Latin Dictionary* has only these two 'military definitions' listed under the word *incurro*.
79. Doidorus (15.32.6) states that Chabrias' men executed their orders at a single word of command and that Agesilaus, marvelling at the discipline of his opponent, thought it was unwise to fight uphill in a hand-to-hand contest and subsequently withdrew. Xenophon (*Hellenica* 2.4.16) outlines the advantages of holding the high ground: '[the enemy], advancing uphill, cannot throw their spears and javelins over the heads of their front rank, while we, with spears, javelins and stones all thrown downhill, cannot miss our target and are certain to inflict casualties ... they will be cowering beneath their shields trying to keep out of the way [of the missiles] so that you [i.e. the men on the high ground] will be able to strike at them where-ever you like, as though they were blind men, and fall upon them and cut them down'. Thus the terrain was also a consideration in the Spartan decision not to engage. It is possible that the 'contempt' that Chabris' men were demonstrating was a well disciplined diregard for the fear that the Spartans normally caused in opposing forces and a clearly visible intention to hold superior ground.
80. Hanson, *Western*, p. 158; see also: Anderson 'Hoplite Weapons' in Hanson, *Hoplites*, p. 15; Lendon, *Soldiers and Ghosts*, p. 71.
81. P. Bardunias, 'The Aspis – Surviving Hoplite Battle' *Ancient Warfare* 1:3 (2007), p. 13.
82. Pritchett, *Greek State IV*, p. 66; Xen. *Cyr.* 7.1.33.
83. J.F. Dickie, 'Crowd Disasters' in R.A. Smith and J.F. Dickie (eds.), *Engineering for Crowd Safety* (Elsevier, Amsterdam, 1993), pp. 93–94; J.J. Fruin, 'The Causes and Prevention of Crowd Disasters' in Smith and Dickie (eds.), *Engineering for Crowd Safety*, pp. 99–104; J.D. Sime, 'Crowd Psychology and Engineering: Designing for People or Ballbearings? in Smith and Dickie (eds.), *Engineering for Crowd Safety*, p. 121; C.E. Nicholson and B. Roebuck, 'The Investigation of the Hillsborough Disaster by the Health and Safety Executive' in Smith and Dickie (eds.), *Engineering for Crowd Safety*, p. 147; P.H. Blyth, *The Effectiveness of Greek Armour against Arrows in the Persian Wars (490–479B.C.): An Interdisciplinary Enquiry* (London, British Library Lending Division (unpublished thesis – University of Reading, 1977)), p. 10.
84. Xen. *Ages.* 2.14.
85. Plutarch (*Pel.* 4), for example, states how Pelopidas could have suffocated under a pile of corpses and Xenophon (*Hell.* 4.4.11) describes how hoplites were crushed and suffocated against the walls of Corinth. Other passages refer to hoplites being trampled underfoot during a rout (Thuc. 5.72, 7.84) but there are no references to crushing or suffocating deaths among the front ranks of an open field engagement during the actual fighting.
86. Luginbill, 'Othismos', p. 54.

87. Cawkwell, *Philip of Macedon*, pp. 151–152; Krentz, 'Nature of Hoplite Battle', pp. 58–59; Fraser, 'Phalanx-scrimmage', p. 15.
88. In his *Bellum Gallicum* Caesar describes how, in an engagement against the Nervii in 57BC, the Roman legionnaires were packed so densely together that they were unable to use their swords properly until they had regained some semblance of their lines (2.25). If the crowding of Caesar's legionnaires prevented the effective use of the small Roman *gladius*, the lengthy hoplite spear would have been even more unwieldy and ineffective under the similar conditions of the style of hoplite warfare that is proposed by adherents of the 'literal model'.
89. Soph. *Ant.* 670.
90. Mitchell 'Hoplite Warfare' in Lloyd (ed.), *Battle in Antiquity*, p. 90; Goldsworthy, 'Othismos', p. 6; Thermopylae: Hdt. 7.224; Coronea: Xen. *Ages.* 2.14; Mantinea: Diod. Sic. 15.86.2.
91. H.L. Lorimer, 'The Hoplite Phalanx with Special Reference to the Poems of Archilochus and Tyrtaeus', *ABSA* 42 (1947), p. 107.
92. T. Everson, *Warfare in Ancient Greece* (Stroud, Sutton Publishing, 2004), p. 140; A.M. Snodgrass, *Arms and Armour of the Greeks* (Baltimore, Johns Hopkins University Press, 1999), p. 90; Sekunda, *Greek Hoplite*, p. 58; Connolly, *Greece and Rome*, p. 58; Anderson, *Military Theory*, p. 21.
93. Xen. *Hell.* 4.4.12; see also Xen. *An.* 6.5.6; Diod. Sic. 15.55.4; Plut. *Pel.* 4; Thuc. 4.38.
94. Hanson, *Western*, p. 156.
95. R. McDermott, *Modelling Hoplite Battle in SWARM* (New Zealand, Massey University, 2004 (unpublished thesis)), p. 57; see also Goldsworthy, 'Othismos', p. 10.
96. Thuc. 4.96.
97. Arist. *Pol.* 1303b13; see also Goldsworthy, 'Othismos', pp. 7–10.
98. Plut. *Mor.* 214C; see also: Plut. *Pel.* 23; Xen. *Hell.* 6.4.13; Diod. Sic. 15.55.3.
99. Polyaenus, *Strat.* 1.10.1; Diodrus (15.55.3) makes no mention of the Spartans being out of order but places the Spartans in a crescent-shaped formation.
100. Due to the Greek charge conducted at the onset, and the shorter weapons held in the overhead posture by the Persians (which would have presented a lesser obstacle to physically closing with an opponent than a long hoplite spear held in the underarm position), the opening clash at the battle of Marathon (490BC) is also most likely to have involved a physical collision of the two formations (although this is not a hoplite vs hoplite encounter).
101. J. Keegan, *The Face of Battle* (London, Penguin Books, 1983), p. 71.
102. Hanson, *Western*, 156, 159; in 1895 Lebon offered a similar theory of crowd dynamics in which rational thought was replaced with the primitive. However, this model has recently been reviewed and dismissed as many of the properties forwarded by Lebon are not evident in modern observations of crowd behaviour. See: Sime, 'Crowd Psychology and Engineering' in Smith and Dickie (eds.), *Engineering for Crowd Safety*, p. 122–129).
103. Xen. *Hell.* 4.2.20.
104. Plut. *Ages.* 18; Xen. *Hell.* 4.3.19; Xen. *Ages.* 2.12.
105. Hom. *Il.* 13.193.
106. Plut. *Aem.* 19.
107. Hanson, *Western*, p. 156; Mitchell, 'Hoplite Warfare' in Lloyd (ed.), *Battle in Antiquity*, p. 96; Cartledge, 'Heroes and Hoplites', p. 16; Anderson, *Military Theory*, pp. 71, 175; Hanson, 'Hoplite Battle' in van Wees (ed.), *War and Violence*, p. 203.
108. Delium: Thuc. 4.96; Coronea: Xen. *Hell.* 4.3.19-20; Leuctra: Xen. *Hell.* 6.4.12–14; similarly, during the First Messenian War, a charge by Messenian hoplites failed to break a

Spartan close-order phalanx (Paus. 4.8.1–3), nor did a Messenian charge break an Acharnian phalanx during the Second Messenian War (Paus. 4.25.7).

109. Hanson, *Western*, 28–29, 154–159; Sekunda, *Greek Hoplite*, p. 27; Anderson, 'Hoplite Weapons' in Hanson, *Hoplites*, p. 15; Hanson, 'Hoplite Technology' in Hanson, *Hoplites*, p. 69; Connolly, *Greece and Rome*, p. 48; Anderson, *Military Theory*, p. 176; Mitchell, 'Hoplite Warfare' in Lloyd (ed.), *Battle in Antiquity*, p. 96; Cartledge, 'Hoplites and Heroes', p. 16; Holladay, 'Hoplites and Heresies', pp. 94–97; Luginbill, 'Othismos', pp. 51–56.

110. Thuc. 4.96.

111. Cawkwell, 'Orthodoxy and Hoplites', pp. 376–377.

112. Pritchett, *Greek State IV*, p. 73; see also Goldsworthy, 'Othismos', p. 21.

113. Although, as previously noted, due to the varied way in which the collision of two loose order formations would occur, some men would already be fighting 'at spear length' rather than pressed up against the shield of their opponent. Such men would have no need to separate to a greater distance. This further indicates the unlikelihood of the push of the 'literal model' occurring right across the line (or at every encounter) as it seems improbable that men already engaged 'at spear length' would give up this kind of position, and raise their spears, only to move forward and push against the man in front of them with their shields.

114. Plut. *Pel.* 7; Plut. *Mor.* 639F; Polyaenus, *Strat.* 2.3.6; Lucian, *Anach.* 24–34, Nepos (*Epam.* 2.4–5) states that Epaminondas' training in wrestling was only enough so that he could grab an opponent, suggesting a somewhat limited use in battle, while he devoted most of his energies to training with weapons, which suggests the common mode of hoplite fighting.

115. Plut. *Mor.* 639F; P. Krentz, 'Continuing the Othismos on Othismos', *AHB* 8:2 (1994), pp. 48–49.

116. Xen. *Ages.* 2.14.

117. Diod. Sic. 15.21.2.

118. This separation of the lines and renewal of the fighting is absent from Xenophon's account of the battle. See: Xen. *Hell.* 5.2.37–43.

119. Paus. 8.10.7.

120. Hdt. 7.211; while not a 'hoplite vs hoplite' battle, Thermopylae did involve two opposing sides engaged in close contact with spears or other short reach weapons.

121. Caesar encountered just such a thing during his encounter with the Belgae in 58BC (*B. Gall.* 2.27): 'the enemy, even in their desperate predicament, showed such courage that when their front ranks had fallen those immediately behind stood on their prone bodies to fight and, when these too fell and the bodies were piled high, the survivors still kept casting javelins as though from the top of a mound'.

122. Matthews (*Thermopylae* pp. 71–72, 79–81, 171–172) suggests that the feigned retreats conducted by the Spartans at Thermopylae were made while the front of the phalanx was abutted hard up against the Persian line and that the process was done in stages, with the rear ranks pulling back first, until only the front few ranks remained engaged. Some of the members of these front ranks then about faced to withdraw while others simply walked backwards, in order to give the impression of the line breaking, before reforming and counter-attacking. However, it seems unlikely that the Spartans would have feigned a retreat in a manner that left only their front ranks to hold the Persian line, exposed the backs of some of their front-line fighters to the enemy once they began to withdraw, and posed possible problems with reforming quickly (i.e. some hoplites walking backwards while others ran etc.). It is more likely that the feigned retreats were conducted *en masse*

during a momentary lull in the fighting as the Persians tried to cross the growing piles of their own dead. For the way in which Laconian formations 'counter-marched' see: Ascl. *Tact.* 10.14; Arr. *Tact.* 24.

123. Xen. *Hell.* 6.4.13; Diod. Sic. 15.55.3–15.56.4.
124. Xen. *Hell.* 6.4.13.
125. Xen. *Hell.* 6.4.13.
126. Xen. *Hell.* 5.4.33.
127. Polyaenus, *Strat.* 2.3.2. See also Polyaenus, *Excerpts*, 14.4; Leonis Imp. *Strat.* 11.8.
128. Luginbill, 'Othismos', p. 56.
129. According to Diodorus (15.56.2), Epaminondas gave many exhortaions at Leuctra; as most likely would any other commander, officer or hoplite in any battle.
130. Polyaenus, *Strat.* 3.9.27; Polyaenus, *Excerpts*, 14.12.
131. Xen. *Ages.* 2.12 see also: Xen. *Hell.* 4.3.19; Xen. *Cyr.* 7.1.38.
132. Goldsworthy, 'Othismos', p. 19.
133. Plut. *Ages.* 18; Diod. Sic. 14.84.2.
134. Xen. *Ages.* 2.14.
135. Plut. *Ages.* 18; Polyaenus, *Strat.* 2.1.19.
136. Polyaenus, *Excerpts*, 32.3.
137. Paus. 4.8.1.
138. Paus. 4.8.3.
139. Paus. 4.8.4.
140. Paus. 4.8.6.
141. Paus. 4.8.7.
142. Paus. 4.8.8.
143. Paus. 4.8.9–10.
144. Warry, *Warfare*, p. 37; Cawkwell, *Philip*, p. 152; J. Kromayer and G. Veith, *Heerwesen und Kriegführung der Griechen und Römer* (Munchen, 1928), pp. 84–85.
145. Plut. *Tim.* 28.
146. It is possible that some men in the front ranks may have tried to flee prior to the rear ranks of a phalanx breaking. However, in doing so, any hoplite who was trying to flee would have dangerously exposed his back to an enemy that was no more than a 'spear length' away, and his way rearward would have been hampered by those in the ranks behind him who would have been trying to maintain the pressure of the attack. It is more likely that, once the front ranks were engaged, they would have had no choice but to continue to fight until somehow relieved, withdrawn due to injury or simply slain in the combat. This explains why the front ranks of hoplite formations were made up of experienced veterans and officers and why kings and commanders generally led from the front.
147. Krentz, 'Continuing the Othismos, p. 45.
148. Hanson, *Western*, p. 156; V.D. Hanson, *Wars of the Ancient Greeks* (London, Cassell, 1999), pp. 128–129; Cartledge, 'Hoplites and Heroes', p. 16; Mitchell, 'Hoplite Warfare' in Lloyd (ed.), *Battle in Antiquity*, p. 96; Holladay, 'Hoplites and Heresies', p. 97; Luginbill, 'Othismos', p. 60; Anderson, *Military Theory*, p. 71; Sekunda (*Greek Hoplite* p. 24) states that this modern perception is incorrect.
149. Anderson, *Military Theory*, p. 176.
150. Goldsworthy, 'Othismos', p. 24.
151. As Asclepiodotus (4.1) points out, the men of the phalanx are not holding on to each other but are separated from each other (ἀπ' ἀλλήλων) by the interval of the formation in which they are in 'on all sides' (πανταχόθεν). See also: Goldsworthy, 'Othismos', p. 3.

152. Thuc. 4.93–96; Xen. *Hell.* 6.4.12-13.

153. Polyaenus, *Strat.* 2.3.15; Xen. *Hell.* 6.4.12.

154. Xen. *Hell.* 6.4.13–14.

155. Diod. Sic. 10.34.10; 11.73.3; Thermopylae: Hdt. 8.24; Polyaenus, *Strat.* 7.15.5; Diod. Sic. 11.7.3; Cunaxa: Xen. *An.* 1.8.17–29; Diod. Sic. 14.23.4, 14.24.3–6.

156. Anderson, *Military Theory*, p. 176; Bardunias, 'The Aspis', p. 13.

157. Thuc. 3.107–108.

158. Xen. *Hell.* 4.2.13.

159. Thuc. 4.93–94.

160. Luginbill, 'Othismos', p. 61.

161. McDermott, *Modelling Hoplite Battle*, p. 62.

162. Luginbill, 'Othismos', p. 59.

163. This mind-set is reflected in the statement made by a Spartan mother who, when handing a shield to her son who was preparing to depart for battle, is reported to have advised him to return 'either with this or on this' (Plut. *Mor.* 241F). In other words, victory or death were the only acceptable options available to a Spartan warrior in battle. Surrender was not a consideration.

164. See Paus. 4.8.6.

165. During the struggle to liberate Syracuse (357BC), those in the rear ranks stepped forward in order to cover those who had fallen in the fronk ranks with their shields (Diod. Sic. 16.12.4) and to no doubt fill the gap created by the fallen and continue the fight.

166. Thuc. 6.67.

167. Xen. *Hell.* 4.2.18.

168. Goldsworthy, 'Othismos', p. 14; Krentz, 'Continuing the Othismos', p. 46.

169. See Anderson, *Military Theory*, p. 160.

170. The figures given in the ancient sources vary greatly. See: Xen. *Hell.* 6.4.9; Plut. *Pel.* 20; Polyaenus, *Strat.* 2.3.8–12; Diod. Sic. 15.52.1–2, 15.53.3; Frontin. *Str.* 4.2.6; see also: Anderson, *Military Theory*, pp. 197–198.

171. Diodorus, for example, states that the intention of the deep Theban formation at Leuctra was to fight to the death (15.55.2), suggesting that the Thebans were prepared to accept considerable casualties in order to obtain victory. This number of casualties could have only been sustained by the use of a deep formation, otherwise the integrity of the phalanx would have become compromised very quickly.

172. Polyaenus, *Strat.* 2.3.8, 2.3.12; Frontin. *Str.* 4.2.6; and Diod. Sic. 15.52.5 all provide varying figures for the two sides. For an analysis of the size of the forces involved in the battle see Anderson, *Military Theory*, pp. 197–198.

173. Anderson, *Military Theory*, pp. 217–220 claims that the Sacred Band was positioned behind the Theban phalanx in an 'ambush' position. However, Plutarch (*Pel.* 18–19, 23) clearly states that the Sacred Band had been positioned in 'the place of danger' (i.e. the front) of the Theban formation since the battle of Tegyra in 375BC and led the attack against the Spartans at Leuctra. Nepos (*Pelopidas* 4.2) also states that the Sacred Band was the first to break the Spartan phalanx and so had to be at the front of the Theban formation. Diodorus states that Pelopidas put his bravest men on one wing with the intention of fighting to the death (15.55.2). Diodorus also states that Pelopidas led the Sacred Band on this wing 'with which he first charged the Spartans' (15.81.2).

174. Plut. *Pel.* 23; Xen. *Hell.* 6.4.12; Polyaenus, *Strat.* 2.3.15; Polyaenus, *Excerpts*, 14.7.

175. Xen. *Lac.* 13.6; Cartledge (*Thermopylae – The Battle that Changed the World* p. 128) incorrectly states that Spartan kings were positioned in the centre of the Spartan line.

294   *A Storm of Spears*

176. Goldsworthy, 'Othismos', p. 8; see also Polyb. 18.31.2–7.
177. Anderson (*Military Theory*, p. 190) equates the Spartan movement at Leuctra with their flanking moves at Nemea and Lechaeum, stating that the best way to overcome a deep phalanx is to attack its flanks.
178. Plut. *Pel.* 23; Paus. 9.13.12; see also: Polyaenus, *Strat.* 1.35.1; Polybius 12.25F calls Leuctra a 'very simple affair' (τοῖς Λεύκτροις κίνδυνος ἁπλοῦς) as only part of the opposing forces were engaged.
179. Xen. *Hell.* 6.4.15; Paus. 9.13.4; Plut. *Mor.* 193B. Diodorus (15.55.2) states that the Boeotian right wing was refused in an oblique line and had instructions to slowly withdraw from the fighting thus drawing the Spartan left wing forward.
180. For the presence of the Boeotian cavalry see: Xen. *Hell.* 6.4.13; Kromayer and Veith, in their topographical reconstruction of the battle and the deployment of the various contingents involved (Map 28 – *Leuktra 371 v. Chr. Schlachtkarte*) show the Theban infantry striking the Spartan line between the first and second *morai* while their left flank is protected by their cavalry. See: Kromayer, J. and Veith, G., *Schlachten-Atlas zur Antiken Kreigsgeschichte* (revised by R. Gabriel (ed.) and re-released as *The Battle Atlas of Ancient Military History* (Ontario, Canadian Defence Academy Press, 2008), p. 32. Cary suggests that the novel tactics used at Leuctra for which Epaminondas became famous were not the deployment of a deep phalanx nor the arrangement of an oblique line (both of which had been used in the past, particularly by the Thebans) but was the co-ordinated use of infantry and cavalry; an innovation that later became the trademark tactic of the Macedonians. See M. Cary, 'Thebes' in J.B. Bury, S.A. Cook and F.E. Adcock (eds), *The Cambridge Ancient History Vol. 6 – Macedon 401–301BC* (London, Cambridge University Press, 1933), p. 82; Tudela calls the cavalry 'the hoplite's second shield' and states that one of the defensive roles of a contingent of cavalry was to protect the flanks (particularly the left) of an advancing hoplite phalanx – see: F. Tudela, 'The Hoplite's Second Shield – Defensive Roles of Greek Cavalry', *Ancient Warfare* 2:4 (2008), pp. 36, 38; see also: I.G. Spence, *The Cavalry of Classical Greece* (Oxford, Clarendon Press, 1993), pp. 151–162.
181. Xenophon (*Hell.* 6.4.12) states that each Spartan *enomotia* was drawn up in three files of twelve. Thus the four units of each *lochos* would possess a frontage of twelve men, and the four *lochoi* of the *mora* would create a frontage of forty-eight men.
182. Vegetius (*Mil.* 3.20) states that this is the main benefit of attacking in a deep narrow formation (shaped like a capital letter 'I') as the enemy cannot outflank the formation due to its depth. Vegetius further states that of all the ways in which an encounter could be fought (for example, with oblique lines, with wedges or simply front on), attacking with a deep narrow formation is the most superior.
183. Matthews, *Thermopylae*, p. 71.
184. Plutarch (*Pel.* 23) says that the Spartans were trying to outflank the Thebans position before the lines met at Leuctra and that this was why the Spartans were not in their regular close-order formation. Regardless of the reason why the Spartans were not in their regular formation, the Thebans may have charged to exploit this opportunity and to deny the Spartans enough time to reform.
185. Plut. *Pel.* 18–19, 23; Diod. Sic. 15.55.3; Nep. *Pelopidas*, 4.2.
186. Xen. *Hell.* 6.4.13.
187. Xen. *Hell.* 6.4.14; see also Diod. Sic. 15.55.4–15.56.4.
188. Xen. *Hell.* 2.4.34.
189. Hdt. 6.113, 9.67–69; Thuc. 4.43–44, 4.134, 5.10, 5.74; *Hell. Oxy.* 7.1; Xen. *Hell.* 3.5.23, 4.2.22, 4.3.19–21, 6.4.15, 7.4.25, 7.5.27; Plut. *Nic.* 6; Diod. Sic. 13.51.7; Polyaenus, *Strat.*

2.32.1; for a more detailed coverage and examples see W.K. Pritchett, *The Greek State at War – Vol. II* (Berkeley, University of California Press, 1974), pp. 246–276; W.K. Pritchett, *The Greek State at War – Vol. III* (Berkeley, University of California Press, 1979), pp. 240–296; Pritchett, *Greek State IV*, pp. 68–71, 246–249.

Chapter 14 – Conclusion: The Nature of Hoplite Combat

1. N. Whatley, 'On the Possibility of Reconstructing Marathon and Other Ancient Battles', *JHS* 94 (1964), p. 130.
2. Coronea: Xen. *Hell*. 4.3.17; Xen. *Ages*. 2.10–11; Plut. *Ages*. 18; Tearless Battle: Xen. *Hell*. 7.1.29; Sicily: Plut. *Tim*. 27–28.
3. Delium: Thuc. 4.93–96; Leuctra: Xen. *Hell*. 6.4.13; Plut. *Mor*. 214C; Plut. *Pel*. 23; Coronea: Xen. *Hell*. 4.3.19; Xen. *Ages*. 2.12.
4. G.L. Cawkwell, 'The Decline of Sparta', *CQ* 33:2 (1983), p. 399.
5. Cavalry: Xen. *Eq*. 9.4; Xen. *Hell*. 3.4.15; Xen. *Ages*. 2.5; Diod. Sic. 15.32.1; Plut. *Mor*. 187B; archers: Xen. *Hell*. 4.2.5, 4.7.6; Xen. *An*. 1.2.9, 4.2.28; Plut. *Mor*. 187B; peltasts: Paus. 4.11.5; Xen. *Hell*. 4.2.5, 5.4.14, 5.4.39–45, 7.4.22, 7.5.10; Polyaenus, *Strat*. 3.9.2, 3.10.9; Plut. *Mor*. 187B.
6. Sphacteria: Thuc. 4.32–35; Lechaeum: Xen. *Hell*. 4.5.11–18.
7. Xen. *Hell*. 3.4.21–24.
8. Thuc. 1.60, 7.27; Xen. *Hell*. 3.1.23, 5.2.21, 6.1.5–6, 6.2.6, 6.4.9; Xen. *Eq. mag*. 9.3–4; Xen. *Lac*. 12.3; Xen. *An*. 5.6.15; *Hell. Oxy*. 21.2; Arist. *Eth. Nic*. 3.8.7–9; Nep. *Chabrias* 1.1–4.3; Nep. *Iphicrates* 1.1–3.4; Nep. *Datames* 8.2; Polyaenus *Strat*. 2.16, 7.14.3–4, 7.16.1, 7.20.1; Polyaenus *Excerpts* 17.1, 19.2–3, 44.1; Dem. 4.21; 4.43–46; Isoc. 4.146, 5.120–123, 7.9; Pl. *Leg*. 630B; Front. *Strat*. 2.3.13; see also: P. Ducrey, *Warfare in Ancient Greece* (New York, Schocken Books, 1986), pp. 119–127; S. Yalichev, *Mercenaries of the Ancient World* (London, Constable, 1997), pp. 100–150; H.W. Parke, *Greek Mercenary Soldiers – from the Earliest Times to the Battle of Ipsus* (Oxford, Clarendon Press, 1933), pp. 14–105; M. Trundle, *Greek Mercenaries from the Late Archaic Period to Alexander* (New York, Routledge, 2004).

Bibliography

Ancient Texts and Translations

Aelian, *Tactics* (trans. J. Bingham), (London, Eliot's Court Press, 1616).

Aelian, *Historical Miscellany* (trans. N.G. Wilson), (Cambridge, Harvard University Press – Loeb Classical Library, 1997).

Aeneas Tacticus/Asclepiodotus/Onasander (trans. Illinois Greek Club), (Cambridge, Harvard University Press – Loeb Classical Library, 2001).

Aeschines, *Speeches* (trans. C.D. Adams), (Cambridge, Harvard University Press – Loeb Classical Library, 1958).

Aeschylus, *Vol. I – Suppliant Maidens/Persians/Prometheus/Seven Against Thebes* (trans. H.W. Smyth), (Cambridge, Harvard University Press – Loeb Classical Library, 1973).

Aeschylus, *Vol. II – Agamemnon/Libation-bearers/Eumenides/Fragments* (trans. H.W. Smyth), (Cambridge, Harvard University Press – Loeb Classical Library, 1971).

Antiphon, *The Speeches* (trans. K.J. Maidment), (Cambridge, Harvard University Press, 1968).

Apollonius of Rhodes, *Argonautica* (trans. R.C. Seaton), (Cambridge, Harvard University Press – Loeb Classical Library, 1967).

Aristophanes, *Vol. I – The Acharnians/The Clouds/The Knights/The Wasps* (trans. B.B. Rogers), (Cambridge, Harvard University Press – Loeb Classical Library, 1967).

Aristophanes, *Vol. II – The Peace/The Birds/The Frogs* (trans. B.B. Rogers), (Cambridge, Harvard University Press – Loeb Classical Library, 1979).

Aristotle, *Vol. XIX – The Nicomachean Ethics* (trans. H. Rackham), Cambridge, Harvard University Press – Loeb Classical Library, 1975).

Aristotle, *Vol. XX – The Athenian Constitution/The Eudemian Ethics/On Virtues & Vices* (trans. H. Rackham), (Cambridge, Harvard University Press – Loeb Classical Library, 1952).

Aristotle, *Vol. XXI – Politics* (trans. H. Rackham), (Cambridge, Harvard University Press – Loeb Classical Library, 1967).

Aristotle, *Vol. XXIII – Poetics* (trans. W.H. Fyfe), (Cambridge, Harvard University Press – Loeb Classical Library, 1965).

Aristotle, *The Athenian Constitution* (trans. H. Rackham), (Cambridge, Harvard University Press – Loeb Classical Library, 1952).

Aristotle, *Politics* (trans. H. Rackham), (Cambridge, Harvard University Press – Loeb Classical Library, 1967).

Arrian, *Anabasis Alexandri Vol. I* (trans. P.A. Brunt), (Cambridge, Harvard University Press – Loeb Classical Library, 1976).

Arrian, *Tactical Handbook* (trans. J.G. DeVoto), (Chicago, Ares Publishers, 1993).

Athenaeus, *The Deipnosophists Vol. VI* (trans. C.B. Gulick), (Cambridge, Harvard University Press – Loeb Classical Library, 1959).

Caesar, *Gallic War* (trans. H.J. Edwards), (Cambridge, Harvard University Press – Loeb Classical Library, 1963).

Cornelius Nepos, *On Great Generals* (trans. J.C. Rolfe), (Cambridge, Harvard University Press – Loeb Classical Library, 1966).

Curtius (Quintus Curtius), *History of Alexander Vol. I* (trans. J.C. Rolfe), (Cambridge, Harvard University Press – Loeb Classical Library, 1971).
Curtius (Quintus Curtius), *History of Alexander Vol. II* (trans. J.C. Rolfe), (Cambridge, Harvard University Press – Loeb Classical Library, 1962).
Demosthenes, *Vol. I – Olynthiacs/Philippics/Minor Public Speeches/Speech Against Leptines* (trans. J.H. Vince), (Cambridge, Harvard University Press – Loeb Classical Library, 1962).
Diodorus Siculus, *Library of History Vol. II* (trans. C.H. Oldfather), (Cambridge, Harvard University Press – Loeb Classical Library, 1979).
Diodorus Siculus, *Library of History Vol. III* (trans. C.H. Oldfather), (Cambridge, Harvard University Press – Loeb Classical Library, 1961).
Diodorus Siculus, *Library of History Vol. IV* (trans. C.H. Oldfather), (Cambridge, Harvard University Press – Loeb Classical Library, 2002).
Diodorus Siculus, *Library of History Vol. VI* (trans. C.H. Oldfather), (Cambridge, Harvard University Press – Loeb Classical Library, 1963).
Diodorus Siculus, *Library of History Vol. VII* (trans. C.L. Sherman), (Cambridge, Harvard University Press – Loeb Classical Library, 1971).
Diodorus Siculus, *Library of History Vol. VIII* (trans. C. Bradford-Welles), (Cambridge, Harvard University Press – Loeb Classical Library, 1963).
Diogenes Laertius, *Lives of Eminent Philosophers, Vol. I* (trans. R.D. Hicks), (Cambridge, Harvard University Press – Loeb Classical Library, 1966).
Elegy and Iambus Vol. I (trans. J.E. Edmonds), (Cambridge, Harvard University Press – Loeb Classical Library, 1978).
Elegy and Iambus Vol. II (trans. J.E. Edmonds), (Cambridge, Harvard University Press – Loeb Classical Library, 1968).
Empedocles, *The Extant Fragments* (trans. M.R. Wright), (New Haven, Yale University Press, 1981).
Euripides, *Vol. I – Iphigeneia in Aulus/Rhesus/Hecuba/Daughters of Troy/Helen* (trans. A.S. Way), (Cambridge, Harvard University Press – Loeb Classical Library, 1978).
Euripides, *Vol. II – Electra/Orestes/Iphigeneia in Taurica/Andromache/Cyclops* (trans. A.S. Way), (Cambridge, Harvard University Press – Loeb Classical Library, 1978).
Euripides, *Vol. III – Bacchanals/Madness of Hercules/Children of Hercules/Phoenician Maidens/Suppliants* (trans. A.S. Way), (Cambridge, Harvard University Press – Loeb Classical Library, 1962).
Frontinus, *Stratagems* (trans. M.B. McElwain), (Cambridge, Harvard University Press – Loeb Classical Library, 1950).
Greek Anthology Vol. I (trans. W.R. Paton), (Cambridge, Harvard University Press – Loeb Classical Library, 1969).
Greek Anthology Vol. II (trans. W.R. Paton), (Cambridge, Harvard University Press – Loeb Classical Library, 1960).
Greek Bucolic Poets (trans. J.M. Edmonds), (Cambridge, Harvard University Press – Loeb Classical Library, 1960).
Hellenica Oxyrhynchia (trans. P.R. McKechnie and S.J. Kern), (Wiltshire, Aris and Phillips, 1993).
Herodotus, *Histories Vol. I* (trans. A.D. Godley), (Cambridge, Harvard University Press – Loeb Classical Library, 1971).
Herodotus, *Histories Vol. III* (trans. A.D. Godley), (Cambridge, Harvard University Press – Loeb Classical Library, 1971).
Herodotus, *Histories Vol. IV* (trans. A.D. Godley), (Cambridge, Harvard University Press – Loeb Classical Library, 1971).
Herodotus, *The Histories* (trans. A. De Sélincourt), (London, Penguin Books, 1996).
Hesiod, Homeric Hymns and Homerica (trans. H.G. Evelyn-White), (Cambridge, Harvard University Press – Loeb Classical Library, 1967).
Hesychius Alexandrinus, *Lexicon Vol. II* (Amsterdam, Adolf M. Hekkert, 1965).

Hesychius Alexandrinus, *Lexicon Vol. III* (Amsterdam, Adolf M. Hekkert, 1965).
Hesychius Alexandrinus, *Lexicon Vol. IV* (Amsterdam, Adolf M. Hekkert, 1965).
Hippocrates, *Vol. I* (trans. W.H.S. Jones), (Cambridge, Harvard University Press – Loeb Classical Library, 1962).
Hippocrates, *Vol. III* (trans. E.T. Withington), (Cambridge, Harvard University Press – Loeb Classical Library, 1968).
Hippocrates, *Vol. VII* (trans. W.D. Smith), (Cambridge, Harvard University Press – Loeb Classical Library, 1994).
Hippocrates, *Vol. VIII* (trans. P. Potter), (Cambridge, Harvard University Press – Loeb Classical Library, 1995).
Homer, *Iliad Vol. I* (trans. A.T. Murray), (Cambridge, Harvard University Press – Loeb Classical Library, 1978).
Homer, *Iliad Vol. II* (trans. A.T. Murray), (Cambridge, Harvard University Press – Loeb Classical Library, 1976).
Homer, *Iliad* (trans. M. Hammond), (London, Penguin Books, 1987).
Homer, *The Odyssey*, (trans. G.P. Goold), (Cambridge, Harvard University Press – Loeb Classical Library, 1980).
Isocrates, *Vol. I – To Demonicus/To Nicocles/Nicocles or The Cyprians/Panegyricus/To Philip/Archidamus* (trans. G. Norlin), (Cambridge, Harvard University Press – Loeb Classical Library, 1966).
Isocrates, *Vol. II – On the Peace/Areopagiticus/Against the Sophists/Antidosis/Panathenaicus* (trans. G. Norlin), (Cambridge, Harvard University Press – Loeb Classical Library, 1968).
Isocrates, *Vol. III – Orations/Letters* (trans. L. van Hook), (Cambridge, Harvard University Press – Loeb Classical Library, 1968).
Justin, *Epitome of the Philippic History of Pompeius Trogus* (trans. J.C. Yardley), (Atlanta, Scholars Press, 1994).
Lucian, *Vol. IV* (trans. A.M. Harmon), (Cambridge, Harvard University Press – Loeb Classical Library, 1969).
Lysias, (trans. W.R.M. Lamb), (Cambridge, Harvard University Press – Loeb Classical Library, 1967).
Lyra Graeca Vol. I (trans. J.M. Edmonds), (Cambridge, Harvard University Press – Loeb Classical Library, 1963).
Lyra Graeca Vol. II (trans. J.M. Edmonds), (Cambridge, Harvard University Press – Loeb Classical Library, 1979).
Lyra Graeca Vol. III (trans. J.M. Edmonds), (Cambridge, Harvard University Press – Loeb Classical Library, 1967).
Minor Attic Orators Vol. II – Lycurgus/Dinarchus/Demades/Hyperides (trans. J.O. Burtt), (Cambridge, Harvard University Press – Loeb Classical Library, 1954).
Minor Latin Poets Vol. I (trans. J.W. Duff and A.M. Duff), (Cambridge, Harvard University Press – Loeb Classical Library, 1934).
Pausanias, *Description of Greece – Vol. I* (trans. W.H.S. Jones), (Cambridge, Harvard University Press – Loeb Classical Library, 1969).
Pausanias, *Description of Greece – Vol. II* (trans. W.H.S. Jones and H.A. Ormerod), (Cambridge, Harvard University Press – Loeb Classical Library, 1966).
Pausanias, *Description of Greece – Vol. III* (trans. W.H.S. Jones), (Cambridge, Harvard University Press – Loeb Classical Library, 1988).
Pausanias, *Description of Greece – Vol. IV* (trans. W.H.S. Jones), (Cambridge, Harvard University Press – Loeb Classical Library, 1965).
Pausanias, *Guide to Greece – Vol. II* (trans. P. Levi), (London, Penguin Books, 1971).
Philostratus, *Gymnastics* (trans. F. Fetz and L. Fetz), (Frankfurt, Limpert Verlag, 1969).
Philostratus, *Life of Apollonius of Tyana* (trans. F.C. Conybeare), (Cambridge, Harvard University Press – Loeb Classical Library, 1969).

Photius, *Photii Patriarchae Lexicon Vol. II* (ed. C. Theodoridis), (Berlin, Walter de Gruyter, 1998).

Pindar, *The Odes* (trans. J. Sandys), (Cambridge, Harvard University Press – Loeb Classical Library, 1968).

Plato, *Vol. I – Euthyphro/Apology/Crito/Phaedo/Phaedrus* (trans. H.N. Fowler), (Cambridge, Harvard University Press – Loeb Classical Library, 1953).

Plato, *Vol. II – Laches/Protagoras/Meno/Euthydemus* (trans. W.R.M. Lamb), (Cambridge, Harvard University Press – Loeb Classical Library, 1999).

Plato, *Vol. III – Lysias/Symposium/Gorgias* (trans. W.R.M. Lamb), (Cambridge, Harvard University Press – Loeb Classical Library, 2001).

Plato, *Vol. IV – Republic* (trans. P. Shorey), (Cambridge, Harvard University Press – Loeb Classical Library, 1970).

Plato, *Vol. X – Laws* (trans. R.G. Bury), (Cambridge, Harvard University Press – Loeb Classical Library, 2001).

Plato, *Vol. XI – Laws* (trans. R.G. Bury), (Cambridge, Harvard University Press – Loeb Classical Library, 1999).

Plato, *Vol. XII – Charmides/Alcibiades I and II/Hipparchus/The Lovers/Theages/Minos/Epinomis* (trans. W.R.M. Lamb), (Cambridge, Harvard University Press – Loeb Classical Library, 1979).

Pliny, *Natural History Vol. II* (trans. H. Rackham), (Cambridge, Harvard University Press – Loeb Classical Library, 1969).

Pliny, *Natural History Vol. IV* (trans. H. Rackham), (Cambridge, Harvard University Press – Loeb Classical Library, 1968).

Pliny, *Natural History Vol. IX* (trans. H. Rackham), (Cambridge, Harvard University Press – Loeb Classical Library, 1968).

Plutarch, *Lives Vol. I – Theseus and Romulus/Lycurgus and Numa/Solon and Publicola* (trans. B. Perrin), (Cambridge, Harvard University Press – Loeb Classical Library, 1967).

Plutarch, *Lives Vol. II – Themistocles and Camillus/Aristides and Cato Major/Cimon and Lucullus* (trans. B. Perrin), (Cambridge, Harvard University Press – Loeb Classical Library, 1968).

Plutarch, *Lives Vol. III – Pericles and Fabius Maximus/Nicias and Crassus* (trans. B. Perrin), (Cambridge, Harvard University Press – Loeb Classical Library, 1967).

Plutarch, *Lives Vol. IV – Alcibiades and Coriolanus/Lysander and Sulla* (trans. B. Perrin), (Cambridge, Harvard University Press – Loeb Classical Library, 1968).

Plutarch, *Lives Vol. V – Agesilaus and Pompey/Pelopidas and Marcellus* (trans. B. Perrin), (Cambridge, Harvard University Press – Loeb Classical Library, 1968).

Plutarch, *Lives Vol. VI – Dion and Brutus/Timoleon and Aemilius Paulus* (trans. B. Perrin), (Cambridge, Harvard University Press – Loeb Classical Library, 1961).

Plutarch, *Lives Vol. VII – Demosthenes and Cicero/Alexander and Caesar* (trans. B. Perrin), (Cambridge, Harvard University Press – Loeb Classical Library, 1967).

Plutarch, *Lives Vol. VIII – Sertorius and Eumenes/Phocion and Cato the Younger* (trans. B. Perrin), (Cambridge, Harvard University Press – Loeb Classical Library, 1969).

Plutarch, *Lives Vol. IX – Demetrius and Antony/Pyrrhus and Caius Marius* (trans. B. Perrin), (Cambridge, Harvard University Press – Loeb Classical Library, 1968).

Plutarch, *Lives Vol. X – Agis and Cleomenes/Tiberius and Caius Gracchus/Philopoemen and Flamininus* (trans. B. Perrin), (Cambridge, Harvard University Press – Loeb Classical Library, 1968).

Plutarch, *Moralia Vol. III* (trans. F.C. Babbitt), (Cambridge, Harvard University Press – Loeb Classical Library, 1968).

Plutarch, *Moralia Vol. VIII* (trans. P.A. Clement), (Cambridge, Harvard University Press – Loeb Classical Library, 1969).

Plutarch, *The Rise and Fall of Athens* (trans. I. Scott-Kilvert), (London, Penguin Books, 1960).

Polyaenus, *Stratagems of War Vol. I* (trans. P. Krentz and E.L. Wheeler), (Chicago, Ares Publishers, 1994).

Polyaenus, *Stratagems of War Vol. II /Excepts/ Leo the Emperor* (trans. P. Krentz and E.L. Wheeler), (Chicago, Ares Publishers, 1994).

Polybius, *Vol. III* (trans. W.R. Paton), (Cambridge, Harvard University Press – Loeb Classical Library, 1966).

Polybius, *Vol. IV* (trans. W.R. Paton), (Cambridge, Harvard University Press – Loeb Classical Library, 1976).

Polybius, *Vol. V* (trans. W.R. Paton), (Cambridge, Harvard University Press – Loeb Classical Library, 1954).

Quintillian, *Institutes Vol. IV* (trans. H.E. Butler), (Cambridge, Harvard University Press – Loeb Classical Library, 1968).

Seneca, *Vol. I – Moral Essays* (trans. J.W. Basare), (Cambridge, Harvard University Press – Loeb Classical Library, 1928).

Sophocles, *Vol. I – Oedipus the King/ Oedipus at Colonus/ Antigone* (trans. F. Storr), (Cambridge, Harvard University Press – Loeb Classical Library, 1977).

Sophocles, *Vol. II – Ajax/ Electra/ Trachiniae/ Philoctetes* (trans. F. Storr), (Cambridge, Harvard University Press – Loeb Classical Library, 1961).

Strabo, *The Geography of Strabo Vol. II* (trans. H.L. Jones), (Cambridge, Harvard University Press – Loeb Classical Library, 1960).

Strabo, *The Geography of Strabo Vol. V* (trans. H.L. Jones), (Cambridge, Harvard University Press – Loeb Classical Library, 1961).

Strabo, *The Geography of Strabo Vol. VII* (trans. H.L. Jones), (Cambridge, Harvard University Press – Loeb Classical Library, 1961).

Theocritus (trans. A.S.F. Gow) (Cambridge, Cambridge University Press, 1965).

Theophrastus, *Enquiry into Plants Vol. I* (trans. A. Hort), (Cambridge, Harvard University Press – Loeb Classical Library, 1968).

Thucydides, *History of the Peloponnesian War Vol. I* (trans. C.F. Smith), (Cambridge, Harvard University Press – Loeb Classical Library, 1969).

Thucydides, *History of the Peloponnesian War Vol. II* (trans. C.F. Smith), (Cambridge, Harvard University Press – Loeb Classical Library, 1965).

Thucydides, *History of the Peloponnesian War Vol. III* (trans. C.F. Smith), (Cambridge, Harvard University Press – Loeb Classical Library, 1966).

Thucydides, *History of the Peloponnesian War Vol. IV* (trans. C.F. Smith), (Cambridge, Harvard University Press – Loeb Classical Library, 1965).

Thucydides, *History of the Peloponnesian War* (trans. R. Warner), (London, Penguin Books, 1972).

Thucydides, *History of the Peloponnesian War* (trans. W. Blanco), (New York, W.W. Norton and Co., 1998).

Thucydides, *History of the Peloponnesian War* (trans. Hobbes), (Chicago, University of Chicago Press, 1989).

Thucydides, *History of the Peloponnesian War* (trans. H. Dale), (London, Henry G. Bohn, 1849).

Thucydides, *History of the Peloponnesian War* (trans. J.P. Rhodes), (Wiltshire, Aris and Philips, 1988).

Thucydides, *History of the Peloponnesian War* (R.B. Strassler (ed.)), (New York, Touchstone, 1996).

Vegetius, *Epitome of Military Science* (trans. N.P. Milner), (Liverpool, Liverpool University Press, 2001).

Xenophon, *A History of My Times* (trans. R. Warner), (London, Penguin Books, 1979).

Xenophon, *Anabasis* (trans. C.L. Brownson), (Cambridge, Harvard University Press – Loeb Classical Library, 1968).

Xenophon, *Hellenica Vol. I* (trans. C.L. Brownson), (Cambridge, Harvard University Press – Loeb Classical Library, 1978).

Xenophon, *Hellenica Vol. II* (trans. C.L. Brownson), (Cambridge, Harvard University Press – Loeb Classical Library, 1968).

Xenophon, *Cyropaedia Vol. I* (trans. W. Miller), (Cambridge, Harvard University Press – Loeb Classical Library, 1968).
Xenophon, *Cyropaedia Vol. II* (trans. W. Miller), (Cambridge, Harvard University Press – Loeb Classical Library, 1968).
Xenophon, *Memorabilia* (trans. E.C. Marchant), (Cambridge, Harvard University Press – Loeb Classical Library, 1968).
Xenophon, *Scripta Minora* (trans. E.C. Marchant).
(Cambridge, Harvard University Press – Loeb Classical Library, 2000).
Xenophon, *The Persian Expedition* (trans. R. Warner), (London, Penguin Books, 1972).

Modern Texts
Adcock, F.E., *The Greek and Macedonian Art of War* (Berkeley, University of California Press, 1957).
Anderson, J.K., 'The Statue of Chabrias', *AJA* 67:4 (Oct. 1963), pp. 411–413.
Anderson, J.K., *Military Theory and Practice in the Age of Xenophon* (Berkeley, University of California Press, 1970).
Anderson, J.K., 'Hoplites and Heresies: A Note', *JHS* 104 (1984), p. 152.
Andronicos, M., *Olympia* (Athens, Ekdotike Athenon, 1999).
Andronicos, M., *Delphi* (Athens, Ekdotike Athenon, 2000).
Baitinger, H., *Die Angriffswaffen aus Olympia* (Berlin, Walter de Gruyter, 2000).
Bardunias, P., 'The Aspis – Surviving Hoplite Battle', *Ancient Warfare* 1:3 (2007), pp. 11–14.
Barley, N., 'Thucydides on Lightly Armed Troops', *Ancient Warfare* 2:1 (2008), pp. 14–17.
Beazley, J.D. and Ashmole, B., *Greek Sculpture and Painting to the End of the Hellenistic Period* (Cambridge, Cambridge University Press, 1966).
Beazley, J.D., *Attic Black-Figure Vase-Painters* (New York, Hacker Art Books, 1978).
Benson, J.L., 'Human Figures and Narrative in Later Protocorinthian Vase Painting', *Hesperia* 64:2 (Apr–Jun 1995), pp. 163–177.
Bertosa, B., 'The Supply of Hoplite Equipment by the Athenian State Down to the Lamian War', *Journal of Military History* 67:2 (Apr 2003), pp. 361–379.
Blyth, P.H., *The Effectiveness of Greek Armour against Arrows in the Persian Wars (490–479B.C.): An Interdisciplinary Enquiry* (London, British Library Lending Division (unpublished thesis – University of Reading, 1977)).
Boardman, J., *Athenian Red Figure Vases – The Archaic Period* (London, Thames and Hudson, 1983).
Boardman, J., *Athenian Red Figure Vases – The Classical Period* (London, Thames and Hudson, 1989).
Boardman, J., *Greek Art* (London, Thames and Hudson, 1996).
Boardman, J., *The Greeks Overseas* (London, Thames and Hudson, 1999).
Bol, P.C., *Argivische Schilde* (Berlin, Walter de Gruyter, 1989).
Boldsen, J., 'A Statistical Evaluation of the Basis for Predicting Stature from the Lengths of Long Bones in European Populations', *AJPA* 65 (1984), pp. 305–311.
Bonfante, L., 'Nudity as a Costume in Classical Art', *AJA* 93:4 (Oct. 1989), pp. 543–570.
Bradford, E., *Thermopylae – The Battle for the West* (USA, Da Capo Press, 1993).
Bryant, A.A., 'Greek Shoes in the Classical Period', *Harvard Studies in Classical Philology* 10 (1899), pp. 57–102.
Buckler, J., 'A Second Look at the Monument of Chabrias', *Hesperia* 41:4 (Oct–Dec 1972), pp. 466–474.
Buckler, J., 'Epameinondas and the Embolon', *Phoenix* 39:2 (1985), pp. 134–143.
Buschor, E., *Greek Vase Painting* (New York, Hacker Art Books, 1978).
Burkert, W., *The Orientalizing Revolution: Near Eastern Influence on Greek Culture in the Early Archaic Age* (Cambridge, Harvard University Press, 1992).

302   *A Storm of Spears*

Burnett, A.P. and Edmonson, C.N., 'The Chabrias Monument in the Athenian Agora', *Hesperia* 30:1 (Jan–Mar 1961), pp. 74–91.

Bury, J.B., Cook, S.A. and Adcock, F.E. (eds), *The Cambridge Ancient History Vol. 6 – Macedon 401–301BC* (London, Cambridge University Press, 1933).

Camp II, J. McK., 'A Spear Butt from the Lesbians', *Hesperia* 47:2 (Apr–Jun 1978), pp. 192–195.

Cartledge, P., 'Hoplites and Heroes: Sparta's Contribution to the Technique of Ancient Warfare', *JHS* 97 (1977), pp. 11–27.

Cartledge, P., *Thermopylae – The Battle that Changed the World* (London, Pan Books, 2007).

Cawkwell, G., *Philip of Macedon* (London, Faber and Faber, 1978).

Cawkwell, G., 'The Decline of Sparta', *CQ* 33 (1983), pp. 385–400.

Cawkwell, G.L., 'Orthodoxy and Hoplites', *CQ* 39:2 (1989), pp. 375–389.

Chase, G.H., *The Shield Devices of the Greeks in Art and Literature* (Chicago, Ares Publishers, 1979).

Chananie, J., 'The Physics of Karate Strikes', *Journal of How Things Work* 1 (Fall 1999), pp. 1–4.

Combellack, F. M., 'Achilles – Bare of Foot?' *Classical Journal* 41:5 (Feb 1946), pp. 193–198.

Connolly, P., *Greece and Rome at War* (London, Greenhill Books, 1998).

Connolly, P., 'Experiments with the *Sarissa* – the Macedonian Pike and Cavalry Lance – a Functional View', *JRMES* 11 (2000), pp. 103–112.

Connor, W.R., 'Early Greek Land Warfare as Symbolic Expression', *Past and Present* 119 (May 1988), pp. 3–29.

Cook, B.F., 'Footwork in Ancient Greek Swordsmanship', *Metropolitan Museum Journal* 24 (1989), pp. 57–64.

Cornelius, F., 'Pausanius', *Historia* 22 (1973), pp. 502–504.

Cotterrell, B. and Kamminga, J., *Mechanics of Pre-Industrial Technology: An Introduction to the Mechanics of Ancient and Traditional Material* (Melbourne, Cambridge University Press, 1990).

Curwen, E.C., 'Spear-Throwing with a Cord', *Man* 34 (Jul 1934), pp. 105–106.

Davey, P.R., Thorpe, R.D. and Williams, C., 'Fatigue Decreases Tennis Performance', *Journal of Sports Sciences* 20:4 (April 2002), pp. 311–318.

Davidson, G.R., *Corinth: Results of Excavations Conducted by the American School of Classical Studies at Athens – Vol. XII – The Minor Objects* (Princeton, American School of Classical Studies at Athens, 1952).

Delbrück, H., *History of the Art of War Vol. I* (Westport, Greenwood Press, 1975).

Devine, A.M., 'EMBOLON: A Study in Tactical Terminology', *Phoenix* 37:3 (1983), pp. 201–217.

Dickinson, R.E., 'Length Isn't Everything – Use of the Macedonian *Sarissa* in the Time of Alexander the Great', *JBT* 3:3 (November 2000), pp. 51–62.

Donlan, W. and Thompson, J., 'The Charge at Marathon: Herodotus 6.112', *Classical Journal* 71:4 (Apr–May 1976), pp. 339–343.

Droysen, H., *Heerwesen und Kreigführung der Griechen* (Elibron Classics, 2006).

Ducrey, P., *Warfare in Ancient Greece* (New York, Schocken Books, 1986).

English, S., 'Hoplite or Peltast? – Macedonian 'Heavy' Infantry', *Ancient Warfare* 2:1 (2008), pp. 32–35.

Epps, P.H., 'Fear in Spartan Character', *Classical Philology* 28:1 (Jan 1933), pp. 12–29.

Everson, T., *Warfare in Ancient Greece* (Stroud, Sutton Publishing, 2004).

Featherstone, D., *Warriors and Warfare in Ancient and Medieval Times* (London, Constable, 1988).

Ferrill, A., *The Origins of War* (London, Thames and Hudson, 1985).

Flower, M.A., 'Simonides, Ephorus and Herodotus on the Battle of Thermopylae', *Classical Quarterly* 48:2 (1998), pp. 365–379.

Forestier, N. and Nougier, V., 'The Effects of Muscular Fatigue on the Co-Ordination of Multijoint Movement in Humans', *Neuroscience Letters* 252:3 (August 1998), pp. 187–190.

Fortenberry, D., 'Single Greaves in the Late Helladic Period', *AJA* 95:4 (Oct. 1991), pp. 623–627.

Fraser, A.D., 'Myth of the Phalanx-scrimmage', *Classical Weekly* 36 (Oct 1942–Jun 1943), pp. 15–16.

Frolich, H., *Die Militarmedicin Homers* (Stuttgart, 1879).

Gabriel, R. and Metz, K., *From Sumer to Rome – The Military Capabilities of Ancient Armies* (Connecticut, Greenwood Press, 1991).

Gardiner, E.N., 'Throwing the Javelin', *JHS* 27 (1907), pp. 249–273.

Geddes, A.G., 'Rags and Riches: The Costume of Athenian Men in the Fifth Century', *CQ* 37:2 (1987), pp. 307–331.

Godnig, E.C., 'Tunnel Vision: Its Causes and Treatment Strategies', *Journal of Behavioral Optometry* 14:4 (2003), pp. 95–99.

Golden, M., *Sport and Society in Ancient Greece* (Cambridge, Cambridge University Press, 1998).

Goldhill, S., 'Battle Narrative and Politics in Aeschylus' Persae', *JHS* 108 (1988), pp. 189–193.

Goldsworthy, A.K., 'The Othismos, Myths and Heresies: The Nature of Hoplite Battle', *War in History* 4:1 (1997), pp. 1–26.

Griffiths, W.B., 'Re-enactment as Research: Towards a Set of Guidelines for Re-enactors and Academics', *JRMES* 11 (2000), pp. 135–139.

Grossman, D., *On Killing* (New York, Back Bay Books, 1996).

Hammond, N.G.L., 'Casualties and Reinforcements of Citizen Soldiers in Greece and Macedonia', *JHS* 109 (1989), pp. 56–68.

Hanson, V.D., *The Western Way of War* (Berkeley, University of California Press, 1989).

Hanson, V.D., *Wars of the Ancient Greeks* (London, Cassell, 1999).

Hanson, V.D. (ed.), *Hoplites – The Classical Greek Battle Experience* (London, Routledge, 2004).

Heckel, W. and Jones, R., *Macedonian Warrior: Alexander's Elite Infantryman* (Oxford, Osprey, 2006).

Hockey, R. (ed.), *Stress and Fatigue in Human Performance* (Chichester, Wiley and Sons, 1983).

Hoffmann, H. and Raubitschek, A.E., *Early Cretan Armourers* (Mainz, P. von Zabern, 1972).

Holladay, A.J., 'Hoplites and Heresies', *JHS* 102 (1982), pp. 94–103.

Homolle, M.T., *Fouilles de Delphes – Tome V* (Paris, Ancienne Librairie Thorin et Fils, 1908).

Hornblower, S., *A Commentary on Thucydides Vol. II* (Oxford, Clarendon Press, 1996).

How, W.W., 'Arms, Tactics and Strategy in the Persian War', *JHS* 43:2 (1923), pp. 117–132.

Hultsch, F., *Greichische und Römische Metrologie* (Berlin, Weidmannsche Buchhandlung, 1882).

Hunt, P., 'Helots at the Battle of Plataea', *Historia* 46 (1997), pp. 129–144.

Hurwitt, J.M., 'Reading the Chigi Vase', *Hesperia* 71:1 (Jan–Mar 2002), pp. 1–22.

Jacoby, F., *Die Fragmente der Griechischen Historiker Vol. II (B)* (Lieden, Brill, 1952).

Jacoby, F., *Die Fragmente der Griechischen Historiker Vol. III (A)* (Lieden, Brill, 1952).

Jarva, E., *Archaiologia on Archaic Greek Body Armour* (Studia Archaeologica Septentrionalia 3), (Rovaniemi: Pohjois-Suomen Historiallinen Yhdistys, Societas Historica Finlandiae Septentrionalis, 1995).

Kastorchis, E., 'ΠΕΡΙ ΤΟΥ ΕΝ ΧΑΙΡΩΝΕΙΑ ΛΕΟΝΤΟΣ', *Athenaion* 8 (1879), pp. 486–491.

Keegan, J., *The Face of Battle* (London, Penguin Books, 1983).

Klinger, D., *Police Responses to Officer-involved Shootings* (Washington, US Department of Justice, 2002).

Kraft, J.C., Rapp, G., Szemler, J.G., Tziavos, C. and Kase, E.W., 'The Pass at Thermopylae, Greece', *Journal of Field Archaeology* 14:2 (1987), pp. 181–198.

Krentz, P., 'Fighting by the Rules: The Invention of the Hoplite *Agon*', *Hesperia*, 71:1 (Jan–Mar 2002), pp. 23–39.

Krentz, P., 'The Nature of Hoplite Battle', *Classical Antiquity* 16 (1985), pp. 50–61.

Krentz, P., 'Casualties in Hoplite Battles', *GRBS* 26 (1985), pp. 13–20.

Krentz, P., 'Continuing the Othismos on Othismos', *AHB* 8:2 (1994), pp. 45–49.

Kromayer, J. and Veith, G., *Heerwesen und Kriegführung der Griechen und Römer* (Munchen, 1928).

Kromayer, J. and Veith, G., *Schlachten-Atlas zur Antiken Kreigsgeschichte* (revised by R. Gabriel (ed.) and re-released as *The Battle Atlas of Ancient Military History* (Ontario, Canadian Defence Academy Press, 2008).

Krueger, G.P., 'Sustained Work, Fatigue, Sleep Loss and Performance: A Review of the Issues', *Work and Stress* 3:2 (April 1989), pp. 129–141.

Kunze, E., *Bericht Über die Ausgrabungen in Olympia – Vol. V* (Berlin, Verlag Walter de Gruyter and Co., 1956).

Kunze, E., *Bericht Über die Ausgrabungen in Olympia – Vol. VI* (Berlin, Verlag Walter de Gruyter and Co., 1958).

Kunze, E., *Bericht Über die Ausgrabungen in Olympia – Vol. VII* (Berlin, Verlag Walter de Gruyter and Co., 1961).

Kunze, E., *Bericht Über die Ausgrabungen in Olympia – Vol. VIII* (Berlin, Verlag Walter de Gruyter and Co., 1967).

Kunze, E., *Bericht Über die Ausgrabungen in Olympia – Vol. IX* (Berlin, Verlag Walter de Gruyter and Co., 1994).

Kunze, E., *Beinschienen* (Berlin, Walter de Gruyter, 1991).

Kunze, E. and Schleif, H., *Olympische Forschungen* (Berlin, Verlag Walter de Gruyter and Co., 1944).

Kurtz, D. (ed.), *Reception of Classical Art, an Introduction* (BAR International Series 1295, 2004).

Kutz, L.R. (ed.), *Encyclopedia of Violence, Peace and Conflict* (Orlando, Academic Press, 1999).

Lawton, C.L., *Attic Document Reliefs* (Oxford, Clarendon Press, 1995).

Lendon, J.E., *Soldiers and Ghosts – A History of Battle in Classical Antiquity* (New Haven, Yale University Press, 2005).

Lloyd, A.B., *Battle in Antiquity* (London, Duckworth, 1996).

Lorimer, H.L., 'The Hoplite Phalanx with Special Reference to the Poems of Archilochus and Tyrtaeus', *ABSA* 42 (1947), pp. 76–138.

Lorimer, H.L., *Homer and the Monuments* (London, MacMillan, 1950).

Lowenstam, S., 'Talking Vases: The Relationship Between the Homeric Poems and Archaic Representations of Epic Myth', *Transactions of the American Philological Association (1974–)* 127 (1997), pp. 21–76.

Luginbill, R.D., 'Othismos: The Importance of the Mass-Shove in Hoplite Warfare', *Phoenix* 48:1 (Spring 1994), pp. 51–61.

Lundy, J.K., 'Regression Equations for Estimating Living Stature from Long Limb Bones in South African Negro', *SAJS* 79 (1983), pp. 337–338.

McDermott, R., *Modelling Hoplite Battle in SWARM* (New Zealand, Massey University, 2004 (unpublished thesis)).

Mallwitz, A., *Bericht über die Ausgrabungen in Olympia XI* (Berlin, Walter de Gruyter, 1999).

Markle III, M.M., 'The Macedonian *Sarissa*, Spear and Related Armour', *AJA* 8:3 (Summer 1977), pp. 323–339.

Markle III, M.M., 'Use of the *Sarissa* by Philip and Alexander of Macedon', *AJA* 82:4 (Autumn 1978), pp. 483–497.

Markle III, M.M., 'A Shield Monument from Veria and the Chronology of Macedonian Shield Types', *Hesperia* 68:2 (April–June 1999), pp. 219–254.

Markoe, G., 'The Emergence of Orientalizing in Greek Art: Some Observations on the Interchange between Greeks and Phoenicians in the Eighth and Seventh Centuries B.C.', *Bulletin of the American Schools of Oriental Research* 301 (Feb. 1996), pp. 47–67.

Marsden, E.W., *Greek and Roman Artillery Vol. II – Technical Treatises* (Oxford, Clarendon Press, 1971).

Matthew, C.A., 'When Push Comes to Shove: What was the *Othismos* of Hoplite Combat?', *Historia* 58:4 (2009), pp. 395–415.

Matthews, R., *The Battle of Thermopylae – A Campaign in Context* (Gloucestershire, Spellmount, 2006).

Meiggs, R., *Trees and Timber in the Ancient Mediterranean World* (Oxford, Clarendon Press, 1982).

Munro, J.A.R., 'Some Observations on the Persian Wars', *JHS* 19 (1899), pp. 185–197.

Nadon, C., 'From Republic to Empire: Political Revolution and the Common Good in Xenophon's Education of Cyrus', *American Political Science Review* 90 (June 1996), pp. 361–374.

Oliver, G., Aaron, C., Fully, G. and Tisser, G., 'New Estimations of Stature and Cranial Capacity in Modern Man', *JHE* 7 (1978), pp. 513–518.

Onians, J., *Classical Art and the Cultures of Greece and Rome* (New Haven, Yale University Press, 1999).

Park, M., 'The Silver Shields – Philip's and Alexander's Hypaspists', *Ancient Warfare*. 1:3 (2007), pp. 25–28.

Parke, H.W. *Greek Mercenary Soldiers – from the Earliest Times to the Battle of Ipsus* (Oxford, Clarendon Press, 1933).

Pearson, L., 'The Pseudo-History of Messenia and its Authors', *Historia* 11:3 (1962), pp. 397–426.

Phytalis, L., 'ΕΡΕΥΝΑΙ ΕΝ ΤΩ ΠΟΛΥΑΝΔΡΙΩ ΧΑΙΡΩΝΕΙΑΣ', *Athenaion* 9 (1880), pp. 347–352.

Pritchard, D., 'Athletics, War and Democracy in Classical Athens', *Teaching History* 39:4 (2005), pp. 4–10.

Pritchett, W.K., 'New Light on Plataia', *AJA* 61:1 (Jan. 1957), pp. 9–28.

Pritchett, W.K., 'New Light on Thermopylai', *AJA* 62:2 (Apr. 1958), pp. 203–213.

Pritchett, W.K., 'Xerxes' Route over Mount Olympos', *AJA* 65:4 (Oct. 1961), pp. 369–375.

Pritchett, W.K., *The Greek State at War – Vol. I* (Berkeley, University of California Press, 1974).

Pritchett, W.K., *The Greek State at War – Vol. II* (Berkeley, University of California Press, 1974).

Pritchett, W.K., *The Greek State at War – Vol. III* (Berkeley, University of California Press, 1979).

Pritchett, W.K., *The Greek State at War – Vol. IV* (Berkeley, University of California Press, 1985).

Reed, N.B., *More Than Just a Game: The Military Nature of Greek Athletic Contests* (Chicago, Ares Publishers, 1998).

Rhodes, P.J. and Osborne, R. (eds), *Greek Historical Inscriptions 404–323BC* (Oxford, Oxford University Press, 2003).

Richardson, W.F., *Numbering and Measuring in the Classical World* (Bristol, Bristol Phoenix Press, 2004).

Richter, G.M.A., *Red-Figured Athenian Vases in the Metropolitan Museum of Art Vol. I* (text) (New Haven, Yale University Press, 1936).

Richter, G.M.A., *Red-Figured Athenian Vases in the Metropolitan Museum of Art Vol. II* (plates) (New Haven, Yale University Press, 1936).

Richter, G.M.A., 'Greek Bronzes Recently Acquired by the Metropolitan Museum of Art', *AJA* 43:2 (Apr–Jun 1939), pp. 189–201.

Richter, G.M.A., *Perspective in Greek and Roman Art* (London, Phaidon Press Ltd, 1970).

Robinson, D.M., *Excavations at Olynthus, Part X – Metal and Minor Miscellaneous Finds* (Blatimore, Johns Hopkins University Press, 1941).

Rose, M., 'Fallen Heroes – Bones of Pericles' Soldiers come to New York for Analysis', *Archaeology* (Mar–Apr 2000), pp. 42–45.

Royal, K., Farrow, D., Mujika, I., Hanson, S., Pyne, D. and Abernethy, B., 'The Effects of Fatigue on Decision Making and Shooting Skill in Water Polo Players', *Journal of Sports Sciences* 24:8 (August 2006), pp. 807–815.

Rubincam, C., 'Casualty Figures in the Battle Descriptions of Thucydides', *Transactions of the American Philological Society (1974–)* 121 (1991), pp. 181–198.

Sabin, P., *Lost Battles – Reconstructing the Great Clashes of the Ancient World* (London, Continuum, 2009).

Salazar, C.F., *The Treatment of War Wounds in Greco-Roman Antiquity* (Leiden, Brill, 2000).

Salmon, J., 'Political Hoplites?' *JHS* 97 (1977), pp. 84–101.

Schauer, P., 'Die Beinschienen der Späten Bronzen und Frühen Eisenzeit', *Römisch-Germanisches Zentralmuseums* 29 (1982), pp. 100–155.

Scullard, H.H. (ed.), *Aspects of Greek and Roman Life* (Ithaca, Cornell University Press, 1977).

Sekunda, N., *The Spartan Army* (Oxford, Osprey Publishing, 1998).

Sekunda, N., *The Army of Alexander the Great* (Oxford, Osprey Publishing, 1999).

Sekunda, N., *Greek Hoplite 480–323BC* (Oxford, Osprey Publishing, 2004).

Shear, T.L., 'The Campaign of 1936', *Hesperia* #6 – *The American Excavations in the Athenian Agora: 12th Report* 6:3 (1937), pp. 333–381.

Siewert, P., 'The Ephebic Oath in Fifth-Century Athens', *JHS* 97 (1977), pp. 102–111.

Skarmintzos, S., 'Armed Passengers – Hoplite Marines', *Ancient Warfare* 2:3 (2008), pp. 16–19.

Smith, R.A., and Dickie, J.F. (eds.), *Engineering for Crowd Safety* (Elsevier, Amsterdam, 1993).

Snodgrass, A.M., *Early Greek Armour and Weapons* (Edinburgh, Edinburgh University Press, 1964).

Snodgrass, A.M., 'The Hoplite Reform and History', *JHS* 85 (1965), pp. 110–122.

Snodgrass, A.M., *Arms and Armour of the Greeks* (Baltimore, Johns Hopkins University Press, 1999).

Sparkes, B.A., *The Red and The Black: Studies in Greek Pottery* (London, Routledge, 1996).

Spence, I.G., *The Cavalry of Classical Greece* (Oxford, Clarendon Press, 1993).

Starr, C.G., *Athenian Coinage 480–447BC* (Oxford, Clarendon Press, 1970).

Stein, A., *On Alexander's Track to the Indus* (New Delhi, Asian Publications, 1985).

Stephenson, I.P., *Roman Infantry Equipment – The Later Empire* (Stroud, Tempus, 1991).

Sternberg, R.H., 'The Transport of Sick and Wounded Soldiers in Classical Greece', *Phoenix* 53:3/4 (Autumn–Winter 1999), pp. 191–205.

Stewart, A., 'Imag(in)ing the Other: Amazons and Ethnicity in Fifth-Century Athens', *Poetics Today* 16:4 (1995), pp. 571–597.

Stroszeck, J., 'Lakonisch-rotfigurige Keramik aus den Lakedaimoniergräbern am Kerameikos von Athen', *AA* 2 (2006), pp. 101–120.

Thompson, D.B., *The Athenian Agora – An Ancient Shopping Centre* (Vermont, The Stinehour Press, 1993).

Thompson, H.A. and Wycherley, R.E., *The Athenian Agora Vol. XIV – The Agora of Athens* (Glückstadt, J.J. Augustin, 1972).

Trundle, M., 'The Spartan Revolution: Hoplite Warfare in the late Archaic Period', *War and Society* 19:10 (Oct 2001), pp. 1–17.

Trundle, M., *Greek Mercenaries from the Late Archaic Period to Alexander* (New York, Routledge, 2004).

Tudela, F., 'The Hoplite's Second Shield – Defensive Roles of Greek Cavalry', *Ancient Warfare* 2:4 (2008), pp. 36–39.

Ueda-Sarson, L., 'The Evolution of Hellenistic Infantry (Part 1): The Reforms of Iphikrates' *Slingshot* 222 (May 2002), pp. 30–36.

Ueda-Sarson, L., 'The Evolution of Hellenistic Infantry (Part 2): Infantry of the Successors', *Slingshot* 223 (July 2002), pp. 23–28.

Van Hook, L., 'On the Lacedaemonians Buried in the Kerameikos', *AJA* 36:3 (Jul–Sep 1932), pp. 290–292.

Van Wees, H., 'The Homeric Way of War: The 'Iliad' and the Hoplite Phalanx (I)', *Greece and Rome*, 2nd Series, 41:1 (Apr 1994), pp. 1–18.

Van Wees, H., 'The Homeric Way of War: The 'Iliad' and the Hoplite Phalanx (II)' *Greece and Rome*, 2nd Series, 41:2 (Oct 1994), pp. 131–155.

Van Wees, H. (ed.), *War and Violence in Ancient Greece* (London, Duckworth, 2000).

Van Wees, H., *Greek Warfare – Myths and Realities* (London, Duckworth, 2004).

Von Bothmer, D., *Amazons in Greek Art* (Oxford, Clarendon Press, 1957).

Walbank, F.W., *A Historical Commentary on Polybius Vol. I* (Oxford, Clarendon Press, 1967).

Walters, H.B., *CVA – Great Britain 4: British Museum* (London, British Museum, 1927).

Warry, J., *Warfare in the Classical World* (Norman, University of Oklahoma Press, 1995).

Whatley, N., 'On the Possibility of Reconstructing Marathon and Other Ancient Battles', *JHS* 94 (1964), pp. 119–139.

Wheeler, E.L., '*Hoplomachia* and Greek Dances in Arms', *GRBS* 23:3 (Autumn 1982), pp. 223–233.

Williams, A., *The Knight and the Blast Furnace – A History of the Metallurgy of Armour in the Middle Ages and the Early Modern Period* (Leiden, Brill, 2003).

Wood, M., *In the Footsteps of Alexander the Great* (London, BBC Worldwide, 2001).

Worcester, D.A., 'Shell-Shock in the Battle of Marathon', *Science* 58:1288 (Sept 1919), p. 230.

Yalichev, S., *Mercenaries of the Ancient World* (London, Constable, 1997).

Reference Texts

A Greek-English Lexicon (eds. H.G. Liddell and R. Scott), (Oxford, Clarendon Press, 1968).

Lexicon Iconographicum Mythologiae Classicae Vol. VII (Zurich, Artemis Verlag, 1994).

Oxford Classical Greek Dictionary (eds. J. Morwood and J. Taylor), (Oxford, Oxford University Press, 2002).

Oxford Latin Dictionary (ed. P.G.W. Glare), (Oxford, Clarendon Press, 1983).

Index

In the index for a book on a topic such as this it would be redundant (and somewhat silly) to list every page that mentions a word like 'hoplite' or 'shield'. As such, the following index contains entries only for passages that contain specific information for the topics that are listed. CM